AF412963

Beyond LANs

Other Related Titles

ISBN	AUTHOR	TITLE
0-07-010889-7	Chorafas	*Local Area Network Reference*
0-07-010890-7	Chorafas	*Systems Architecture and Systems Design*
0-8306-9690-3	Chorafas	*Handbook of Data Communications and Computer Networks*
0-07-060360-X	Spohn	*Data Network Design*
0-07-019022-4	Edmunds	*SAA/LU6.2 Distributed Networks and Applications*
0-07-054418-2	Sackett	*IBM's Token-Ring Networking Handbook*
0-07-004128-8	Bates	*Disaster Recovery Planning: Networks, Telecommunications, and Data Communications*
0-07-020346-6	Feit	*TCP/IP: Architecture, Protocols, and Implementation*
0-07-005075-9	Berson	*APPC: Introduction to LU6.2*
0-07-005076-7	Berson	*Client/Server Architecture*
0-07-012926-6	Cooper	*Computer and Communications Security*
0-07-016189-5	Dayton	*Telecommunications*
0-07-016196-8	Dayton	*Multi-Vendor Networks: Planning, Selecting, and Maintenance*
0-07-034243-1	Kessler/Train	*Metropolitan Area Networks: Concepts, Standards, and Service*
0-07-051144-6	Ranade/Sackett	*Introduction to SNA Networking: A Guide for Using VTAM/NCP*
0-07-051143-8	Ranade/Sackett	*Advanced SNA Networking: A Professional's Guide to VTAM/NCP*
0-07-033727-6	Kapoor	*SNA: Architecture, Protocols, and Implementation*
0-07-005553-X	Black	*TCP/IP and Related Protocols*
0-07-005554-8	Black	*Network Management Standards: SNMP, CMOT, and OSI*
0-07-021625-8	Fortier	*Handbook of LAN Technology, 2/e*
0-07-063636-2	Terplan	*Effective Management of Local Area Networks: Functions, Instruments, and People*
0-07-004563-1	Baker	*Downsizing: How to Get Big Gains from Smaller Computer Systems*
0-07-046321-2	Nemzow	*The Token-Ring Management Guide*
0-07-032385-2	Jain/Agrawala	*Open Systems Interconnection: Its Architecture and Protocols, rev. ed.*
0-07-707778-4	Perley	*Migrating to Open Systems: Taming the Tiger*
0-07-033754-3	Hebrawi	*OSI Upper Layer Standards and Practices*
0-07-049309-X	Pelton	*Voice Processing*

To order or receive additional information on these or any other McGraw-Hill titles, in the United States please call 1-800-822-8158. In other countries, contact your local McGraw-Hill representative. **MH93**

Beyond LANs

Client/Server Computing

Dimitris N. Chorafas

McGraw-Hill, Inc.

New York   San Francisco   Washington, D.C.   Auckland   Bogotá
Caracas   Lisbon   London   Madrid   Mexico City   Milan
Montreal   New Delhi   San Juan   Singapore
Sydney   Tokyo   Toronto

Library of Congress Cataloging-in-Publication Data

Chorafas, Dimitris N.
    Beyond LANs : client/server computing / Dimitris N. Chorafas.
       p.   cm. — (McGraw-Hill series on computer communications)
    Includes index.
    ISBN 0-07-011057-3
    1. Client/server computing. I. Title. II. Series.
  QA76.9.C55C48 1994
  650′.0285′436—dc20
                                                      93-24640
                                                          CIP

ISBN 0-07-011057-3

The sponsoring editor for this book was Jerry Papke, the editing supervisor was Ruth W. Mannino, and the production supervisor was Suzanne W. Babeuf. This book was set in Century Schoolbook by McGraw-Hill's Professional Book Group unit.

Contents

Chapter 17. Beyond Client/Servers: The Federated Database Solution   339

Chapter 18. Handling Heterogeneity in a Federation of Databases   361

Chapter 19. Knowledge Engineering and Interoperability in Client/Server Environments   385

Appendix A. Who Can Help in the Transition Period?   407

Preface

During the late 1980s and early 1990s, the image of the classical mainframe grew smaller and smaller. By 1993 it had vanished into a tiny point of light. Market forces saw to it that those computer companies that stuck to mainframes as their vital product line suffered a massive hardware attack. They are still not at the end of their pain.

A similar outlook of doom and gloom applies to computer user organizations that are run by mainframers and by old concepts. Even companies that used to be ahead in computers and communications are falling back, because mainframes not only strangle information technology (IT) perspectives but also stifle personal initiative and imagination.

In light of these developments, and of the need for renewal, this book focuses on the new solutions that leading-edge organizations are adopting to revamp and revitalize their communications, computer, and software operations. Among leading-edge organizations, *innovation* is at a premium, as is *quality* of information technology services.

There are prerequisites to adopting such a policy. As Ross Perot has suggested: "I think one thing I might be able to bring to bear at this stage in my life is a keen sense of the *balance* between *human ingenuity* and *advanced technology*. When the two fit together, we can avoid the enormous wastes I have seen when relying too much on technology to the exclusion of people." This balance can be achieved by bringing computer power to the end user through *client/server solutions*—as we will see in chapter after chapter of this book.

The concept behind the client/server solution is concurrent, cooperative processing. It is an approach that presents a single systems view from a user's viewpoint; involves processing on multiple, interconnected machines; and helps provide coordination of activities in a manner transparent to the end users.

These are the main themes of this text. It has been written both for decision makers in information systems investments and for computer specialists. It presupposes no deep expertise in computers and software; hence, it also has appeal to managers who wish to gain an understanding of the major transitions currently taking place in information technology.

The book is divided into three parts. Part 1 addresses the basic issues associated with client/server architecture. Chap. 1 offers the reader the key elements for appreciating the new approach to computer-based solutions. But effective systems implementations must respond to business perspectives. To this end, Chap. 2 discusses the nature and extent of business challenges—and explains how to face them effectively.

The focal point of Chap. 3 is how to capitalize on the evolution of computing through *true* client/server models. The emphasis on the word *true* is essential, since there are a number of fakes around. Chap. 4 makes the reader aware of the *pseudo*-client/server approaches advanced by some vendors and suggests how to avoid them.

The transition from mainframers to client/servers must be smooth and well studied. Chap. 5 shows how this can be done, using one of the best examples of mainframe to client/server conversion I have seen in American industry. Since the company prefers not to be identified, its name here has been changed to ALPHA.

There are plenty of successful case studies in Chap. 7. Citibank, Merrill Lynch, and Reuters are specific examples. They have been selected because their solutions are quite different from one another—yet they converge on the same principles.

Effective implementation of client/server solutions calls for the use of *open systems*. These, too, are concepts as well as practical implementations of computer technology, and go beyond what local area networks (LANs) have been able to offer.

The issue behind open systems is no different from that characterizing open societies. In order to survive, both must be *open to change*. This is what mainframes and mainframers cannot deliver.

Part 2 focuses on interconnection and high-performance problems. Chap. 8 defines what is meant by an open systems environment. Chap. 9 expands upon this definition by introducing the concept of an ongoing normalization effort and the role played by standards organizations.

Open systems solutions are practically synonymous with highly distributed architectures. Chap. 10 elaborates on this issue and explains how, by capitalizing on distributed processing and database environments, the leading user organizations have been able to escape the technological cul de sac still blocking the growth of many companies.

Chap. 11 underscores the cost-effectiveness of client/server solutions by presenting the contributions of high-performance computers and the benefits that clear-eyed user organizations derive from them. Supercomputers are increasingly becoming a major focus of prime IT users, from number crunching all the way to visualization and inter-active visualization.

New solutions with local area networks are the theme of Chap. 12. Interconnecting computer systems through wide area networks is the focus of Chap. 13. Whether local area or wide area, interoperative communications underpin the 1990s and constitute a pillar of twenty-first-century systems engineering.

Of course, new solutions must go beyond LANs and master the domain of networked heterogeneous databases. Explaining why and how this can be achieved is the goal of Part 3.

Chap. 14 sets the perspective by explaining how an environment of networked databases works in a client/server setting. Planning and managing a heterogeneous database environment takes a good deal of foresight and insight. Chap. 15 presents the criteria characterizing a fully distributed architecture.

Just as there exist pseudo-client/servers, so there are fake distrib-uted databases masquerading under the name of information ware-houses or some other fuzzy term. Chap. 16 elaborates on this issue and emphasizes the importance of avoiding self-indulgence, focusing instead on the development and implementation of sound remote data access solutions.

One of the key issues beyond client/servers is the federated data-base. Chap. 17 explains the meaning of a database federation and presents concrete examples of how it can be achieved. The theme of Chap. 18 is heterogeneity in a database federation and ways to han-dle it most efficiently.

Knowledge engineering and interoperability in client/server environ-ments are the focal points of Chap. 19. Able solutions also call for a properly planned transition period—a topic covered in the Appendix.

Good management will initiate and follow a coherent, convincing transition path even when confronted with slippery subjects that may threaten the transition from legacy to competitive applications of computers, communications, and software. By contrast, bad manage-ment will often stumble in its decisions, and the transition policy will leave much to be desired. This book presents a series of convincing examples from both cases—the good as well as the bad.

Dimitris N. Chorafas

Acknowledgments

My gratitude is extended to everyone who contributed to making this text successful: to my colleagues for their advice; to the organizations I visited for their collaboration and their initiative in communicating competitive parts of their work; and to Eva-Maria Binder for the artwork, the typing of the manuscript, and the index.

The senior executives and system specialists of the following organizations participated in the 1992 and 1993 research projects that led to the contents of the present book and its documentation.

United States

Bankers Trust

1. Dr. Carmine Vona, Executive Vice President, Worldwide Technology
2. Shalom Brinsy, Senior Vice President, Distributed Networks
3. Dan W. Muecke, Vice President, Technology Strategic Planning
4. Bob Graham, Vice President, Database Management

One Bankers Trust Plaza, New York, NY 10006

Citibank

5. Colin Crook, Chairman Corporate Technology Committee
6. David Schultzer, Senior Vice President, Information Technology
7. Jim Caldarella, Manager, Business Architecture for Global Finance
8. Nicholas P. Richards, Database Administrator
9. William Brindley, Technology Officer
10. Michael R. Veale, Network Connectivity
11. Harriet Schabes, Corporate Standards
12. Leigh Reeve, Technology for Global Finance

399 Park Avenue, New York, NY 10043

Morgan Stanley

13. Gary T. Goehrke, Managing Director, Information Services
14. Guy Chiarello, Vice President, Databases
15. Robert F. De Young, Principal, Information Technology

1933 Broadway, New York, NY 10019

16. Eileen S. Wallace, Vice President, Treasury Department
17. Jacqueline T. Brody, Treasury Department

1251 Avenue of the Americas, New York, NY 10020

Goldman Sachs

18. Vincent L. Amatulli, Information Technology, Treasury Department

85 Broad Street, New York, NY 10004

J.J. Kenny Services, Inc.

19. Thomas E. Zielinski, Chief Information Officer
20. Ira Kirschner, Database Administrator, Director of System Programming and of the Data Center

65 Broadway, New York, NY 10006

Merrill Lynch

21. Kevin Sawyer, Director of Distributed Computing Services and Executive in Charge of the Mainframe to Client/Server Conversion Process
22. Raymond M. Disco, Treasury/Bank Relations Manager

World Financial Center, South Tower, New York, NY 10080-6107

Teachers Insurance and Annuity Association/College Retirement Equities Fund (TIAA/CREF)

23. Charles S. Dvorkin, Vice President and Chief Technology Officer
24. Harry D. Perrin, Assistant Vice President, Information Technology

730 Third Avenue, New York, NY 10017-3206

Financial Accounting Standards Board

25. Halsey G. Bullen, Project Manager

26. Jeannot Blanchet, Project Manager

27. Teri L. List, Practice Fellow

401 Merritt 7, Norwalk, CN 06856

Massachusetts Institute of Technology

28. Dr. Stuart E. Madnick, Information Technology and Management Science

29. Dr. Michael Siegel, Information Technology, Sloan School of Management

30. Patricia M. McGinnis, Executive Director, International Financial Services

31. Prof. Peter J. Kempthorne, Project on Non-Traditional Methods in Financial Analysis

32. Dr. Alexander M. Samrov, Project on Non-Traditional Methods in Financial Analysis

33. Robert R. Halperin, Executive Director, Center for Coordination Science

34. David L. Verrill, Senior Liaison Officer, Industrial Liaison Program

Sloan School of Management, 50 Memorial Drive, Cambridge, MA 02139

35. Dr. Kenneth B. Haase, Media Arts and Sciences

36. Dr. David Zeltzer, Virtual Reality Project

Ames St., Cambridge, MA 02139

Santa Fe Institute

37. Dr. Edward A. Knapp, President

38. Dr. L. Mike Simmons, Jr., Vice President

39. Dr. Bruce Abell, Vice President Finance

40. Dr. Murray Gell-Mann, Theory of Complexity

41. Dr. Stuart Kauffman, Models in Biology

42. Dr. Chris Langton, Artificial Life

43. Dr. John Miller, Adaptive Computation in Economics

44. Dr. Blake Le Baron, Non-Traditional Methods in Economics

45. Bruce Sawhill, Virtual Reality

1660 Old Pecos Trail, Santa Fe, NM 87501

**School of Engineering, University of
California, Los Angeles**

46. Dr. Judea Pearl, Cognitive Systems Laboratory

47. Dr. Walter Karplus, Computer Science Department

48. Dr. Michael G. Dyer, Artificial Intelligence Laboratory

Westwood Village, Los Angeles, CA 90024

**School of Business Administration,
University of Southern California**

49. Dr. Bert M. Steece, Dean of Faculty, School of Business
    Administration

50. Dr. Alan Rowe, Professor of Management

Los Angeles, CA 90089-1421

Prediction Company

51. Dr. J. Doyne Farmer, Director of Development

52. Dr. Norman H. Packard, Director of Research

53. Jim McGill, Managing Director

234 Griffin Street, Santa Fe, NM 87501

Simgraphics Engineering Corp.

54. Steve Tice, President

55. David J. Verso, Chief Operating Officer

1137 Huntington Drive, South Pasadena, CA 91030-4563

NYNEX Science and Technology, Inc.

56. Thomas M. Super, Vice President, Research and Development

57. Steven Cross, NYNEX Shuttle Project

58. Valerie R. Tingle, Systems Analyst
59. Melinda Crews, Public Liaison, NYNEX Labs

500 Westchester Avenue, White Plains, NY 10604

60. John C. Falco, Sales Manager, NYNEX Systems Marketing
61. David J. Annino, Account Executive, NYNEX Systems Marketing

100 Church Street, New York, NY 10007

Microsoft

62. Mike McGeehan, Database Specialist
63. Andrew Elliott, Marketing Manager

825 8th Avenue, New York, NY

Reuters America

64. Robert Russel, Senior Vice President
65. William A. S. Kennedy, Vice President
66. Buford Smith, President, Reuters Information Technology
67. Richard A. Willis, Manager International Systems Design
68. M. A. Sayers, Technical Manager, Central Systems Development
69. Alexander Faust, Manager Financial Products U.S.A.
    (Instantlink and Blend)

40 E. 52nd Street, New York, NY 10022

ORACLE Corporation

70. Scott Matthews, National Account Manager
71. Robert T. Funk, Senior Systems Specialist
72. Joseph M. Di Bartolomeo, Systems Specialist
73. Dick Dawson, Systems Specialist

885 Third Avenue, New York, NY 10022

Digital Equipment Corporation

74. Mike Fishbein, Product Manager, Massively Parallel Systems
    (MAS-PAR Supercomputer)
75. Marco Enrich, Technology Manager, NAS

76. Robert Passmore, Technical Manager, Storage Systems

77. Mark S. Dresdner, DEC Marketing Operations

146 Main Street, Maynard, MA 01754
(Meeting held at UBS New York)

UNISYS Corporation

78. Harvey J. Chiat, Director Impact Programs

79. Manuel Lavin, Director Databases

80. David A. Goiffon, Software Engineer

P.O. Box 64942, MS 4463
Saint Paul, MN, 55164-0942
(Meeting held at UBS in New York)

Hewlett-Packard

81. Brad Wilson, Product Manager, Commercial Systems

82. Vish Krishnan, Manager R + D Laboratory

83. Samir Mathur, Open ODB Manager

84. Michael Gupta, Transarc, Tuxedo, Encina Transaction Processing

85. Dave Williams, Industry Account Manager

1911, Pruneridge Avenue, Cupertino, CA 95014

IBM Corporation

86. Terry Liffick, Software Strategies, Client/Server Architecture

87. Paula Cappello, Information Warehouse Framework

88. Ed Cobbs, Transaction Processing Systems

89. Dr. Paul Wilms, Connectivity and Interoperability

90. Helen Arzu, IBM Santa Teresa Representative

91. Dana L. Stetson, Advisory Marketing IBM New York

Santa Teresa Laboratory, 555 Bailey Avenue, San José, CA 95141

UBS Securities

92. A. Ramy Goldstein, Managing Director, Equity Derivative
    Products

299 Park Avenue, New York, NY 10171-0026

Union Bank of Switzerland

93. Dr. H. Baumann, Director of Logistics, North American Operations

94. Dr. C. Gabathuler, Director, Information Technology

95. Mr. Shrikantan, Director, Telecommunictions

96. Roy M. Darhin, Assistance Vice President

299 Park Avenue, New York, NY 10171-0026

United Kingdom

Barclays Bank

1. Peter Golden, Chief Information Officer, Barclays Capital Markets, Treasury, BZW

2. Brandon Davies, Director of Financial Engineering

3. David J. Parsons, Director Advanced Technology

Barclays Bank

4. Christine E. Irwin, Group Information Systems Technology

Murray House, 1 Royal Mint Court, London EC3N 4HH

Bank of England

5. Mark Laycock, Banking Supervision Division

Threadneedle Street, London EC2R 8AH

Association for Payment Clearing Services (APACS)

6. J. Michael Williamson, Deputy Chief Executive

14 Finsbury Square, London EC2A 1BR

Abbey National Bank

7. Mac Millington, Director of Information Technology

Chalkdell Drive, Shenley Wood, Milton Keynes MK6 6LA

8. Anthony W. Elliott, Director of Risk and Credit

Abbey House, Baker Street, London NW1 6XL

NATWEST Securities

9. Sam B. Gibb, Director, Information Technology
10. Don F. Simpson, Director, Global Technology
11. Richard E. Gibbs, Director, Equity Derivatives

135 Bishopsgate, London EC2M 3XT

ORACLE Corporation

12. Geoffrey W. Squire, Executive Vice President and Chief Executive
13. Richard Barker, Senior Vice President and Director, British Research Laboratories
14. Giles Godart-Brown, Senior Support Manager
15. Paul A. Gould, Account Executive

Oracle Park, Bittams Lane, Guildford Rd, Chertsey, Surrey KT16 9RG

Virtual Presence

16. Stuart Cupit, Graphics Engineer

25 Corsham Street, London N1 6DR

Valbec Object Technology

17. Martin Fowler, Ptech Expert

115 Wilmslow Road, Handforth, Wilmslow, Cheshire SK9 3ER

Scandinavia

Vaerdipapircentralen (VP)

1. Jens Bache, General Manager
2. Aase Blume, Assistant to the General Manager

61 Helgeshoj Allé, Postbox 20, 2630 Taastrup-Denmark

Swedish Bankers' Association

3. Bo Gunnarsson, Manager, Bank Automation Department
4. Gösta Fischer, Manager, Bank-Owned Financial Companies Department

5. Göran Ahlberg, Manager, Credit Market Affairs Department

P.O. Box 7603, 10394 Stockholm-Sweden

Skandinaviska Enskilda Banken

6. Lars Isacsson, Treasurer
7. Urban Janeld, Executive Vice President, Finance and IT
8. Mats Andersson, Director of Computers and Communications
9. Gösta Olavi, Manager SEB Data/Koncern Data

2 Sergels Torg, 10640 Stockholm-Sweden

Securum AB

10. Anders Nyren, Director of Finance and Accounting
11. John Lundgren, Manager of IT

38 Regeringsg, 5 tr., 10398 Stockholm-Sweden

SVEATORNET AB of the Swedish Savings Banks

12. Gunar M. Carlsson, General Manager

(Meeting at Swedish Bankers' Association)

MANDAMUS AB of the Swedish Agricultural Banks

13. Marie Martinsson, Credit Department

(Meeting at Swedish Bankers' Association)

Handelsbanken

14. Janeric Sundin, Manager, Securities Department
15. Jan Aronson, Assistant Manager, Securities Department

(Meeting at Swedish Bankers' Association)

Gota Banken

16. Mr. Johannsson, Credit Department

(Meeting at Swedish Bankers' Association)

IRDEM AB

17. Gian Medri, Former Director of Research at Nordbanken

19 Flintlasvagen, 19154 Sollentuna-Sweden

Austria

Creditanstalt Bankverein

1. Dr. Wolfgang G. Lichtl, Director of Foreign Exchange and Money Markets
2. Dr. Johann Strobl, Manager, Financial Analysis for Treasury Operations

3, Julius Tandler-Platz, 1090 Vienna

Bank Austria

3. Dr. Peter Fischer, Director of Treasury
4. Peter Gabriel, Deputy General Manager, Trading
5. Konrad Schcate, Manager, Financial Engineering

2, Am Hof, 1010 Vienna

Association of Austrian Banks and Bankers

6. Dr. Fritz Diwok, Secretary General

11, Boersengasse, 1013 Vienna

Aktiengesellschaft für Bauwesen

7. Dr. Josef Fritze, General Manager

2, Lothringenstrasse, 1041 Vienna

Management Data of Creditanstalt

8. Guenther Reindl, Vice President, International Banking Software
9. Franz Necas, Project Manager, RICOS
10. Nikolas Goetz, Product Manager, RICOS

21–25 Althanstrasse, 1090 Vienna

Germany

Deutsche Bundesbank

1. Eckhard Oechler, Director of Bank Supervision and Legal Matters

14, Wilhelm Epstein Strasse, D-6000 Frankfurt 50

Deutsche Bank

2. Peter Gerard, Executive Vice President, Organization and Information Technology
3. Hermann Seiler, Senior Vice President, Investment Banking and Foreign Exchange Systems
4. Dr. Kuhn, Investment Banking and Foreign Exchange Systems
5. Dr. Stefan Kolb, Organization and Technological Development

12, Koelner Strasse, D-6236 Eschborn

Dresdner Bank

6. Dr. Karsten Wohlenberg, Project Leader, Risk Management, Simulation and Analytics Task Force, Financial Division
7. Hans-Peter Leisten, Mathematician
8. Susanne Loesken, Organization and IT Department

43, Mainzer Landstrasse, D-6000 Frankfurt

Commerzbank

9. Helmut Hoppe, Director, Organization and Information Technology
10. Hermann Lenz, Director, Controllership, Internal Accounting and Management Accounting
11. Harald Lux, Manager, Organization and Information Technology
12. Waldemar Nickel, Manager, Systems Planning

155, Mainzer Landstrasse, D-60261 Frankfurt

Deutscher Sparkassen und Giroverband

13. Manfred Krueger, Division Manager, Card Strategy

4 Simrockstrasse, D-5300 Bonn 1
(Telephone interview from Frankfurt)

ABN-AMRO (Holland)

14. Mr. Schilder, Organization and Information Technology

(Telephone interview from Frankfurt)

Media Systems

15. Bertram Anderer, Director

6, Goethestrasse, D-7500 Karlsruhe

Fraunhofer Institute for Computer Graphics

16. Dr. Martin Goebel
17. Wolfgang Felber

7, Wilhelminerstrasse, D-6100 Darmstadt

GMD First—Research Institute for Computer Architecture, Software Technology and Graphics

18. Dr. Wolfgang K. Giloi, General Manager
19. Dr. Behr, Administrative Director
20. Dr. Ulrich Bruening, Chief Designer
21. Dr. Joerg Nolte, Designer of Parallel Operating Systems Software
22. Dr. Matthias Kessler, Parallel Languages and Parallel Compilers
23. Dr. Friedrich W. Schroer, New Programming Paradigms
24. Dr. Thomas Lux, Fluid Dynamics, Weather Prediction and Pollution Control Project

5, Rudower Chaussee, D-1199 Berlin

Siemens Nixdorf

25. Wolfgang Weiss, Director of Banking Industry Office
26. Bert Kirschbaum, Manger, Dresdner Bank Project
27. Mark Miller, Manager Neural Networks Project for UBS and German banks
28. Andrea Vonerden, Business Management Department

27, Lyoner Strasse, D-6000 Frankfurt 71

UBS Germany

29. H.-H. von Scheliha, Director, Organization and Information Technology
30. Georg Sudhaus, Manager IT for Trading Systems
31. Marco Bracco, Trader
32. Jaap Van Harten, Trader

52, Bleichstrasse, D-6000 Frankfurt 1

Switzerland

Bank for International Settlements

1. Claude Sivy, Director, Controllership and Operational Security
2. Frederik C. Musch, Secretary General, Basel Committee on Banking Supervision

2 Centralbankplatz, Basel

CIBA-GEIGY AG

3. Stefan Janovjak, Divisional Information Manager
4. Natalie Papezik, Information Architect

Ciba-Geigy, R-1045,5.19, 4002 Basel

The Client/Server Architecture

1

Appreciating Client/Server Solutions

1.1 Introduction

Interoperability is the No. 1 item on the agendas of computer users today. The request is for services that are both cost-effective and on line to an increasing range of computer resources—precisely what is supported by *client/server* solutions.

User organizations must understand the reasons behind the new generation of layered operating systems, database management systems (DBMS), and transaction processing monitors (TPMs), as well as the functionality necessary for a solution to be acceptable. For this purpose, it is wise to start with the environment for which the new implementation concepts are designed. This approach requires doing both information processing and knowledge handling at the same time.

In the background of requirements regarding functionality, and of the demands posed by business and industry, is *competitiveness* in a market more demanding than ever. This is what Sec. 1.1 highlights by placing emphasis on the roles that are played by leading-edge organizations.

Business leadership requires that we steadily renew our concepts and solutions. Under this dual aspect, *client/servers* are both an architecture and a marketing buzzword applied to a wide range of equipment as well as design methodologies. In the background of this distributed information processing approach is the ability to:

- Maximize the benefits of each individual computing platform within a given implementation

- Provide solutions that are flexible and modular, and implemented at an affordable cost

Figure 1.1 highlights the synergy that exists between clients—mainly workstations—and servers. Although there are many types of servers, in the general case the focus is placed on database managers and communications services.

Clients and servers must be characterized by seamless access to each other's resources. Solutions to interoperability problems must not only be technically sound but also combine flexibility, security, and reliability. They must provide advanced communications capabilities and raw computing power to handle demanding applications, as well as graphics user interfaces (GUIs) and knowledge-enriched approaches.

Well-designed solutions will ensure that resource-intensive implementations currently resting entirely on large mainframes and their cycle-hungry DBMS can be downsized to run on local area networks (LANs), file servers, and workstations. With such architectures, processing power is far less expensive than what the old centralized solutions can provide.

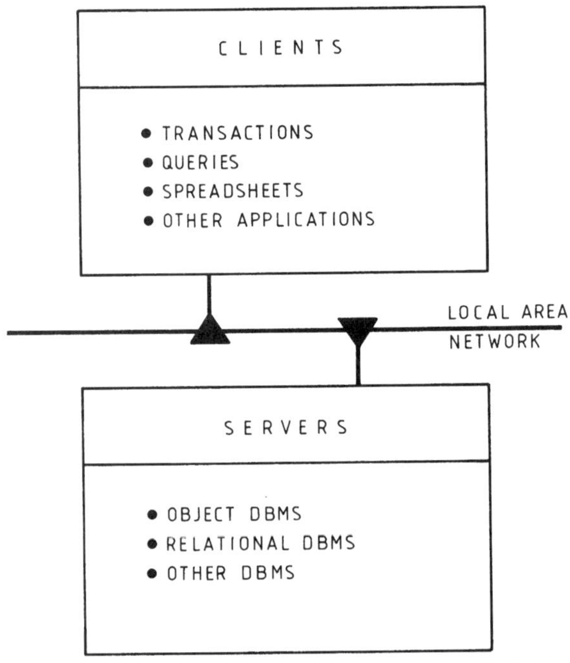

Figure 1.1 A client/server synergy across a spectrum of applications.

The concepts we implement have to be ingeniously worked out, as the distributed client/server platforms handle a range not only of applications but also of operating systems, database management systems, and network protocols. Without the appropriate integrative capabilities, we will find ourselves obliged to rely on incompatible, discrete island approaches, one for each individual application.

1.2 Client/Server Functions

Starting with the fundamentals, a *server* is a unit providing services to requesting processes. Generally, it does not send information to the requester until the requesting process tells it to do so. But the server must also manage synchronization of services as well as communications once a request has been initiated.

Processes that request services from a server are *clients* of that server. The client may initiate a transaction with the server, while normally the server does not initiate a transaction with the client.

The client is therefore the more active partner in this association, requesting specific functions, accepting corresponding results from the server, and acknowledging the completion of services. The client, however, does not manage the synchronization of services and associated communications.

The general case of client/server implementation is shown in Fig. 1.2. With the client/server computing model of distributed operations:

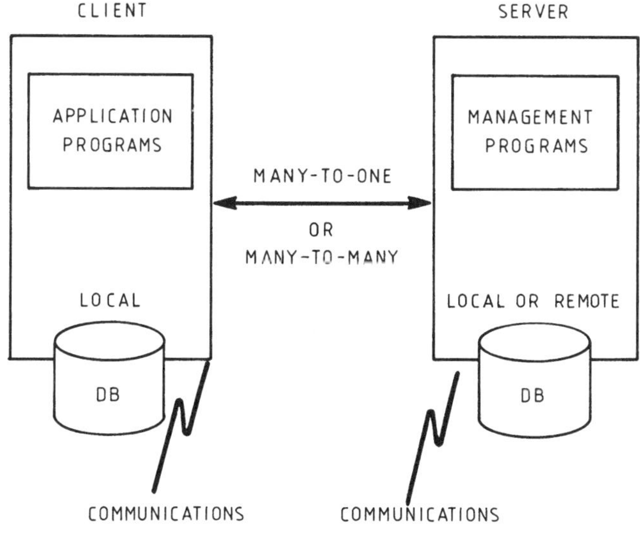

Figure 1.2 The general case of client/server implementation.

- Many clients may share one server.

- The same client may access many servers, both logical and remote.

The client, the server, or both can be a workstation. The server can also be a supermicro, a database computer, or a supercomputer. Purposeful old minis and obsolete mainframes have not been included in the definition.

Since server-based supports can be complex, the term *server* does not necessarily refer to a piece of hardware, a database unit, a gateway, or a special-purpose processor dedicated to run software. The concept is much broader: Servers require both software and hardware for a range of functions—though typically each server is specialized.

The technical solutions should be able to assure networkwide shared access by applications processes that address databases, number printers, gateways, and other resources. The environment can be:

- Simple, such as a small work group sharing applications and peripherals

or

- Complex, resulting from wider sharing across multiple systems and topologies

Whether the solution we are after is simple or complex, totally new or a conversion of mainframe applications, a basic design principle is never to build a system to support the current organizational divisions and their departments. A great deal of the necessary flexibility can be provided by solutions that are modular and independent of current structures.

A different way of making this statement is that the information technology (IT) solutions we develop must be organization-independent:

- They should not reflect the current organization chart.

- They should be immune to structural changes—hence flexible.

- They should integrate with existing resources, assuring the end user of seamless access to them.

The goal of the solutions sought through client/server computing is to enable a client program anywhere in a network to request services from anywhere else in the network in a way that is both transparent and independent of any particular interconnected software and hardware. This reference raises a number of questions:

- What computers, communications, and software solutions should be used to create a client/server network?

- What range of functionality should be targeted to optimize cost-effectiveness?

- How can the system be kept flexible to develop new applications, add new users, and enhance its own structure?

- How can we ensure that server platforms and client stations will deliver the high availability demanded by the most competitive applications?

- What facilities will be able to manage all the nodes and links in the client/server network, distributing the software and controlling the physical assets?

Not all approaches that represent themselves as client/server models can answer these questions in an able manner. Without any doubt, exceptions should be made of mainframes and nonintelligent terminals connected to mainframes or minis.* As we will see in Chap. 4, these are fake client/server architectures.

Another major exception is the "stand-alone workstation." Under no stretch of the imagination can it qualify as a client/server model, although some vendors try to sell it as such.† A PC or any other unit that is not networked is not a workstation.

Integrating what has been said so far, we are converging toward a definition that client/servers are excellent multiuser systems with a flexible but all-defined applications perspective. These applications must be designed to work together through adherence to rules.

The foregoing concepts are not necessarily new. To a substantial extent, they have existed for four decades in computing. What is new is the truly peer-to-peer structure of the implementation environment.

The wider acceptance of the outlined solutions largely depends on the functionality provided by the system as a whole. What makes the client/server architecture distinct from mainframe-based processes are its distributed but cooperative applications characteristics:

- Clients and servers function across platforms within the network, whether in a local or in a wide area.

- Distributed software artifacts execute on multiple platforms within the supported architecture.

- Processes on the network can be dynamically distributed to the most appropriate (and available) platform for execution.

---

*Some vendors call these nonprogrammable terminals (NPTs).

†For instance, this is IBM's Environment 1.

Graphics applications can be assisted through graphics processors. A numerically intensive process within an application can be migrated from a client to the network's number cruncher server, and a complex database query may access a different database server if the information elements it requires are themselves distributed. This emphasizes the need for first-class solutions in networking.

1.3   The Integrative Role of Networks

Within the integrative role provided by the network, the concept of client/server computing is to assure that end users have transparent access to any computing resource needed across the company and its business partners.

Indeed, a common characteristic of clients and servers is their communications capability. In this setting, the programming complexities of distribution across a network may be handled by the called service or by the calling mechanism, but in every case such distribution complexities should be transparent to the client application—that is, the calling program:

- The client requests services by calling appropriate routines available as part of the underlying distributed operating system.

- Given the facilities provided by the network operating system, the client does not need to distinguish between local and remote server services.

This architecture and its distributed support are evolutionary, in both topology and functionality. The network solution being provided should be any-to-any but also pay great attention to security, because client/server architectures will see a great increase in external users.

Superficially, it may seem that there is a contradiction in the statements made in the preceding paragraphs. On the one hand we intend to increase the number of internal and external users, and on the other hand we are downsizing the available resources. In reality, however, there is no contradiction at all. What we do is downsize the costs, not the computer power, by capitalizing on the incredible cost-effectiveness of the microprocessor. Commodity microprocessors today offer 20 million instructions per second (MIPS) at a very low cost—and in a couple of years they will provide 100 MIPS. A mainframe of equal power today costs more than $7 million.

Precisely for these reasons, some clear trends lie on the horizon. For instance:

- Mainframes will continue to disappear.

- The value of classical in-house programmers will diminish.
- Open systems environments will grow, with a number of developing alliances.
- Solution selling will be the dominant characteristic of IT investments.

One of the most imaginative projections is that information technology managers will become business managers in order to survive; and they will perceive conversion to client/server and downsizing as one of their most important duties.

Nevertheless, it should not be forgotten that downsizing available computer resources creates challenges in many technical domains, one of them being networking. The interconnection between the LAN-based production system and the traditional mainframes is typically done through a wide area network (WAN) employing leased or dial-up lines. If a company has not yet rationalized its WAN strategy, it will find obstacles in its downsizing efforts.

The wide area network provides the backbone upon which the distributed system will build. With a strong base in place, an effective way to view geographically dispersed LANs is to see them as physical and logical extensions of the corporate network, with downsizing distributing the processing and database functions among these LANs, their clients, and their servers.

From an implementation viewpoint, the WAN is used to transfer queries and transactions between workstations and servers as well as the mainframes still remaining in the system. From a support perspective, the corporate WAN can be used to:

- Distribute software
- Upload and download database contents
- Perform version control
- Provide remote network control functions
- Assure server backup and recovery

The systems solution to be adopted must offer a central repository and a distributed applications library, whose on-line access would be at the core of systems programming and commodity software support.

As client/server implementations evolve, communications networks will provide the biggest opportunities for developing new applications. But to gain the potential benefits of the expanding networked computer base we must get beyond the old multidrop and point-to-point lines, or even X.25 protocol, into asynchronous transfer mode (ATM) and frame relay.

The goal should be to create powerful and innovative communications networks. For this, we need high-capacity bandwidth—because information of the 1990s will be multimedia, requiring the ability to create, store, and transmit not only voice and data but also images, graphics, text, and compound electronic documents.

1.4   The Systems Integration Market

Prerequisites are needed to answer, in an able manner, the systems requirements of a company. The first major task is to identify the business needs and objectives of the end users who are clients. Then solutions must be devised, and the best client/server architecture as well as migration path must be thoroughly selected.

When such definitions are well done, they make fairly simple the task of properly describing hardware and software components as well as networking requirements. Typically, this should be an evolutionary approach:

- Reflecting an extensible information model

- Supporting multiple software paradigms

- Making feasible growth and configurability

- Featuring industry standards, as far as they exist

This strategy protects investments in computers, communications, and software and combines the best features of new technologies with the evolving standards.

Such solutions, however, call for a significant amount of experience and skill as well as for novel approaches to systems management and truly distributed applications software. Without a high level of integrated network management, tasks performed at the workstation level take longer and require more computer literacy from the end users. This takes a toll on productivity, flexibility, and costs.

As the boundary between local, metropolitan, and wide area networking becomes blurred, we need to ensure a better control over resources. Sun Microsystems introduced the phrase "the network is the computer" to describe its view of the merger of the two technologies. Crucial questions requiring a factual reply include:

- What is the strategy we should adopt to meet the requirements of production subsystems?

- What technology changes might further enhance client/server applications?

- What evolution will client/server architectures experience in the coming years?

- Which network control system should be selected in a company-wide setting?

- Which software tools are needed for interoperability and integration?

Underlying most of these questions is the fact that much tighter integration is needed between application software and networking software. As suggested in Fig. 1.3, the technological evolution in computers and communications can be seen as a stage-by-stage development: mainframes to PCs and LANs, then onward to cooperative client/server and integrated architectures.

This transition is much more than a change in hardware and logical software platforms. Embedded into it is a very significant evolution in applications and, even more, a large degree of transparency in computer resources—as far as the end users are concerned.

Up to a point, the bad news is that such transparency cannot be carried forward to the programmers, since they may well be using multiple different computers and operating systems. Indeed, present technology is only just coming to terms with:

- The concept of remote procedure calls (RPCs)

- Many of the cooperative processing approaches that have come into existence

Some classes of cooperative processing solutions are relatively easy, particularly if the basic logical processing is on one system and the data manipulation on another. However, there are many different

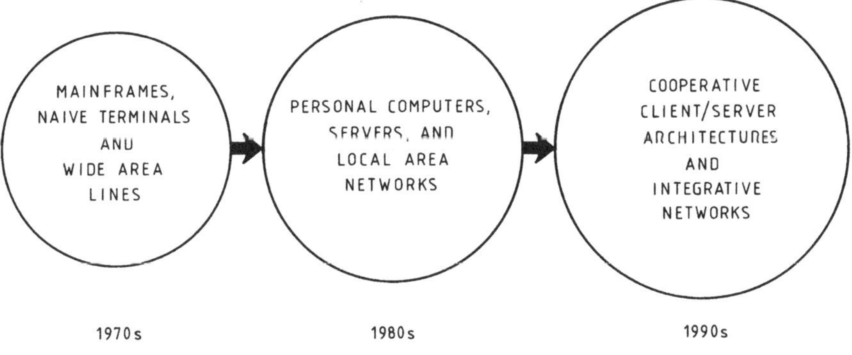

Figure 1.3 The technological evolution in computers and communications over three decades.

classes of workstation applications that dictate different client GUI tools, as well as some differences in database server requirements.

What makes the distributed processing solutions of the 1990s different from those of the 1980s is the growing amount of complexity:

- Rising user requirements make the tasks ahead of us more difficult and call for a new departure.

- The real challenge is complexity that past approaches cannot handle and that the human brain, unassisted, cannot comprehend.

During the 1980s, the availability of affordable LANs, with personal computers and easy-to-use software, gave user organizations the ability to distribute their computing to several sites. However, the distribution of computing tasks which was not planned appropriately resulted in diversity of hardware and software. It is not uncommon for the same enterprise to have a variety of machines (even from the same vendor) with incompatible operating systems, DBMS, and protocols.

The challenge in the 1990s is to interconnect all these different computers into a unified information-sharing network. A fundamental problem is that mainframes, minicomputers, workstations, and servers run incompatible software. Even when networked together, they still cannot cooperate because they cannot share data—unless valid integrative solutions are provided. The network can serve as the backbone of integrative solutions that:

- Are able to leverage the company's existing application investment

- Provide expanded capabilities to the end user

- Reduce overall systems costs by capitalizing on technological opportunities

These are the guidelines for action. A careful case-by-case examination of projects shows that companies that have been successful in achieving downsizing objectives have many characteristics in common. One of the most important is strong user support and an emphasis on standard platforms. Although industry standards are not quite as stringent as user organizations might have liked to see them:

- The evolving norms by standards bodies are critical to new implementations.

- There is growing evidence that proprietary approaches ultimately limit long-term opportunities.

- However, at the same time the size of technology investments strongly suggests the wisdom of multisourcing.

In conclusion, both technological change and return on investment (ROI) requirements alter the style of the application perspectives, moving the computers, communications, and software concepts toward *information integration.* Competitive leadership in the 1990s is defined by the ability to provide an effective service in an integrative manner. This is what experts with insight and foresight suggest.

1.5 Beyond LAN Solutions

As conceived in the late 1970s and widely implemented through the 1980s, a local area network is a communications facility that covers a limited topology and interconnects in an effective manner different types of servers and workstations, more particularly personal and professional computers. This definition has remained valid for more than 10 years, but as we will see there are also a number of other subjects that have changed.

The pillars on which a LAN rests include the physical and logical transport media as well as the workstations that servers have been evolving over time. The same is true of the concepts and processes underlying LAN operations.

In the steady search for productivity at the workbench, new solutions from small firms rival those from billion-dollar corporations in a field that is only a few years old but is dynamic and fast-growing. With computers and LANs—that is, with a *myriaprocessor*—the features:

- Are supported at an affordable price by an evolutionary technology

- Are distributed across a broad spectrum of devices, which themselves are rapidly changing

In my first book on designing and implementing local area networks,* I described the environment in which a LAN can best be put to work, its distinguishing characteristics, architectural issues, and the systems design associated with them—according to the state of the art supported at the time. I also discussed the real-life possibilities of myriaprocessors and the fundamental requirements for a successful application.

Fewer than 10 years later, significant changes occurred in this domain because of both rewarding experiences and a number of constraints that had to be overcome. These evolutionary changes came as a result of major developments in technology on which the flexible

---

*D. N. Chorafas, *Local Area Networks,* McGraw-Hill, New York, 1984.

workstations, servers, and LANs have been able to capitalize—while the monolithic mainframes in their glass houses missed the chance to renew themselves and their software.

As the number of believers in myriaprocessor solutions multiplied, the applications to which LANs have been put have grown. What 10 years ago was called a networked PC or workstation is today a *client* characterized by rich software: powerful OS, DBMS, TPM, and end user interfaces.

Capitalizing on their experience with PCs and LANs, user organizations have come to appreciate that client hardware and basic software not only must be a platform adequate for a growing range of applications but should also enable networkwide user access to resources available elsewhere within the larger communications support system. At the same time, the client should in principle be *a lowcost machine* in view of:

- The competitive environment in which we live

- The cost-effectiveness requirements the company must satisfy in order to survive

Along a similar frame of reference, the server needs increasingly sophisticated hardware and software support to manage the shared resources it makes available to users. Knowledge engineering artifacts help the server to respond more efficiently to clients' requests, communicate with other servers, manage databases, and/or perform gateway functions. Like the client, the server must also be offered at an affordable cost.

In a nutshell, these are the background reasons that servers are purchased, installed, and configured. They are also the reasons that there is a trend away from mainframes whose image grows smaller and smaller in users' appreciation and nearly vanishes into a tiny spot of light.

- Clients, servers, and LANs are typically characterized by a very competitive cost/performance ratio and ease of operation.

- Client/server solutions offer the possibility of flexible incremental investments in an existing system that performs functions related to the end user.

- At the heart of this model is the concept of network-based computing, which has introduced a new dimension in computers, communications, and software—permitting applications to be developed where they are executed.

Some companies call the network-based approach *supercomputing,* as contrasted with the supercomputer, which is typically one single machine. However, the newest generation of high-performance computers uses massively parallel computing. Hence, these engines are a microscopic view of network-based computing the way we have been examining it in this section.

There is as well a different way of looking at the difference between *supercomputing* and *supercomputers*. If an organization moves out of the ossified mainframes in order to modernize and revitalize its information technology

- A change to *supercomputing* will be motivated by the desire to significantly reduce costs at same or better performance

- The adoption of *supercomputers* will primarily emphasize much greater performance at the same or lesser cost

From client, server, and LAN to supercomputing, advanced computer and communications technology has become the key to survival of a great many financial institutions and industrial concerns. No words can better explain its role than the General Electric (GE) dictum: "Automate, emigrate, or evaporate"—which was said 10 years ago and is still going strong.

In fact, since the early 1950s, having called the able application of high technology "the most important undertaking of this century," GE has engaged in a farsighted program of steadily retooling. As generations of machines and software succeed one another, new, exciting tools and techniques are used in three broad areas of interest:

The technology base.   Accelerating advances in productivity and product quality

The thrust for generic solutions.   Developing concepts and standards for applications, demonstrating possibilities, and providing experimental facilities

Enlarged application support.   Assuring specialized skills through education by seminars, workshops, and dissemination media

Along this frame of reference, the evolution beyond LANs is perceived as an integrative multiuser computing system built from a set of discrete machines and software modules. As we will see in this book, these are interconnected by a high-speed, reliable mechanism whose structure is transparent to the applications running on the system.

Within this implementation perspective, there is flexibility in the choice of approaches and solutions revolutionizing computers, communications, software, and business systems. This suits the goals of a knowledge-driven society to which the generation of mainframes, with its image problems, is adjusting with difficulty. But that's life.

1.6   Bringing a Business Sense to the Client/Server Architecture

The shift of market power toward information originators and information providers is an invitation for senior management to make the tough choices it has avoided for years. Unless management revamps its information technology in a radical manner, today's leading firms will be tomorrow's losers.

Both organizational and technological reasons lie behind this statement. When during the 1980s companies began to restructure themselves internally around the flow of information, top management found that it did not need many intermediate reporting levels. As a result,

- The lesson started seeping in that an organization needs far fewer management layers than in the past decades.

- The able use of information technology significantly increases the span of control and cuts in half the intermediate levels of management.

Because networked databases are changing the pattern of physical distribution of information, many industries are discovering that much of what they knew and did in the past is becoming redundant or outright obsolete. Topmost retailers, such as 7/11 in Japan, now handle most merchandise without any intermediate storage. It goes directly from the manufacturer to the racks serving the clients.

Even when the manufactured goods transit through a warehouse, they are not held there. Supported through powerful mathematical models, just-in-time (JIT) inventory management sees to it that they go out within hours. As a result, the warehouse is changing function, becoming a marshaling yard instead of a parking place.

Propelled by computers, communications, and software, this new business perspective also has significant financial aftermaths. Both manufacturing and merchandising networks need much less of the financing that provided banks with their most lucrative business: short-term lending on inventory.

The sharp drop in the demand for loans explains in large measure why banks, even in good times, are seeing their commercial loan business shrink. The trend has major implications for the economy, but also points toward a specific direction in terms of desired technological solutions.

The change in business perspectives is so high that no middle-of-the-road plan can really succeed. The need is for architectural solutions that lead away from the beaten path and are able to end the cost explosion of legacy applications.

- Existing technology (read: mainframes and midsize computers) and the solutions it affords are costing too much and giving too little.

- A radical restructuring is necessary to gain business advantages by capitalizing on information services, and to promote cost-effective solutions.

It is precisely for these reasons that the client/server model is establishing itself in the minds of many user organizations—and there is no turning back. This statement is documented not only from the meetings held with leading user organizations in the 1991–1992 time frame but also from working meetings with such vendors as Oracle, Microsoft, IBM, DEC, and Hewlett-Packard.*

The client/server model, for example, seems to be seeping into the IBM organization and its culture, though the latter is still split down the middle between two trends:

- The AIX architecture, which is client/server

- The SAA architecture, which uses mainframes as a curious server breed.†

"The network solution to be provided should be any-to-any," said the chief information officer (CIO) of one of the better-known American firms. "That's why the importance of SNA will diminish over time— and with it of SAA." It is good advice, but vendors have their own fixed ideas and don't listen to what the market says.

"What is meant by a client/server solution in a practical sense?" asked another CIO, answering the question: "The client is the computer on which the user is working—typically, a personal computer or workstation. From the client, the user issues instructions in the machine's operating system primitive or, more typically, applications programming language. The new job of the information systems experts is to facilitate this process."

For instance, a workstation might call an object or record or ask for transaction execution. The application residing with the client sends these instructions as messages to the server, a nearby or remote system in which the desired records reside.

The chosen architecture must ensure that the server monitors a communications line for incoming messages sent to it by the clients in the network.

---

*Both the vendor meetings and those with user organizations have provided the background material for this book.

†The same reference is valid for Unisys, Bull, Siemens-Nixdorf, Fujitsu, Hitachi, NEC, and other mainframers.

1.7 Promoting the Interoperability of Applications

Interoperability among networked computer resources requires a good deal of software functionality to be properly executed, particularly when the client addresses many servers in connection with a given transaction, whether serially or in parallel.

- Ensuring the able execution of an operation on one server is sometimes conditioned by the execution of associated subtransactions on another server.

- Contrary to the simple transactions of past decades, many current transactions are complex and their handling reflects some of the challenges associated with a distributed environment.

The applications environment characterizing the 1990s is significantly different from the one for which legacy programs were written 20 or even 10 years ago. Competitiveness is attained through logically integrated operations that go well beyond the old solutions.

Just-in-time inventory management, for example, requires a very close coordination among the databases of business partners: from the raw materials vendors to the manufacturer, wholesaler, and retailer. Transactions spanning computer networks are complex and recently have become known as *long transactions*.

- They may take considerable time to complete, owing to multifunctional requirements.

- Each is composed of several subtransactions that may be executed in heterogeneous computer systems.

A superficial view of computer hardware installations in the retail trade, for example, may lead the observer to the conclusion that many retail shops just have a mini and some workstations around. Chains, for example, do so in every store. Although correct, this is an incomplete observation.

The careful examiner will see that on these platforms, user organizations implement point-of-sale (POS) systems that capture each sale by customer and by item. Machine-readable customer identification comes from credit cards, debit cards, check-cashing cards, or some form of frequent-shopper cards.

Along with other inputs such as goods and money, client identification at points-of-sales interests many independent but logically interrelated users. The same is true of item identification for inventory control and ordering purposes—and several other operations.

Those who command the best information systems structure have a competitive advantage over their competitors. This has led to a shift of market power toward information providers, that is, toward companies that are able to capture the buying habits of individual customers.

By getting ahead in information technology, product manufacturers and distribution chains position themselves for leadership in design trends as well as for targeting specific promotional campaigns at individual buyers. They target consumers who tend to buy new products on the basis of television advertising, those who tend to buy on price alone, or those who always buy premium products.

- By having a better profile of its customer base, the store improves its inventory forecasting.

- Customers receive better service, with frequent customers being rewarded with special promotions and incentives.

As we will see in Chap. 2, vastly improved inventory control has major financial aftermaths, from fewer loans to finance purchasing and holding goods in store to better cash flow. Vital sales statistics collected on line assist in improved turnover and therefore profitability, if and only if there is immediate exploitation of such information through networked solutions.

In the sense of a continuous interoperability, the system must manage user interaction, focusing on the specific application being done. It must not only accept input but also perform data validation. Another major systems contribution is preparing and issuing requests for services:

- Reading or writing an object or record
- Forwarding a data stream to clients and servers
- Sorting and prioritizing different operations

The work executed through this architecture takes place so that multiuser applications do not burden the attached servers by performing relatively simple but resource-intensive tasks—as is the case with mainframes. Such operations belong to the client level but cannot be done through nonintelligent terminals.

Prioritizing the operations to be executed in a client/server architecture, and localizing some of them, permits implementing a high-performance, multiuser, multitasking environment at reasonably low cost. This is what is giving client/servers the *20:1 advantage* over mainframes that many companies say they have found in client/server implementation.

Superficially, the infrastructural facilities that accomplish cross-database services, preemptive multitasking, and applications programming interfaces (APIs)* are very similar to those found on mainframe settings. This, however, overlooks a principal difference between the implementation of such functionality on a mainframe and under the LAN model of operations.

On a mainframe all operations take place on one system, timesharing one very expensive processor. This is what has been done for over 30 years, but it is:

- Highly costly, hence unwise

- Characterized by inflexibility

- Quite slow because of contention

- Low in reliability

By contrast to this monolithic approach, Fig. 1.4 demonstrates the client/server's layered structure, which provides a low-priced robust solution to user requirements. This approach permits downsizing production subsystems while allowing the clients and servers the necessary tools and facilities to control, manage, and tune the environment in which they operate.

Most client/server solutions are also very attentive in matters of security. Access to any resource can be defined to the file level, with such access being controlled through identification and authorization. Logically defined closed-use groups can be set up to enable the enhancing of security measures by network administrators.

Through knowledge-enriched software, changes made at one server or a domain can be automatically transferred at all other servers. Replicators automatically distribute changes in files or directories to other servers, and systems support can be extended to cover an expanding implementation perspective without disruptions from human intervention.

1.8 Capitalizing on the New Communications Opportunities

By implementing client/server solutions, leading-edge organizations have been promoting applications that can fill the ever greater network bandwidth that is available at affordable prices. But there is a systems problem. Today's model of the existing relationship between communication networks and computer-based services does not nec-

---

*An applications programming interface is a set of software commands that provides an interface to server applications such as file transfer, data extraction, and import/export.

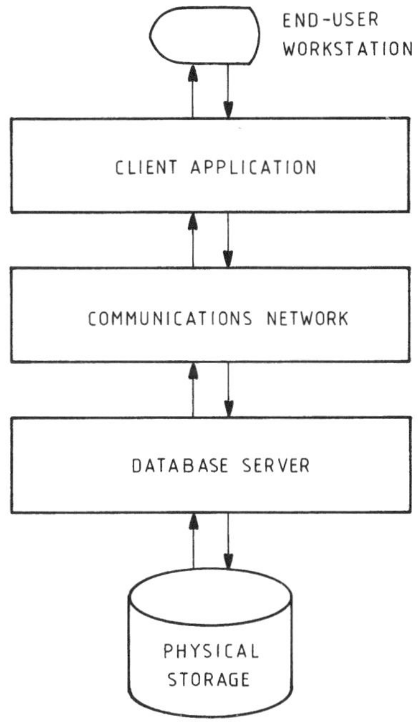

Figure 1.4 A layered approach to computing enhances functionality and increases flexibility, speed, and reliability at low cost.

essarily work for tomorrow, because by the year 2000 the roles of computers and communications will be reversed. Communications will be the master subject, and computers will be doing server jobs. Two problems highlight the aftermaths of this radical change:

1. *Skills obsolescence,* as nearly all the experience we have accumulated since the early 1950s comes from the time when computers were the masters and were faster than the communications channels serving them. The major systems change we are discussing radically alters this perspective. By the year 2000 the relationship which highlighted nearly 40 years of computer applications will be reversed. Communications will work faster than computers, even if the latter feature teraops (trillion operations per second) capacity.

2. Fiber-optic communications will be significantly cheaper than copper-based approaches, thus altering the economics of the architectural solutions that have characterized data communications in the last three decades.

This fact has numerous consequences. For example, as costs are turning into prices, prices fall dramatically and the market relations which prevailed in the past are turning upside down.

Concepts such as multimedia, data compression, database distribution, user interfacing, and so on need to be reexamined to see how they fit with the new landscape. Each one of these terms takes on a new meaning, since by the end of this decade the relationship among them will be quite different from the one we presently know.

We must already plan on how to capitalize on the developing telecommunications opportunities. We can do so if we appreciate that both the systems concepts and the tariff structure will be influenced by, and at the same time affect, the new generation of communications-intensive services.

- Seen in this perspective, today's models are wrong because they are based on assumptions that are becoming obsolete.

- But how soon will network operators and user organizations grasp the opportunities offered by the new technology?

A valid answer to this question has to be based on an ability to predict coming events. But since the dynamics of new technology change very fast, it is not possible to make long-term forecasts with a significant degree of assurance—hence the wisdom of being *flexible,* a strategy supported through client/server systems.

Today, we can predict quite accurately what technology will be like in 5 years. But no one can forecast the needs of the market 10 years down the road—that is, into the twenty-first century. Two points are, however, certain:

- It is economically impossible to completely reconstruct public switching, transmitting, and wiring facilities.

- The wise approach, therefore, is to view developments as evolutionary—avoiding wide-scale service changes while taking advantage of new offerings as they present themselves.

No doubt, the evolving technology will be instrumental in easing what is today a difficult task. For example, by switching light streams instead of electronic ones, photonics exchanges will eliminate the need to convert signals at each end of a communications transmission, thus making switching 10 to 100 times faster than is now possible.

However, only the most advanced companies in the First World countries, particularly those with deregulated telephone services, can offer such solutions.

To realize the full potential of technologies such as photonics there must first be widespread fiber subscriber connections end-to-end.

This implementation should take years to complete given the prevailing replacement policies and new-installation rate in public networks—unless the installation of new communications disciplines accelerates through initiatives due to competitive pressures.

Significant attention should also be paid to the choice of protocols that can permit efficient communications between networked resources. Some of the protocols used for client/server architectures are shown in Fig.1.5.

- The best choice available today is TCP/IP.

- The most backward, and yet most widely used, is the 3270.

The 3270 represents the way dumb terminals have been interconnected for 20 years to mainframes. IBM's 3270 information display system was introduced in the early 1970s and has since been widely used—but user organization after user organization is now converting into more efficient protocols such as TCP/IP and Novell's IPX.

A similar statement regarding modernization can be made relative to applications software. This is written in full understanding that legacy-type (DP) and communications programming products will have to coexist over an interim period. But by putting all new implementations on client/server architectures, using for applications development a policy of prototyping and generators, and applying

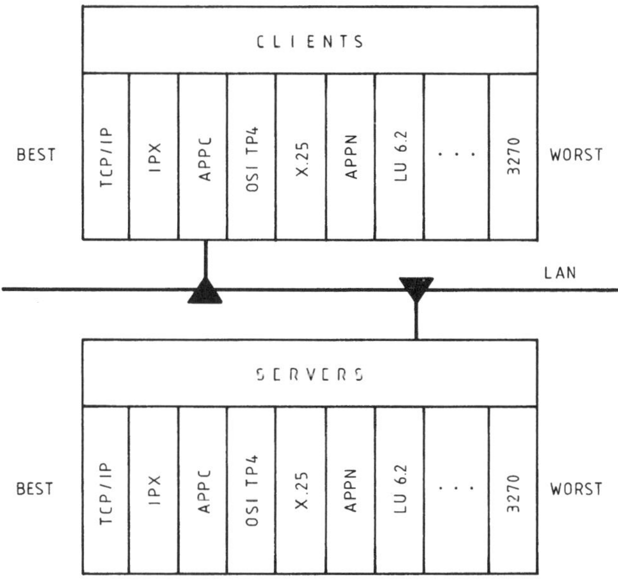

Figure 1.5 From best to worst, network protocols in clients and servers.

knowledge-engineering-enriched software solutions, a company can position itself in a way that capitalizes on the forces of the 1990s. This amounts to a significant competitive advantage in terms of the bottom line, that is, profits.

In conclusion, the need for capitalizing on the best options currently available on the technology front is just as true of communications and of software as it is of computer hardware. In all these areas, project management must be organized to maximize the visibility of available benefits, as we will see in Part 2. This, too, means a change in past policies, accounting for the fact that as a whole users want to see a clear evidence of benefits.

2

Business Challenges and Client/Server Architectures

2.1 Introduction

The first major challenge for businesses today is staying competitive in a changing global market. Success, even survival, depends on getting information to the executives and professionals who need it—all the way from the sales floor to the boardroom.

The ample supply of knowledge and information requires more than simply extending the company's already heavy computer investments. It calls for integrating communications and computer systems with advanced applications, employing the best and most cost-effective solutions technology can provide. Such solutions were offered:

- In the 1960s by centralized mainframes
- In the 1970s by minicomputers, as distributed data processing
- In the 1980s by personal computers (PCs) and local area networks (LANs)
- In the 1990s by *true* client/server architectures which use as servers products ranging from Unix and NT boxes to database computers (DBCs) and supercomputers

The reason the word *true* is emphasized is that some architectures are as fake as $3 bills. (See Chap. 4.) Pseudo-client/servers come in the form of expensive and obsolete mainframes rebaptized as "servers." Clear-eyed managers know that they have to guard against such eventuality.

Companies that have moved out of the mainframe backwater, to true client/server architectures have found three major advantages.

1. *A technology that is more flexible and responsive to user needs.* This is an aftermath of the fact that an effective utilization of intellectual resources demands the on-line sharing of knowledge and information, as well as easy access to applications solutions and databases.

2. *A significant reduction in data-processing costs, representing millions of dollars per year.* As stated in Chap. 1, cost/effectiveness ratios of 20:1 in favor of client/server solutions versus mainframes are not uncommon. Management accounting should reflect not only what is paid for hardware but also basic software license fees. When the cost of applications and operations is accounted for, the benefit ratio becomes much more important.

3. *An increase in business competitiveness as the market edge turns toward merchandising.* For this and the above two reasons, a growing number of mainframe users are now actively considering downsizing. Since the new architectures are very appealing, current mainframe customers are a major market opportunity for firms specializing in mainframe to client/server conversion—as the case studies presented in this chapter help document.

2.2 The Shift of Market Power toward Information Brokers

There is a synergy among market developments, effects of on-line operations through real-time networks, and expanding use of mathematical models for optimization and resource allocation. With such synergy power in the leading economies of the world has been shifting from manufacturing to marketing, distribution, retailing, and finance.

The companies that are best positioned to benefit from the shift taking place in the market are those able to act not only as intermediaries but also as information originators and providers—the *information brokers.* The key to this switch in market emphasis is the ability of firms with control over information to gain the upper hand over the operations of their main suppliers. Information brokers are able to tell their suppliers in no uncertain terms:

- What should be produced

- In what mix

- In what quantities

- When it should be delivered

- Through which channels

- At which time
- To which places

With a surprising number of products, a few very large distributors actually write the specifications for the products they want. Sometimes they even help in designing them. They also specify the delivery schedules.

For instance, the chains of hypermarkets that have come to dominate food retailing in many western European countries control the product mix, manufacturing plans, and deliveries of their main suppliers. This is also true of the huge discount chains in America.

- Knowledge and information create the leverage base.
- With them comes the financial power that makes business leadership possible.

It is wrong to think that the whole deal is in marketing. The leverage rests on real-time information, and the systems supporting it must be capable of capturing the pulse of the market. This is as true in finance as it is in merchandising—in short, throughout the information brokerage business.

That's why, as Fig. 2.1 suggests, return on investment (ROI) in information technology can be high if, and only if, it is characterized by *new departures,* not by old concepts and the beaten path.

- The return is high if investments are oriented toward product innovation, and low if a predominantly replacement policy is followed.

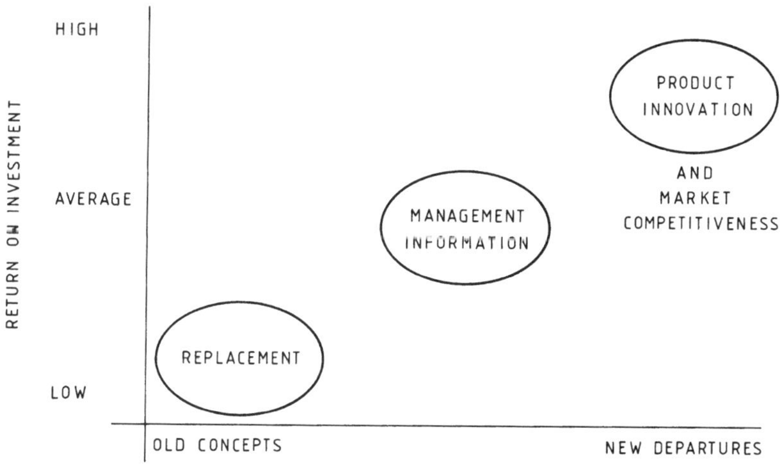

Figure 2.1   Return on investment is high with innovation, not with replacement of machines.

- A new departure is the highly modular, distributed client/server architecture which can reach the market's pulse on-line.

- Replacement policies of mainframes by mainframes or a swarm of medium-sized computers are simply extending the uncompetitive legacy applications where ROI is trivial or nonexistent.

The change characterizing the marketplace and the requirements it poses in terms of knowledge and information should not be taken lightly. Product innovation and market competitiveness depend on them.

An interesting phenomenon in merchandising and in finance is that the leading-edge real-time information processes are increasingly concentrated in a few firms. By contrast, manufacturing tends to splinter as large distributors are becoming less and less dependent on the producer company's established brands.

What underlies this shift in market and financial power is information technology and the ability to extract meaningful knowledge from customer and product information in distributed databases. This is true all the way from the market and the sales floor to the designers, the producers, and the salespeople.

Flowing from the sales floor directly to the factory, knowledge about the market and information on the goods bought by the customers—as well as their buying habits—has eliminated the wholesale levels of old. Networks reach the manufacturers in real-time, automatically converting vital data into products, schedules, and delivery instructions:

- What to ship
- Where to ship
- When to ship
- How to ship

Traditionally, about a fourth of a product's retail price went toward getting merchandise from the producer's plant to the retailer's store—typically keeping inventory in three warehouses: the manufacturer's, the wholesaler's, and the retailer's. This approach is no longer valid.

Networks, computers, and mathematical models see to it that the different intermediate levels and their associated costs are largely eliminated. This is leading to very significant savings and better response to market drives. That's how the new fortunes are made.

The ongoing major switch in business practices sees to it that the high technology merchandisers have become both *market-driven* and *customer-driven.*

- As long as management did not have rapid access to market information, decisions were basically of a manufacturing type, controlled by trademarks.

- The priorities have changed. The new technology-intense landscape both makes feasible and favors the *real-time marketplace.*

Management decisions are increasingly based on what goes on where the ultimate customers take buying action. This is the *true* market economy. The fact that these decisions are largely controlled by merchandisers means that the corresponding power is shifting toward them.

Billions are made by exploiting this knowledge-and-information potential. In just 20 years the late Sam Walton turned the Wal-Mart Stores into a great power in merchandising—and in October 1992, Forbes 400 list of the richest Americans said the third to seventh places were taken by his heirs.

As the cutting edge of technology takes its toll, old practices and obsolete systems become a handicap. Companies have to restructure their plans for flexible response to market drives. From manufacturing to finance:

- Survival depends on product design and production organized around the flow of market information.

- Profitability no longer correlates with stagnant practices, just as it is no longer geared around the flow of materials.

The more technology advances, the more important a flexible response to market drive becomes. If we don't take the necessary modernization steps, we will be at a disadvantage with regard to our competitors. Emphasis therefore must be placed on restructuring the organization around real-time market information. Such a change is simply unfeasible through old methods.

2.3   The Concept of Business Engineering

Centralized computer operations are absolutely incapable of answering the requirements posed by a flexible organizational structure and an evolving marketplace. Client/server solutions are better equipped to reach this goal. There is, however, no single way to implement them, since many alternatives exist and the approach to be chosen has to consider:

- The current competitive environment

- Projected new requirements

- Needed networkwide interoperability

Only a systems approach that observes these three prerequisites can permit the exchange of data and applications in a global real-time sense. And such an approach needs an architectural perspective that also makes business sense.

Among topmost firms this growing wave of information technology restructuring is becoming known as *business process engineering,* or simply business engineering. In its background is the quest for a much more efficient management of resources, to permit a rapid time-to-market policy.

Japan's Toyota provides a good example of how this policy applies. Its stated goal for the year 2002 is to produce a custom-made car, at client specifications, in $3\frac{1}{2}$ hours. It's an impressive goal which exemplifies how far flexibility has to go to remain competitive.

The most advanced financial institutions, merchandising firms, and manufacturing companies have come to appreciate that knowledge and information are now as important as labor and capital.

- Timely, accurate, management-oriented information is crucial in conducting business, both day to day and over the longer term.

- For this reason, the top populations to serve through technology are the client's and the company's own managers and the professionals.

This is something the data processors never did in an able manner. For more than 30 years most user organizations have made very bad information technology investments, as evidenced by the fact that less than 5 percent of their applications on mainframes have a management orientation. Finally, among foremost firms policies are changing.

The new awareness in terms of direction evidently calls for a conversion policy as well as for one of coexistence between legacy applications and competitive applications. This need is examined further in Chap. 3, but the careful reader must appreciate that there are constraints as well.

As we will see in this chapter, constraints come from two sources: polarized skills and huge investments in legacy applications. An example is the $1 billion investment in accounting-type computer programs that Fuji Bank is said to have made. Something similar is true of many other companies, and such investment has to be protected through the appropriate policies of reusable software.

Under no condition, however, should such policies inhibit new departures—hence the decision by Fuji Bank to stop investing in old technology and start an orderly process of conversion. Start to finish, this is expected to take 6 years along the path of an accelerated client/server introduction.

Within the perspectives of business process engineering, a conversion strategy raises issues connected to computer architecture. Real-time applications and on-line transaction processing (OLTP) offer totally different solutions from batch. But mainframes have been designed for batch processing.

- Real time and multithreading are best served through a large number of commodity processors, for better efficiency and lower cost.

This is the architectural solution featured by client/server as well as by the new operating systems for workstations and for massively parallel supercomputers—that is, by the modern approaches characterizing the new wave of information technology.

- Batch is single-threaded; and the bigger the processor, the better the throughput, if memory transfer and basic software support it.

The lesson is that mainframes are made for batch, and so is the mentality tooled around them. It is a sad fact that today 70 percent of every dollar spent on corporate information systems goes toward maintaining the old mainframe-based infrastructure.

The lesson a clear-eyed management will derive from such statistics is that only 30 percent of the huge amount of funds it allocates to information technology is available for developing new applications, and this money is rarely well spent. By contrast, with true client/server systems, the ratio can be turned on its head.

Let's, however, keep well in perspective that to capitalize on new technology a company needs firm policies which are not only established but also executed. The goals should be spelled out. For example:

- Greater market competitiveness

- Improved customer service

- Truly timely information

- Reduced systems costs

- More efficient operations

- Increased employee productivity

Such goals have to be expressed company by company, and the plans being made should include the priorities that business engineering implies.

Top management should appreciate that viable solutions promoting business process engineering will not come of their own will.

Somebody has to plan for them and execute them competently. *Speed* is of the essence and the same is true of *quality.*

Companies serious about getting an edge through high technology are quick to realize that many of their software development projects today take 2 or 3 years or more—and often the resulting quality is substandard. For many firms, the solution is more decentralization by:

- Segmenting the applications software by business unit

- Adopting state-of-the-art prototyping tools

- Steadily training human resources

Steady training is part of the new perspective that business process engineering brings to bear. Training is also the best way to implement astute fine-tuning in business practices.

In conclusion, when we look at new departures, it is quite important to examine all features entering into the competitive landscape, from the computer literacy of the company's human capital to conversion strategies toward a client/server architecture. Within this frame of reference, as far as the users are concerned, there has to be documented evidence of benefits—and the information technologists must be able to sell their concepts and their projects to management as well as to end users.

2.4   Deciding on Technology Investments for the 1990s

We have seen in Chap. 1 that return-on-investment perspectives have changed over the years. Most significantly, they keep on changing to match the evolution taking place in the marketplace and the requirements this imposes.

Since the funds available every year for investing in computers, communications, and software are finite, one of the missions given to business process engineering is to assure that the money being spent offers a good return on investment. Some companies, such as Bankers Trust and the Mellon Bank, have a policy of better than 20 percent ROI.

An acceptable return on investment will not be obtained unless the applications to which our computers and communications resources are put give tangible results. For 35 years or so, this has rarely been the case. A worldwide study done by Peat, Marwick in 1988 documented that, in spite of huge amounts of money being invested, most banks suffer from technology.

Some institutions have, however, learned a lesson. The Industrial Bank of Japan estimates that 60–70 percent of capital budgets in the

1990s, in Japan, will be spent on labor-saving projects as well as on developing and supporting new products. This is a sound guideline for all future investments in technology; it can respond to characteristics of this decade, namely:

- Open, increasingly competitive markets

- Demand for sophisticated services

- Competition in every field of operations

- Products and companies no longer protected through national barriers

- Greater emphasis on human capital thanks to technology

- Rapid maturity and decay of products and services

Because of the spreading telecommunications networks, and the computers and software artifacts populating them, information technology eliminates geographic distances. Therefore, trends and patterns must be carefully monitored to assure that we keep on the right course.

Figure 2.2 presents in a block diagram the systems architecture that the foremost companies follow to capitalize on the means and media that technology makes available. It is a layered approach to systems design. The client applications layer supports:

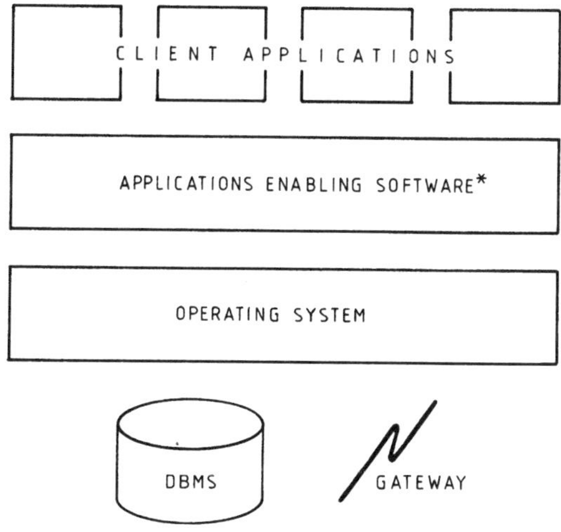

Figure 2.2 Capitalizing on technology through a layered approach to system design. Examples include transactional routines and/or graphics support.

- Interactive graphics presentation
- User-friendly solutions
- Experimental capabilities beyond "what if"
- Use of color for exceptions
- Data capture at point of origin

Most important, the solution capitalizes on the pricing of the different tools—and therefore on economics. When we talk of mainframes, maxis, or minis—that is, machines of the 1950s to 1970s—we are referring to computers which are no longer being priced competitively. Their cost-effectiveness is so low that anybody investing in them for new applications needs to have a brain exam. Therefore:

A growing number of leading organizations have decided to move not only out of mainframes but also beyond LANs to client/server architectures. And they are saving a lot of money.

A pattern is now developing which speaks volumes about how user organizations feel about computer technology. During a May 1992 working meeting in New York in the course of a research project I was doing, Oracle mentioned that its client base is rapidly changing:

- In 1989, some 60–65 percent of the Oracle DBMS business came from VMS.
- In 1992, more than 60 percent of the Oracle DBMS business came from Unix environments.

Not only the mainframes but also the maxis and minis have proved to be a very bad investment, and those user organizations lagging behind must finally take notice of this fact. In terms of price and performance, mainframes, maxis, and minis are far outpaced by high-performance, massively parallel computers and client/server approaches.

In a 1992 Cupertino meeting, Hewlett-Packard mentioned that its new Business Systems Server will take care of 90 percent of IBM-installed computer bases—at a small fraction of the cost. The rich description Microsoft gave during a similar 1992 meeting in New York, regarding its SQL Server, is another first-class example of the changing pattern of computer usage.

Oracle, Microsoft, and Hewlett-Packard are targeting not only IMS database installations but also DB2. In terms of business, the IMS client base may be vast, as it is said to represent an amazing $80 billion in investment.

- VSAM and IMS each have a much greater client base than DB2.

- IMS and VSAM each constitute a fruitful case for conversion to client/server.

- But DB2, too, has major weaknesses, particularly its mainframe base and its inability to handle the growth stream of transactions.*

The same is true of past products of the other mainframers. That is why computer vendors and software firms with proven client/server architectures are targeting their installed base with the aim of replacing the existing constrained installations—and because of technological breakthroughs, winner takes all.

Any vendor attacking the installed base of old, shared-everything solutions needs to be really strong in transaction processing. Its wares must feature high performance, high availability, and automated systems management—all at a small fraction of mainframe costs.

Every single one of the competitive features being mentioned in connection with distributed transaction processing requires a new OS departure with knowledge engineering and object orientation embedded into the operating system. Competitive vendors understand this reality.

- The policy of these competitive vendors is aggressively to go after the installed base of mainframes.

- The policy of mainframers is a defensive one—and therefore a weak position.

- The strategies are different, but the incumbents have now started using the tools of knowledge engineering and object-based solutions, just like the challengers.

As the architecture of Pink† helps document, IBM and its challengers appreciate that closely related to the choice of an operating system is an object orientation—and it is just as critical. Chapter 3 documents the benefits an object orientation can offer.

In conclusion, the strategy of any forward-looking organization should be rapidly shifting toward client/server computing built on networked workstations with graphics user interfaces and server-based information sources. The company should be steadily downsiz-

---

*Which recently led an IBM bastion in banking to move out of DB2.

†This is the operating system jointly being developed by IBM and Apple Computers.

ing its mission-critical business applications to the new architectural environment—in light of the compelling economics and the flexibility offered by the underlying technological infrastructure.

2.5 Is Technology Affecting the Way in Which We Operate?

The evidence provided in Chap. 1 as well as in the first sections of this chapter suggests that the way in which computer technology is evolving (and the pace) greatly affects how businesses operate. If we want to stay ahead, we have to adapt to the ongoing changes.

The justification for adopting a client/server architecture can be stated simply. The centralized data processors of the past cannot match the cost-effectiveness, flexibility, or power of present solutions. That's why:

- The glass houses of mainframe centers are giving way to client/ server products and services.

- New implementation concepts characterize the support that technology provides to major business strategies.

But major business strategies must rest on a solid architecture that is open, uses industry standards, and transcends the changes in computers and communications.

Just because the technological future is difficult to predict, we should not restrict ourselves to a single vendor. Instead, we should ask half a dozen vendors and a dozen or so peer organizations—then make up our own minds.

Short of this approach, which is largely based on research, there will be an *architectural chaos* in competitive organizations. There is no substitute for thinking about alternative solutions and their consequences. IT must be planned on the basis of multivendor sourcing and on an open architecture defined by the organization in order to fit its requirements in the best possible manner.

The specified architecture has to be integrative, without concern over the fact that multivendor sources mean heterogeneity:

- In the decade of the 1990s, no vendor or user organization can pretend that its communications and computing environment is homogeneous.

- Heterogeneity can be managed if people really care about doing a good job. We will see how in Part 3.

A sound, rigorous approach to the heterogeneity problem is necessary because a company's competitive position depends on how fast information gathered at local sites is processed into regional and corporate information resources. We have seen practical examples in Chap. 1.

The systems architecture that is developed should definitely account for the fact that decay caused by batch processing and other discontinuities can be fatal. The loss of time in connection with mission-critical applications costs the company, in terms of both profits and market share.

- Diverse, isolated, piecemeal proprietary applications approaches no longer make the grade.

- Such approaches can break corporate leadership and cost dearly in terms of profits.

At a time when communications networks effectively link in real-time remote operations into one point in space, that is, in *real space,* those unable to face the challenges fall behind the competition. By contrast, companies in control of their technology are able to see that this is an interconnected heterogeneous world where solutions should and can be provided.

As noted several times, precisely because no single best approach exists for all companies and all problems, management must assure that the solution to be adopted is flexible. Figure 2.3 provides an example by means of an end-user-oriented query environment which hosts different incompatible programming interfaces.

LINGUISTIC TOOLS				
APPLICATIONS				
	SQL INTERFACES			
RUN-TIME INTERPRETER	TRANSPARENT GATEWAYS	SQL ACCESS GROUP API	IBM API DRDA	PRECOMPILER
ACCESS PROCEDURES				
DBMS I	DBMS II	• • •		DBMS N

Figure 2.3 An end-user-oriented query environment could host different applications programming interfaces.

This layered approach to software tools permits taking maximum advantage of a client/server solution. The approach makes it feasible to build complex, full-function applications that are:

- Multiuser

- Transaction oriented

- Mission-critical

- High volume

The layered approach also helps in creating attractive, easy-to-use applications that take full advantage of graphics user interfaces (GUIs), as well as in developing applications that maximize the use of prototyping tools and are fully integrated with workstation-level software.

In terms of server capabilities, the goal is to assure a virtual database homogeneity that is able to offer competitive advantages in spite of incompatibilities existing in the system. Cross-database possibilities can help organizations better respond to their line of business requirements, as we have seen in Chap. 1.

The message conveyed here is that we have to plan for the fact that the computers, communications, and software serving our businesses make up a world of heterogeneous systems and competing standards. We need to know not just which products work in this new environment but which are most appropriate to *our* case.

- The business of companies standardizing on outmoded technology simply because it feels safe, will suffer.

- They will be left with the past "traditional" legacy operations— while their competitors employ far more efficient systems.

Most companies fail to understand that they are developing new applications that are simply stillborn. The irony is that even this they do far too slowly in relation to the dynamic behavior of the market.

For many companies, one of the biggest obstacles to greater efficiency is the low level of innovation in their information technology and the rigidity of their software. The cross-database tools briefly examined in Chap. 3 (and presented more fully in Part 3) provide evidence that even if the environment is heterogeneous, data accessibility is fairly simple.

Information elements at multiple sites can be easily accessed and modified, though for global consistency and concurrency, knowledge-enriched software is necessary to coordinate activities and guarantee operations.

- Data dictionaries are needed by the drivers and other utility routines running on workstations.

- The import/export of information elements requires code translation and other messaging operations, but this is do-able.

Whether the case is homogeneity or heterogeneity, the system must support location transparency. End users and applications should not need to know where the information elements come from. Apart from the necessary directory services, other facilities include synonym maintenance, which should be standard and simple.

The most flexible and scalable environment is that of site autonomy, with each local database controlled at the place where it belongs. This way there is no central point of failure, though all local databases are available globally for cross-network transactions and queries.

In the context of the solution being suggested, each database node can speak the native network protocol for that environment. Management should not enforce a common protocol, given the conversion, operating changes, costs, and risks of failure this requires—but the technologists should provide in a networkwide sense cross-database access.

2.6 Processing Bandwidth and Databasing Bandwidth

Communications bandwidth is very important and so is the cost at which it comes. This, however, does not mean that the solutions necessary for the 1990s will depend strictly on the availability of the appropriate networks. An integrative solution is much more complex than that and involves many more factors.

From end-user level to that of the distributed resources, there are 10 layers to account for, and each one of them requires great attention in its design—as well as in interfacing. As Fig. 2.4 suggests, the best approach lies in a modular structure that emphasizes bandwidth at three levels: processing, databasing, and communications.

Networkwide interoperability rests on both bandwidth and the existence of the appropriate software for connectivity. The latter is conditioned by implementation of a given architecture and the specific software routines associated with its execution—but the term *network bandwidth* is known and needs no explaining.

- *Processing bandwidth* means computer power and should be counted at the levels of both central and distributed resources—the latter concerning departmental computers and personal workstations.

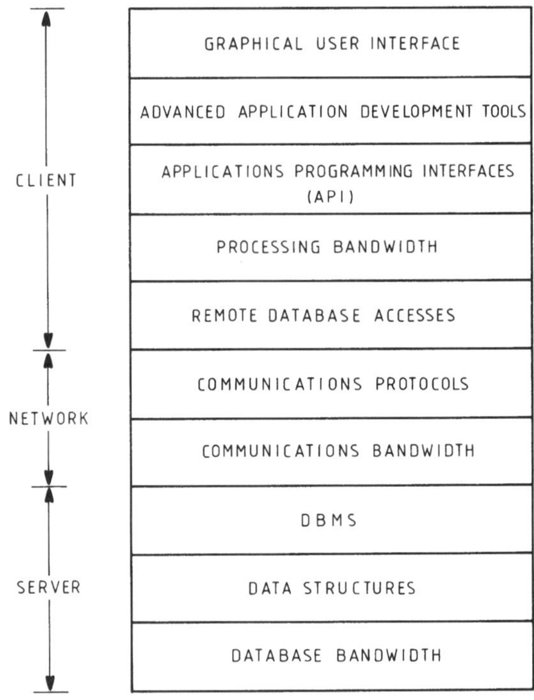

Figure 2.4 A layered data structure from the graphical user interface to database bandwidth.

Processing bandwidth is not a usual term in computer literature, yet it helps to describe fairly accurately the giga-instructions per second (GIPS) and tera-operations per second (teraops) which are becoming available. These are necessary not only for processing per se but also to meet deadline requirements for servicing ongoing connections.

For instance, we pay in computer-processing cycles for the agility and flexibility of the object-oriented methodology—hence the need for processing bandwidth. At the same time, the processing strategy we employ, as well as the different concurrent control mechanisms, must be established in a way to assure customization and adaptation. This, too, requires processing power.

Precisely because the requirements for processing bandwidth are quite significant and growing, it makes no sense to attach 30 or 40 million instructions per second (MIPS) workstations to 50 MIPS mainframes. Yet this is what most companies are still doing in a curious violation of basic systems design principles.

To get the best advantage of available physical solutions, today's powerful workstations should be networked to high-performance computers which work at 10,000 MIPS or greater capacity. This will provide the user organization with the ability to exploit processing bandwidth, which is available at low cost.

A well-designed client/server solution with the appropriate processing bandwidth can tie together existing mainframes,* internal and external databases, input systems, analytical tools, and artifacts such as dynamic customer profiles. As it grows in sophistication, this approach will be able to support entirely new ways of doing business.

Processing bandwidth is also necessary to promote the use of graphics user interfaces which facilitate ease of use and ease of learning for all personnel.† For instance, through GUIs the local sales staff with no particular expertise in computers can have sales order information integrated with detailed customer records that are maintained in distributed servers.

GUI permits a consistent user interface to be applied even when the underlying supports employed by the different clients or suppliers and the company's own personnel are running on heterogeneous machines. The concept is to greatly improve the user interface by moving from unintelligible characters and codes, which are needed with traditional dumb terminals, to full graphics capabilities.

Processing bandwidth is also necessary to allow rapid prototype development where the prototype works directly with the database and evolves into the finished application. Any solution for the 1990s should encourage iterative software development through the use of icons and design tests.

In this manner, by working interactively with distributed systems resources, sales staff can be more effective in responding to customer needs. Greater processing bandwidth permits detailed analysis of customer requirements and buying habits, this information being tied to word processors for automatic generation of follow-up letters, confirmation notices, invoices, and other communications.

- *Database bandwidth* is necessary to handle the large volume of bit streams necessary for oncoming storage requirements—from vectorized raster images to other graphics, text, data, and voice objects—that is, *multimedia.*

In the not too distant future, terabytes will become the unit of measurement in database size. Terabytes of storage are employed today by large organizations, but they are not yet a unit of measurement. Eventually this, too, will be a narrow bandwidth.

---

*These as a matter of policy should be slowly phasing out.

†See also D. N. Chorafas, *Intelligent Multimedia Databases,* Prentice-Hall, Englewood Cliffs, NJ, 1994.

To better understand the concept of multimedia databases, it is necessary to examine what the term *media* means in the database context. Like *data, media* is noun singular. The Latin word *medium** has been widely used in the field of communications to mean: "The message is the medium."

The end-user exploration of databases with a large bandwidth is assisted by *hypermedia.* This is a flexible and effective approach to information management, permitting navigation in distributed databases; but it also poses bandwidth requirements. Two basic principles are involved:

- Intelligence-enriched artifacts are stored in a network of nodes connected by links.

- Such nodes can contain information meant to be viewed and manipulated interactively.

Hypertext solutions are a subset of hypermedia. They involve issues, systems, and applications mainly connected to text. Among the basic concepts are cognitive aspects of using and designing the primitives of hypermedia systems, including:

- Means for supporting collaborative work

- Management of complexity in large information networks

- Strategies for effective use of browsing

The facilities that hypertext and hypermedia provide come from the fact that the supportive mechanism has intelligence embedded into it. This is as important with text as it is with information combined from various sources—text, data, graphics, audio, and video—in a nonsequential manner. Such information elements may lie in incompatible storage devices and feature diverse data structures—but must be presented coherently and in unison with one another.

The more the database bandwidth expands, the more we need knowledge engineering artifacts to filter and exploit its contents. Citibank, for instance, is currently working on projects of knowledge robots (knowbots) which reside at network nodes and are activated through message passing to automatically perform an increasing array of tasks.

---

*There is also the Latin word datum. Both datum and medium have Greek origins. In Latin, the plural forms of datum and medium are data and media. In information science, data and media are nouns singular.

TABLE 2.1   Cost and Transaction Throughput Employed as Indicators by User Organizations in Evaluating Their Solutions

Simple transactions	Mainframe 3090/150		Client/server Unix box (Sequent)
Throughput	150 TPS		450 TPS
Cost	$2.5 million		$0.5 million
	Cost/effectiveness ratio	15:1	
Complex transactions*	3090/600		Hypercube architecture
Throughput	50 TPS		300 TPS
Cost	$8.0 million		$1.2 million
	Cost/effectiveness ratio	40:1	
Long transactions	3090/600 E/VF		KSR supercomputer
Throughput	20 TPS		140 TPS
Cost	$9.0 million		$3.0 million
	Cost/effectiveness ratio	21:1	
Analytical queries	2 × 3090/150		Unix boxes (Hewlett-Packard)
Throughput	80 QPS		400 QPS
Cost	$5.0 million		$1.0 million
	Cost/effectiveness ratio	25:1	

*With about 1,000 disk accesses per transaction.
TPS = transactions per second.   QPS = queries per second.

2.7   Financial Bandwidth with Client/Servers

As noted earlier in this chapter, between client/server solutions and mainframes there is a very significant difference in cost-effectiveness. Advantageous ratios of 15:1, 20:1, 30:1, or more are not uncommon to workstations, servers, and LANs.

Table 2.1 presents throughput and cost from four different implementation studies, three from America and one from Europe. The cost/effectiveness ratio varies from 15:1 to 40:1 in favor of the client/server solution—and, in one case, to the advantage of a supercomputer.

Another benchmark between old technology and new technology focuses on peak performance in megaflops considering IBM's 3090/600 E/VF versus Intel's iPSC/860-128 hypercube. A careful study has shown:

- The cost of the top-of-the-line IBM computer has been $7,840 per megaflop.

- The cost of the hypercube engine was $450 per megaflop.

- The resulting cost/effectiveness ratio is 17.4:1.

As these examples help demonstrate, the difference in cost and effectiveness between old and new solutions is well beyond an order of magnitude. Yet such crushing statistics are not always able to lead user organizations out of their mainframe shells. Typically, those companies that are least willing to change old habits find the greatest trouble down the road.

"There are two things that most senior executives know about information technology," advises Dr. Pamela Gray. "The first is that it costs too much and the second is that it never works." Some companies find this fact out the hard way—but the market is voting with dollars against the mainframe approaches.

Not long ago, a bank in New York bought a 3090/150 mainframe for $2.5 million. As the project for which the purchase was made dropped by the wayside, a year later the so far unused mainframe was put on the block and the highest bid for it has been $150,000—or 6 percent of the paid price.

In Europe, a financial institution had the same experience. A year after its purchase it put up for sale a 3090/150 and it fetched $200,000—again 6 percent of its original price. That is what mainframes are worth: $1/16$ or less of the money paid to purchase them. This is what is meant by "The market votes with dollars," and the market's response establishes beyond doubt the *financial narrowband* of mainframe equipment.

Even when such dry holes are not apparent, companies are using money unwisely by sticking to traditional mainframe approaches, though they may not be aware of it. Oracle made a study on financial bandwidth which proved that *one transaction per second* (TPS) costs:

- $57,000 on an IBM 3090/600S

- $23,000 on a Vax 6360

- $8,000 on Sequent Symmetry

- $1,000 on a PC with i386 chip

The conclusion to which this Oracle benchmark leads is that much lower costs per TPS can be achieved by smaller, more cost-effective approaches than by the mammoth monolithic mainframes. Even if the i386 is overlooked in favor of a Sequent Symmetry server, the cost per TPS stands at 7.13:1 in favor of the Unix box.

Not surprisingly, an increasing number of firms are getting eager to capitalize on new technology that downsizes their mainframe environment. Wise management does not allow itself to be tempted by mainframe adventures that lead into a cul de sac.

According to Dataquest, more than 46 percent of American mainframe users are actively considering downsizing to client/servers. As we have seen, huge cost savings are realizable by this move.

The move out of mainframes and toward vastly more efficient client/server solutions is growing. The following real-life conversions from mainframe to client/server were discussed during meetings that I had in New York in May and October 1992:

- Citibank, by Citibank

- Merrill Lynch, by Oracle and Merrill Lynch

- J.J. Kenny, by Oracle and J.J. Kenny

- Avis, by Avis

- State Farm Insurance, by Hewlett-Packard

- Eurocar, by Perot Systems

- British Petroleum, by Oracle

- Kodak, by Microsoft

- Smith Klein Beecham, by Microsoft

- Intermec, by Microsoft

- National Center for Manufacturing Sciences (NMCS), by Microsoft

In later chapters we will look more closely at some of these cases, which in themselves help demonstrate that conversion from mainframe to client/server is not only do-able but also highly profitable to the user organization undertaking it. No company can afford to miss this opportunity. Yet, because of inertia and fear of the unknown, that's what many companies do.

In a growing number of cases, an important ingredient of the conversion is the opportunity to renew and revamp the applications environment. Behind this fact lie two important points:

- Less than 5 percent of applications on mainframes currently have management orientation in them.

- Yet management and professional applications is where return on investment is the highest—and where two-thirds of the salaries go.

Slowly, the excuses used to avoid conversion from the paleolithic technology of mainframes to the new wave are fading. Here are two of the excuses often heard: "The difficult part of using workstations as a scalable multicomputer is the low-bandwidth communications links that limit their applicability to long-engrained problems." "The mainframes served us in the past; they will continue doing so in the future."

Companies that have received the benefits of the client/server approach point out a number of positive results from the new environment. The top five among them are:

1. Step-by-step increment rather than paying for lots of onward horsepower

2. A much greater flexibility and adaptability

3. Better response to developing business needs

4. Much faster development timetables

5. Graphics user interfaces rather than character user interfaces

Among other benefits that organizations with experience in implementing client/server solutions notice are a reduction in data duplication, better approaches to integrity problems, the ability to control the applications backlog, and systems that are more easily modifiable for enhancements.

All this amounts to a significant improvement in the financial bandwidth—the benefits a company gets for its investments. There is more than one way to serve a firm's continuing existence, and optimization has to be based on cost/effectiveness—not on hanging on to old computer vendor connections.

Capitalizing on the Evolution of Computing

3.1 Introduction

To face the requirements of the 1990s, leading manufacturing companies, merchandising firms, and financial institutions install multimedia networks spanning the world in T-1 and T-3 lines.* They also integrate into these networks databases of terabyte capacity and employ both client/servers and supercomputers. Manufacturing companies use mathematical simulators and expert systems. So do financial institutions aiming to map the global market into the machine.

Figure 3.1 provides some insight on how much new types of software such as knowledge engineering and prototyping weight in serving three classes of financial applications:

1. Risk management, option-adjusted spread evaluation, and liquidity analysis

2. Credits and loans, investments, asset management

3. General ledger and other accounting-type practices

As is to be expected, the first class depends by almost a 2:1 ratio on knowledge engineering, simulators, and prototyping. Of the remaining 35 percent the larger share is taken by fourth-generation languages (4GL) and spreadsheets. Precisely the opposite ratios prevail

---

*T-1 lines operate at 1.54 megabits per second (MBPS). The capacity of a T-3 line is 27 times that of a T-1.

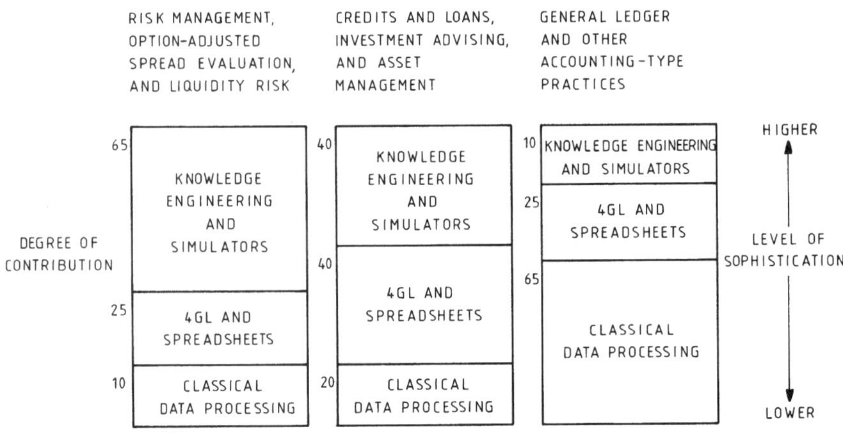

Figure 3.1 The share of old and new types of software in three different applications areas.

in the class of accounting-type applications, in which the classical data-processing routines dominate.

Between these two groups of high-risk and low-risk domains, imaginative applications are performed to match the needs of sophisticated, demanding, and lucrative clients. The knowledge and information requirements posed by such clients bring up the need for advanced implementations—hence the 40-40-20 percent ratios in the third class in Fig. 3.1.

However, the common ground for these three implementation areas is that sought-after solutions have to be fully networked with a seamless passthrough to databases. Architectures must be chosen on their ability to be flexible and expanding, but also to permit downsizing.

Two more across-the-board suggestions relate to the adoption of advanced development tools which should aim to:

- Improve analyst/programmer productivity by a scale of 500 percent to 1,000 percent

- Enable end users to develop their own software

Both aims are do-able with the new shells of fourth- and fifth-generation languages, which permit interactive prototyping and employ generators as well as reusable software.

Client/server solutions fit this frame of reference because they are more open to prototyping approaches and the productivity tools we are examining. They also provide a unique opportunity for change in the information systems culture of the organization.

While going in the direction of client/server solutions in itself provides no guarantee of success, keeping on the beaten path of the mainframes assures that there will be no value differentiation to justify the huge expenses. Eventually the facts of life are catching up with the data processors, and they have severe consequences for competitiveness and careers.

3.2   From Batch Transactions to a Valid Information Technology Plan

A valid information technology plan has to account for all the batch programs in the company's library—that is, the legacy applications, which may be 10, 15, or 20 years old.* If we convert them on line as, for instance, the Dai-Ichi Kangyo Bank has done, how many transactions per second are we talking about? Are our mainframes able to face the challenge?

A relic of the past, batch programs are a hindrance to the efficiency of computer operations. Their conversion to on-line applications makes sense for operational reasons, but the results have to be delivered at really low cost. Low cost evidently should be the guiding criterion as well for the more modern applications currently under development—by using advanced technology as suggested in Sec. 3.1.

This is not just the better way to think about applications environments. It is the only way if we really care about return on investment. As Ross Perot suggested: "I think one thing I might be able to bring to bear at this stage in my life is a keen sense of the balance between human ingenuity and advanced technology. When the two fit together, we can avoid the enormous wastes I have seen when relying too much on technology to the exclusion of people."

It is precisely this sense of balance between human ingenuity and advanced technology that provides the basis for benefiting from the implementation of computers, communications, and software. But not every user organization has a strategy that permits it to capitalize on Perot's advice.

Efforts to continue using old technology consume a huge amount of money—and they finally end by crashing. This has been the fate of, among others, the IBM–Westpac Banking project, which started in 1985 and came to an abrupt end in 1991, leaving a $200-million loss at the Westpac side.† The way Westpac Banking management sees it:

- The Core System for the 1990s (CS 90) project was not able to sell itself to the bankers,

---

*At a recent meeting in London, a British bank mentioned that it had in its library programs that were written before the programmers maintaining them were born.

†For greater detail see D. N. Chorafas and Heinrich Steinmann, *Do IT or Die,* Lafferty Publications, London and Dublin, 1992.

- There was no perceived added value to be derived from this large investment.

The way other bankers and technologists look at it, there have been seven other reasons for this mammoth mainframe project crash: (1) long development timetables, (2) split project management (IBM, Westpac), (3) too much centralization of effort, (4) obsolete development technology (AD/Cycle), (5) unsettled software (repository, OS/2), (6) high project cost, and (7) lack of milestones and design reviews.

The IBM–Westpac Banking catastrophe is far from being alone. When in 1991 the U.S. Postal Service abandoned Project Star, which was supposed to revolutionize information technology through mainframes, it was left with a dry hole of $500,000,000. In Switzerland a similar PTT (post and telecommunications) project crashed, taking along with it SF60,000,000 ($44,000,000)—and the man in charge of IT committed suicide, leaving behind wife and children.

Playing with mainframes, hence with fire, French banks went just as deep in the red. Quite recently, for example:

- Crédit Agricole's Project Varalpin cost FF400,000,000 ($80,000,000) and took 7 years,

- The original budget called for FF7,000,000 ($1,400,000) and 1 year to get the deliverables.

This project was done on mainframes with IDS II as the DBMS. A similar Crédit Agricole project, also on mainframes but with DB2, ended in a comparable disaster. The French savings banks were more ambitious. They tried to work the same project under DB2 and IDS II at the same time. Three years later the project crashed and left a hole of FF500,000,000 ($100,000,000).

Other financial institutions more sensitive to their profit-and-loss account have taken a totally different road. Figure 3.2 suggests an approach based on the client/server architecture. This provides a substitute for a major mainframe configuration with transaction-type applications running under MVS and DB2.

- The transaction processing monitor is AT&T's Tuxedo.

- The DBMS is Oracle.

- The OS is Unix.

- The LAN is Novell.

As transactions get bigger and more frequent, all must be handled in distributed networked servers. The goal is high performance which is really low cost through client/server implementation.

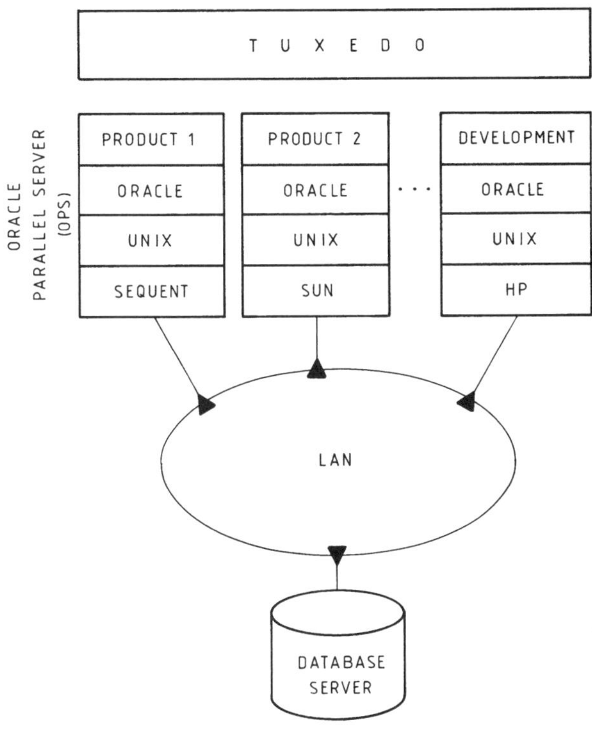

Figure 3.2   System configuration with the changeover
from DB2 and CICS to client/server.

In an interview in *Datamation* (August 1, 1992), Lawrence J.
Ellison, chairman and CEO of Oracle, aptly suggested that we can
"take a very poorly written application and throw tons of iron at it."
We could improve the response time for poorly written programs and
make them virtually instantaneous—by capitalizing on high technology, therefore client/servers and supercomputers, not by sticking with
mainframes.

3.3   Strategies for the Conversion
to Client/Server

Companies with experience in establishing and executing conversion
plans from mainframes to client/servers suggest that there are three
strategies among which to select. Each has its advantages and disad-
vantages depending on the type of company, the available skill, and
the variety and mass of applications.

1. *Global conversion.*   This will take time to execute and should be done with full support of top management.

2. *Selective approach to existing applications.*   An example is the area of operations under one director.

3. *Focus on new applications.*   This means leaving the old ones as they are while providing a soldering iron.

Strategy No. 3 is essentially a strategy of soft conversion, depending to a large extent on program renewal in order to move out of mainframes. Because of stringent requirements for interoperability between old and new applications, its success depends on the efficiency of the bridge or bridges to be established with the legacy programs.

Figure 3.3 outlines the solution adopted along the line of conversion strategy No. 3 by Dun & Bradstreet Software. A bridge is established between mainframe-based legacy applications and the new value-added software which is on client/server. Eventually the former will transit into the latter environment, but without a rush.

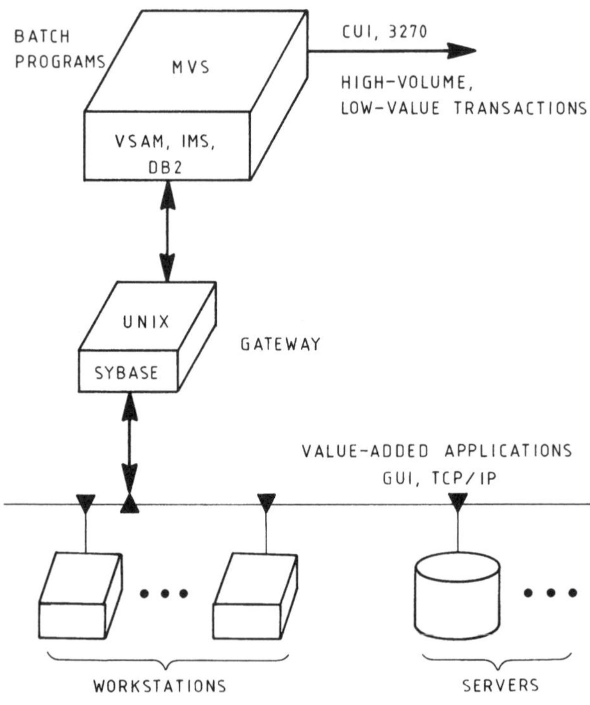

Figure 3.3 Establishing a bridge between legacy applications and competitive client/server developments.

Notice, however, that end users on the client/server setting are much better served than those attached to the mainframes. They benefit from graphics user interfaces (GUIs) rather than character user interfaces (CUIs), and they communicate by means of the TCP/IP protocol rather than 3270. That's why value-added applications are done exclusively on the client/server platforms.

It is precisely the goal of better service to the end user that guides the hand of the proponents of conversion strategies No. 1 and No. 2. Smaller organizations target strategy No. 1, as the transitory period can be kept at the level of less than 1 year. In Chap. 6, we will see an example with the case study focusing on the ALPHA Bank.

By contrast, when we talk about converting 15, 20, or more million Cobol statements and operations running on many mainframes, a division-by-division change provides a more prudent policy. Here again bridges have to be established between the old applications and the new, and cross-database access has to be assured at all times— but the transition timetable will generally be shorter than that characterizing strategy No. 3.

Whether strategy No. 1, 2, or 3 is chosen, it is advisable to observe basic design principles in establishing the architecture of the new environment. Among many issues under this heading, three are outstanding.

There should be a clearly established, well-thought-out conversion schedule.

At company X, for instance, the first priority that management thrust upon itself was to visit peer company sites and learn both the good news and the bad news of the ongoing conversion effort. When the obtained results were judged to be satisfactory, senior management asked the IT department to proceed with benchmarks.

The lessons learned during "get acquainted with the client/server architecture" visits served another purpose. The field research demonstrated that two alternative paths should be studied:

- The so-called linear conversion process

- The policy of accelerated conversion

With either plan, both technical and financial issues must be considered in the conversion of current mainframe applications to client/servers. Because of the existing skill set of employees and of the large investments in software, the current applications running on central mainframe computers can be expected to present a level of resistance. Hence, there has been a sort of queue in the conversion process, even with the accelerated conversion plan.

The solution must assure any-to-any connectivity, at every stage of the transition period.

This practically means any workstation to any workstation and any server, as well as any server to any workstation and any server. This is a subject to which some mainframers pay only lip service, while the majority avoid talking about it because they do not have the needed technology to answer the resulting requirements.*

As cannot be repeated too often, high-performance networks are a prerequisite to competitiveness. Having very efficient communications links becomes a key factor in the success of manufacturing companies, merchandising firms, and financial institutions. This statement has many other aftermaths besides any-to-any networking.

- The traditional separation between voice-oriented wide area networks (WANs) and data-oriented LANs is fast disappearing.

- Global internetworking with its bursting high-speed profile requires new solutions.

- Worldwide deregulation and liberalization are generating market opportunities for global network providers.

The evolving marketplace is being approached aggressively by the established, large telecommunications carriers as well as by new entrants. User organizations are now confronted with a choice of supplier-offered technologies like frame relay and ATM, and new concepts like outsourcing the needed communications facilities.

What the success stories have in common is that they rest on market-oriented, competitive bases. By applying advanced technologies, including LAN routers, intelligent network management, and network partitioning, they aim to offer efficient services that are designed to meet current and future needs. The key features are open architectural solutions, cost-effectiveness, and contribution to a competitive strategy designed for survival.

For each information element there must be one entry, many uses.

Of all the many and varied failures of mainframe mentality, the repetitive entry of the same information elements would seem by far to be the most damaging.

A rate of 70 percent reinput done at least once is not uncommon. Some companies fare better than that; others input the same data

---

*The result of such policies widely followed in the past has been discrete islands of applications. We will see what this means in Sec. 3.4.

four or five times. Though multiple entry concerns a small part of the whole lot, it still adds a great deal to errors, delays, and costs.

That's how money is thrown down the drain with the mainframe mentality and the inefficiencies it implies. Correcting such inefficiencies is a matter both of improving systems performance and of practicing much-needed cost control. Anything short of these two corrections will be *short on judgment*—both in a technical and in a managerial sense.

3.4   The Computer-Integrated Business

The classical structure of an industrial or financial organization is built in multiple management layers. Such a structure has little to do with computers, and until recently computers have not been used as they should have been to:

- Eliminate unnecessary management layers

- Flatten the organization to make it more efficient

- Close the gap between the plant and different islands of business activity

A computer-integrated business perspective addresses itself specifically to this problem: The aim is integrative resource management bringing a leaner organization, greater flexibility, and better cost control perspectives.

The message conveyed here is that the currently discrete islands on applications on heterogeneous equipment with incompatible databases and many repetitive inputs should be relegated to the time closet. It is not enough to convert to a client/server architecture; we should also *integrate* these islands into one well-knit system.

Figure 3.4 presents six of the most renown cases of discrete and incompatible computer applications islands in today's implementation landscape. There are many more, as each one of them is often further subdivided. For instance, production planning can divide into scheduling, on-time tracking of production orders, just-in-time inventory control, efficient energy administration, maintenance management, reduction of waste, quality assurance, and so on.

In the search for computer-based integration, emphasis must be placed on the user organization as a whole. Further, we must appreciate that there exist diverse functional requirements which utilize as well as support potentially integrative activities. Among them:

- *Order entry locations.*   Equipped with on-line workstations, sales offices must be able to enter or change orders, make inquiries

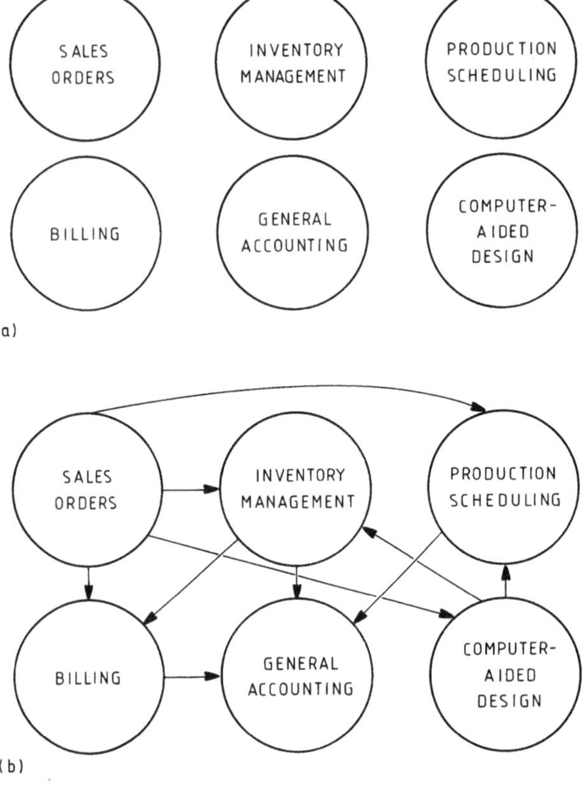

Figure 3.4 The discrete islands of computer applications have to be integrated into one system. (*a*) Mainframe-based legacy applications. (*b*) A computer-integrated solution.

regarding existing orders, customer accounts, and inventories, and enter information regarding new customers. For every information element the principle must always be: "One entry, many uses."

- *Stocking points.* Inventory locations, such as warehouses or central distribution centers, may use on-line workstations to enter shipping information regarding orders executed, scheduled, or rescheduled. These workstations may also be used to report receipts of stock transfers and customer orders.

- *Accounting.* Not only should invoices be provided to the accounting organization on line—and payments information as well as credit control data received in the same manner—but also this must be integrated with the general ledger.

- *Planning and decision support functions.* Headquarters must be able to conduct analytical studies and handle ad hoc queries, as well as monitor exceptional conditions. This is important for reasons of planning the allocation of resources and also for supervisory control.

Another area where systems integration enriched with knowledge engineering can make significant contributions is in enhancing the synergy which should exist among research and development (served through computer-aided design), manufacturing engineering, production management, inventory control, marketing, and sales. An integrative perspective should be established:

- By customer, for all customers

- By product, for all products

- By production center, for each and every center

- By cross-customer, product, production, and sales center

All this is written in full understanding that computers, communications, and software perform no miracles. A company needs organizational restructuring in order to successfully proceed with the outlined types of applications. A key question management should ask itself is: "Technology is at *our* service, but is *our* company organized for its able usage?"

It serves nothing to confuse the *systems studies* with the *organizational requirements*. Throwing money at the problem by buying machines, basic software, applications routines, or whole systems can be highly counterproductive.

- It is in itself ineffectual.

- It hides the really crucial issues.

Chances are that the salient issues are *organizational, structural, and cultural*. These are not being solved through technological advances; they have their own prerequisites.

When it comes to the implementation of computer-integrated business solutions, account should also be taken of the fact that variations do exist by industry as well as within a certain industry. Hence specialization is needed, though all industries face common requirements:

- Focusing on competitiveness

- Restructuring their management layers

- Rethinking and retrofitting their product lines

- Improving quality

- Swapping costs

- Integrating the so far discrete islands of technology implementation into a coherent total system

To be successful in business, companies must not only cope with day-to-day operations but also be somewhat ahead in technology to benefit from the effects that new types of software have on managers, professionals, and clerks. That much was noted in Chap. 1 in examining the aftermaths of corporate restructuring on middle management.

Together with the organizational perspectives to which we must be attentive, to succeed with computer-integrated business we must focus on *training* and upgrading our human resources. This has already been underlined in Chap. 2. It may sound strange repeating it so often in connection with client/servers, yet it is the pillar on which able solutions are resting.

3.5 Remote Queries, Remote Transactions, and Object Orientation

Addressed to a client/server environment, remote data access capabilities are necessary to select information elements from one or more nodes and the databases attached to them. To be properly executed in a heterogeneous environment, the distributed query should be able to perform joins between the distributed relational tables environment or, better, it should operate in an object-oriented manner.

Security measures should be projected to protect database contents, as client/server solutions derive a good deal of their strength from the execution of remote transactions. A distributed transaction environment modifies information elements at two or more nodes and therefore poses complex security and housekeeping requirements.*

To competently handle the resulting challenges, user organizations and some vendors look toward object-oriented software technology, which can customize applications and distribute them among computer networks. Hewlett-Packard's Distributed Object-Computing Program, for example, offers features compliant with Boston-based Object Management Group's Object Request Broker. This is a specification intended to let object applications be distributed among heterogeneous computer networks, simplifying programming and to a large measure doing away with program customizing.

The flexibility offered by object solutions can be vital because a key benefit of object-oriented systems is the ability to break up huge databases and distribute them across a client/server enterprise network. This makes it easier to build a distributed object computing environment that integrates different software and hardware components.

In fact, Hewlett-Packard plans to capitalize on this feature to integrate its NewWave desktop tool kit and office automation platform;

---

*See also D. N. Chorafas, *Long Transactions*, IEEE Computer Society Press, Los Alamitos, CA, 1993.

HPVue, a graphics user interface; OpenView, its network management product; SoftBench programming tools; and the Open-ODB object-oriented relational database management system.

Among software producers Borland International* chose to base its future strategy on object-oriented programming. This makes feasible a modular approach to producing software that experts are calling the single greatest change in programming since the introduction of computing 50 years ago.

Object-oriented approaches enhance systems modularity by providing a basis for dynamic but perishable inheritance characteristics. Whether for ad hoc queries or for transaction processing, the modular approach promises to do for software what the industrial revolution did for manufacturing. The effect will be a significant change:

- From custom-made, built-from-scratch huge programs

- To assembly from prefabricated software pieces

The power of the new generation of tools lies with the fact that in object-oriented programming, modules can be reused in combination with other modules in a network sense. Because of this, not only Borland but also the other major personal computer software developers like Lotus and Microsoft have used object-oriented programming for their own development purposes.

As far as the user organization is concerned, the able employment of object-oriented paradigms rests on three pillars, which among themselves create the needed infrastructure for new departures:

1. The culture change among the company's technologists to make feasible capitalizing on the new tools

2. The careful study of the legacy applications to assure that the fragmented, discrete islands of applications can be interconnected through software bridges

3. Client/server implementation for all new applications and the orderly transition from old toward the new applications environment

During the No. 2 and No. 3 aspects of the work, it is necessary to pay a great deal of attention to the efficiency necessary to handle both queries and transactions. In the expanding landscape of computers and communications, transactions and queries will in all probability be distributed. But their requirements are not the same, as each type

---

*Borland is third largest after Microsoft and Lotus Development.

has its constraints—and we have to deal with long transactions, as already explained.

Complex queries are the result of analytical requirements of management and, as we will see in Sec. 3.6, they demand a totally different systems solution than that needed for the naive SQL-type operations.

Senior management must be able to test different options, evaluate hypotheses, and manipulate information elements—without necessarily changing them. This is a totally different approach than what the transactions which appeal to accounting-type (hence, legacy) applications usually do.

But this too is changing. Even at the lower level of the organizational pyramid, where simple transactions are typically handled, their manipulation becomes increasingly complex. This is to a substantial degree due to the fact that the computer and communications environment is growing in size and the different databases need to be interconnected, as we saw in Sec. 3.4.

The newer and more potent aspect of transaction complexity is, however, the fact that one single application now involves many interdependent transactions for the completion of one and the same operation. This is the meaning of the *long transaction* defined in Sec. 1.7.

3.6 Commodity Software for Cross-Database Access

Remote, ad hoc analytical queries can be handled in an efficient manner by referencing central, departmental, and even personal databases. A company can significantly increase the usefulness of all its database information resources—both for query and for transactional purposes—if it is able to do so in a fully automatic manner.

Today and for the rest of the 1990s any technical solutions in a computer and communications environment will be partial and incomplete without support for *cross-database access*. The approach to be adopted must be able to reach across:

- Heterogeneous DBMS

- Incompatible data structures

Every company must become conscious of such a need, and there exist old and new solutions. In the past, companies facing the growing requirements for database access had to develop ad hoc approaches. Figure 3.5 gives three examples along these lines: NTT's MIA, GTE's IDA, and EPRI's DAIS.

NTT's Multivendor Integration Architecture (MIA) is operational. Of the two major parts composing it, Version 1 has been running since early 1992; Version 2 is expected in a couple of years.

1.0 Initiatives by User Organizations
1.1 MIA by NTT (probability and interoperability supporting transactions and queries)
1.2 IDA by GTE (queries only)
1.3 DAIS by EPRI (queries only)

2.0 Initiatives by Software Companies
2.1 CONNECT by Oracle (mainly queries)
2.2 DATALENS by Lotus (queries only)
2.3 Q + E by Microsoft (queries only)

3.0 Initiatives by Computer Vendors
3.1 RDB Star by DEC (object-oriented for relational environments only)
3.2 OPEN ODB by Hewlett-Packard (object-oriented for relational and object environments)
3.3 EDA/SQL by IBM (queries only)
3.4 DRDA by IBM (only for IBM's own heterogeneous relational DBMS)
3.5 DAL by Apple

4.0 Solution by Consortia
4.1 RDA by ISO, ANSI, and SQL access group

Figure 3.5 Cross-database capabilities in a heterogeneous environment.

- Version 1 primarily addresses *program portability* among five incompatible OS by IBM, DEC, Fujitsu, Hitachi, and NEC.

- When available, Version 2 will address *cross-database interoperability* for both transactions and queries, but only for relational DBMS.

Contrary to MIA, both IDA and DAIS have been projected for queries only. DAIS by EPRI is a set of specifications. IDA by GTE operates using knowledge engineering support. Such ad hoc solutions were necessary till the early 1990s because vendors could not provide commodity software for cross-database access. But this situation has radically changed.

Three offerings by American software companies are worth reviewing. They have been introduced to the market as programming products by:

- Lotus Development

- Microsoft

- Oracle

In April 1991 during the Kyoto Symposium on Parallel and Distributed Computers, Lotus Development presented *DataLens*.* This

---

*See also D. N. Chorafas and H. Steinmann, *Solutions for Networked Databases*, Academic Press, San Diego, CA, 1993.

cross-database programming product works in conjunction with the Lotus 1-2-3 spreadsheet, capitalizing on its data dictionary facilities. Over 20 incompatible databases are handled on line through this solution—relational, hierarchical, and so on.

An important feature of DataLens, which characterizes other commodity database products as well, is the use of drivers—one per heterogeneous database being addressed:

- The user of the spreadsheet poses his or her data requirement without being bothered about where the information elements are stored.

- The spreadsheet connects to the applications programming interface (API), which provides the bridge between the user program and the drivers.

- Using directory facilities, the drivers address the distributed environment of heterogeneous databases, extracting and fetching the information using code conversion if necessary.

Microsoft's Query and Edit (Q + E) cross-database software is a competitive product to DataLens, developed by Pioneer Software. Figure 3.6 shows the layered structure of this cross-database commodity software and the relational DBMS it currently supports.

Microsoft brought the Q + E programming product to the market in 1992 to answer requirements from customers like Bankers Trust,

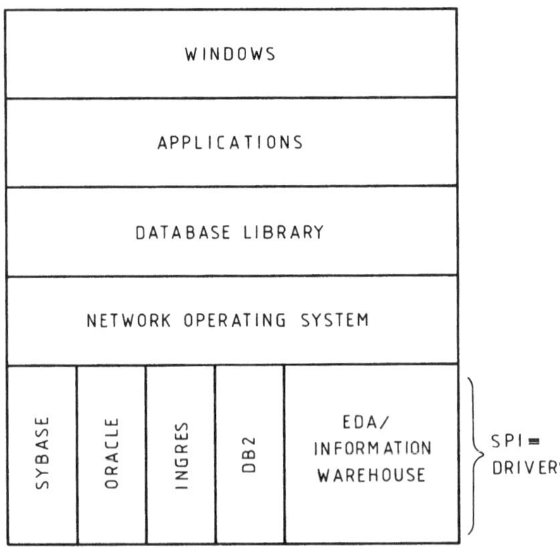

Figure 3.6 The layered structure of Microsoft's Q + E for relational cross-database access.

Eastman Kodak, Smith Klein Beecham. Operating cross-database, Q + E addresses heterogeneous databases and can supplement user needs for cross-database access connected to Microsoft's Excel.

Among the reasons the Q + E commodity product is promoted by Microsoft is to strengthen its presence in the DBMS market. Following its acquisition of the Fox Company and its DBMS, Microsoft is expanding the range of server engines to include microDBMS at the client level.

- One of the first targets to optimize is downloading and uploading of files between client and server.

- Expanding upon this application comes the need for the Q + E facility to access a growing range of heterogeneous databases.

Key to the overall functionality is the server process interface (SPI), essentially composed of drivers. Unlike DataLens by Lotus, for the time being Q + E addresses only relational DBMS.

Another good commodity cross-database programming product available today is Connect by Oracle. This too is built around a gateway concept. Most specifically:

- A transparent gateway

- A procedural gateway

Connection to the procedural gateway calls for special software to be written by the user organization in PL/SQL, a language developed by Oracle. By contrast, the transparent gateway connectivity is automatically assured and addresses the following list of DBMS and data access commodity products:

- Relational DBMS: RDB, SQL/DS, DB2, nonstop SQL (Tandem), Hitachi RDBMS

- File management: VSAM, ISAM, RMS, PACE (Wang)

- Inverted file: Adabas, Sesam

- Codasyl: IDMS, Prince DBMS

- Hierarchical: IMS, Turbo Image

- Data access: RDA (SQL Access Group), DRDA

The benefits that commodity cross-database solutions in a heterogeneous environment can offer are evident enough, so there is no need to detail them here. The competitive advantages of these programming products are just as evident. They offer both time and money savings to the user organization—hence, they constitute a solution with significant aftermaths in cost-effectiveness.

As Fig. 3.5 has shown, major vendors also offer commodity products for cross-database access. However, there exists a huge difference in terms of cost-effectiveness, in regard to what software companies and computer vendors can provide.

DataLens and Q + E run on PC under MS DOS, which costs $2,000 or so a unit. For the same job, IBM's EDA/SQL* needs a mainframe under MVS, with the smallest unit coming at the cost of $2.5 million.

- In terms of cost-effectiveness, the difference is three orders of magnitude.

- This is how money is literally thrown out of the window with mainframes.

Like DataLens, EDA/SQL addresses about 20 heterogeneous databases, including hierarchical, Codasyl, and relational; nothing more, nothing less. To repeat: EDA/SQL, DataLens, and Q + E handle only queries.

3.7 Factoring Response Time Requirements into the Systems Solution

Response time is a critical variable of the total system and of each of its component units. Companies terminalize their business partners, managers, professionals, secretaries, and clerks to help them speed up and improve the quality of their work—not to discourage them with slow computers.

One of the reasons end users get disenchanted by the technological supports put at their disposal is the long time it takes to gain a usable response.

- In principle, response time should be subsecond.

- EDPers usually try to divert management's attention from this important fact.

Long response times are unacceptable. They inhibit rather than contribute to greater productivity, and at the end-user side they create the impression that the information technologists cannot deliver. This is particularly true with variable response time, which significantly increases at peak utilization rates, as shown in Fig. 3.7.

How should the response time be calculated? There is no unique answer to this question, but there are some good models.

Traditionally, the practice has been that response time is counted from the time the last character of a transaction or query has been

---

*EDA/SQL was written for IBM by Information Builders.

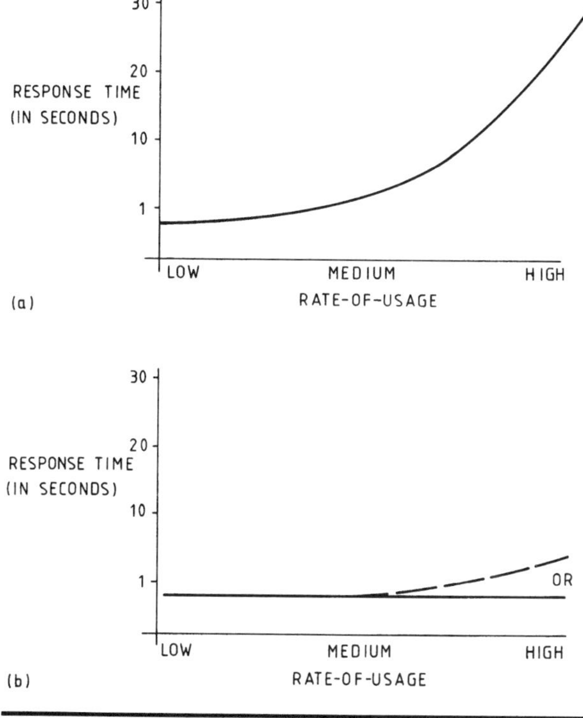

Figure 3.7 (*a*) With mainframes, response time increases at peak usage. (*b*) Response time can be held steady with client/servers and database computers.

entered on the keyboard until the first character of the response appears on the screen. This algorithm, however, has the disadvantage of rewarding slow and awkward input/output devices and protocols.

In order to provide a more all-inclusive (hence better) representative response time, many companies now distinguish between two different metrics, the second being a subset of the first. *Response time* as seen by the end user includes two parts:

1. User-level time

2. System turnaround time

According to this definition, response time extends from the first character of the input to the last character of the output. All this is, of course, giving a significant advantage to the graphics user interface over the character user interface, which is the right way to look at this issue—GUI is superior to CUI in many ways.

However, *user-level time* involves not only input/output but also local applications programs, protocols, and interfaces. This distinction reflects the slow motion of obsolete protocols like 3270. That's why today companies include in response time the delay till the complete answer is visualized.

Greater detail may also be necessary for fine-tuning the user-level part of the response time, which can be divided into three components at workstation (client) level:

- Input
- Output
- Software functions

In a similar manner, the *systems turnaround time* involves all functions not at client level, which essentially amount to:

- *Communications time,* including the LAN and/or WAN delay, both ways
- *Computer time,* for kernel commands, systems calls, database searches, and the like
- *Idle time,* arising from contention, interlocks, and other mishaps.

Within this perspective, systems turnaround time should be subsecond for about 90 percent of all cases of user access, with the balance being less than 2 seconds. This is a good standard, permitting flexibility in systems design without undue costs. It can be nicely met at reasonable expense through client/servers but not by mainframes.

Long years of experience with on-line applications help document that the more centralized the system, the greater the systems turnaround time—a fact mainframers prefer to forget. As the number of processors increases, so does the cost/performance ratio.

Based on these facts, Dr. Michael Stonebraker of the University of California at Berkeley has advanced another important metric. The principle behind it states that every time the *number of processes* exceeds the *number of processors* in a system, the solution that has been implemented is in trouble.

To properly account for response time, Dr. Stonebraker and his associate Dr. Wei Hong proposed the following algorithm:

$$\text{Cost function} = \text{resource consumption} + (W \times \text{response time})$$

W is a judgmental factor valuing response time over the cost of resources. Response time is calculated in seconds and expressed in absolute value.

- If end-user time is expensive, W can equal 5 or more.
- For clerical work W may be equal to 1.

The major advantage of the Stonebraker-Hong metric lies in the visibility it brings to the real costs. Every time the response time increases, so does the systems cost, since it is conditioned by the *cost function.*

Experiments done at the University of California help document that this cost function can be instrumental in determining resource allocation, all the way from the purchasing of new equipment (hardware and software) to its usage. It is a simple and very effective equation that can help in answering queries such as:

- What are the documented advantages of client/server over mainframe?

- How powerful a system will be needed?

- How much throughput will be required?

- How many servers and workstations will be necessary to handle the workload?

- What kind of software will be called for?

- How much training should take place to reduce delays in user interactivity?

Such estimates will, of course, require a number of assumptions. Configuration decisions will have to be made before a firm systems design can be generated, but so far obtained statistics suggest that cost/benefit results are outperforming mainframes.

For the same installation and the same application, greater response time is due to a variety of factors which have to do both with the systems configuration and with the number of users. The cost function is particularly negative with centralized mainframe solutions.

In conclusion, the Stonebraker-Hong algorithm puts attention where it really belongs, not only at the level of the computer and communications resources but also at the end-user level. This dual perspective makes the client/server solution a double winner over mainframes:

- At the level of resources and their costing

- In reference to the time the user spends on terminals and workstations

In fact, the Stonebraker-Hong algorithm can be nicely extended to cover the shuffling of paper files. This will really help dramatize the huge hidden costs which are usually embedded into paper-based administrative and back-office systems.

Being Aware of Pseudo-Client/Server Models

4.1 Introduction

In an era of rapidly changing software and hardware, no self-respecting organization that depends on computers and communications for its business can risk being locked into a monolithic technology. Instead, it needs easy-to-use workstations with full graphics capability and servers that can be dimensioned in a modular manner.

The irony of a mainframe-based approach is that if a company uses conventional technology it will finish with a brand-new but obsolete system—even if its efforts are successful. Surprisingly, this is precisely what some vendors are proposing to their clients.

No doubt the irrational advice to turn the mainframe into a client/server of sorts does not stem from bad intentions. But there is a conflict of interest, and user organizations should be aware of the fact that there exist plenty of pseudo-client/server models.

Something similar is happening with pseudo-open systems. Because open architectures and client/servers are the "in" things, over the next few years traditional mainframes will continue to evolve toward supporting distributed environments.

- Vendors will speak of increasingly "open" networks featuring their proprietary and incompatible OS, DBMS, and protocols.

- The policy statement these vendors will advance is that this will be done by adopting industry standards.

- But they will also add "under the umbrella of their own architecture," which raises doubts about how open their "open" systems will be.

Some computer experts think that as far as mainframers are concerned, client/server is nothing more than cooperative processing, which is about 20 years old. Nothing really changes. Other cognizant people believe that adoption of a more open architecture by the mainframers is a matter not of choice but of market thrust. Both are right.

There are many techniques that can be explored for interconnecting mainframe equipment at levels that include PCs and Unix boxes. What is forgotten in this argument is that these approaches offer facilities that largely provide:

- Terminal emulation

- File transfer

But these are old hat, hardly worth talking about today. The approaches they offer are very limited—and a far cry from client/server concepts. Besides this, each major computer vendor has its own approach—which is incompatible with that of the others.

This point is particularly important when it comes to interconnecting equipment from different vendors. Because of IBM's size, it is mainly emulation of SNA terminals such as 3270 that is provided on Vaxes, Unix boxes, and personal computers. As a result, in spite of vendor claims, there is relatively little connectivity from IBM to DEC—and this is valid of other makes as well.

The difficulties lying in the way of an efficient IBM-DEC interconnection are further compounded by the two incompatible IBM networking systems: SNA and APPN, even if by submitting to market pressures both IBM and DEC are introducing OSI options in SNA and DECnet. Computer experts find it difficult to say how much this is a practical case and how much it is marketing hype. The same is true with pseudo-client/server approaches.

4.2   Shared-Nothing, Shared-Disk, and Shared-Everything Solutions

A lot of traditional computer companies (read: mainframers) are building the so-called symmetric-multiprocessing boxes (SMBs). They are conveniently forgetting to define the limit of these approaches in a true client/server implementation sense. To better appreciate the point made at the beginning of this chapter, we should briefly examine the differences among the three solutions known as:

- Shared-nothing

- Shared-disk

- Shared-everything

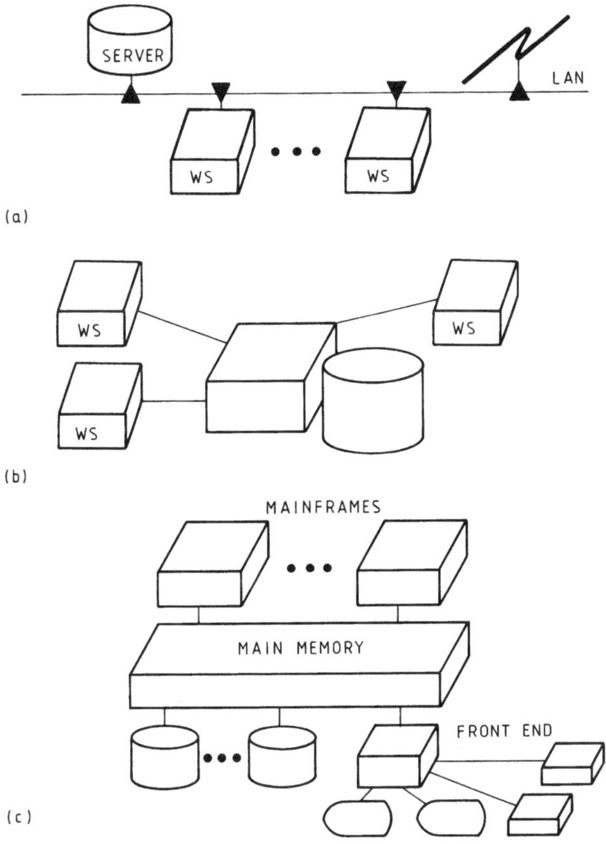

Figure 4.1 Computer applications as we know them today can be classified into three alternative architectures: (a) shared-nothing; (b) shared-disk; (c) shared-everything.

Parallel and distributed systems are based on shared-nothing designs. In this, processors communicate with one another only by sending messages via an interconnecting network, as shown in Fig. 4.1a.

The *shared-nothing* architecture has its prerequisites. Relational database solutions along the shared-nothing principle, for example, see to it that tuples of each relation in the database are partitioned across disk storage units attached directly to each processor.

■ Partitioning allows multiple processors to scan large relations in parallel.*

---

*These architectures were pioneered by Teradata in the late 1970s and by several research projects. The design is now used by Teradata, Tandem, NCR, Oracle-nCUBE, and others.

- The basic architectural concept is one of independence of action while each component part of the system works in unison with the others.

In its fundamentals, a client/server architecture follows the principles just outlined. As suggested in Chap. 3, this is the better approach because when we have more processes than processors we have to provide not only efficient queuing solutions but also a significant amount of complex software—and we are heading for trouble.

- Shared-nothing minimizes interference, by radically reducing resource sharing.

- The architecture can exploit the evident advantage presented by commodity microprocessors and main memory modules.

In contrast to shared-nothing, where each main memory and disk is owned by the processor to which it is attached and acts as a server—and where mass storage is distributed, *shared-disk* solutions alter the stated relationship. Each processor has direct access to all disks, though each has its own main memory. An example is given in Fig. 4.1*b*.

Shared-everything, also known as shared-memory, is the typical configuration of a tightly coupled system. All processors share direct access to common global main memory and to all disks. This is the classical IBM/360/370 architecture as well as that featured by all mainframers. Whether single or interconnected (multiprocessors), mainframes exemplify this design. An example appears in Fig. 4.1*c*.

In the mainframe world, many processes can operate on one processor by partitioning and timesharing the shared-nothing structure. This, however, creates many of the skew and load balancing problems faced by traditional configurations and their legacy applications.

- The design is too naive for modern dynamic environments.

- The approach reaps none of the simpler hardware interconnect benefits.

- Shared-everything does not economically scale down.

In order to ameliorate the interfacing problem, some vendors have adopted a shared-disk approach. If the disk interconnection can scale to thousands of disks and processors, an answer can be provided for large read-only databases and for those where there is no concurrent sharing.

This means that shared-disk solutions are not very effective for applications that read and write in a shared database. Although it improves upon the awkward shared-everything concept, for shared database read-write purposes the shared-disk approach is more expensive than exchanging high-level transactions and queries among clients and servers.

Cost-effectiveness, flexibility, and scalability in computer systems can be achieved only by using distributed memory designs. This avoids the bottlenecks that arise in shared-memory structures and at the same time improves systems reliability.

Some experts would answer that the programming paradigm of shared-memory architecture is attractive nevertheless, since it facilitates the program-writing task because of an inherent uniform address space. But there are techniques available today to handle the individual address space of each node. Moreover, the address space argument is just as present with heterogeneous shared-everything computers.

It is important to note that the speed of a shared-everything architecture is not determined by how fast access to memory is. With virtually an infinite amount of money, mainframers can build memory fast enough to support perhaps 250 or 300 MIPS of computing power. But this is peanuts today.

As shared-everything architectures, mainframes cannot benefit from the faster and faster microprocessors. Specially designed chips alone don't make fast servers because the shared-memory bottleneck remains while costs skyrocket. To get rid of the shared-memory bottleneck:

- We have to move away from the shared main memory in systems design, that is, away from the shared-everything concept.

- We have to adopt a networked shared-nothing environment, that is, a true client/server solution.

Let us never forget the great importance of cost factors in business. No company can spend useless money and prosper. A 10,000 MIPS supercomputing engine cost just a fraction of the 120 MIPS mainframe, and it opens a horizon toward parallel and distributed solutions that the old-hat advice given by mainframers cannot match.

4.3 The Wrong Way to Look at Client/Servers

Lawrence J. Ellison aptly suggested in a *Datamation* interview (August 1, 1992): "Old, slow, expensive hardware is going to pass. This is a well-tuned assault on the virtual monopoly in computing that mainframes have held." This is a message that every information technology executive and systems specialist should write in block letters.

When it comes to central resources, supercomputing is not just the better alternative; it is the only one. Client/server is the engine for all new competitive applications to be done in this decade.

However, as Chap. 3 has underlined, because of the huge investment in mainframe programming codes, client/servers and massively parallel computers will not replace all mainframes at once. Over a number of years they will work in conjunction with some of them, as happened in the 1980s with the PC.

As the user community has begun to realize this fact, different mainframers are trying to emulate the newer, more effective solutions through the old concepts and wares they are still marketing. IBM is used as an example in this section, but the references being made are just as true of Unisys and other remnants of the BUNCH.*

Starting with the facts, as of September 1992 the IBM personal-computer operation was reborn as the IBM-PC Company—an independent business unit. But aside from the new name and the revamping of an existing IBM marketing arm, little has changed: same management, same products; same concepts, same problems.

One of the problems is a shrinking market share. In 1992, the IBM-PC mastered only a 13 percent share of shipments to the American market, down from 14.5 percent in 1991 and 16.5 percent in 1990. Moreover, after years of steady effort OS/2 has conquered only a small fraction of the booming market for workstations.

If this is what happens at the workstation level, how is the server side doing? Is a new, truly parallel processing architecture in the making? Is IBM really serious about remaking itself? "That has been the question on the minds of analysts, investors, competitors—even IBM employees," suggests *Business Week* (September 21, 1992). "The IBM mainframe, the biggest cash cow in the computer industry, is no longer the sacred cow of Armonk, N.Y."

The way Wall Street firms look at this broader issue of renewal and survival is that the facts do not suggest that IBM is reinventing itself and the computer business, as it should have done. Rather, the now-independent business units spun off from mainframe operations:

- Are cloning the old mainframe concepts and marketing approaches

- Are not innovative with a *true* client/server architecture

No doubt, a company has to protect its installed base, and because multimillion-dollar mainframes have been so profitable to IBM they

---

*Burroughs, Univac, NCR, Control Data, Honeywell. Burroughs and Univac merged into Unisys; NCR was bought by AT&T, and Honeywell sold its computer interests to Bull.

retain their clout. But the mainframe market is shrinking. Revenues from sales of traditional mainframes are flat. The big machines are losing ground to true client/server technology.

- Theoretically, there is a change in policy. Practically, the more it changes the more it stays the same.

- Theoretically, Application Business Systems (ABS) is not in the mainframe business. Practically, it is an SAA concept centered around the AS/400 midrange computer rather than the 3090 or the ES/9000.*

The solutions being heralded—for example, offering the user organization the possibility of saving money by "downsizing" work to lower-cost minicomputers—are coming too late and present too little in terms of savings.

When we talk about implementing a client/server solution, we are implying *more than 90 percent* cost reduction for similar services—as compared with mainframe costs. Most important, we speak of a new design philosophy, not an adaptation of the old one.

There was, therefore, little credibility when the news hit the wire that ABS was giving the AS/400 extra hardware power and software functions. The ABS chief, suggests the *Business Week* article, even hired 150 engineers from IBM's mainframe development facility in Endicott, NY, when his laboratory activities were merged with those of IBM's central mainframe development site in Poughkeepsie, NY.

More surprising is the reference, made in the same article, that IBM's own software group has started to redirect a key initiative away from mainframes: "Called AD/Cycle, the scheme was designed at least in part to keep mainframes at the center of computer networks.... Now, AD/Cycle is being reworked so the repository can be a microcomputer-based server."

In other words, the more this mainframe spirit changes, the deeper it gets into mainframe depths. AD/Cycle has been around since the mid-1980s. It is a fully mainframe-oriented mentality that unfortunately (for IBM and its customers) has failed to make any impact.

- Void of any significant innovation in software development, AD/Cycle acts as a cycle sponge.

- The concepts embedded in the different tools in the toolkit date back to the 1970s, starting with the Cross-System Product (CSP).*

---

*According to ABS General Manager John M. Thomson, even larger AS/400 models than midrange are in the wings.

*CSP was developed 20 years ago by IBM's laboratory near Rome, Italy.

- Largely provided by third parties, other tools integrate poorly with one another.

- None of these tools is renowned for significant enhancements in programmer productivity.

All this is simply an anathema to client/server solutions. Behind it is still the policy of keeping control through the big-ticket, high-profit-margin systems that have been for so long an awesome cash machine. The approaches being heralded as a "new era" have nothing really to do with true client/server solutions or with end-user and programmer productivity.

4.4   Steamrolling the Mainframe through the New Environment

Downsizing from proprietary mainframes to distributed client/servers may be justifying dire predictions of great mileage to the buck, but mainframers will not submit to it without a fight. Neither will they pay more than lip service to open systems, although they would admit that these give users the option of purchasing compatible hardware from several different suppliers.

- The strategy of the old (and often aged) computer companies is to assure that downsizing does not necessarily mean that mainframes are replaced.

- The strategy is to see to it that mainframes are incorporated into the new distributed systems, remaining their focal point and their heart.

"Mainframes still have several advantages compared with minicomputers, workstations, or personal computer networks," the old computer vendors typically tell their clients. "What is really inhibiting the open systems trend is the shortage of data-processing managers experienced in their use, not the fact that mainframes remain as the centerpiece."

- More than 80 percent incorrect, this argument forgets altogether that the much lower prices of client/servers are a big point of attraction.

- There has been a shift of power in information technology from the data-processing center manager to the end-user community.

Most operating department managers now have their own computers and software budget. The new holders of the IT purse have no loy-

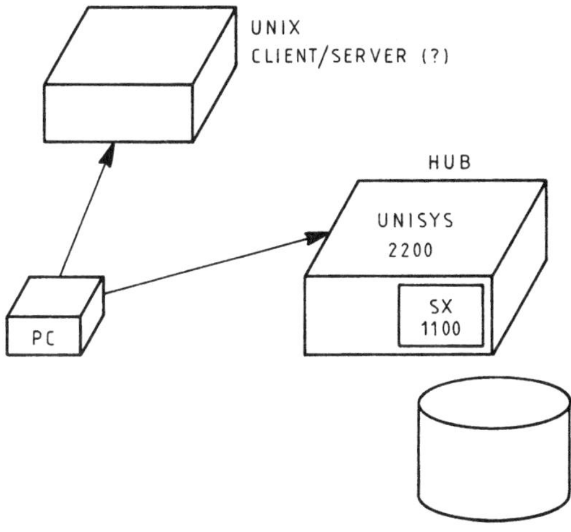

Figure 4.2 Taking the wrong way just to put a
mainframe into the system: high cost and low
reliability.

alties to the old computer suppliers and their mainframes. Hence,
they are quite often exploring client/server solutions.

The alternative of putting squarely into the picture the mainframers is not at all exciting. Based on an example by Unisys*—just
to take the heat off IBM—Fig. 4.2 shows why such an "alternative"
exemplifies precisely what *should not be done.*

- The mainframe serves as a hub. It is evidently a shared-everything
  approach.

- The SX1100 (a parochial Unix of Unisys) rides on the mainframe
  as a virtual machine.

- The use of two overlapping OS consumes many cycles—but this
  does not bother the vendor.

- The PC has a split personality and looks toward both the mainframe and a client/server of sorts.

- To make things worse, the vendor promises to put on the 2200
  mainframe file management, middleware, DBMS, RDBMS, and
  Mapper.

- The reliability of this setup is very low, and so is the efficiency, but
  the costs are high.

---

*The example was presented by a senior Unisys representative during a meeting in
New York, in May 1992.

These are the "solutions" mainframe mentality advances in spite of their unsupportable overheads. Putting two OS and three DBMS plus "middleware" on the mainframe will consume about 90 percent of its cycles. Only third-class user organizations would fall into this vendor trap.

The approach is so awkward that apart from the unwarranted high cost, the user organization faces a horde of dilemmas when it comes to upgrading or expanding its computer systems. It must either undertake a costly expansion of this make-believe "solution" or have the courage to break from the traditional mainframe and become part of the *real* client/server.

Incidentally, this is also a challenge with users of old operating systems, VSE being an example. Not surprisingly, the rate of conversion to client/server solutions taking place among these users is higher than average. Some surveys reveal that companies employing VSE are twice as likely to switch to new types of systems, as are users of MVS or VM mainframe OS.

To sell their equipment in spite of awkward systems design and obsolete OS, mainframers have in the past generally counted on marketing prowess and their ability to provide superior maintenance service. But today in the most dynamic market segments, such as the workstation business, service and support count less than speed. Hence, to maintain market control the old computer companies have to be offering technology that matches the industry's most advanced standard. If they don't understand that, then they understand nothing.

Survival has to be based on solutions, not just machines, and solutions have to have impressive specifications. Workstations work at a top speed of 40–70 million instructions per second (MIPS). They have color graphics that can be created exceptionally quickly and other advantages that can in no way be matched through naive terminals and dumb protocols.

Solutions based on client/server engines steal sales from the aged vendors' product lines. It serves little to argue that MIPS is only one measure of computer performance and that mainframes still surpass workstations at moving large amounts of data quickly. The argument fails in its fundamentals, and it becomes counterproductive.

4.5   Putting Unix on the Mainframes

Apart from the fact that the mainframers' argument reflected in the closing paragraph of Sec. 4.4 is questionable at best, the numbers have definitely turned against the old computer companies and their wares. Table 4.1 shows what this means by using as an example ES/9000 models, the top of IBM's line.

**TABLE 4.1 MIPS and Processors in
the ES/9000 Series**

Model	Processors	MIPS
9021/740	3	124
9021/660	2	86
9021/640	2	84
9021/520	1	44
9121/610	4	73
9121/570	3	56
9121/490	2	40

The MIPS attained are, to say the least, pitiful. Yet not long ago, in 1991, IBM unleashed a barrage of more than 100 new products tied to its *ES/9000 mainframe family,* including seven new models of the main processor. The careful reader will notice the following:

- The 9021/520 and 9121/490 (the latter is multiprocessor) deliver less than what Sun Microsystems' workstations feature—though they cost millions of dollars.

- The newest chip by Intel is rated at 100 MIPS, which is nearly 20 percent more than three mainframes taken together: one 9021/520 and the dual 9121/490.

The power configuration of this mainframe line is ill conceived. It provides a significant performance overlap between the 9021 *watercooled* machines and the 9121 frame-mounted models. Mainframe fans were quick to notice that the top-end 9121/610 rates at some 73 MIPS. Big deal.

Looking for a moment into basic physical characteristics, just the idea of having around a water-cooled machine is preposterous. This has to be done to gain a few MIPS, for which millions of dollars are paid—while much more MIPS could be bought for a very small fraction of that money.

Besides this, in an engineering sense the 9021 and 9121 series are both aberrations. Marketingwise, however, they suggest that IBM has lost none of its notorious skill in pushing mainframes.

- Its salespeople try to sell the 9021 as hard as they can until it seems likely they will lose the sale.

- Then, they can switch to the 9121 to show that it is a cheaper option than a second user or PCM machine.

How much this push is worth to the user organization can be seen through an example already given in the preceding chapters. To repeat: A leading bank in New York purchased an IBM 3090/150 for

$2,500,000. Not quite a year later, the project had led nowhere and was dropped.

- The bank tried to sell the 3090/150 to the secondary market.

- The best offer it could get from an interested party was $150,000— or 6 percent of the money it had paid.

That is what the mainframes really are worth in terms of market value: less than 6 percent of their list price, and even that is not justified in cost/performance terms.

Again, to refresh the reader's memory, here is a far better deal the careful client could have: The smallest configuration of the massively parallel Mas-Par computer comes at $125,000, a little less than what the sale of the useless mainframe could bring. Its power, however, is 13 times bigger than that of the IBM 3090/600 vector processor mainframe and of the fairly comparable 9021/740 mainframe—to the tune of 1,600 MIPS—hence, the 80:1 performance ratio in favor of Mas-Par.

While Unix boxes don't yet offer 124 MIPS,* they can nicely match the lower end of the 9021 and 9121 mainframe series—at a very small fraction of the cost. Here again 80:1 cost/effectiveness ratios are not uncommon and they tend toward 100:1—a difference of two orders of magnitude.

The magic, of course, is not in the word "Unix," though this OS helps as a platform for program portability. The magic is in the effectiveness of commodity microprocessor hardware that is not only modern but steadily upkept in a technological sense—and capitalizes from a mass market.

- This is the reason Sun Microsystems and Hewlett-Packard/Apollo have been able to capture a total of 55.1 percent of the market to which they appeal.

This is shown quite clearly in Fig. 4.3, which shows that Sun Microsystems and Hewlett-Packard/Apollo run head to head for first position, with the only other company capturing a two-digit share of the market being DEC—while IBM runs sixth, with an insignificant 1.8 percent market share.

That is also why IBM faces an uphill fight in breaking into the computer industry's hotly contested workstations market, as financial analysis suggests.

But people who believe in miracles may think of other reasons. Interestingly enough, introduced with the ES/9000s was a new

---

*They will be offered before too long.

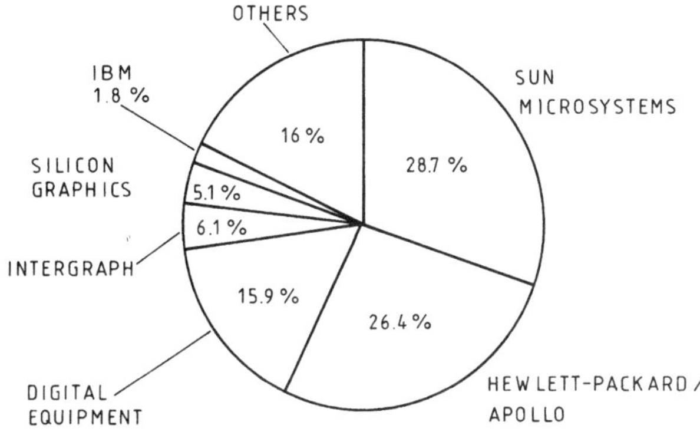

Figure 4.3 Share of the workstation market based on
worldwide revenues.

release of AIX (IBM's version of Unix) called AIX/ESA. It is said to be
based on the OSF/1 release from the Open Software Foundation—a
statement which is only partially true, since OSF/1 presupposes a
Mach kernel.*

In retrospect, the past 2 years give evidence of the inaccuracy of a
statement made at the time: "The effects of AIX/ESA will be felt most
in the technical computing environment. This will be real Unix OS-,
Berkeley-, and System 5-compliant.† The vector capabilities of the
9000 will be unleashed and unlocked and OSF/1-based. You name it
and it's there, as rich and featured as any Unix."‡

IBM and other mainframers with similar ideas about the role of
magic in computer sales could have learned a lesson, and saved themselves the trouble, by studying what has happened with Japanese
mainframers. We should always be keen to learn from other people's
successes and failures.

Some of Japan's leading computer makers did offer Unix on their
mainframes. Hitachi, for example, tried for a while to sell mainframe
Unix, but the market did not bite and the vendor decided the product
was not worth the effort.

Subsequently, as years of trying to sell Unix on a mainframe yielded negative results, Hitachi shifted its Unix focus into workstations.
NEC, meanwhile, decided not to offer Unix on its mainframe, insist-
ing that the operating system is better suited for workstations and for

---

*This is the knowledge engineering enriched Unix version by Carnegie-Mellon
University.

†The promise was still another miracle.

‡See *Electronic World News,* September 23, 1991.

its supercomputers. Only Fujitsu continues its push into mainframe Unix, and the result is not brilliant.

4.6 Paying Attention to Available Options
Prior to Commitment

The ES/9000 mentioned in Sec. 4.5 is an important addition to IBM's product line, replacing the existing ES/3090, ES/9370, and ES/4300 products. As such, it is a workhorse for the 1990s and unfortunately for IBM is not competitive—either in price or in MIPS. But that is typical of what mainframers have to offer.

Even if the question of unreasonable costs was left out for a moment, that of computing power is enough to cancel out the mainframe option. How many MIPS really remain after the overhead of OS, DBMS, and TPM has been accounted for? As performance benchmarks of workload under MVS and DB2 have documented:

- About 50 percent of available cycles was consumed by OS and DBMS.

- Some 30 percent was consumed by the ES/9000 communications subsystem (not even counting presentation services).

- Another 10 percent of available cycles was allocated to the transaction processing monitor (with 5,000 instruction programs per message).

- The remaining 10 percent went to other activities, including housekeeping.

These statistics are unsettling because they bring to the forefront one of the greatest mainframe weaknesses that user organizations rarely consider prior to commitment. Some 90 percent of the very expensive mainframe computer power is allocated to the tasks of managing the system rather than getting the job done.

It helps precious little to say that the communications load is taken care of by the front-end processor (FEP). Or that in addition to improving the performance of the mainframe the vendor has announced an effort to substantially improve the overall performance of its front-end processors.

It is beyond any doubt that this has to be done and will be done. But the client/server option also evolves. Any vendor aims to substantially improve information transfer to and from LANs connected via WANs. It is not just the token rings connected to the mainframes FEP that are undergoing improvements.

Meaningful comparisons can be made only when we accept that the available evidence is very, very negative for mainframes. What the different mainframers essentially propose to their clients is a systems design turned upside down.

Front-end processors have been around for 20 years. Their reason for being, in the early 1970s, was to unload the communications chores from the even then overburdened mainframe. But during these two decades the whole concept of how to design computers and communications systems has radically changed.

The reference just made to front-ending brings into perspective the issue of the network architecture—a vast subject which in itself would justify a whole book. "SNA enters a new era," IBM is suggesting, and other mainframe vendors say just the same about their communications software—which is, all the same, aging.

The challenge for the traditional computer vendors is to retain what they brought to the market 20 or 25 years ago, and is embedded in their clients' applications, while at the same time trying to present alternative paths to multiprotocol networking. IBM moved in this direction through the multiprotocol router, the 6611 announced in early 1992, and advanced peer-to-peer networking (APPN).

To IBM's credit, APPN is a break from the mainframe-based approach to data communications. Cognizant systems specialists, however, suggest that doubts remain over the approaches proposed by the mainframer—while others question the technology being used by suppliers of SNA multiprotocol routers.

Let's review the fundamentals. Multiprotocol routers allow user organizations to consolidate SNA and non-SNA systems.

- IBM gave this concept credibility with its 6611 router, a recognition of the spread of local area networks.

- Subsequently, the APPN announcement of March 1992 seems to have ended the company's policy of promoting hierarchical networks based on mainframes.

- The problem remains that maintaining separate SNA and non-SNA networks is expensive, and can create islands within computer networks.

We have examined the negative results that such discrete islands have to the user organization's business system in Chap. 3.

Besides this, industry watchers are pointing out that new SNA multiprotocol routers must still be proved in the marketplace. Many companies would likely take time to consider the risks involved. "Routing with SNA is less efficient than with other protocols, but it *might* still be justified," some experts suggest.

IBM seems to have compounded these kinds of doubts by omitting delivery dates and pricing for several key APPN components in its original announcements. This left users with the question of whether their corporate network plans will coincide with IBM's direction.

At the same time, many user organizations have embarked on other strategies, building non-SNA networks for such tasks as interconnecting local area networks. A strategic question then is: "How many SNA networks will the new announcement save from going to non-IBM solutions?" No immediate answer can be given to that query.

4.7   The Straightjacket of Obsolete Communications Protocols

While many fallacious, if not outrageous, statements are being made regarding pseudo-client/server models, none is more so than keeping alive the 3270 protocol*—a subject which has already received attention here. Its presence alone is able to degrade a system even if every other component in it, hardware as well as software, is first class.

The 3270 protocol, a product of the 1980s, should have been retired long ago. In spite of claims to the contrary, it can very badly support:

- End-user interactivity

- Multimedia solutions

- Network independence

- Protocol transparency

- Program and process portability

As a matter of basic principle, we have to be very prudent in our choices. Many people think that way but few companies appreciate what real prudence means.

Back in the 1980s, it was still a mainframe-and-3270 world even in the most advanced IT shops. But even then some organizations had made strategic decisions about the computer, communications, and software systems they wanted to employ. Such decisions left out the choice of open architectures—decisions that seem common enough today.

Companies that have gone the open systems route have by now enough experience to realize that a policy decision is one thing and its technical implementation is another. One of the main challenges is to determine the right mix of:

- Client/server software

- Network operating systems

---

*It is good to keep in mind that even if old and naive, the 3270 protocol does two things: It handles the data strings driving a device and it provides SNA transport.

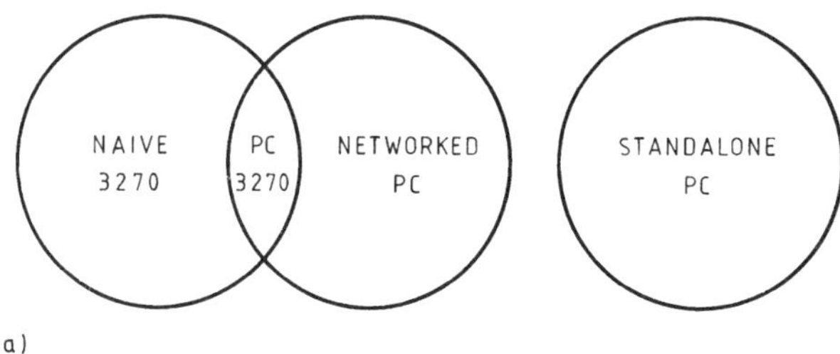

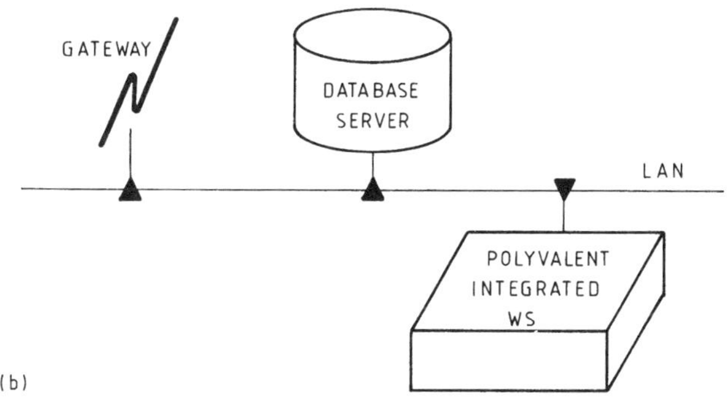

Figure 4.4 Moving out of the naive 3270 protocol is a strategic decision to be implemented organization-wide.
(a) Current status. (b) Rational solution with TCP/IP.

- Session- and transport-layer protocols
- Network interface cards
- Client/server hardware with universal interoperability

An equally important challenge is to move out of half-baked solutions
with naive 3270—a relic of the past—into an efficient solution with
Transmission Control Protocol/Internet Protocol (TCP/IP).

Figure 4.4 conveys that much, advising a move out of the naive
3270 connection and the stand-alone PC to a fully networked environment, characterized by polyvalent integrated workstations and
servers. This is the way to look to the challenges of the 1990s.

Some vendors would say that their mainframe-based wares with
distributed access and presentation through 3270 are, after all, client/
servers. This argument is misleading, and when the user organization
points this out, the vendor typically suggests that it is equally possible
to "take the logic and split it."* Less cryptically this means putting:

---

*This is a split-logic proposition anyway.

- On the one side the workstation with the user applications

- On the other side the front end and behind it the mainframe with data access

- In the middle an SNA link

Extending this split-logic approach a bit further, the vendor even offers an SNA multiprotocol router of the type we saw in Sec. 4.6. This merely puts SNA traffic into TCP/IP packets, rather than actually converting it. It is an approach pulled by the hair, but it can help in keeping the customer under control.

User organizations would be smart to see the ploy of the pseudo-client/server approach. Without doubt this is not a solution which answers their interests in the best possible way; hence, it is not the solution to adopt. Confronted with quite a similar problem, a leading financial organization responded to the vendor in this way:

- "It is a folly to do client/server solutions with this form of distribution."

- "It will never really satisfy our end-user requirements; neither will it be able to answer the need for flexibility in a reasonable manner."

When the vendor hears this sort of response, it may make another suggestion leading to an approach as unwarranted as the one that has just been discarded:

- Replace SNA by APPN

- Replace 3270 by APPC or LU 6.2.

The vendor can even sweeten the second part of the deal by throwing in TCP/IP. The savvy user organization which hears this offer should answer: "No, thanks!" Such a twisted way of facing networking requirements will end up costing a lot of money, keep intact old machines and old concepts, and in exchange provide very limited results.

Compromises that try to mix old protocols and new are for those companies that have decided to relegate their networks to third-rate solutions and an unreliable connectivity. First-rate connectivity requires new departures (with a protocol like TCP/IP or IPX) which are well supported and are currently available for common communications services. This is the strategy any serious user organization will follow, minimizing current risks while maximizing the ability to exploit future products.

5

Converting from Mainframes to Client/Servers

5.1 Introduction

A solid disk or a circular frame connected by spokes to a central hub and capable of turning on a central axis is one of history's greatest inventions. It took imagination to make a polyvalent means for transport and other purposes out of the wheel.

The wheel, however, was invented thousands of years ago, and it makes no sense to spend time today making it less round. Yet this is precisely what a depressingly large number of companies are proposing to do with some of their computer, communications, and software projects.

Typically, companies with money to spend on doing nothing have a significant number of "chief architects" devoting their time to redesigning the wheel. All this in spite of the fact that, as we saw in Chaps. 1–4, there exist today:

- Fairly clear concepts of what makes a good client/server architecture

- Plenty of programming products that can be purchased as commodities at very reasonable cost

One of the messages being sent by the different "chief architects" is that their work on Cloud 9 is necessary because of the improvements they can make over what has been achieved so far. While we should always be keen to improve upon what we have done, we should not make this an excuse for having no deliverables.

Therefore, while a plan for converting from mainframes to client/servers is established, priority should be given to acquiring assistance from people and companies with real practical experience in the changeover domain. Two principles should be kept in mind in this regard:

1. Huge improvements are to be made by moving out of the current paleolithic information technology structure.

2. There are alternatives to choose from in selecting a partner for the conversion from mainframe to client/server, and each alternative should be weighed carefully.

These alternatives are essentially three: consulting companies that have done the mainframe to client/server conversion a number of times; software vendors which for at least part of their business specialize in conversion procedures; and workstation/server manufacturers going aggressively after the current mainframe landscape.

Whichever solution is chosen by the user organization, it is wise to keep in mind that while the partner in the conversion procedure may have experience in this domain, the individual people it puts on the project may not. It is therefore wise to carefully scrutinize the curriculum vitae of the experts assigned to the job and to insist that the most experienced people be put on this assignment.

Strategically speaking, the conversion from mainframes to client/servers is also a golden opportunity for the organization and its people to change information technology *culture.* Executives and systems specialists should convert from "owners of information" to *facilitators,* as we will see after some real-life case studies convey the message of what is involved in a mainframe to client/server conversion.

5.2 Avis, Eurocar, and British Petroleum Move to the Client/Server Architecture

Many well-known companies have, after careful study, opted for the client/server architecture. By doing so, they have moved away from the monolithic mainframe environment, increased their competitiveness, and improved their profit figures. These real-life examples are important for several reasons:

- They identify the on-going trend among leading user organizations.

- They help assure that conversion in information technology is indeed successful.

- They help build confidence in regard to the decisions for architectural changes. We can always learn from what other companies have successfully done.

In early 1992, Avis Rent A Car Systems, Inc., shifted its core business applications to a client/server architecture.* Through this switch, Avis replaced a series of IBM 3270 terminal applications which had outlived their time.

The revamp in information technology that Avis has gone through includes the fourth iteration of Wizard, the company's reservation business program. Avis says it chose client/server computing for three good reasons:

1. A graphics user interface (GUI) helps to cut training costs.

2. Productivity increases because employees work on multiple windows.

3. Still, manual procedures too costly to run on a mainframe can be successfully automated on microcomputers.

Prior to the conversion of its core business, Avis did a prototype of applications to be converted. These have been operated by about 100 users at 20 locations in the United States.

As these prototype applications pass inspection, Avis management deploys them at 1,400 U.S. locations; the transition will take about 2 years. Subsequently, management will examine implementation of client/server software at 3,500 offices outside the United States.

Other car rental companies have made a similar move in the direction of client/server implementation. In May 1992, Perot Systems got a major multimillion-dollar contract with Eurocar aimed to fully replace the company's current information technology infrastructure.

- Eurocar's current system rests on IBM mainframes.

- Its replacement will be Unix-based client/servers.

The new solution targets an integrated network spanning all countries where Eurocar operates, reaching a level of 1,000 branches. Perot Systems won the contract in competition with IBM, AT&T, and GM/EDS, each of which had proposed a much similar objective.

For clients who know how to read the future trends and calculate cost-effectiveness, IBM seems ready to oblige replacing its own monolithic mainframe and SAA structure with AIX-oriented client/servers. But not all customer organizations are in this class, and those who do not know or care are left in the old, inefficient environment.

Indeed, only the foremost companies have the courage of moving out of the asphyxiating mainframes and their concepts of the past, a

---

*See *Communications Week International,* February 17, 1992.

case in point being British Petroleum. BP recently faced this basic problem:

- It wanted a new European common accounts system able to offer much greater flexibility than anything attempted so far.

- Management decision support was given priority, and this meant restructuring a number of applications.

- The system also had to handle in a homogeneous manner the sales of oil products in all countries where the company operates.

Management decided that a package solution would be the best and bought software that runs on an open system (which will be fully defined in Chap. 8). One of the prerequisites is that this package had to handle multicompany as well as multicurrency accounts, with a different language interface by country.

BP's current mainframe solution features SAP software under VSAM, for general ledger and all associated accounting, costing, and billing procedures. With the switch, all these applications, including the general ledger, moved to Sequent servers—through a project which BP has granted to Oracle Corporation.

The technical problems associated with this important conversion have been minor. The major issue was political, particularly in Germany, where IBM actively fought to retain management support for mainframes.

But the millions of dollars in savings carried the day with top management at BP, which gave a flat order that conversion to client/servers had to be done. Even so, problems persisted with the EDPers, whose political clout remains strong. As a result, to overcome local resistance BP management used a policy of rotation of systems experts—for instance, employing Americans in Germany and Britons in America.

Another oil company, which prefers not to be identified, was to underline that there have been major operational benefits apart from the significant cost reduction obtained by moving from mainframes to client/servers. An example concerned the interactive development of criteria able to identify profitable areas of activity.

- Client profiles
- Client service quality
- Instruments to lead over competition
- Low cost in added-value offerings
- Higher reliability of the information system
- Better implementation of the network concept
- Possibility of new management-oriented applications

Every one of these factors is important in maintaining competitiveness, particularly in a tough market such as oil. In Rotterdam, where the oil spot market is, some oil companies have trained a few of their people as airplane pilots. Their job is to fly over the competitors' refineries and depots and record how high the floating decks are.

This flyer input helps management judge the oil supply for the spot market. It also reveals a lot about the significant competitive advantage that on-the-spot information helps assure.

5.3   A Policy of Capitalizing on On-the-Spot Assistance

By being flexible as well as close to the floor where information originates and/or is interactively reported, client/server computing provides the needed on-the-spot assistance. It is also instrumental in making the independent business unit, into which modern industry tends to divide, truly autonomous.

- "Divide and control" does not mean pitting the parts against one another.

- The goal is to keep big organizations divided into smaller, more manageable entities.

To be successful, this solution requires a rigorous architectural background. A system is not a cake to be cut into pieces. It is an integrated structure and—when the job is properly done—the whole is bigger than the sum of the single parts.

To this organizational perspective should be added the reduction of overhead from downsizing, as well as important technical services such as ad hoc analytical queries and DBMS optimization. In the past, the typical optimizer strategy has been based upon the syntax of the query itself.

This allows skilled programmers to manipulate query procedures more efficiently. However, it makes no allowance for end users who cannot follow the technical rules needed for optimum query execution.

To correct the situation, some DBMS vendors focusing on the client/server market introduced the idea of a cost-based optimizer at the distributed database level able to provide a better method for the less skilled user. The optimizer does so by:

- Employing statistics on table populations

- Providing for their on-line manipulation

This helps to generate an automated query strategy, rather than relying upon the skill of the programmer. For instance, statistics on table populations are gathered through use of an "analyze table" command, whose execution flushes out old, inappropriate query plans. "Select" statements allow the user to proceed with tuning queries as necessary.

A thorough conversion study will look at all outstanding requirements and make a grand design for handling them competently. Based on a study by a leading financial institution, this is what Fig. 5.1 practically suggests. Three major areas of interest have been examined in depth:

- Telecommunications

- Office automation

- Databases

Specific interests within these domains were found to overlap. Workstations (WS), for example, are the end of the communications line and the beginning of the client environment.

With client/server solutions, telecommunications interface to databases through LANs. A common ground of databases is data processing (DP). Most importantly, the motor at the core of profitable new applications was found to be artificial intelligence (AI).

One of the key issues to which particular attention is paid by companies downsizing to client/server is user interactivity and with it

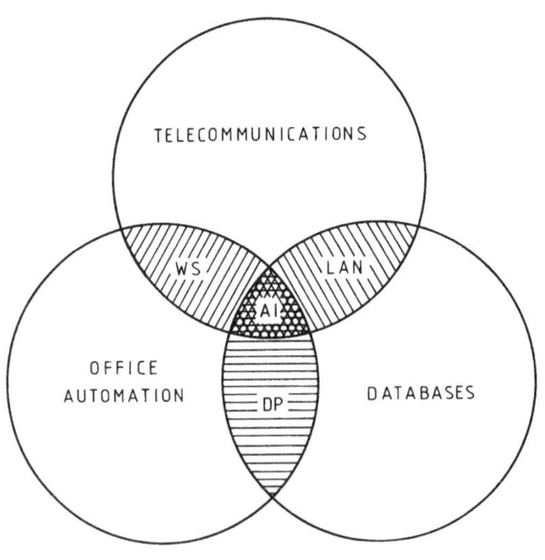

Figure 5.1 Telecommunications, databases, and office automation interrelate—the kernel is artificial intelligence.

visualization—including screen technologies, graphics modes, character-mapped displays (alphamosaics), bit-mapped displays (alphageometrics), keyboard, mouse, joy stick, tracker ball, infrared controller, pads (graphics tablets), and image-digitizing systems. Such companies are also concerned with issues connected to resolution, compatibility, and monochrome versus color.

Every one of the enumerated devices presents distinct advantages with client/server models. The concept is to promote graphics user interfaces. Visualization is the eyepiece of the computer, able to present through a human window everything from simple graphics to the behavior of complex dynamic systems. Advanced implementations include:

- *Visibilization,* making visible very small and very big items or concepts

- *Visistraction,* making visible phenomena lacking a direct physical interpretation

Both visibilization and visistraction require knowledge engineering support. As leading-edge organizations recognize, the interest in the sophistication of visualization is fed by end-user demand. It is also propelled by the fact that by the mid- to late 1990s:

- Microprocessor-based workstations could reach a peak of 500 Mflops, providing 25,000 flops per dollar, or 10 times the projected cost-effectiveness of a supercomputer.

- With the advent of high-definition television (HDTV), low-cost, very high definition video can be distributed directly to the desktop. As a by-product, users would have video conferencing and telepresence.*

However, multimedia and visualization are for an interactive environment, not for batch; and they require TCP/IP or IPX protocols, not 3270. Furthermore, to properly exploit the advantages visualization presents, the whole concept of programming has to change.

Another issue in need for thorough revamping is the concept of direct user input, as well as the systems events being supported at the workstation level. Among the types of events that need normalization and streamlining are initializing, finalizing, zooming, resizing, activation, and deactivation.

There is a reason for having inserted these issues between two sections of the chapter devoted to case studies on the conversion from

---

*See also D. N. Chorafas, *Intelligent Multimedia Databases,* Prentice-Hall, Englewood Cliffs, NJ, 1993.

mainframe to client/server. The reason is to dramatize the fact that a significant range of issues require attention, well beyond program conversion as such.

One more key point should be mentioned about the user interface which has classically been very badly served through mainframes and 3270. Systems designers must appreciate the importance of this interface:

- It is the sole means of attending to user queries, transactions, and visualization requirements.

- It is the channel through which the user can command information retrieval and analysis.

- It is the channel for presenting the results of one or more queries or commands.

The client and the server may use a naive language (such as SQL) or a more sophisticated one. The choice may be a standard of sorts or a proprietary language specifically designed for the end user's job.

The workstation may use caching and optimization techniques to reduce queries addressed to the server or perform security and access control checks. In all these issues, and there are many more, the conversion study must be specific and provide solutions—it should not just rest on principles and generalities.

A client may need the ability to check the integrity of queries or commands requested by the end user. Sometimes it may not be necessary to send a query to the server at all, as the workstation may itself perform the requested processing by the user and satisfy the query or command.

As these technical references help document, from management-level decisions to goals such as cost reduction and better end-user service, client/server models have a significant role to play. Their flexibility can afford huge advantages over mainframes. These advantages are known to many, but there are also many others who prefer to live and die in yesterday's technology world.

5.4   Kodak, Smith Klein Beecham, and Medical Laboratory Results

Value-added resalers using Microsoft's SQL server have replaced a number of mainframes through client/server architectures. The list includes Eastman Kodak, Smith Klein Beecham, Intermec, American International Group (insurance), Dun & Bradstreet, J. P. Morgan, Chemical Bank, and Bankers Trust.

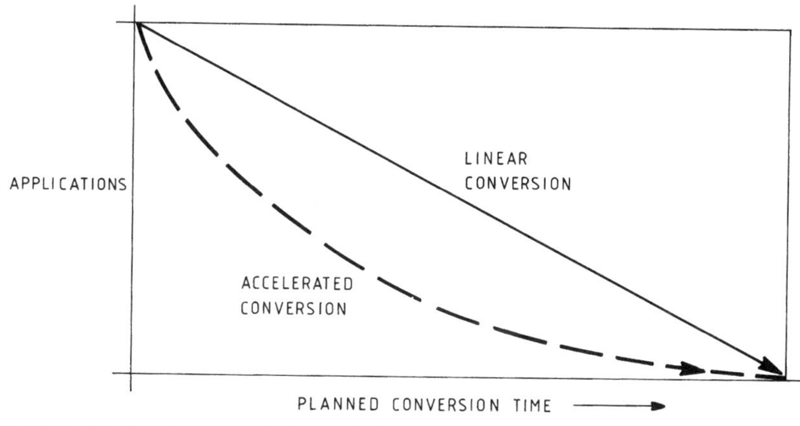

Figure 5.2 Conversion to client/server architecture will not happen overnight. It has to be planned.

Whether in manufacturing or in the banking industry, these implementations are characterized by a fairly similar concept. Therefore, the examples provided by some of them can be applied to other implementation environments.

One of the basic concepts is that, as underlined in Chap. 3, the conversion to client/server architecture will neither take place all by itself nor happen overnight. It has to be planned. Figure 5.2 shows two alternatives:

- Linear conversion

- Accelerated conversion

My personal choice is for the accelerated path. This is suggested through personal experience but also by means of a significant number of case studies.

Eastman Kodak uses an electronic data interchange (EDI) solution permitting customers to intercommunicate. The networked stations range from photo labs and graphic arts suppliers to shops which sell Kodak products. Based on client/server architecture, this system permits Kodak customers to:

- Quickly and easily place orders from on-line personal computers

- Access in real-time information about more than 80,000 of Kodak's products and parts

When this interactive approach was first projected on mainframes, the company sought to achieve simplicity in user interfaces. But such simplicity had as its counterpart a complex systems solution for on-line order entry and processing. Hence, the move out of the mainframe world.

Today, Kodak's infrastructure for this interactive, client-oriented solution is a local area network using Microsoft's SQL server. The system operates nonstop, handling customer calls 24 hours per day, 7 days per week, through a cost-effective solution.

Typically, customers use Kodak-developed software on their workstations and hook on to the General Electric Information Services (GEIS) for wide area networking. Kodak customers are able to dial in and access more than a gigabyte of product information from the SQL server.

Having handled the interactive requests from the customer as they come, the LAN sends orders to the appropriate regional order-processing location. The chosen solution allows customers access in real-time information from corporate databases. Kodak also has in operation a LAN server that can handle high transaction volumes.

Some 3,500 client PCs reside in the offices of Kodak's customers. The hardware ranges from 8088 to 80486, and operates under MS DOS.

- When a client logs on, the system checks the hardware configuration.

- Accordingly, it adjusts the available functionality to optimize on-line service.

Eastman Kodak uses the client/server architecture for metals, X-ray film, and Sterling drugs. The company developed a new generation of applications to enable customers to hook directly into the client/server landscape, replacing the more restrictive mainframe implementation that was used till then.

- Kodak is now proceeding with full on-line order handling.

- The system replaces 150 to 200 people employed for data input purposes.

Smith Klein Beecham provides another good example of client/server benefits. During a May 1992 meeting in New York, an audio-visual presentation by Microsoft quoted a Smith Klein Beecham executive saying:

> We were mainframe jockeys...
> Had data centers in 22 countries...
> And still could not get the information *we* needed for our work3...
> Then we chose the client/server model.

The point Smith Klein Beecham was making interests practically every dynamic company. Many applications today require analyzing data worldwide and these can no longer be provided the old way. Bankers Trust did precisely the same thing in terms of management information and customer service.

Vendors who know how to survive are very sensitive to these requirements. As we have seen in Chap. 3, to help in answering demanding requirements from customers, Microsoft developed Query and Edit (Q + E) as cross-database software addressing heterogeneous databases. It also expands the range of server engines to include microDBMS at client level. The aim is to optimize downloading and uploading files between different DBMS such as Sybase and Fox.

The benefits cross-database solutions can offer to business and industry in a heterogeneous environment are exemplified by a case study from Japan. In one of the medical applications, the establishment of common database access led to concurrent medical work.

Such a solution has been quickly adopted by Japanese medical laboratories. Through it, the medical labs brought down the analysis of blood samples:

- From 36 hours, prevailing in America and Europe

- To only 20 minutes, using concurrent medical analysis

The approach has been instrumental not only in improving speed and quality in customer service, but also in effecting sharp cost reduction. Some 85 percent of the cost of medical laboratory analysis is labor, a statistic found in many other industries as well.

5.5   Intermec and National Center of Manufacturing Sciences

Some of the examples on the successful conversion from mainframes to client/server architectures come from the manufacturing world. Intermec is a leading producer of data collection equipment, a $190 million company that assembles and distributes more than a dozen lines of products. Included in this product range are bar code printers, laser scanners, and radio-frequency network devices.

Intermec's product line is very appealing to manufacturing firms reexamining the automation of their product line. The implementation of just-in-time (JIT) inventory has been found to require a prompt flow of accurate information, and the appropriate devices to support it.

- JIT has created an increased demand for Intermec's products, causing the company to reevaluate its information systems strategy.

- New solutions had to be found which were more prompt, cost-effective, and flexible than the old ones.

Of particular interest to management during the strategic IT study was the ability to accurately track and prioritize parts in inventory, to keep the manufacturing lines running smoothly. Up to a point in time, Intermec had managed its inventory on an IBM AS/400, including some additional paperwork. But:

- Throughput was in excess of a quarter-million transactions per month.

- The existing AS/400 and paper-tracking procedures clearly had to be replaced.

- What the company needed was an efficient on-line system at affordable cost.

Management wanted a flexible solution that could be quickly reconfigured as goals and requirements changed. A task force determined that warehousing was a good candidate for downsizing the IT costs, while improving systems performance. The task force made a list of design criteria that a client/server network would have to meet:

- Manufacturing has to be able to send orders and receive status updates on-line.

- The warehouse needs to disconnect from the minicomputer during periods of peak usage.

- Finance should be in a position to interactively collect inventory data for cost analyses.

- The solution has to allow integration with the existing AS/400 legacy programs.

- The LAN needs to work transparently, being a key element of a larger system.

Another major goal was that, for greater data access efficiency, the network should be run by one database management system. The chosen solution was Microsoft's SQL server.

A third party, MIDAK, was given the client/server implementation project with the added mission of upgrading the Inventory Management and Control System (IMACS) to meet Intermec's specific needs.

- In a wide area sense, the adopted solution now provides interactive on-line data services to more than 50 clients.

- At Intermec itself, as parts move through the warehouse, the AS/400 tracks only whether or not parts requests have been filled.

- The SQL server handles all necessary details such as part locations and JIT inventory management procedures.

IMACS uses the easily accessible server information to verify inventories throughout the day. Soon after the client/server system was installed, this approach enabled the warehouse to achieve 97 percent picking accuracy—well beyond what the old approach could produce.

The advantages that true client/server solutions provided and continue to provide to business and industry are so widespread that national associations, too, engage in client/server research for the benefit of their members. The following is an American example along this line.

National trade associations require able information technology solutions to meet their own operational requirements. Almost always the first basic step is to assess the current situation, giving factual and documented answers to managerial and technical questions.

The National Center for Manufacturing Sciences (NCMS) is a consortium of manufacturing technology users. Its members include General Motors, Ford, Rockwell International, Digital Equipment, AT&T, and Texas Instruments. More than 100 organizations are involved in NCMS, collaborating in the development of new controllers, testers, tooling devices, and robots.

Incorporated in 1986, NCMS began shopping for an information system to support its growing activities. This has been a *new-start* experience, unlike that of many established organizations which must leverage technology purchased in the 1970s, the 1960s, or even the 1950s.

Today, NCMS relies on Microsoft's SQL server to track and manage its diverse projects. This solution permits its members to quickly access the status of:

- Any project in which they participate

- In any stage of the project's development

- Anywhere within the organization

Standard and ad hoc reports are handled by objects created in C++. Each object makes a separate SQL call, thereby shielding users from directly accessing or managing relational tables and assuring a simple, friendly on-line environment.

These case studies help document that both as a first-time application and as a conversion procedure, client/server computing is not only do-able but also beneficial to the user organization. No doubt, by the end of this decade new forms of computing will emerge. But until then it is unwise to stay with inefficient and costly systems when client/server solutions are available.

5.6 Who Is *Your* Partner for the Conversion to Client/Server?

Few topics are more fashionable in mainframe to client/server conversion today than outsourcing. Section 5.1 has made reference to this fact.* An outsourcing skill is rapidly becoming a hedge against the likelihood that, left alone, the internal human resources may not be up to the task.

Third-party assistance, some companies reason, helps add value and avoid repeating the same mistakes, hence rediscovering the wheel. But other companies either oppose wholesale outsourcing or take a cautious approach to its use.

There is value to both viewpoints. Third-party assistance in downsizing should not be a one-way street, outsourcing all the work which must be done.

- The user organization should put its own people full time on the mainframe to client/server conversion project.

- The prudent course is to rely on technology transfer by the third party rather than to delegate all the work.

This being said, which are the best candidates to help in the conversion which has to be done? What are the alternatives in doing this job? Who are the reengineering players in the market?

All told, the best partner will be a third party that understands well how the world is moving from machines to brains. This is a concept which has not yet been accepted by many people and many companies. Using these premises, we can proceed with the selection of the right partner by default.

It would be a laughing matter simply to call one of the mainframers to save *our* company from its mainframes. This would resemble having the wolf guard the lambs. In any case, mainframers do not have the client/server know-how; neither do they have the systems culture which goes with it.

---

*See also the Appendix to this book: "Who Can Help in the Transition Period?"

By contrast, Microsoft, Oracle, Perot Systems, EDS, CAP GEMINI, and Arthur Andersen are systems suppliers—hence players in the field. Hewlett-Packard has had good experience in converting from mainframes to client/servers, and the same is true of other workstation and server vendors. A valid solution will, in any case, see to the following:

1. The contract is well negotiated and includes penalty clauses.

2. Tough timetables are established for the conversion and the tests.

3. The applications development shell is resolved to the user organization's satisfaction, and that of its end users.

4. The brains and know-how of the third party's people who will do the job, are agreed upon prior to starting the project.

5. Regular design reviews are established to take care of any deviations in the project.

6. The overall cost to the user organization is reasonable as well as acceptable.

Though cost is very important, quality rather than cost should be the No. 1 factor in the decision to choose third-party assistance. And with it should come timeliness as well as the right methodology.

As for timeliness, the deliverables should be well specified in advance through a sound conversion program structure that fully observes the transition toward client/server architecture. Deliverables should not only be demonstrated by means of a prototype but also properly tested and implemented.

In terms of methodology, needed information includes dataflows, access files and their size, a list of applicable programs, a description of their complexity, and critical performance issues. This is practically synonymous with establishing a *bill of materials* (BOM) for information systems resources. Most particularly:

Databases: Input, files, reports, interactive requirements, and current and projected information element distribution

Processes: Procedures, programs, modules, links to information elements, and projected process distribution

Similarly, the user interface requirements mentioned in Sec. 5.3 should be well outlined. And as noted in Part 2, the same is true of the communications network—its links, nodes, and protocols. We have seen some examples of what to do and what not to do in Chap. 4.

As suggested in Fig. 5.3, it is wise to start with a grand design which is divided into modular parts or subsystems. Each of these

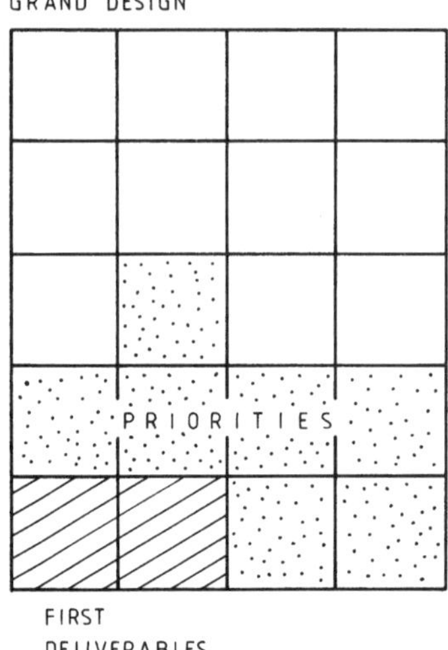

Figure 5.3 Starting with a grand design, dividing it into modules, establishing priorities, and following up with the deliverables.

modules must be evaluated in terms of its contribution to the infrastructure as well as the prevailing priorities and choices made on which modules should be attached first.

Through steady design reviews and exceptional major audits, deliverables should be evaluated in terms of planned vs. actual performance with respect to budgets, timetables, and product quality. Control action should be taken without delay when deviations occur. It is bad policy to leave quality control to the end of the project.

5.7 Changing Culture: From Being an Information Owner to Being Consultant and Facilitator

As noted in Sec. 5.1, changing culture is an issue that *should be* close to the heart of information technology executives and computer professionals. The title of this section describes the career paths for the 1990s.

The lesson to be derived from the real-life case studies in this chapter, and from other projects, is that information technology managers and systems specialists have more important things to do than to baby-sit old concepts and obsolete equipment. This is the policy of losers—not of winners.

The message is that to help the company for which they work—as well as themselves—traditional data-processing personnel must adopt a new role. To repeat once again: Computer, communications, and software professionals must change

- From being information owners
- To being teachers and facilitators

This is an entirely new and different way of looking at IT management, but it is both the new strategy among leading-edge organizations and a professionally rewarding approach.

Computer professionals can profit by realizing the strategic value of their skills. However, without a steady renewal such value is perishable. Only with a clear vision of how different the view of technology is from a 1990s perspective will systems specialists professionally survive and assure continuing demand for their skills.

Let's first look into the wrong way of going about renewal in professionality. Figure 5.4 illustrates the case of a manufacturing company that used a Unisys computer for the marketing division and IBM mainframes for manufacturing.

Although they depended on the same head of IT, the two groups of software developers—one for the IBM the other for the Unisys machines—worked independently.

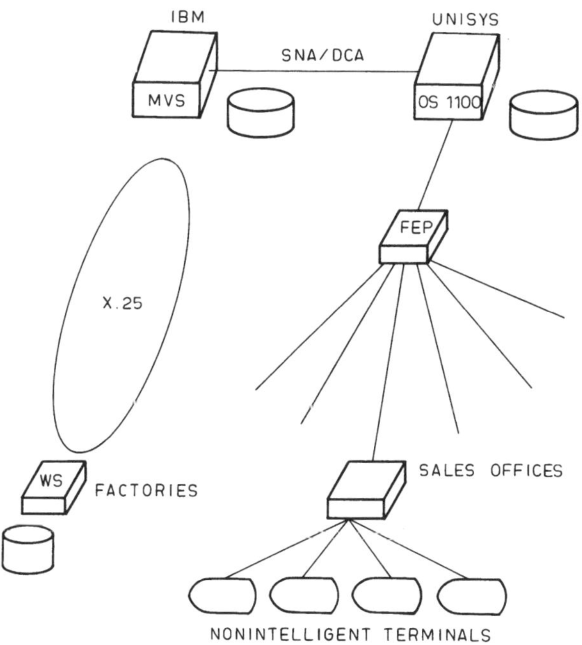

Figure 5.4 The wrong way of going about on-line computer solutions.

- In terms of databases, there were duplications as well as inconsistencies, given that the two discrete islands of applications had many files in common.

- Still worse, miscoordination between sales and manufacturing resulted in excessive inventories.

A newly elected president convinced the board that something had to be done to correct this situation, but internal company politics saw to it that the solution was left to the EDPers.

Instead of using this opportunity to engineer a new departure, the data-processing department focused its attention on two issues:

- Hooking up the mainframes at the center through a dubious SNA/DCA link

- Establishing a private X.25 network to interconnect the workstations at the factories* with the manufacturing mainframe

Nothing changed on the sales network side, and this put the company at a competitive disadvantage. Twenty years ago such a solution might have been acceptable, but for the 1990s it was just dreadful. The approach was fraught with delays, costs, and risks of failure, since the duplications still persist.

Besides being unwise in terms of cost-effectiveness and representing the negation of a modern systems architecture, the idea of different, incompatible networking solutions has a huge built-in inefficiency. The people who promote it have failed to sort out their priorities—and those of the companies for which they work.

As noted, one of the primary goals of this structure is to coordinate sales and manufacturing in real time. The result, however, suggests that manufacturing has *yesterday's* sales data. And users who want today's data must input the transactions manually!

These concepts come out of the Dark Ages and serve the end user in no way. Not only was money tossed down the drain, but the whole approach soon became a liability to the firm rather than really assisting sales and manufacturing objectives—in spite of the money thrown at the problem.

Yet available technology would have permitted the adoption of a very competitive solution. (See also Chap. 17, on federated databases.) The solution is capable of providing seamless cross-database access:

---

*Until then, dial-up lines were used at a reduced rate in late hours.

- From anywhere

- To anywhere

- At any time

Who says cross-database access means networked databases including help-desk activities to be supported automatically in real time through expert systems? Rather than installing silly links like SNA/DCA, the company should have purchased commodity software to serve cross-database access as well as to enhance data access security. Over and above this commodity software, the company could add knowledge engineering routines.

But client/servers and new types of software alone will not make all the difference. At a level much higher than hardware and software solutions, a cultural change is evidently imperative. Turning the IT specialists into consultants and *facilitators* is at the core of the cultural change just described.

Being a facilitator means giving up strict control of the computing environment. It demands a good amount of research to find the best solutions and give the end users the tools they need to access critical data ad hoc. It also necessitates looking at problems the way users look at them.

This is diametrically contrary to what is happening today where the false issues being promoted typically revolve around the creation of intermediate databases which will be full of error, while what they offer is too late and too little.

- In the past, companies with InfoCenters stored their management data there.

- Today isolating such data on the old systems simply wastes them.

By referencing central, departmental, and even personal databases in a networked manner, a company significantly increases the usefulness of all its databased information resources without wasteful ventures. Why take unwarranted risks?

An Example of Mainframe to Client/Server Conversion

6.1 Introduction

ALPHA is a well-established financial services company. Like most firms, it used to support its information technology requirements through mainframes. In 1991, ALPHA performed a thorough study with associated benchmarks, demonstrating that client/server solutions are vastly more efficient, for the following six reasons.

1. The cost-effectiveness ratio between mainframes and client/servers is 15:1, in favor of the client/server.

2. It is possible to implement step-by-step increments rather than acquire one-shot horsepower which will be only partly used.

3. Workstations, servers, and local area networks (LANs) provide greater flexibility than mainframes.

4. Client/servers offer a faster and more focused response to developing business needs.

5. Software is characterized by much faster development cycles and a simpler type of maintenance.

6. Client/servers employ graphics user interfaces (GUIs) rather than character user interfaces (CUIs) usually supported by mainframes.

As ALPHA management underlined, fundamental to this conversion is the concept of change—of steady evolution in information technology. Associated with this transition is the need to be:

- Outward-going in terms of connecting to end users and their requirements

- Forward-looking regarding improvements in computers and communications—in software, hardware, and costs

The technologists of the ALPHA company emphasized that client/server solutions are basically an evolution reflecting years of experience with distributed data processing. Their architecture mirrors the huge strides technology has made:

- GUI is both a friendly interface and one appealing to the end user.

- New and effective tools are now available on workstations.

- Client/server solutions permit quick response to user requests.

- The overhead can be kept very low because of the lower costs of semiconductors and microprocessors.

The original feasibility study at the ALPHA company, subsequent benchmarking, and the work so far accomplished in converting from old concepts and platforms document that the change from mainframe processing to client/server is smooth and fairly rapid. Basically, the conversion involves a changeover of procedures:

- From mainframes to workstations, servers, and LANs

- From CICS* and DB2 to Tuxedo and Oracle

Part of the overall strategy was to reengineer the legacy applications. Another goal was to make server resources seamlessly available, permitting the end user to integrate applications as they develop.

A third objective was to provide a more homogeneous implementation landscape. While CICS-DB2 was the major part of the old system, there was also a need to change from other heterogeneous environments such as DEC VMS, Hewlett-Packard, Perkin Elmer, and PC-LAN.

6.2   A Real-Life Experience
Capitalizing on Client/Servers

Like any other company truly aiming at getting out of the mainframe straitjacket, ALPHA proceeded step by step. It started with a distributed data-processing experience, then moved to distributed databases—and with this out of DB2 and into Unix boxes.

While this change in concepts and supports took place, the company was very careful to evaluate mission-critical applications, provid-

---

*IBM transaction processing manager that is 21 years old.

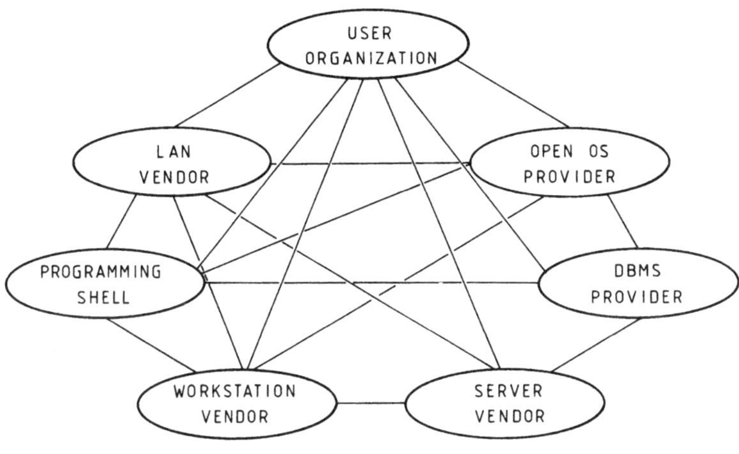

Figure 6.1 A web of vendor relations has to be managed because it underpins the client/server solution.

ing documented evidence that the new model was not only vastly superior in cost-effectiveness but also much more dependable.

Dependability, of course, relies to a large extent on vendor relations. Therefore ALPHA studied the different vendors as partners in the mainframe to client/server conversion. Figure 6.1 shows the web of vendor cooperation and hand holding necessary for a successful project. It involved not just two or three but six other parties:

- Open OS provider
- Workstation vendor
- Server vendor
- LAN vendor
- DBMS provider
- Open programming shell provider

This web of close vendor relations is necessary not only during the mainframe to client/server conversion but also as new applications develop. In fact, such a relationship makes a good part of the difference between:

- A closed, proprietary one-vendor environment, which features just one provider

and

- The implementation of an open architecture with many providers whose relationship must be effectively managed

"When we started, most of the products we use today were not there," suggested ALPHA's chief information officer (CIO). "Since new products come at a rapid pace, we have to keep our options open, and this requires a very efficient process of coordination."

- Both conversion and coordination are key words in capitalizing on technology's strides.
- Conversion will end within a relatively short timetable, but coordination is a steady process.

Coordination must be both internal with the user departments and external with the vendors. In the ALPHA case, the applications environment was pulled into a homogeneous landscape in coordination with the mainframe conversion. This involved an impressive range of sophisticated applications.

- Pricing securities
- Description of bonds
- Rating of bonds
- Bond trading
- Sale of information on bonds
- Client billing
- Other software important to the financial industry

Pricing securities is a major application. A complex pricing model takes some time to develop. But as ALPHA's information technology management suggested, value-added work through modification of an existing model to fit a new product perspective can be done in a few hours if:

- The proper tools are available
- There is a policy of speedy development

The aforementioned applications have had a variable life cycle. Some were written around 1990, but others were much older. All together, the programming constructs represented 2 million rows of primary tables with individual tables 10 million lines long.

Benchmarking and planning the conversion work was done by a team familiar with both DB2 and Oracle.* The CICS environment that characterized the mainframe applications involved several hundred programs operating both on-line and batch.

---

*Oracle is the DBMS used with the client/server architecture.

The transition from CICS and DB2 to Tuxedo* and Oracle has been across the board. The conversion effort was benchmarked with the most time-consuming applications to gain confidence that downsizing and migrating to oracle posed no real problems.

- On-line programs written in CICS Cobol were converted using the Gupta Fourth Generation Language (4GL).

- Batch programs were converted from Cobol to MicroFocus Cobol.

Indeed, incompatibilities among MicroFocus Cobol, ANSI Cobol, and Oracle's ProCobol led to the decision to convert in two stages:

- CICS Cobol to MicroFocus Cobol
- MicroFocus Cobol to Oracle's ProCobol

The impact on maintenance was felt to be nil. The key benefit is the fact that a well-documented source code is now available.

Improvements are well integrated into the system. All on-line applications use graphic, not character, user interfaces, as was true in the past. GUI permitted add-ons in quality and functionality never before possible with CUI.

For example, some of ALPHA's structured on-line applications, using the Gupta 4GL and a GUI environment, have five interacting screens. This is very hard to do with Cobol.

The conversion of CICS to Tuxedo through Gupta provided a 300 percent improvement in favor of the new solution. Hence, Gupta worked well. For batch, the MicroFocus Cobol compiler was used to avoid program rewriting.

6.3 Benefits from Prototyping and Fourth-Generation Languages

As the experience described in Sec. 6.2 helps document, information technology projects must rely on the most advanced computer-based tools, both for development and for maintenance. End users must be able to program their own applications through prototypes and powerful shells.

Other policy decisions are just as important. Modern computer programs are written to operate on multimedia information: text, data, graphics, images, voice. Hence, they must execute across different platforms. Enabling tools assist in user-made applications, with the

---

*A transaction-processing monitor (TPM) originally developed in the late 1980s by AT&T, Tuxedo runs under Unix.

systems experts focusing on the tough jobs—for instance, to satisfy database access needs.

Precisely because past commitments in hardware and software see to it that the computer and communications environment is heterogeneous, project management should be keen in supporting open systems with a policy that promotes multivendor sourcing.

Open systems typically observe norms and standards. This makes possible greater choices, which are further enhanced by an open-vendor policy. The framework abides by standards under which different products can interoperate. Other major requirements surrounding a policy of efficiency and interoperability include:

- Reusable software

- Modularity in design

Modularity is essential to program efficiency, which must be the basic characteristic of the solution adopted in connection with software development. *Compatibility* and *interoperability* with database resources are other basic requirements.

Management policies, however, must be not only be established but executed. When Abraham Lincoln won the 1860 election, he turned to reporters and said: "Well, boys, your troubles are over now. Mine have just begun." The person responsible for shaping and then executing the management policies is the chief technology officer.

The chief technology officer should see to it that the persons leading software projects are in the front line in terms of salary and position in the organization—and therefore have to deliver results.

- Rewards are called for when projects are executed correctly in terms of budget, timetable, and quality.

- This need is well understood by cutting-edge organizations.

The required change in IT culture is a major challenge that user organizations must face single-handedly, because most vendors remain hardware-oriented and steer their clients down the old dead-end road. That is another reason the ALPHA experience is so important: By providing its own well-managed solutions, it avoids the arm twisting of computer manufacturers.

Along with the adoption of open systems, the Gupta Fourth-Generation Language permitted the ALPHA organization to become much more effective in the management of information system applications. It made feasible:

- Laying out processes on the screen and having them evaluated by the users practically in real time

- Effectively integrating helps, prompts, and hypertext—thus gaining in quality and flexibility

Conversion aside, the development of new software has been tremendously aided by the new environment. ALPHA's chief information officer stated that, at equal levels of complexity:

- Applications programs now take 7 labor-days to develop in 4GL
- In Cobol they required 3 to 4 labor-months

Some of the programs in ALPHA's legacy library were in C and were easily converted to Gupta. Conversion from Cobol to Gupta was more difficult and required training. The phase-by-phase productivity improvements follow:

- The writing of functional specs and design specs required about the same time.
- In the coding phase, there was a 300 percent to 600 percent productivity improvement.
- During testing and systems integration, productivity also showed significant improvement.

The hardest element to change, however, was the mentality of those who would be using the new system. In addition to 2 weeks of training for each computer specialist, cultural change was assisted by:

- Observing the favorable user reaction to the new environment
- Demonstrating the great increase attained in productivity and throughput

Significant benefits were also obtained by the change from CICS to Tuxedo for transaction processing. Tuxedo allows going through heterogeneous databases within the relational DBMS domain. Also, according to ALPHA management, it offers good housekeeping tools, for instance, for handling in-flight transactions.

The decision to move to Unix Database Server* was based on a pilot study that addressed three key issues:

- Availability of commodity-relational DBMS

---

*The system called for Unix on Sequent machines for servers, but Microsoft Windows for clients and Novel LANs. Wide area networking was X.25. Another server under examination was n-Cube, for massively parallel database access. However, n-Cube does not work with Tuxedo.

- Performance evaluation of the old and new environments

- A sound and well-supported open systems approach

To improve upon obtainable results, ALPHA management chose to divide the maintenance group from the development group—the latter operating all the way with 4GL. Database design was done by systems specialists, but screen design was performed together with the end users. The same was true of dataflow studies affecting interactive screen usage. Much of this was done on the fly.

The first implementation in the new environment brought up other interesting results. These pointed to the fact that the benefits from prototyping as well as the use of fourth- and fifth-generation languages will be that much greater if there is a simultaneous conversion of end users toward tools such as the mouse.

To help end users learn and like the distributed interactive environment with GUI interfaces, ALPHA set up some games to arouse their interest and make them comfortable using the tools. ALPHA also bet on the positive effects of windows and electronic mail.

Further improvements in user interfaces are planned. For instance, to move the cursor, a new IBM PC features a joystick that works like a mouse. However, the hand need not move away from the keyboard, since the joystick is part of it.

In conclusion, computer literacy is a basic prerequisite to the adoption of a new policy with computers, communications, and software. One of the basic reasons information technology is badly managed in so many firms is that it is incomprehensible to senior management and top professionals. The notions underpinning software development and systems integration are totally alien. The ALPHA company has scored successes on both fronts.

6.4 Taking a Systems Look at Rejuvenating Computer Operations

The strategy employed by ALPHA brings into perspective an interesting dichotomy between the practices of the first 40 years of computing and the needs and requirements of the 1990s and beyond. The basic characteristics of the new environment include the simultaneous presence of:

- A dynamic execution of increasingly complex operations with transactions that take a long time to complete and/or with analytical as well as fuzzy queries

- The need for coexistence with the more classical but large number of simple operations, characterized by rather short transactions and crisp queries

To a significant extent, the first issue is brought up by global transactions which should be seamlessly accessing objects in a cross-database sense. It also represents the evolving pattern of applications management. The second issue concerns local databases and their global networking.

Management-type applications typically perform fewer but much more complex and polyvalent queries that have semantic meaning. Then they operate on the results. Such activities often involve large amounts of data, but the following factors also come into play:

- Flexibility

- Ad hoc characteristics

- Versioning

- Visualization prerequisites

- Response-time constraints

Because of these, today's management simply cannot afford to retrieve the needed information elements from mainframe-based database and their bulky DBMS. In contrast to the flexible client/server solutions, old approaches usually take an order of magnitude longer to retrieve the distributed information elements and process the user transactions or queries—much longer than the on-line application can afford to wait.

The managerial and technical consequences are many. Clear-eyed companies realize that their developing applications environment is both *data-intensive* and *computer-intensive*. Such duality often requires local processing and memory resources whose management is more effective through client/servers and the new wave of object-oriented DBMS and transaction processing monitors (TPMs).

This fact is, indeed, in the background of the growing interest for more advanced types of software that take full advantage of global and local resources. At the same time, there is a need for minimizing the effects of network traffic while making feasible cross-database accesses.

What successful solutions have in common is that they reflect current conditions but also establish a transition plan that, correctly, proceeds in phases. At the ALPHA company:

Phase 1 still featured the IBM 3090, DEC Vax Cluster, Hewlett-Packard, and other hardware.

But the system converted to a LAN environment, linked token rings to Ethernet gateways, and introduced Unix platforms and Novel servers. The different departments and their end users, as well as all development work, were supported through networked workstations.

All developers were moved to client/servers working on a LAN. The same was true of networked user departments—research, evaluation, trading, portfolio pricing, portfolio management, and so on. All new applications were also client/server-oriented.

The on-line network served some 200 interactive terminals, mainly PCs working through 3270 emulation. The database on the mainframe was about 70 gigabytes, with another 10 GBs of table storage. But much of this changed during the next phase.

Phase 2 did away with the mainframes, clusters, and other heterogeneous hardware and software, aiming at a more uniform configuration.

Of the diverse, heterogeneous platforms that were used in the past, only the tape and print services remain. In this second phase *the main database was moved from DB2 to Oracle on Sequent Unix servers.*

A thorough cost/benefit evaluation suggested the wisdom of making soft changes rather than hard changes, through reprogramming. Therefore, as a first step all on-line applications were converted to CICS on OS/2 with standard ANSI calls. This choice was made for two reasons:

- CICS on OS/2 has a DB2 connection. (For CICS on RS 6000, the DB2 connection is not yet established.)
- OS/2 on PS/2 costs much less than AIX on RS 6000.

Most impressive has been the conversion timetable. It was possible to move the massive DB2 contents to Oracle 7.0 on Sequent in about 2 weeks, with another 2 weeks needed for thorough testing. This effort of less than one month can best be appreciated if we recall that one of the toughest jobs in any conversion procedure is moving the database contents.

Some basic choices improvements were, however, necessary. For instance, since GUI has been a policy decision, the Presentation Manager of OS/2 was used because CICS on Windows did not provide satisfactory results. At the same time, since Tuxedo is the target TPM, every application other than those still on CICS was made to work on Windows.

Experience with Phase 1 permitted fine-tuning during the Phase 2 process. The initial proposal on conversion to client/server was to rewrite CICS through 4GL at a cost of $750,000 to $1 million. This alternative, however, would have meant that tangible benefits from the conversion would have shown up in the third year. Instead, by adopting the solution of using Tuxedo for new applications and using CICS for legacy programs, but executing both on the server, ALPHA was able to show significant financial benefits from the first year of conversion.

Another strategy that was adopted for rapid payoff was to keep the 3270 emulation for a year in order to spread the cost and accelerate the changeover to client/server. This step avoided immediate rewriting into 4GL, though such change was scheduled for the next phase.

The procedural improvement saved time as well as money, since OS/2 was already in place. Essentially, the downside was remaining with Cobol for some more time. But such a drawback would soon change, as savings showed up in the first year. The 4GL conversion is budgeted to permit further benefits.

6.5 Appreciating the Streamlined Applications Environment

The streamlined applications environment which comes with *Phase 3* is outlined in Fig. 6.2. This environment is a peer-to-peer client/server model that, in addition to clients, servers, and LANs, features a *disk farm*.

Architecturally, peer-to-peer denotes the lack of central authority commanding over the operations of the network and its component parts.

■ The LAN provides the linkage to a federation of communicating workstations and servers.

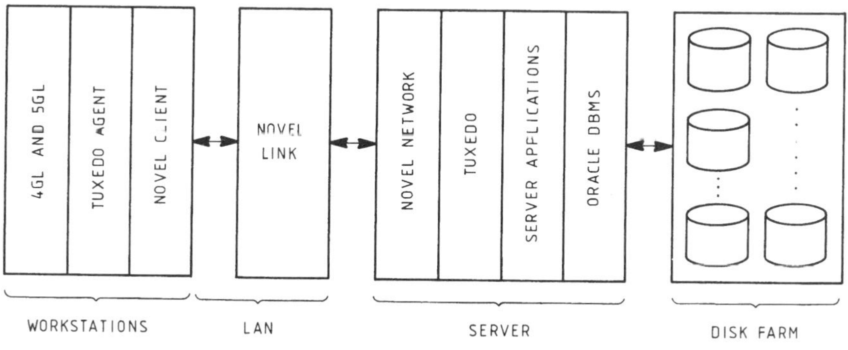

Figure 6.2 The integrative approach in a streamlined applications environment.

- Each component subgroup handles its local transactions but also shares global transactions.

Figure 6.2 presents a true case of peer-level operations. This contrasts with the limited, vendor-oriented approach in which the peer-to-peer model is given only lip service.

Phase 3 takes advantage of every feature supported by modern technology. *Multithreading* with OS/2 and NT is one example. Multithreaded servers reduce memory usage and help balance CPU usage in multiprocessing configurations.*

Typically, a listening process watches out for any clients which are requesting services and assigns a dispatcher. The dispatcher manages the interaction between clients and the systems environment. The client can be not only a networked device but also an application. In accordance with requirements, systems personnel can tune:

- The number of dispatchers and servers
- The way in which they are created and destroyed

Tuning is necessary for the implementation of large, performance-critical applications and for complex transaction processing. Just as important is the ability to integrate existing routines with the client/server architecture as it develops.

In systems configuration and implementation perspective at ALPHA, workstations are dedicated by product. The adoption of an across-the-board Tuxedo TPM enriched with load-balancing capabilities helps in promoting interoperability.

The policy is to choose workstations and servers that accept field upgrades of the CPU. This is a relatively recent development. "Never buy a workstation or server which cannot be field-upgraded. No matter what it costs, it costs too much," said a cognizant executive in another firm.

With the use of Tuxedo came a parallel server solution that according to ALPHA, gives good reliability through replication of crucial information elements in the database. "We cannot afford to be down for more than a couple of minutes," said the chief information officer.

Another important requisite of the project was the rapid timetable for the conversion.

---

*NT has been tested both on workstations and on servers (Sequent) and has yielded good results.

- The overall effort demanded 18 to 24 calendar months.

- The team of people engaged in the effort was been small but well trained.

A similar process by Yamaichi Securities was projected at 2 to 3 years for total conversion—say about 30 calendar months. The work team varied from 12 to 15 people. Hence, the investment represented roughly 400 labor-months.

In terms of timetable, in the ALPHA case, project evaluation was done in September and October of 1991, followed by careful planning and the initiation of Phase 1.

- The first client/server applications went on stream in December 1992 and currently operate on Oracle 6.03. They include the parallel servers and cluster of Unix processors, making available a core implementation system.

- The second set of client/server applications went on stream in January 1993.

- Two more sets of applications were instituted in April and June of 1993.

Each set of client/server applications has been subjected to 3 months of parallel testing. Hence, the whole lot is expected to be operational by the end of 1993.

Part of the client/server strategy implemented at ALPHA was to reduce the number of platforms used in the system. After getting rid of all the different, incompatible hardware and basic software, management sought to make homogeneous the applications software environment, including the languages being used.

Homogeneity in hardware and software is one of the significant benefits to be obtained through open architectures—most specifically, through client/server solutions. Yet surprisingly few companies are able to reason in these terms.

Experiences like ALPHA's help document that apart from the much better systems performance obtained, the financial gains to the user organization are significant. These gains are essentially reflected in terms of:

- Much lower cost per transaction

- Much lower software licensing fees

- Cost saving from personnel reduction

More important still are the flexibility and adaptability the client/ server strategy provides. According to one executive: "There have been tremendous savings, but this is *not* our No. 1 goal. Our No. 1 goal is *time*—that is, *product to market*—and the possibility to grow rapidly in an *economically sound* manner."

6.6   The Multiple Benefits of Conversion to Client/Servers

Unlike the ALPHA company, many corporations become mired in a stagnating 30-year-old mainframe environment. The cause is typically computer illiteracy at the level of top management, along with a CIO and other information scientists who have few sparks of technological courage and no clear direction. Meanwhile:

- The computer, communications, and software budget is at sea, with no return on investment goals in sight.

- The amount of money thrown down the drain on mainframes grows by the year, without a clear sign of whether and when the budgetary waste will end.

When top management is illiterate in terms of computers, communications, and software, backward-looking CIOs and their disciples know that the members of the board are willing to turn according to the vendors' wind.

In a meeting in London in late 1992, the chairman of a $7-billion institution noted that his bank bought packages from Hogan Systems to run on its mainframes. Then he added that his EDPers adopted a policy of changing these packages all the way.

The purchase of the Hogan packages had occurred 3 years earlier, in 1989, on the premise that they would be adapted to the bank's needs rather than the other way around. To do so, the bank hired 70 new programmers and a number of project leaders—and still the project of package conversion has another 2 or 3 years to go.

This timetable represents 210 labor-years to do what should not have been undertaken in the first place. With another 200 labor-years still committed, the bank is faced with more than 400 labor-years of thrown-out money. It is foolhardy, but not unusual. A long roster of companies spend 400 to 500 labor-years to change packages.

Such a policy violates three basic principles at once, and shows how big money is spoiled:

1. Changing a package rather than applying it *as is*

2. Upsizing rather than downsizing computer resources

3. Using a team of programmers to massage old software

The result is sinking further into the EDP quagmire—and being unable to answer end-user requests. The chairman of the bank agreed that something odd was happening, indeed. But then he added: "What can I do? I don't understand anything about computers, and I am too old to learn."

When the EDPers hear such talk, they know that they can have a free rein. Can the board retrieve its position on technology? The answer is *yes, but* only by being bold instead of foolhardy in the use of financial and human resources.

This is precisely what the board of Irish Life Insurance did. It took the time to learn what the problem was and then made the right decision in terms of policy—and computer operations had to follow. Business strategy led the technology strategy, rather than falling into the hands of the big-spender clan.

The board of Irish Life is literate enough to appreciate that for the last 7 or 8 years insurers, banks, merchandisers, and manufacturing companies have been the sponsors of the mainframe industry—*against* their own best interests. This has drained their resources through unwise and unnecessary expenditures.

In order to survive in a fiercely competitive market, business and industry need systems solutions that are able to act and respond the way people act and respond. That is, they must react not in an unintelligible, naive manner—the way the large numbers of computers work today—but through induction and deduction directly applicable to problem solution. (See Fig. 6.3.)

In implementing a more efficient information technology strategy, Irish Life converted from mainframes to client/servers. The resulting cost of the system is 30 percent of what it used to be. Most important:

- The number of people servicing the system has been reduced by 60 percent.

- The end users are better served in their requests for information.

- Response time to client requests has been significantly decreased.

Such changes in the way technology—and associated modernization of systems and procedures—are treated are important because in order to survive a company must maintain effective parity with its competitors, but at lower cost. Or, alternatively, companies must target being *service leaders* way ahead of the competition—but at equal cost.

6.7 Why, Where, When, and How

Both strategies—equal service quality at lower cost and higher service quality at equal cost—can be effectively implemented through

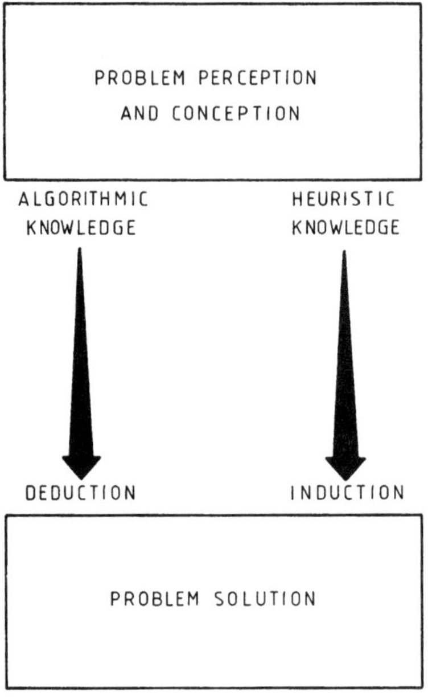

Figure 6.3 Systems solutions should be able to act the way people act, not in a naive manner.

high technology, all the way from the client/server infrastructure to the shells and languages chosen to increase programmer productivity significantly.

We must be very hard-nosed on why, where, when, and how we make our investments. When AT&T Capital Holdings decided to convert its fast-growing retail auto leasing program from a mainframe-based system to graphics client/server technology, it not only took the right path in infrastructure but also focused on the tools offering the needed power.

A significant increase in the power of the programming tools was necessary for team development of a sophisticated application, bringing it up and running in a few months, not years. The necessary elements were

- Ease of use
- Good graphics
- Systems performance

These were important criteria because AT&T telemarketing representatives approve or deny credit in real time. Also in real time they structure financing arrangements.

The choice was PowerBuilder because of its latitude in allowing developers to optimize stored procedures for each application. The tool made this feasible without a choice between power vs. graphics capabilities, power vs. database control, or some other unacceptable tradeoff.

Most of the applications in the client/server environment were built using DataWindows objects and some C extensions for complex windows. The DataWindows object is an intelligent SQL object that integrates PowerBuilder with Sybase in such a way that the developer can graphically paint applications without writing code.

The DBMS is Sybase and runs on an i486 platform, connecting with 386 end-user workstations via Ethernet LANs. Using the PowerBuilder application it is possible to transfer:

- 9,000 records back to the WS in less than 1 minute

- 200–300 records in about seconds

The tool permits users to utilize stored procedures at the DBMS. Hence, the application appears to be running on the server because the response is so fast. Such an achievement is simply not do-able through mainframes and Cobol. Both have outlived their time and should be put to rest.

It is rewarding to compare this rapid applications development, assisted by powerful graphics programming tools, to the naive and self-destructive policy of the banking institution discussed in Sec. 6.6. Having 70 programmers labor through paleolithic tools and rusty concepts to reinvent the wheel undermines the entire systems engineering profession.

Unfortunately, this approach is still widespread, particularly among companies whose top management has not yet understood that global competition requires *quality*. In these cases, top management and its EDPers alike are mired in tradition and other employees are following suit.

When innovation is ignored, quality suffers, waste is huge, and costs are high. Simply put, any company that behaves this way has decided to destroy itself.

Client/Server Policies of Major Users

7.1 Introduction

Single vendor offerings no longer satisfy the requirements of knowledgeable user organizations. The systems functions required in a distributed processing and databasing environment demand complete solutions and a thorough understanding of the links among the various components of the computer and communications aggregate.

This statement becomes even more valid as vendors of information technology face increasing customer demands, decreasing profit margins, the growth of open systems environments, and the greater need for software solutions for demanding clients. The only valid way to respond is by offering solutions that are:

- More comprehensive

- Better integrated

- Enriched with knowledge engineering

To do so, the old, established vendors have to change their culture. Short of this, they will not be able to keep pace. In fact, a change in culture is key—both for vendors and for user organizations—to competitiveness and survival.

Clients demands for basic service and add-ons in the 1990s can no longer be met by mainframes, obsolete protocols, and naive software. As noted in Chap. 6, organizations need to have knowledge constructs that tell them:

- *What* the problem is

- *How* to handle it

Leading-edge organizations appreciate the need for new departures, as the three case studies in this chapter help document. By contrast, laggards have no evident strategy to stop what looks like a slide toward decay.

It is up to top management to appreciate that confidence has to be restored, because in business a bright image is invaluable. People and companies like to buy products and services from winners, not losers—and a firm cannot be a winner if its technology is in shambles.

This is tantamount to saying that mainframes are spent, and their vendors with them. And while the overcentralized, expensive, and incapable hardware continues to decay, there is a crisis in software as well.

Today in a large number of user organizations, only 25 percent of systems analysts and programmers work on development. The balance work on the maintenance of old software—a task that gets more onerous year after year. By sticking to mainframes, Cobol, and 3270, companies:

- Are unable to face the increasing applications complexity

- Find it difficult to better program development productivity

- Are at a loss in assuring integrated applications

- End with an inconclusive software effort which demands an unreasonably long development time

As the case studies examined in this chapter help document, successful systems integration projects encompass not only the required systems components and their integration but also development of the proper understanding needed for new solutions. An integral part of this process is achieving end-user acceptance.

7.2   Promoting Client/Server Policy at Citibank

Citibank is one of the leading financial institutions which is taking existing mainframe applications and moving them down to the client/server environment. In parallel, it is getting out of the 3270 protocol toward:

- LU 6.2 for connectivity to the remaining IBM hosts

- TCP/IP (Transmission Control Protocol/Internet Protocol) for all other applications

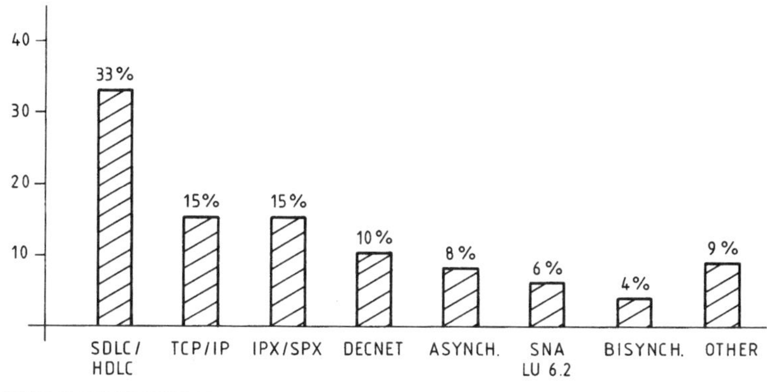

Figure 7.1 The percentage of traffic in the United States running on different communications protocols today.

Figure 7.1 suggests that counting the traffic running on the different protocols that are presently supported, TCP/IP is far more popular in America than LU 6.2. The No. 1 in terms of networking is SDLC/HDLC in SNA and X.25 environments. It masters about the same traffic as TCP/IP and IPX/SPX taken together—but at the same time, the three most popular protocols control among themselves roughly two-thirds of the market.

IPX/SPX by Novel is the de facto protocol standard supporting logical addressing, while TCP/IP features physical addressing. Since logical addressing has advantages, this explains the popularity of IPX/SPX—which, however, is not an open standard.

Since open systems currently dominate the communications and computer market, in order to establish and promote an open protocol standard 13 leading computer and communications equipment vendors met in October 1992 to begin work on advanced peer-to-peer internetworking (APPI).

- Known as the APPI Forum,* this initiative represents an effort to establish a fully open alternative to IBM's Advanced-Peer-to-Peer Networking (APPN) protocol.

- The aim of APPN is to allow computers in a systems network architecture to treat one another as peers.

- APPI's goal is to assure peer communications perspectives in a cross-database manner—hence an open standard.

---

*Among the APPI Forum members are Alcatel, Cisco, Digital Equipment, Hewlett-Packard, Infonet Services, and Sun Microsystems.

The APPI Forum's goal is to submit the full specification of an open peer-to-peer protocol, based on TCP/IP, to the Internet Engineering Task Force. The next step will be APPI's productization.

Citibank felt that for the time being, even if LU 6.2 was not a popular protocol, its employment was a necessary compromise. Problems associated with so-called legacy systems and the remaining mainframe jobs are not always simple and easy to overcome. "This is our bleeding edge," suggested a senior executive. "IBM said that running TCP/IP on mainframes is not a good idea."*

The transitory phase will not take long. As Citibank underlined, benchmarks have indicated that TCP/IP is a far better solution than LU 6.2. Both higher performance and lower costs have been obtained through this steady conversion and downsizing effort.

One of the problems that Citibank management brought into perspective was the challenge posed by the legacy applications. Conversion has to allow for coexistence. Legacy applications represent the installed base of software.

- They are typically based on closed (proprietary) operating systems.

- They may not be easily accessible as open protocols are implemented.

To overcome such a deficiency, technologies are being developed to access existing databases and take advantage of legacy systems without compromising the new applications in terms of their sophistication, polyvalence, and cost reduction.

In America today a lot of companies are working on access to legacy databases, with the foremost user organizations also addressing problems associated with the needed update and optimization of these aging systems through conversion to client/server architectures.

Companies with good experience in the technology domain, and Citibank is one of them, suggest that two of the key problems with the old legacy systems are that they:

- Are quite difficult to maintain

- Have many overlapping functions

Downsizing to client/server will not, by itself, solve these problems. But it will reduce the cost and make feasible a more friendly environment with a view to replacing the legacy programs gradually, starting with the most unmanageable ones.

---

*Neither is it a good idea to run mainframes in the first place.

In Citibank's view, moving out of the mainframe landscape toward efficient client/servers requires a new and pragmatic evolutionary strategy. The grand design is important but just as vital is:

- Defining the direction of change

- Creating digestible steps

- Moving through the steps rapidly during the conversion process

During conversion, the action shifts from the main data-processing center(s) to a structure characterized by storage hierarchies. The systems of the 1990s have a multimedia focus but are also of a federated nature.

The CPU becomes a smaller and smaller part of costs. Storage becomes the crucial issue, and the requirements posed by global storage management must be competently addressed. The same is true of a number of other requirements—such as *long transactions* and *ad hoc fuzzy queries*. Hence, object-oriented solutions must be found.

Like many leading companies, Citibank is keeping up with the age of technology. By contrast, other companies are unable to invest the *time, money,* and *training* necessary to deploy advanced technology. They are reluctant to recast production operations in order to change to a new, more cost-effective architecture. But Citibank is putting forth the effort needed for conversion. The same is true in the next case study.

7.3   The Changeover from Mainframes to Client/Servers at Merrill Lynch

The changeover from DB2 to client/server operations at Merrill Lynch is a much more complex process than that occurring in a number of other organizations. But it also seems to be much more rewarding in terms of both savings and service:

- The response time with client/servers has been significantly better than that with mainframes and DB2.

- The cost of the new client/server configuration is around one-twentieth that of the old and obsolete environment.

In addition to the significant cost reduction, the resulting system is more powerful than the one it replaces. It is also far more flexible and easier to operate, featuring a significant downsizing in installation and personnel expenditures.

In all, 12 major applications have been converted to date. This mainframe to client/server process started in 1989, but accelerated significantly in 1991 after the appropriate experience was gained.

The client/server implementation at Merrill Lynch started in with the treasury function. Other applications include:

- Finance
- Controllership
- Taxation
- Corporate credit
- Human resources
- Telecom administration

These conversions to client/server and associated applications have been realized by Merrill Lynch's distributed computing services department, which was established at group level with the aim of helping all organizational divisions implement the new architecture.

However, though a group-level department coordinates the whole effort, software development is distributed to the operating units. Not only client/server conversion but also graphics and imaging are at the top of the agenda. This is no different from the procedures many other companies have adopted in getting out of the old and inefficient mainframe culture into new, optimized perspectives in information technology.

Client/server implementation begins with a strategic business study on how to rationalize the company's operations. Correctly, this study integrates organizational issues and also focuses on:

- The best possible access to information at lowest cost

- Optimal support to managers and professionals through timely and accurate information services

This approach led the Merrill Lynch study groups to focus on database technology and on how to convert data into knowledge to assist the managerial task. Every user organization is faced with the same challenge.

Though many vehicles for getting at information were examined and benchmarked, cognizant company executives concluded that networked workstations were "the most effective means." The client/server project involves:

- Using workstations to exploit the information in the company's databases

- Database-mining the information contents to better the results that workstations provide

In all conversion procedures from mainframes to client/servers, cost-effectiveness has been the final justification—but not necessarily the real driver. The driver is the added value to be obtained through distributed solutions in order to significantly improve performance.

As with the conversion procedures established by other user organizations, Merrill Lynch found that some compromises had to be made. For instance, in Phase 1 of the conversion, one DB2 application with 100 users was downloaded into 20 OS/2 servers because the analysts were concerned about putting all 100 users into one Sequent server.

This was, however, an interim approach. Phase 2 has the goal of removing both systems and managerial overhead by:

- Maximizing the amount of horsepower

- Minimizing the amount of money the solution costs

For this reason, Phase 2 moves out of the OS/2 interim solution into a Unix-based client/server environment. This, too, resembles the steps other companies have taken to assure continuity in the conversion process.

Given the size of Merrill Lynch's operations, it is estimated that the conversion from mainframe and DB2 to the new environment will require a low two-digit number of database servers. However, the exact number will be determined by a group of factors, including response time and overall systems reliability.

If greater efficiency in end-user service and cost reduction are the two top goals of the conversion, streamlining of databases and processes can be rated as the third. Streamlining is very important to all companies. A well-known financial institution noted that over the years it had developed:

- Some 63 securities master files for different applications

- Many of these files had overlapping records

This is no rare or isolated example. It comes up time and again, and mainframe to client/server conversions are a good opportunity to correct some of the errors of the past.

One of the lessons learned from converting from mainframes to client/servers is the importance of proper specifications. Done in advance, this work can guarantee the proper procedure for the company to follow—a procedure regarding the legacy applications—as well as help to define the magnitude of the benefits to be obtained.

7.4 Commitment Control and Cost Justification

Postmortem studies have been instrumental in evaluating how successful each stage in the client/server conversion has been. "We are doing the right thing," suggested the executive in charge at Merrill

Lynch. "Everybody on the users' side is very happy with it, and data-processing costs have significantly decreased."

To assure that cost-effectiveness criteria are observed, the company established a *commitment control* process which rests essentially on two pillars:

- Project by project, for conversion purposes and new implementation, there is a $2 million value limit.

- In excess of that amount, the user department and IT operations have to develop *financial economics*—meaning an a priori justification of costs.

Profitability studies for IT projects are conducted through *project analysis,* executed through the firm's controller group. Provided the return on investment (ROI) is acceptable, the project is authorized.

ROI on a business-by-business basis follows quantitative criteria. The latter depend on the activity under study. For example, capital asset analysis requires a 15 percent ROI.

The sophistication of the application is a key to providing higher benefits. Merrill Lynch prides itself on a well-developed *risk management* implementation on client/server systems, permitting senior management to have an overview of the company's trading books.

The observance of strict timetables has also been a priority issue—and it was found to be of great assistance in that rules were observed. The conversion of the finance application, for example, started in May 1992; by mid-October 1992 one subsystem was already running and two subsystems had been delivered for final tests.

Some development work has been compressed down to weeks. The policy is that as client/server experience is gained, new software development should take months rather than years.

A lot of attention is also being paid to security. Cognizant Merrill Lynch executives observed that servers turn out to be quite secure as well as reliable. Still, steady work is being done to improve security at the network level, using MIT's Kerberos software.

Let us turn to another example to see how greater reliability is achieved. At State Farm Insurance, the conversion from mainframe to client/server was assisted by Hewlett-Packard. Instead of a costly and monolithic mainframe environment, State Farm Insurance today features:

- 600 to 700 remote client/servers

- Working together unattended and

- Constituting a very reliable network

The strategy chosen to enhance reliability is that of remote backup, which has proved to work very well with both real-time and real-enough-time (RET)* applications. The latter are background processes that have effectively replaced the batch routines, providing results on line but on a second-priority basis.

The change from the old IMS and DB2 system to the new client/server architecture has been as beneficial to State Farm Insurance as it has to many other user organizations. Obtained benefits have fully justified the conversion costs.

In fact, to ease the needed conversion procedures, Hewlett-Packard advises using its Conveyor product. This software construct takes CICS programs and translates them into Cobol. While some calls may need to be done manually, the conversion procedure as a whole seems to be about 90 percent automatic.

At Merrill Lynch, a validation exercise—along with the methodology necessary to handle the more difficult cases resulting from the conversion—has proved to be a fairly significant step in assuring that end users have the right information.

For instance, systems moved out of the mainframe to the client/server have batch reporting, which, in a transitory step, is handled through emulation of batch to prove similitude. Regression techniques are employed by the user department. Other means are in place to assure that end users feel comfortable with the integrity of the data.

7.5 Successive Implementation Steps in the Conversion Procedure

As noted in Sec. 7.4, at Merrill Lynch ROI analyses on the mainframe to client/server conversion were made to assure a cost justification prior to taking the proverbial long, hard look in systems terms: databases, LANs, and workstations. This led to a methodology that rests on three successive steps.

Step 1 calls for understanding where a given application is today.

Since systems tend to be interconnected, an application review is not done strictly on a local basis. Dependencies must be understood in order to avoid upsetting current solutions until their replacements are in place and functioning well.

---

*This is the author's own jargon.

The internal methodology of Step 1 rests on peer project review to assure that the proper analysis is being made. Peer project evaluation is essentially a design review, and it is taken to be inseparable from project management.

A bill of materials has been developed to assist in the peer project review process. A central repository keeps track of mainframe systems and their applications. Client/server procedures and their supports are tracked locally.

One of the most challenging assignments faced by distributed computing services was to set priorities for conversion of legacy applications. The decision was made one by one for different applications domains. Finance, for instance:

- Started moving off the *back-end* systems

- Converted into interactive *front-end* systems

Under the chosen methodology, essentially the traditional back-office operations still stay on mainframe. A number of technical questions, however, arose during the conversion processes.

Originally, for example, the Merrill Lynch analysts thought of converting IMS to DB2, but this idea was dropped not just for the major difficulties it presented but also because moving to the client/server architecture was found to be more cost-effective. "One of the reasons for the client/server choice is to make the solution we adopt applications independent," suggested one executive.

At the same time, through networking solutions the company sought to gain greater flexibility. This has been evaluated against a multifunctional background permitting:

- Changes as well as enhancements to applications programs

- The support of distributed databases

Implementation is facilitated by the bill of materials defined in Step 1. Knowing in a factual and documented manner what is being done now—how and why—make advancing to the next step possible.

Step 2 standardizes the evaluation process in terms of hardware platform, database engine, and tools for software development.

Senior management made a "statement of direction" that the DBMS on which database operations would rest were Oracle and Sybase. Two DBMS were chosen for their varying, different strengths. According to Merrill Lynch:

- *Sybase* has a higher performance in transaction processing, as is required in the trading and credit areas.

- *Oracle* is good for consolidation purposes, as required in finance applications.

Management suggested that double-sourcing helps in negotiations with vendors as well. The company also found it necessary to develop cross-database software. This was done internally, and the developed product is known as Darwin.

The strategy now is for all corporate databases to be networked and shared. The same is true of those databases that are divisional and departmental, as well as geographically distributed worldwide.

- The cross-database policy avoids constantly rebuilding file management routines.

- Applications become a set of screens—many with universal appeal.

Merrill Lynch is also actively using communications teleports to interconnect its distributed databases client/server to client/server. The size of interconnected local resources ranges from 300 and 400 MB to 25 GB—with some of the systems components still on mainframes.

Downloading is used more frequently than remote access. But duplication of information is not very significant because of a distributed locality of databases. The information resources of some applications are more streamlined than others. Finance is a good example.

A similar open-sourcing policy has been followed with hardware platforms. These operate almost entirely under Unix, but come from different vendors: Sun, Sequent, and IBM's RS 6000. Most workstations are Sun and PCs.

- All workstations use windowing.

- The development tool is Powerbuilder.

- A policy decision was made to focus on programmer productivity and pay for it with greater workstation power.

Applications development is now done mainly through prototyping, using Powerbuilder, some Oracle tools, and SQL windows. Project teams are kept small, and attention is paid to end-user training—for instance, through the use of windows. Both on-the-job training and follow-up training are used.

Management feels that LAN-based applications have become very mature and stable and has adopted three local network standards:

- Novel

- Banyan

- TCP/IP

The choice of which one to use depends on the platform being employed.

Unlike the ALPHA company, Merrill Lynch feels that TCP/IP gives better flexibility. "Looking at the history of LAN," said an executive, "office automation applications were dominated by Novel, and IPX had the day. But now we think of addresses—though getting uniform TCP/IP support is still an issue."

The LAN solutions are kept flexible in order to meet changing user requirements and to capitalize on technological evolution. Like many other companies, Merrill Lynch is moving from bridges to routers, and it has devised a plan for placing them strategically.

The studied and documented response to the problems posed by Step 2 led to a further evolutionary step in the implementation of the client/server architecture and the associated conversion routines.

Step 3 calls for solutions capable of assuring steady, reliable operational support.

Support involves the description and establishment of functions such as network system administrator (NSA) and database administrator (DBA). A distinction has been made between the corporate DBA function and the local DBAs.

Cost justification both affected the adoption of this administrative infrastructure and is influenced by it. Management clearly stated that, with proper organization, payoffs from the client/server architecture are quite high.

- The payoff period ranges from 1 to 3 years.

- The typical development time for a client/server project is less than 1 year.

- The typical payoff takes 1 more year.

Only a few of the converted procedures required more than 1 year on either side of the equation. An example is *deal financing,* done for investment banking and calling for the conversion of many financial system routines, including commitment control. Given its size, this project was broken up into modules:

- Data collection

- Profitability analysis

- Further automation of invoicing and payables

- Internationalization of the deal-financing application

Significantly, with the client/server architecture, there is a change in how an application is defined. Downsizing has affected not only the physical characteristics of the data-processing system but also, and more importantly, the logical aspects of system design. Greater efficiency has been the net result.

7.6 Learning from the Reuters Experience

In recent years, Reuters has made a significant change in contractual policy as an information provider. While this domain may seem far apart from that of computer vendors, in reality there are similarities.

- The driving force behind the new policy is an able response to market drives.

- The key message to be retained is the need for a steady adjustment.

Unlike some of the mainframers, Reuters is aware that the market is in full evolution, and the company aims to lead rather than be overrun by market forces. The new policy alters the way in which the company will operate in the 1990s and presents a significant opportunity in terms of licensing—as well as in employing Reuters information.

- So far global, country, and local fees characterize the information provider's real-time component.

- The new pricing structure foresees a flat fee that makes it possible to feed financial information into the company's database.

The new pricing structure promoted by Reuters will also consider the decay curve of the feed. It will lower the entry point for data-feed pricing, adding value through API interfacing.

The opportunity for user organizations comes from the fact that the new fee structure is not yet fixed, and therefore it can be influenced prior to being cast. Reuters is currently reviewing its whole pricing scenario, segmenting the dataflow and putting it into buckets to lower the fee per channel. This is essentially an unbundling policy.

To understand how the pricing schemes promoted by Reuters have developed over the years, and therefore to strengthen the hand of negotiators, it is advisable to review the evolution of Reuters services—particularly the change which took place through mergers and acquisitions.

Reuters characterizes itself as being an information utility providing not only real-time but also historical data. In terms of the evolution of its product line, Reuters has undergone the following:

- More than 30 years ago, in 1962, Reuters was a news service only.

- Subsequently, some financial price quotations were added, but the system really did not come alive until 1972.

- In 1973, Reuters started operating the *monitor,* with contributions to its quotations made by major banks.

- Nine years later, in 1982, transactions were added to the quotations system, which graduated to *monitor dealing.*

In other words, by 1982 the idea had arrived of using the terminal installed at a subscriber site to create a trade, replacing telex exchanges.

- 1985 saw the acquisition of Instinet, a service for institutional investors started in 1970.

- With the acquisition of I. P. Sharp (in the late 1980s), Reuters got control over Instantlink and Blend.*

- In 1991, Reuters offered third-party database access.

- In 1992 came the Dealing 2000/Globex venture.

Dealing 2000 provides for automatic matching of trades and has still to prove its wider market appeal. Reuters also beefed up its monitor by several thousand pages, charging page-by-page fees.

Under the Globex agreement, Reuters is the systems supplier with a 20-year exclusive contract. Its responsibilities include:

- Designing the network

- Providing for software development

- Providing facilities management

For networking purposes, Reuters supports three main processing centers in London, New York, and Tokyo. There will be a fourth one in Geneva.

Because of stiff competition and the high cost of networking, current operations are not very profitable. "It is unlikely that we will develop our own network again," a senior Reuters executive commented.

7.7   Client/Servers and Seamless Access to Databases

The evolution of product line and market strategy by Reuters illustrates that the fact that business policy should both *precede* and *master* the technological solutions being adopted. This is the first important lesson to be learned from the case study on Reuters.

---

*When these applications domains were passed to Instinet, they were losing money and have since had no turnaround in profitability. Therefore, Reuters put these two products on the blocks.

As business strategy evolves, technology must follow. For instance, today for its Market Stream and Market Feed, the Reuters network uses many proprietary protocols, but is currently moving toward international standards.

Some norms, in fact, start showing up at the workstation level. The current OS are Unix V.4 and Windows. "NT will be the convergent software," Reuters said. "But for some time Unix will remain the basic operating system."

At the workstation level, Reuters has provided a complete and user-friendly software environment. The aim is to enable customers to program their own applications by means of knowledge-enriched software supports.

In a networking sense, the No. 1 goal at the present time is to provide seamless solutions to Reuters clients. This is essentially a cross-database problem with two aspects:

1. *Seamless access* to heterogeneous databases

2. *Navigation* capability assured at the client site

The solution to this dual problem is highly challenging, since the Reuters network features quotations from about 130 exchanges, largely with automatic feed—as well as textual sourcing. This information is databased.

To help control an explosion in databases, Reuters' current policy is to stop building special database answers per product line and to integrate the different operations under a common scheme. This is partly a response to problems which develop when a new acquisition brings in incompatible languages and structures—like APL with I. P. Sharp.

The new management policy is to work on Reuters' own integrative Reference Database (RDB).* A first step is to converge different reference databases, starting with historical time series that represent 15 years of data. In addition:

- Reuters has 5.5 million events per day with a maximum of 400 updates per second, done in real time.

- There are 100 updates per second on the average, and at the end of day prices occupy 150 gigabytes.

For the selection of a new transactional system, Reuters examined DEC, Tandem, and Teradata—all with front-end capabilities. The decision was to go with DEC, using a cluster back end and the

---

*This is not to be confused with DEC's RDB.

Reliable Transaction Route (RTR) protocol—developed for Sofex* by DEC and Arthur Anderson. The basis for this choice was greater availability.

Since Reuters looks at NT as the OS of the 1990s, it seems likely that the Reliable Transaction Route protocol will be ported to NT. Major reasons for the RTR choice were:

- A better disaster backup than that provided by alternative schemes

- An ability to run both the old and the new software

At the completion of its evaluation, Reuters management ended up questioning some of the basic hypotheses and concepts it had been using for the past 20 years.

In terms of cost-effectiveness, the Tandem offer stood at twice DEC's cost. "Tandem and its people are accustomed to bid against IBM," suggested a Reuters executive. "Therefore, they are not cost-effective." The Reuters study also found that Tandem had a long program development cycle.

- The Reuters programming goal is fast development and delivery.

- The systems goal is to achieve a distributed high availability.

- The target is to go well beyond disaster tolerance at the center, toward the support of the client environment.

This is a goal that every company should adopt for its own network—all the way from the proprietary bank's resources to the on-line endpoints to be installed at client sites.

Regarding systems availability, Reuters' goal is set at 15 minutes downtime per quarter, or about 1 hour per year—a *99.98 percent* systems reliability. This goal could not be answered by Tandem. Other criteria included:

- Quality
- Scalability
- Cost
- Speed

Questioned about possible adoption of DB2, Reuters responded in the following way: "For our databases we are looking at a triple criterion of costs, flexibility through distributed resources, and 99.99 relia-

---

*The Swiss software running on the Zurich commodity exchange under the same name, which has been sold to the Frankfurt and other exchanges.

bility.* We don't see IBM in this game." Several factors lie behind this negative answer:

■ IBM's approach to high availability is through Stratus, which is essentially a Tandem-type solution.

■ DB2 is not as high in quality as it should be. Neither is it part of the wave of the future.

■ As a service provider, Reuters simply cannot afford ending up with database corruption—and IBM could not convince Reuters specialists that it could handle the challenge.

On the basis of the experience gained from the most recent market-and-technology studies, Reuters management has added a number of strategic criteria to its technical ones—for instance, documented positive cost/benefit ratios, systems flexibility, scalability, and factual references from other sites. The main lesson to be learned from this study, Reuters suggests, is the wisdom of:

■ Establishing beforehand qualitative and quantitative selection criteria

■ Doing a thorough investigation of the references that vendors provide

■ Assuring that the chosen solution can pass the test of time in terms of absorbing load increases and client requests

Quite definitely, the aim is not to provide dying computer vendors with life support, but rather to assure the user organization's own survival in a dynamic, competitive environment. Both strategic and tactical top management guidelines are needed: the former using *foresight* and the latter being more technical and benefiting from astute fine tuning.

---

*That is, slightly better than 1 hour downtime per year.

Solving the Interconnection and High-Performance Problems

Chapter

8

The Open Systems Environment

8.1 Introduction

Part 1 of this book provided factual and documented evidence that the idea of the centralized mainframe with terminals attached to it through dumb protocols such as 3270—with practically all software development done in Cobol—is no longer valid.

- The cost-effectiveness of such obsolete approaches is rock bottom.

- The problems they present are big and growing.

Effective solutions require distributed client/server systems like those we examined through case studies in Chaps. 6 and 7. They also call for *open architectures* in which software and hardware from different vendors can be effectively interconnected, as defined in Sec. 8.2.

Easy, matter-of-fact interfacing among attached resources is very important in an on-line environment. The availability of networked systems capabilities allows user organizations to effectively share computers and communications resources—and today's new technology makes this feasible at an affordable cost.

Solutions will be reached in a more flexible and cost-effective manner if *open systems* principles are observed, and with them *industry standards*. That's the best way to use technology. Moreover, such a strategy is in synergy with new management policies demanding that:

- Investment in applications be protected and provide benefits evident to the users

- Solutions be increasingly built on top of an open, extensible architecture

The days when the central data-processing department made all the computer choices and handled all the software development and maintenance are gone. Central data processing no longer controls everything that happens in EDP.

The time of the CIO as the czar of information technology is forever gone. A lot of systems development work is going on in operating units, including

- Design and engineering

- Manufacturing

- Marketing

- Field and customer service

Every one of these operations has its own database, and because many information-processing issues transcend each one, it is necessary to establish an effective, seamless access among these incompatible databases. This is the meaning of distributed databases and federated structures, which are examined in Part 3.

The central computing department may have different names: data processing (DP), management information systems (MIS), information technology (IT), and so on. Whatever the name, the role has changed. More and more, central computing plays a supporting role, and the best professional stance for its systems experts is to assist the operating units as knowledgeable consultants.

8.2 The Search for Open Systems

Architectural characteristics are important because the hardware and special software platforms* that support a distributed environment must work together. This is not always the case, and the result is often a low level of overall performance with inadequate results.

A well-chosen and properly implemented systems architecture must support distributed, diversified, heterogeneous structures. It must be able to integrate all the facilities offered by the computer industry in the absence of firm standards and norms. Hence, the chosen architecture should provide:

1. A way for different products to operate together in a consistent manner

2. A structure within which functions and configurations can evolve over time

---

*These include operating systems (OS), database management systems (DBMS), transaction processing monitors (TPMs), shells, languages, compilers, and utilities.

3. A flexible continuity to protect the investment made in applications and other resources

But there is nothing standard about systems architectures. The available lot features a variety of levels of sophistication. Quite often, systems architectures are released in stages, with the first release typically serving only a kernel of the functions which have been announced and which might be featured in future releases.

Is there any reliable way to differentiate architectural supports? The answer is yes—by classifying them into *open* and *proprietary* (that is, *closed*) systems.

- *Open architectures* help integrate wares from different vendors, with a variety of design characteristics.

The goal here is to adhere more or less to industry standards. There are, however, different degrees of "openness." Not only is this term sometimes misused, but even when it is properly used it does not necessarily identify a truly cross-vendor servicing environment. Nonetheless, it remains a better solution than its alternative.

- *Proprietary architectures* typically refer to a given vendor's own systems software. But it is a mistake to think that there is only one per vendor.

In the 1970s, for example, IBM launched its System Network Architecture (SNA), which was centralized and mainframe-based—and supposed to serve its clients' needs till the end of the century. But as user organizations moved toward distributed environments, in the mid-1980s IBM introduced the Low Entry Network (LEN) architecture (eventually revamped into APPC), which is not necessarily compatible with SNA.

Also, in the mid-1980s, IBM announced the System Application Architecture (SAA). The goals of SNA and SAA are not the same. The former addresses network interconnection and is presented as a subset of the latter, which has a broader scope. But this is not necessarily technically correct.

There are, of course, similarities between the two offerings. Both SNA and SAA are tooled around mainframe concepts, with MVS the pivotal operating system. By contrast, another IBM announcement—the AIX architecture*—is more of a peer-to-peer type and is centered on Unix. As such, it is incompatible with SAA.

---

*IBM's proprietary version of Unix.

Hence, anybody who thinks that a vendor's proprietary architecture is *the* solution is sorely deceived. Not only at IBM but also industry-wide, major confusion at the architectural level seeps all the way down to the special software artifacts.

Open architectures, too, have definitional problems. Until quite recently, much of the discussion on *open systems* revolved around one key technical issue: the operating systems. Adjunct to this were protocols and user interfaces. At the core, however, are more fundamental issues that affect the bottom line of any business:

- Developing advanced software to support product and market competitiveness

- Supporting in-place legacy applications and extending their productive life

- Providing for greater accuracy and easy update of the databased information elements

- Supporting federated databases* with locality and global bearing

- Increasing the effectiveness of retrieval through database mining

- Assuring an integrative, intelligent companywide network approach

- Making it easier to deploy new, more advanced systems solutions while promoting reusable software

- Reducing perceived complexity at the user end

- Making user-machine communication most friendly through GUI and agile interfaces

Because these issues are many and demanding, user organizations (as well as the end users themselves) welcome the concept of an open architecture at all levels. But even at the more limited level of the OS, real life is not always what it seems.

Unix is an excellent example, since it is the operating system which brought about the open systems concept. Today, there are many Unix OS, the majority of them being incompatible. To name a few: System V.4 by AT&T; Berkeley Software Distribution; OSF/1; Mach by CMU†; and the parochials such as AIX, Ultrix, and UX. This issue is examined in greater detail in Chap. 9.

---

*Contrary to distributed databases, *federated databases* are locally autonomous but participate in a global network. This works, so to speak, through a process of *reverse delegation* from the periphery to the center.

†OSF/1 integrates Mach as a kernel, but IBM has announced plans to use AIX in the kernel role.

MS DOS has been closer to the true concept of an open OS, having been adopted by nearly every vendor. The same will most likely be the case with Microsoft Windows' New Technology (NT). How does this compare with, say, OSF/1? Both NT and OSF/1 claim to be open OS, which up to a point is true—but they are incompatible.

To move up one notch further: At the DBMS level, open systems are in principle those supplied by third parties that can be ported on many different OS:

- DB2, SQL/DS, SQL/400, SQL/OS2, and RDB are vendor proprietary—hence, *closed* systems.

- Sybase, Ingres, Oracle, and Informix (among the relational DBMS) and Ontos, Versant, Gemstone, and Object Store (among the object-oriented DBMS) can be seen as *open* systems.

One of the focal points of open systems is their portability and integrative capability. Another, equally important issue is procurement. Today companies are preoccupied with the effect of proprietary special software on their procurement policies—hence, on *cost*. That is why many are changing to an open systems policy.

8.3 Adopting an Open Systems Policy

The adoption of an *open systems policy* is a matter not of novelty but rather of cost-effectiveness. But what does choosing an open systems policy mean in practical terms? Can we carry this concept all the way to the basic level of hardware and software?

At the bottom layer—that is, *hardware*—an open systems policy means a basic choice between reduced instruction set computer (RISC) chip and alternatively the iX86 microprocessor. The special proprietary chips of IBM and DEC, for example, are *not* open systems, no matter how they are billed by the vendor.

By contrast, because of its widespread use in the computer industry, iX86 can be seen as an *open,* de facto industry standard. Not only does the iX86 series, with few exceptions, underpin the better-known personal computer offerings but it also has continuity in development and upward compatibility:

- Intel's i386 microprocessor features 5 MIPS and has become the computer industry's best-known cash cow.

- The i486 state-of-the art offering is upwardly compatible and four times more powerful than i386.

- The i586 (P5) in its advanced development has five times the power of i486, reaching 100 MIPS.

- A new, much more powerful P6 is in the midst of research, and the P5 designers plan to retool for P7.

As we saw in Sec. 8.2, at the OS level, Unix, NT, and MS DOS are open systems. The proprietary MVS, VM, DOS/VSE, and VMS are *not* open systems, and the same is true of AIX by IBM and Ultrix by DEC—the parochial and incompatible versions of Unix.

In fact, NT is much more of an open OS than Unix because, as stated, the latter comes in several versions. Careful choices must be made. Only two of the Unix versions qualify as semiopen OS: System V by AT&T/Sun and OSF Unix (the main stuff, not its dialects).

In the past, many companies found themselves on the wrong track by staying with one and only one vendor in the belief that they would have no problems with heterogeneity and incompatibility. Nothing is more untrue.

In the 1980s, one of the best-known companies in Europe had only one vendor—IBM. But there were nine incompatible OS in its environment. This meant large duplication of effort in software development and therefore very significant costs. It also called for very costly solutions in interfacing, where serious technical problems were present and the lack of program portability resulted in throwaway software.

Many companies have come to the conclusion that this way of facing computer challenges no longer makes sense. Over the years, user organizations have found out the hard way that what the vendor says about compatibility and program portability and what the reality is are two different, even contradictory things.

By contrast, when the protocols and external interfaces are the same across the different platforms that applications programs will run, software portability, which should be the user's objective, is assured. Since vendors are not highly sensitive to this argument, some major user organizations took the task of finding and implementing homogeneous solutions into their own hands.

During an April 1991 meeting in Tokyo, Dr. Fukuya Ishino* stated that the motivating factor for Nippon Telegraph and Telephone's (NTT) development of its Multivendor Integration Architecture (MIA) was the need for software portability across different computer platforms.

---

*Dr. Ishino is director of the Information Technology Laboratory of NTT, in Yokohama, Japan. For a thorough discussion of MIA, see D. N. Chorafas and H. Steinmann, *Solutions for Networked Databases,* Academic Press, San Diego, CA, 1993.

- When the MIA decision was reached, NTT was served by five different computer vendors and had about 30 million statements in software inventory.

- An internal study established that if there had been a unique OS rather than five incompatible ones, 15 million statements would have been sufficient to provide support for the programmed functions.

Cutting the software costs by half, from development to maintenance, means a great deal in terms of saving money, time, and labor. Thus, the ability to get the necessary service from 15 million statements rather than 30 million represents a saving of over 4,500 labor-years in software development effort alone.

The evidence provided in this chapter suggests that the open systems strategy is equivalent to an *open-vendor policy*—in which the user organization depends not just on one vendor but on many. But the user organizations are well advised to control whether the open systems policy it adopts will make it feasible:

- To port its applications software from one platform to another

- To do so without manual intervention in changing the existing programs

Figure 8.1 highlights this open-vendor policy and what it involves. Emphasis is placed on portability standards at the level of OS, DBMS, TPM, and so on. These greatly affect software and systems integration.

The solution presented in Fig. 8.1 can be extended all the way to the total corporate procurement policy for computers, communications, and software. An end-to-end solution must, by definition, be bidirectional:

- From hardware to special software and from there to systems integration

- From systems integration to performance criteria, cost-effectiveness, and organizational issues all the way to hardware and software.

Basic software is the enabling technology permitting this two-way flow in portability, and it sits right in the middle of any solution to be adopted. Hence, it has to be studied with special care.

In the 1980s the motto was that software sells hardware. Today, a wiser approach is to make the open-vendor policy a platform for selling both software and hardware. Always keep in mind that systems and their components are coming from many vendors and need to be architectured.

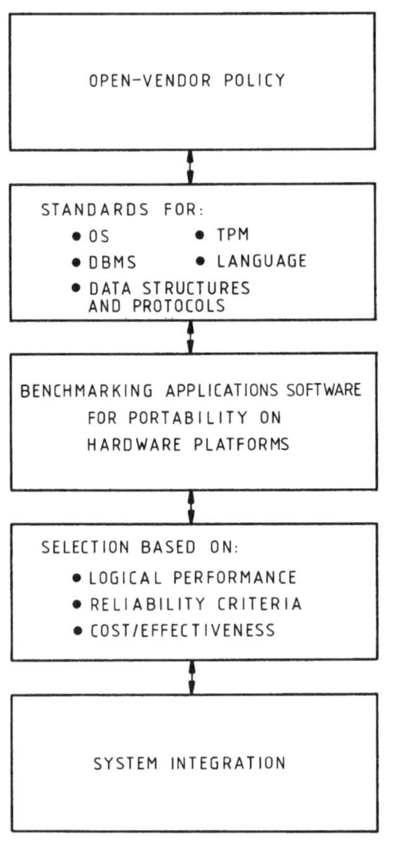

Figure 8.1 An open-vendor policy rests on standards, program portability, and systems integration.

8.4 Principles Applicable to Architectured Solutions

Architectured solutions must be robust and secure since they underpin the whole network of workstations, databases, number crunchers, and communications nodes—as well as the system's ability to handle services of value to the enterprise.

- Architectural approaches are not made in the abstract. They take place to support a distributed environment and do so in a cost-effective manner.

- Architectural offerings should feature, and the systems architects must understand, critical integrating factors for a range of applications.

Both technical prerequisites and know-how lie behind this proposition. There is also the need to overcome shortsightedness in systems solutions. Companies have to stop seeing only the immediate and relying on vendors to look to the future.

Able approaches to the integration challenges would help smooth the diversity in OS and DBMS characteristics, enabling a heterogeneous environment with dissimilar platforms to work as one unit. But even though distributed database management and network management have become synonymous, there are basic rules to observe in both of them—rules that are not necessarily compatible.

Part 1 brought into perspective the fact that a valid architectural design should distinguish among five different layers, at the same time providing the means to integrate them into one system. Figure 8.2 builds upon this concept.

A layered architecture is necessary to promote the expanding applications horizons of this decade and to permit the able exploitation of technological resources at our disposal. IBM talks of a three-layered systems structure: data processing, databases, and networking. Figure 8.2 expands this framework to include the all-important end-user interfaces and infrastructural issues.

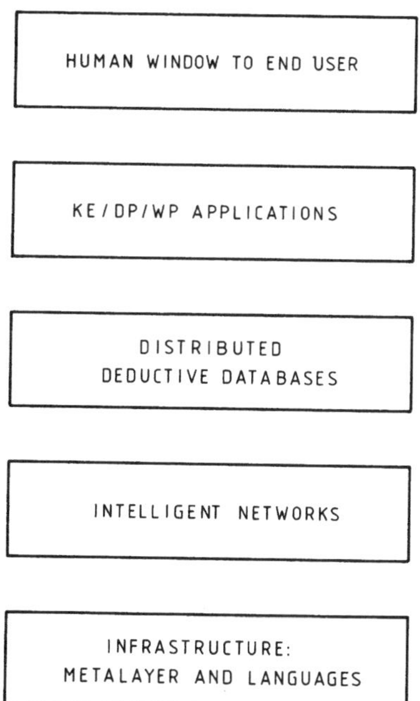

Figure 8.2 The five fundamental layers composing a systems architecture.

The PC revolution of the 1980s has distributed processing power to end users on an unprecedented basis, but it has also made mandatory the development of *human windows.* This term refers to agile and friendly user-machine interfaces, preferably enriched through engineering.

Human windows are fully distributed artifacts residing at every workstation. Just as distributed is the second layer in Fig. 8.2, which integrates:

- Knowledge engineering (KE)

- Data processing (DP)

- Word processing (WP)

Price Waterhouse surveyed companies in the United States, Japan, Australia, and the United Kingdom about their plans for using knowledge-based systems. Over 80 percent said they now use or plan to use knowledge-oriented technology in their applications, and that it will have a significant impact on their business.

Distributed databases constitute the third architectural layer, which, as we will see in Part 3, is increasingly enriched with artificial intelligence artifacts. There is no question that this is the way of the future. The challenge is:

- How to manage with integrity the growing distribution of function and databases

- How to synchronize distributed structures as well as assure privacy and security

This is not a matter concerning servers alone. It affects central databases as well. Information elements today transit and are manipulated throughout the enterprise over a variety of networked workstations.

Fundamentally, it is no longer a question of whether text data, graphics, and other information will be distributed. This is done de facto with a variety of tools, such as spreadsheets, and it characterizes supports like microfiles, which are embedded at every workstation.

The fourth layer in Fig. 8.2 is that of networks and distributed communications: their nodes, links, protocols, and software. We have come a long way from the days of star networks and start-stop protocols, even if the majority of circuits for data communications are still working in an asynchronous manner.

- Protocol efficiency and sophistication have increased tremendously, making the 3270 and its likes obsolete.

- Even 15-year-old protocols, like X.25, are today put on the back burner, replaced by frame-relay solutions.

The architectural solution should also define a rational computer and communications infrastructure. This requires establishing the technology and standards for linguistic developments, not only for applications but also for interconnecting in real-time database resources and workstations.

The systems architecture must assure a structure that provides consistent, transparent access to information resources across the enterprise. Needed here are specifications, conventions, software interfaces, and protocols that developers use to create common applications, as well as a *metalayer* that acts as the *intentional* structure.

Infrastructural needs should not be underestimated. From designers to analysts and programmers, applications developers must have available tools that—on the user's side—assure data and applications transparency but also help to streamline connectivity. Agile, high-level tools must be able to manipulate database and query interfaces to achieve consistent access:

- Assuring that information anywhere in the network is available to the application and its users

- Appreciating the fact that modern implementation environments are communications-intense

Hence, the language—and therefore the developer—must have available a communications interface that is callable by simple commands and capable of sending and receiving information elements, both selectively and in lots.

In any interactive system, this communications interface should provide the foundation for cooperative processing. Different parts of an application may reside in different places and platforms, yet they must function as if they were a, seamlessly integrated whole.

Architectural solutions should enable developers to work out applications that are consistent, easy to use, and structured to access all attached resources. Applications users become more productive through agile, friendly, and uniform interfaces that facilitate faster and more comprehensive work.

8.5 Can an Open Architecture Be Uniquely Defined?

Since the mid-1980s the term *open architecture* has had a variety of definitions, with many computer manufacturers claiming that their solution is "the only valid one." But the bottom line is that an open architecture means *an open interface* architecture—and even that is not a sure thing. A better way to view an open architecture is in a market-oriented sense. Does the architecture make possible:

- Wider competition among suppliers?

- A better range of choices in hardware and software?

- Greater cost-effectiveness in terms of implementation?

All three issues have attendant benefits and implications. One of the benefits is that of actively participating in the dramatic changes we are witnessing in information processing, which essentially can be grouped into four epochs:

1. Single vendor, single machine

2. Single vendor, multiple computers

3. Multiple vendors, multiple computers

4. A developing open-vendor policy

From the early 1950s to the mid-1960s, the single vendor, single machine approach dominated. As a practical matter, however, this was a multiple systems environment, since each machine had a unique hardware architecture and associated operating system. Hence, an application written for one machine had to be totally rewritten to work on newer equipment—not a very appealing choice.

From the mid-1960s to the mid-1970s, the single vendor still dominated, but the new landscape featured multiple machines per vendor. Some, but not all, of these computers, could run the same operating system, and applications programs could be moved to the newer machines with some effort. But portability disappeared as multiple, incompatible OS from a single vendor proliferated.

Beyond the problems of diversification, user organizations found themselves locked into the machines of a particular vendor. A great deal of effort was required to port applications programs to a different operating system—for instance, from DOS-VSE to MVS. Hence, the practice was discouraged even if the vendor advised the transition.

The third epoch lasted from the mid-1970s to the mid-1980s, with a policy characterized by multiple vendors, multiple machines, and multiple operating systems. Somehow user organizations learned to live with the not-so-elegant situation. At the same time, companies were faced with a variety of machines from different computer manufacturers running under proprietary (hence, incompatible) operating systems.

In their effort to develop better, more advanced computer solutions many companies found themselves handicapped by the inability to port applications programs from platform to platform. To a significant extent, the popularity of Unix stems from the fact that it presents a common OS ground—but in reality, as we have already seen, there are many incompatible Unix versions.

As a result of these incompatibilities, a trend emerged in the mid- to late 1980s toward adopting an *open systems* policy, provided the appropriate supports could be found. This fourth epoch is much more visible at the workstation level, with Unix and MS DOS, than it is with maxis and mainframes—though operating systems currently being introduced (like NT and OSF/1) may significantly change this pattern.

Accepting that open systems are not uniquely defined, and are themselves a concept in transition, what are the main characteristics of an open-vendor policy? Can we use some yardstick to distinguish proprietary and open systems? The answer is yes, and the two main lines of demarcation are:

- *Interoperability*—sharing information elements across heterogeneous databases

- *Applications portability*—running an application on all computing platforms in the enterprise

These are the stated goals of practically all organizations seeking to streamline their applications environment. If achieved, they promise to provide greater flexibility and scalability, as well as lower software costs and investment risks. But such a solution is not so easily achieved.

Interoperability—starting with seamless cross-database remote access—is a subject which has been seriously approached during the last few years. Largely based on knowledge engineering, the first solutions which appeared in the late 1980s were made by user organizations and have been proprietary. Only in 1991 did vendors start introducing community software for heterogeneous cross-database access. (See Part 3.) However, there are problems:

- Most of these approaches are query-only.

- They are not made for transactions.

Transaction-processing capabilities are a vital and integral part of any business solution. The long-delayed transition from batch programs, which rest on concepts of the 1950s and 1960s, to on-line operations hinges on meeting the transaction-handling challenge.

One of the basic reasons the batch bottleneck persists is the massive amount of work required to break it. Some user organizations have had the courage to do so. For instance, between 1984 and 1988 Japan's Dai-Ichi Kangyo Bank succeeded in eliminating batch. Today it executes all its dataprocessing requirements in real-enough time, as background processes operating on line.

Another basic reason for the persistence of most batch bottlenecks is that classical programming approaches cannot help. Only knowledge engineering appears to have the needed solutions in regard to:

- Transaction handling in heterogeneous environments

- Portability of programs among different platforms.

- Conversion of batch to real-enough time.

Today, applications program portability among heterogeneous computers is real only within a limited perspective, even with a supposedly standard OS such as Unix. Every time users hear "This version is better," they should read "It is incompatible with what already exists."

The statement by many vendors that their operating system version is "95 percent compliant" with a given norm or standard is nonsense. What it really means is that the new system further confirms the incompatibilities pervading the computer, communications, and software industry.

No doubt, standards organizations play an important role in establishing a framework for open systems, as we will see in Chap. 9. But many areas are not addressed by the de jure standards-making process. The reasons:

- Computer technology, particularly in software, is too new to settle into norms.

- Nonstandardized solutions have always met with user acceptance.

- No down-to-earth agreement can be reached among the major vendors, as each sees the proprietary approach as a competitive advantage.

These stubborn historical and political reasons must be overcome in order to attain truly universal standards and architectural platforms. No doubt work on normalization will go on, but so will the deviations and disagreements.

8.6   Who Will Certify the Open System?

Since the market likes the idea of open systems, every vendor tries to make its wares sound like they are following open systems norms—even though this is usually far from the case. Quite often, new software products and revamped old ones add the word "open" to their name. There is, for example, Open VMS.

Initially, information systems from different vendors were not designed to interoperate. But with computer-integrated manufacturing and computer-integrated business perspectives, a way had to be found to do so. Hence, interest in multiprotocol routing grew, even though the wares offered by vendors were not as compatible with standards as they should have been.

In a way, the growing interest in multiprotocol routing and other supports reflects the user organizations' disenchantment with *open products* from computer, communications, and software vendors.

- Users insist that very few vendors live up to the claim of openness at all levels of connectivity for systems that are typically incompatible.

- A vendor claim of "more or less *open*" is meaningless marketing hype. Yet the term is widely employed and has caught the fancy of users, unaware of what it really means.

Setting aside the marketing issue, we need to realize that in a technical sense the idea behind open systems in information technology is *not* simple. In such an environment, software and hardware have to be built to a set of common standards so that:

- Equipment from one manufacturer can work with equipment from another, providing for interoperability

- Software can be easily moved from one computer platform to another, providing for portability

As we have seen, these goals are rarely met. Worse yet, they do not seem to appeal to the different vendors and, up to a point, to the user organizations. This is particularly true of companies with highly centralized computer environments. Normalization will make them lose part of the hold they have on the information technology of their entire operation.

Good business sense, of course, points the other way. There is little doubt that open systems solutions—hence, enforceable standards—lie at the heart of our future ability to integrate and fully exploit computers and communications systems in every sector of business and industry, all the way to client/servers and distributed database structures. But this is a concept based on rationality, not on company politics.

- Unlike proprietary solutions, open systems reduce computing equipment to a series of commodity products.

- In such an environment, competition increases and price becomes a dominant factor in purchasing decisions.

Conformity means that truly open systems will abide by norms governing a plethora of common interconnection devices—such as gateways, repeaters, bridges, and routers—and will be able to accommodate device emulation, internet transmission, and interstation information exchange.

Open systems are still far from perfect. In their practical applications, they are as different as the companies that build and use them. Each one features a blend of different ingredients, such as:

- Local bridges

- Remote bridges

- Multiprotocol routers

- Protocol converters

- Application gateways

- Intelligent hubs

These devices are based on all sorts of technical approaches which are not even compatible within the same vendor organization. Integrative solutions remain an important goal. They are necessary to hold together the different heterogeneous computers, operating systems, and networks.

Precisely because the cross-systems approaches that are supposed to be homogeneous are not necessarily so, there is an explosion in demand for different internetworking protocols. The worldwide market for such devices hit about $700 million in 1992 and is projected to reach $1.3 to 1.5 billion by 1995.

An important consideration is the fact that open systems solutions are more expensive than proprietary gateways that allow different systems to interoperate. Many user organizations admit that their long-term preference for open systems is compromised by their short-term business requirements.

Beyond the investment issues, the fact remains that norms will have weight only when user organizations can be given the assurance that in extending the functionality of a system they will not be locked into an awkward design philosophy. Knowledgeable user organizations look for assurances that they will not need to completely redesign their systems, including extensive software rewriting.

Ironically, this is exactly what happens when nonstandard proprietary components are used. But many companies somehow have accepted it as part of life, while they are more suspicious of open systems offers.

User organizations will be convinced to go for standards if both in the shorter term and in the longer run the resulting system proves to be more portable, decreases the requirement for repeated special training, and serves the organization's design characteristics effectively.

Behind this approach lies the fact that as networks grow and spread, they must be better understood and controlled. Internetworking is necessary not only for operational reasons but also for monitoring the network for faults in equipment and lines, permitting those faults to be fixed efficiently and reliably.

In conclusion, whether vendors like it or not it is not the standards organizations* or the computer, communications, and software manufacturers themselves that will certify what is or is not an open system. The *market* will do so, voting with dollars. The bottom line is that the user organizations themselves have to provide the open systems certificate—often through a hard-gained experience turned to profit.

8.7 Open Systems and Fake Open Systems

As we saw in the preceding sections, despite the constraints that exist with open systems, they do make a difference in the sense that no vendor really has a lock on the user organization. For marketing purposes, vendors will always try to create supposedly "better versions"—or dialects—which are incompatible with the normalized open systems standards. Hence, user organizations must be on guard.

In many respects, the issue of open systems vs. fake open systems resembles that of client/servers vs. pseudo-client/servers, examined in Chap. 4. In both cases, the computer vendors seek to show they are really getting ahead of market trends—while in reality they do not intend to do so.

One of the reasons knowledgeable user organizations like to deal with a truly open system is that its underlying strengths are *conceptual*. Using a metaphor from thermodynamics:

- *Open systems* do not absorb and hoard entropy; hence, they don't wear and tear like closed systems.

- Closed, *proprietary systems* are thought to be self-contained; yet they provide little or no flow of ideas, matter, and energy between themselves and their environment.

In contrast to closed, proprietary approaches, open systems are self-organizing and hence can evolve. If, as is often the case, the level of

---

*As we will see in the next chapter, these organizations do not even have the charter to engage in certification.

requirements increases in a systems sense, open solutions can always deal with it—a distinct advantage.

Once a closed system reaches its limits or breaks down, there is little hope of putting it back together again. But open systems are by their nature subject to steady change. They do so by absorbing input and adapting themselves to environmental stimuli.

The underlying strength of open systems has an ironic edge. As a process, the drive toward open systems is fueled by the economic necessity of the user community. What the user community really wants is to leverage existing investment in computing:

- Software

- Hardware

- Protocols

- Gateways

- Operating systems

- DBMS

- TPM

- Applications programs

Given the multiplicity of these issues and their interconnection, we should always look to the experience of other companies which faced

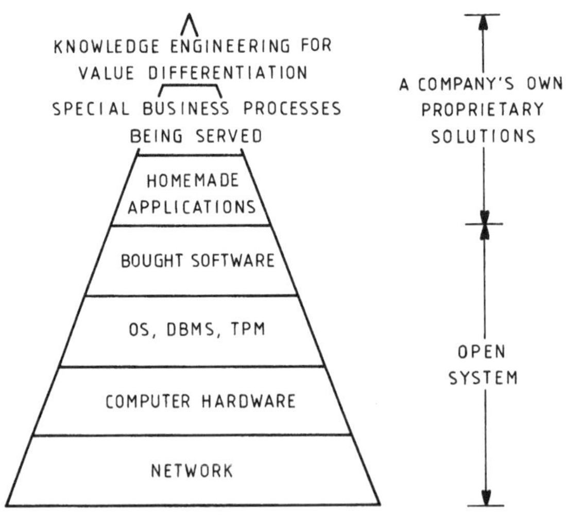

Figure 8.3 Layers for open and proprietary solutions from a user organization's viewpoint.

the open systems challenge earlier on and have established a practice in this regard. Figure 8.3 illustrates the blending of value differentiation with an open systems policy at the County NatWest Investment Bank in London.

The strategy of County NatWest answers in a very effective way the argument made by some computer user organizations that they would not like to find themselves at the "bleeding edge." What such companies fail to understand is that if they stay with closed systems, they will be de facto at the bleeding edge of technology.

Using the experience it has gained through an open systems policy, NatWest now distinguishes successive layers in its IT solutions for the 1990s and beyond:

The top three layers are the bank's own proprietary solutions, whose goal is to add value and sharpen the competitive advantages to be derived from technology.

This is particularly true of the topmost layer: *value differentiation.* However, what is today value differentiation—NatWest advises—will be slipping down to the second and third levels, as competition closes the gap created through an advanced solution. Therefore, says County NatWest, developing high technology must be a steady effort.

The bottom layers are open systems that were once vendor-proprietary. These are the layers that have opened up through standards.

The great value of this model is that it makes visible a little appreciated yet very important fact. The bottom line in adopting an open systems approach is to lower installation, maintenance, and implementation costs. "If we are not very careful on costs," says County NatWest, "we will lose the benefits from open systems."

Companies that are careful on costs will also be aware of *fake open systems* and do something about them. To put it bluntly, the adoption of an open systems policy is a matter not of novelty but of cost-effectiveness.

Section 8.3 has explained, in practical terms, what choosing an open-vendor policy at the microchip and basic software levels means. When so many fake open systems are being pushed in the market, it is wise to keep the real vs. fake distinction in mind.

The same caveat applies to network solutions. The closed systems alternatives are those using proprietary protocols and architectures:

- SNA, SAA, and AI by IBM
- DCA by Unisys

- DNA and DECnet by DEC

- XNS by Xerox and others

The search for open systems approaches and architectures also requires an evaluation of leading integrator products applicable to network protocols. Alternatives include NetView, Net/Master, Accumaster, EMA, OpenView, and Allink.

Network protocols such as IBM's LU 6.2 are closed, proprietary solutions. They are also aging and rapidly losing effectiveness—though LU 6.2 is much better than the technically archaic 3270 protocol that IBM continues to aggressively market to its customers. (See Part 1.)

An open systems solution for network protocols, based on TCP/IP, has been worked out by the U.S. Department of Defense and adopted by a myriad of companies. These companies are reluctant to lock themselves into a closed system—thus being at the mercy of "this" or "that" vendor. Once again, the TCP/IP open systems approach involves:

- An internet environment

- ARPA/DDN architecture

- TCP/IP protocol and lower-level elements

- Higher-level elements, such as Telnet and FTP

- Addressing, routing, and network management

All this creates an open systems environment that forward-looking organizations should be keen to adopt as policy for the 1990s and beyond. This will, however, require a definite board decision—and a policing action to make sure that policy is executed. If implementation is left to lower levels of the organization, the political pressures exercised from above will make a mockery of open systems policies.

Standards Organizations and the Normalization Effort

9.1 Introduction

The open systems interconnection (OSI) reference model was formally initiated by the International Standards Organization (ISO) in March of 1977. It has been promoted in response to the growing need for an open set of communications standards, aiming to provide an architectural reference point for developing normalized systems and procedures.

Among the aims of ISO/OSI is to facilitate effective interconnection among networks of the same or similar type and to serve as a common framework for the development of services and protocols. In that sense, ISO/OSI has helped promote the offering of interoperable, multivendor products and services. The response, however, has been mixed.

To begin with, OSI is divided into seven layers. (See Fig. 9.1.) Because the functions to be performed at each layer are described rather than defined, OSI has remained an abstraction, with the following results:

- Each vendor interpreted OSI in its own way, and after twisting some of the basic notions, proudly announced that its wares were "OSI-compliant."

- Each ISO/OSI layer included a number of incompatible protocols, creating a fair amount of confusion.*

---

*See also D. N. Chorafas and H. Steinmann, *Intelligent Networks,* CRC Press, Los Angeles, CA, 1990.

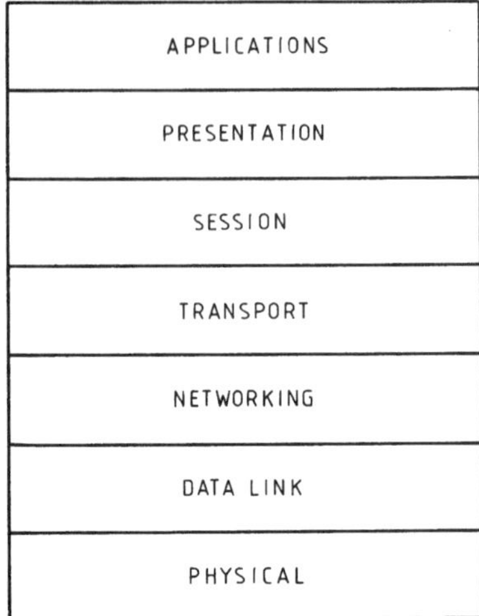

Figure 9.1 The layered architecture of the OSI
reference model.

■ Since 1988, ISO has attempted to look beyond the seven layers of
  OSI to open distributed processing (ODP).

The groundwork of ODP is carried out by the architectural group
within OSI. Some elements of what might become ODP—for example,
the security framework—already exist, but not much more than that
has been established. Open distributed processing is in essence an
attempt to provide the same sort of structure for distributed processing that OSI offers for interconnection.

Both ODP and OSI are of significant importance to client/server
solutions, since they aim at normalization. Still on the drawing board,
ODP addresses a wider set of issues than OSI—for instance, operating system interfaces. It also ties together OSI, Unix/Posix, and applications portability.

Even though OSI does not go beyond the descriptive level, and
therefore is open to biases and misinterpretations, it has made a couple of major contributions to information technology. One of them is
to "raise consciousness" about the importance of having standards to
rally around.

Another of OSI's main technological contributions is its advance-
ment of the layered model (seven layers in OSI's case). Layering permits specialization of systems functions level by level. Unlike monolithic approaches, it also enhances flexibility by making radical
changes in one of the layers feasible without upsetting the aggregate.

Essentially, the orderly replacement of one layer without affecting the total system is what a modular approach offers, and its benefits extend to networking as well as client/server computing models.

9.2   Standards, Computers, and Networks

As networks become increasingly global, businesses view them as a core component in gaining a competitive edge. But the acceleration of technological progress has deepened the complexity of the system itself, and therefore of the standards-making process pertaining to it.

In the face of rapid technical progress, standardization now requires much closer collaboration from industry sectors spanning telecommunications, computers, and software technology, as well as from other industries such as radio and broadcasting. At the same time, by freeing the reigns of competition, and therefore of diversity, deregulation has led to demands for closer collaboration between manufacturers and users.

As we saw in Sec. 9.1, to assist in meeting such challenges, the International Standards Organization developed the open systems interconnection to address issues associated with network protocol standards. (Refer again to Fig. 9.1.) ISO's lowest layer is physical. Above it is the data-link level. Taken together, they provide physical control and data-link services for effective communications.

The networking layer selects routing procedures, segments blocks and messages, assures error detection, and performs recovery and notification. Its functionality is exemplified by the X.25 protocol developed by CCITT.* The problem here is that the new technologies of frame relay and asynchronous transfer mode (ATM) eliminate the need for a networking layer. Essentially, data link and networking collapse into one and the same level.

Here is where ISO/OSI's flexibility comes into play. The differences between CCITT and ISO are instructive. These two important international standardization bodies differ in their approaches toward several issues, one of them being quality of service:

- CCITT is oriented toward the overall quality of network service.

- ISO leans toward individual user perceptions of supported functionality.

Such a difference in viewpoint creates confusion for many implementors, and it is not an isolated example. Indeed, on a global scale,

---

*This is the Consultative Committee for International Telegraph and Telephone.

there seem to be little coordination among the many standards groups that are currently addressing various issues of normalization.

The ISO/OSI transport layer controls point-to-point information interchange, data packet, size determination, and transfer, as well as connection and disconnection of session entities. This is where TCP/IP fits in. For its part, the session layer stands above transport and serves to:

- Organize and synchronize the applications dialog between presentation entities

- Manage the normal and expedited exchange of data during the session

- Monitor the establishment and release of transport connections as requested by session entities

The presentation layer is responsible for the meaningful display of information to applications entities, assuring finer programmatic interfaces. It also identifies and negotiates the choice of communications transfer syntax and the subsequent data conversion or transformation.

The top-of-the-line application layer is, to start with, a misnomer. Its job is to address the interfacing of applications processes with interconnection facilities in order to assist with information exchange. Theoretically, it is also responsible for management of applications processes (including initialization), maintenance and termination of communications, prevention of deadlocks, transmission security, and so on.

This is the OSI layer with the most built-in contradictions. Today many incompatible protocols from different vendors address applications-level services—and the irony of it is they don't even complete that job.

To help in squaring out the needed functionality of the applications layer, ISO works on an ASN.1 norm. It specifies a self-describing data format which can be used for the transmittal of information between heterogeneous machines.

Addressing the issue of interoperability, ISO has established the remote data access (RDA) working group. Its charter is to elaborate the formats and protocols necessary for cross-database operations among SQL-based relational DBMS applications. Productization of the RDA committee's work has been undertaken by the SQL access group.*

---

*See also D. N. Chorafas and H. Steinmann, *Solutions for Networked Databases,* Academic Press, San Diego, CA, 1993.

For all practical purposes, the effort to establish norms with industrywide impact is never ending. In fact, a surprising number of people believe that the notion of standardization is a relatively recent one. Nothing could be more untrue.

The layout of the QWERTY keyboard, for instance, was introduced in 1873—and it was designed to slow down typists so they would not jam the keys. That criterion for advancing a norm quickly disappeared, yet all attempts to replace QWERTY with something faster have been thwarted, with productivity cost doubtless in the billions of dollars.

There are two morals to this story, and they are contradictory.

- Picking a standard too soon can lock you into obsolete technology.

- Even a mediocre standard is better than none.

Both lessons should be kept in mind in light of the proliferation of norms institutes and associated efforts over the last few years. The result is that standards today are drafted and ratified by a maze of institutions with input generated from quite diverse interests. Some examples are reviewed later in this chapter.

In the computer, communications, and software field, no single organization can realistically claim preeminence in the definition of international standards. Three reasons can be cited:

- Fragmentation in the field seriously stretches the ability of any one company or group to participate in, and exert influence over, the definition of standards.

- Standardization has become a dynamic process in which pressure for speedier norms definition encourages the trend toward ad hoc organizations for setting standards.

- Working at too fast a pace, these organizations end up making it more difficult to achieve a single international standard with staying power.

For instance, of 89,000 standards used in the United States, only 17 have been directly adopted by the International Standards Organization. Many standards for integrated services are being developed independent of national and international standardization procedures.

The end result is that both the vendors and the user organizations are bombarded by incompatible technological solutions. Multivendor settings such as the Open Software Foundation, the OSI/Network Management Forum, the X/Open Consortium, and the Open Token Foundation have bloomed, with the intention of bridging the gaps among proprietary computer systems. That's all there is to it: the *intention.*

The proliferation of standardization bodies is not the only issue. The tensions among engineering perfection, timeliness, and marketing demands shape most of today's debates over computer standards, especially those involving the management of computer networks. But nobody really thinks that the industry can operate without, at least, some standards.

9.3 Systems Interoperability and Incompatibilities in the Standards Effort

Another reason that norms for the able management of computers, communications, and software are so hard to develop is that they have to be built on lower-level networking technologies, which themselves are evolving. The layered approach of ISO/OSI could be turned around to address this issue, but there has to be general agreement to do so.

ISO/OSI does recognize the importance of layer-by-layer standardization, and that's a good start. But services for the seven layers of the OSI model have been developed independently and do not necessarily work in unison. In several (though not all) cases, each has a specified quality of service that corresponds only to that particular layer, not to the next.

While user applications depend on all seven layers, if the protocols of one of the layers are incompatible, the whole system is at risk. Since the semantics of the parameters in the OSI model have not been defined, a message transmitted through incompatible layers may not be understood and acted upon.

For instance, within the specifications for X.25 certain parameters are defined. However, if a particular communication happens to cross at some point through a local area network running an incompatible protocol, there is no way to establish a standard for how end-to-end quality of service will be met—or for what action should be taken if this is not the case.

As noted in Chap. 8, vendors interpret standards differently for a variety of reasons. There are often incompatibilities in the way norms are established as well as implemented. Whether such incompatibilities are slight or significant, the result is an inability to transmit information in an integrative way.

Politically (and most particularly in a marketing sense), vendors resent the pure form of standards set by international bodies. As the market forces them to adopt early versions of a norm, which they do to defend their market share, they interpret that version as they please—with twists and add-ons. Typically, the result is additional incompatibilities.

Even in good faith, vendors may interpret ambiguously stated standards, then try to influence the way other vendors interpret that same norm. Supposedly to alleviate some of these problems, conformance-testing organizations have come into being. The most prominent are:

- Corporation for Open Systems International (COS), in North America

- Standards Promotion and Application Group (SPAG), in Europe

- Promoting Conference for Open Systems Interconnection (POSI), in Japan

Their purpose as standardizations bodies is to identify uniform interpretations of norms or profiles and to test and certify vendor products for compliance.

However, no two conformance-testing organizations take the same approach, since there are not even standards for testing! Each has adopted a set of protocol profiles and testing methodologies that reflects the way local vendors like it. This is why the only true test of conformity to standards is the market.

- Each conformance body's interpretation of a standard does not necessarily include the same set of features, functions, and protocols required by the others.

- The consequent incompatibilities in results occur both within and among products tested for conformance to standards.

In a way, such deviations from what should have been a normalized standards-testing procedure are worse than variations in norms among vendors, which are bound to exist even if profiles from conformance test houses do match. Because of differences in normalization profiles, user organizations still cannot be certain that products will truly interoperate.

Largely as a result of these factors, the testing and evaluation community has defined three levels of interoperability testing, as shown in Fig. 9.2.

1. *The bottom level is one of theoretical conformance.* The product's technical design documentation is compared with the definitions of a de jure standard in an effort to flush out any differences that exist. One of the problems at this level is that conceptual performance does not necessarily catch minor deviations of the "version type."

2. *The middle level includes test sequences to verify that the product operates in accordance with the standard.* Each function is tested in

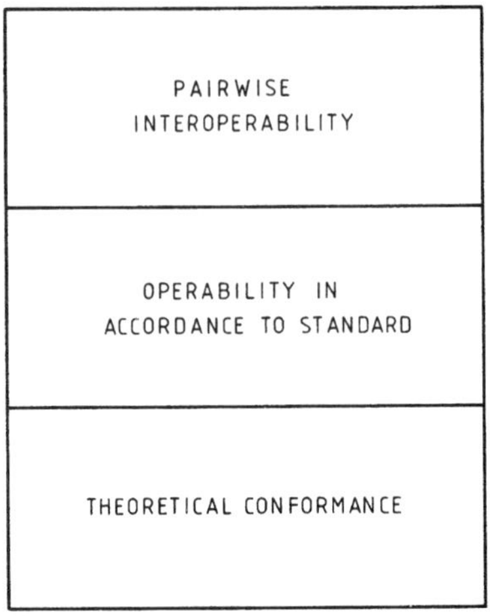

PAIRWISE
INTEROPERABILITY

OPERABILITY IN
ACCORDANCE TO STANDARD

THEORETICAL CONFORMANCE

Figure 9.2 A layered approach to interoperability testing for the normalization of standards.

isolation, using specialized equipment. The problem here is that conformance houses have adopted different approaches to such testing, with each house favoring its own tools. For this reason, computer equipment that passes one set of tests may not pass another.

3. *The higher level is the so-called pairwise interoperability.* The aim of this check is to assure that a piece of equipment will interoperate with another vendor's product using the same standard. However, as the pairwise reference indicates, this takes place two by two, not necessarily with many systems in tandem. Furthermore, such tests typically evaluate isolated protocols. Yet often products that operate in a single-protocol mode fail when multiple protocols are used. Hence, a still higher level is projected:

- *Full-suite* testing aiming to overcome the single-protocol limitation

So far, there is no fully international conformance-testing network, though regional efforts are being made in America, Europe, Japan, and Australia. In any case, while necessary, full-suite testing is not enough. There should also be a still higher level:

- Systems *tuning* and *balancing,* addressing the top level of interoperability

A tune-up has to be performed by users and vendors in a joint initiative and should include both required and optional features. The aim should be not only to assure performance testing but also to evaluate the product's parameters for the best possible performance.

It is clear that assuring the interoperability of products entails much more than simply purchasing equipment or software that has passed conformance tests. User organizations must carefully balance *standards* and *sourcing* against the need to maintain independence of vendors and avoid lock-ins.

Interoperability can be a double-edged sword. As desirable as it is, it entails many problems. And once again, there is no guarantee that the products of one and the same vendor will interoperate. That is why Chap. 8 concludes with the suggestion that the user organization is the ultimate arbiter of how *open* an open system may be.

9.4 Criteria Affecting Systems Interoperability

A sound solution to interoperability can be built in only at the design stage of systems development, with all due care paid to flexibility and extensibility. Any systems study has lots of prerequisites, so close attention must be paid to the relationships among the various parts—whether they come from the same vendor or through multisourcing.

For reasons of vendor independence as well as flexibility and cost-effectiveness, multisourcing is the better alternative. But we must keep in mind that at run time, user applications typically call upon different types of resources and may need to access them simultaneously:

- Computer software and hardware

- Public and private networks

- Local and wide area interconnections

Theoretically, the tools for, integrating systems components should conform to one or more standards. But as we have seen, the different standards are incompatible. Therefore, design perspectives and the appropriate actions must be precisely specified, outlining the particular requirements to be observed.

As we will see in Chap. 10, interoperability among heterogeneous systems and components, as well as high performance requirements, call for close attention to formal specifications of needed services. Included here are such critical parameters as:

- Quality level

- Reliability

- Availability

- Security

- Response time

- Cost

Since interoperability is likely to be created through resources that are subject to dynamically changing conditions, an open architecture is advisable to assure future flexibility.

User organizations are well advised to take an active stance on interoperability, developing aggressive procurement and implementation strategies. Also, they should be prepared to devote considerable time as well as resources to understanding the issues in order to avoid expensive pitfalls as the deployment of the system unfolds.

Key questions that user organizations should ask their vendors cover not only whether the products being offered conform to standards but also how conformance will meet specific implementation requirements.

- Is the computer or even the network going to operate at the lowest common denominator?

- Which of the normalized features will affect each specific user the most?

- Can these crucial features truly interoperate in a networkwide sense?

Even if the vendor gives every assurance that this will happen, it is proper to press on with both systematic and ad hoc tests. One ad hoc method is to take selected user requirements and follow their execution as well as servicing in a systemwide sense.

Attention should be paid to the level at which conformance and interoperability testing has to be performed. Ad hoc tests should take place not only in a controlled environment but also, if not primarily, in a live environment—with a protocol being kept of issues and problems arising during these tests.

Prior to deciding on the supplier, the user organization should insist on reviewing the test results of other customers. Pilot testing of a small-scale version is also advisable.

Before awarding a contract, the user organization should see to it that real interoperability is a specific condition of sale. The alternative is over-reliance on the vendor's interpretation of past results, which may not be in line either with what the user organization requires or with events that unfold as the application proceeds.

For instance, in testing a client/server solution, the user organization should be keen in examining the client *and* server characteristics offered by each vendor, both individually and in unison:

- Client characteristics must not be confused with a PC connected to a LAN, which downloads all the necessary files from a server or a host and does the processing locally.

- The client runs a process, or a set of processes, all of which must exist on the server machine which provides support to the end user.

It all boils down to the fact that the final arbiter of service quality and its functionality is no one else but the end user. That opinion should account for 10; the opinion of the systems specialist, for 5.

In a similar manner, the server does not provide an abstract type of support to the client. The service is valuable only when it is focused. The nature and extent of such support must be defined by business goals. In other words:

- It is not a matter of the server merely responding to the queries or commands from networked clients.

- The real challenge is that of effectively maintaining a conversation.

One of the principles of client/server design is that a good server hides the entire composite system from the client and the end user. This principle should be appropriately verified during testing.

- A client communicating with a server should be completely unaware of the server platform and its hardware and software.

- The communications technology used should make no difference to the maintenance of the client-and-server conversation.

The same is true of servers communicating with one another. The system must have knowledge of the existence of multiple servers. This is what is meant by a distributed processing environment, as discussed in Chap. 10.

It is up to the client/server architecture to divide an application into individual processes operating on separate machines that are connected over a network. This arrangement forms a loosely coupled system, dividing the user-defined task into subtasks to be completed either by the client or by the server(s) within the constraints posed by business goals.

9.5 Organizations Aiming to Standardize Unix

The Open Software Foundation (OSF) was established in 1988 by IBM, DEC, HP, and other computer companies as a nonprofit research and development outfit committed to open software. In addition to the different computer manufacturers, user organizations are on OSF's membership list. In fact, Unix International also includes user organizations in its membership.

OSF/1, the operating system of OSF, was initially to be derived from IBM's AIX Release 3, a Unix clone based on AT&T's System V Release 2. But reasons of greater performance and multiprocessor support led OSF to select the Mach operating system as kernel. Mach is a Unix version enriched with knowledge engineering derived from work done at Carnegie-Mellon University.

The OSF/1 version of Unix is based on POSIX which has been projected as a standard OS by the Institute of Electrical and Electronic Engineers (IEEE). For some time, IEEE has been involved in the standardization of the Unix operating system, and it is this work which brought forward the POSIX specifications.

Figure 9.3 presents a list of the various groups seeking a definition of POSIX-compliant OS, including issues of security. Subsequent to the POSIX work, IEEE focused on standardizing its extensions in various areas, including:

- Real-time computing

- Threads

OSF products are selected through a process known as open *requests for technology* (RFTs). Member and nonmember companies

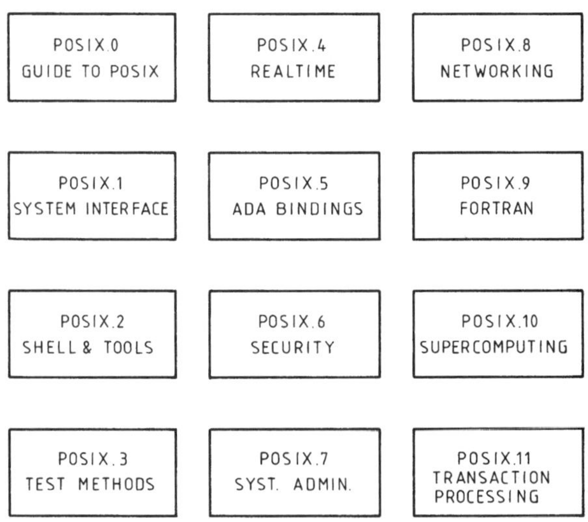

Figure 9.3 The 12 POSIX working groups, by IEEE, working on standardization projects.

are solicited to submit technology-oriented proposals that address a particular problem. OSF has released a number of RFTs. The first issue regarded a graphics user interface (GUI) and subsequently led to the choice of Motif as OSF GUI.

The second RFT by OSF focused on a *distributed computing environment* (DCE). The aim has been to standardize:

- Remote procedure calls (RPC)

- Network file systems

- Global directory services

- Other system aspects of distributed computing

A proposal made by DEC, HP, and other companies was selected as the winner, in preference to a proposal spearheaded by Sun Microsystems.

For its part, Sun Microsystems has worked with AT&T in developing the Unix version supported by Unix International (UI). A normalization competitor to OSF, Unix International capitalizes on the fact that the Unix operating system was originally developed by Bell Telephone Laboratories, strictly for internal purposes.

As is well known, Unix was subsequently licensed in source code form by AT&T to computer manufacturers that wanted to offer Unix on their machines. Parallel to this process, however—and for a variety of reasons—hardware and software vendors developed their own versions of Unix. For many years Xenix by Microsoft was the most popular version in the trade.

If vendors created their own incompatible Unix dialects, so did universities. Berkeley Software Distribution (BSD) by the University of California and Mach by Carnegie-Mellon are the best-known examples.

To further its goals, AT&T now uses Unix International as an advisory body whose purpose is to set the direction and content of future Unix releases. UI consults the Unix System Laboratories (USL), which was recently separated from the AT&T company.* USL has been AT&T's Unix research and development group. UI working-group activities include:

- Transaction processing

- Multiprocessing

- System interfaces

---

*With Novel taking a major share.

- User interfaces

- File management systems

- Licensing and conformance

UI and USL can be seen as the drive behind X/Open, a London-based international body composed of hardware and software vendors as well as users. Its goal is to turn de jure and de facto industry standards into an interface capable of assuring a certain measure of portability of software across hardware platforms.

The latest version of AT&T's Unix is System V Release 4 (SVR4). It represents a blend of earlier releases of AT&T Unix, incorporating many features from the Unix work done at the University of California at Berkeley and refined by way of joint work between AT&T and Sun Microsystems.

The aim of SVR4 was to produce a single, unified version of Unix to set the de facto standard. This did not happen, and SVR4 is now one of several Unix versions, a major competitor being OSF/1.

- Both SVR4 by Unix International and OSF/1 are expected to be POSIX-compliant

- Each one of them offers significantly different features to the applications developer.

The spread of normalization efforts toward open systems, particularly among user organizations, has led to industry-specific bodies. This process began with the Manufacturing Automation Protocol (MAP) initiative. Originally, General Motors designed MAP for its own use, but in 1980 GM started a MAP movement defining open systems for manufacturing. The aim was to encourage suppliers to meet the needs of large companies.*

Other similar initiatives include the U.S. government's GOSIP and European Procurement Handbook for Open Systems (EPHOS). With billions of money to spend on information technology, governments and government agencies can be instrumental in defining implementation of their standards. A prime example is the U.S. Department of Defense (DoD).

These initiatives typically take existing OSI standards and refine them to make OSI *profiles*. Such profiles select from the options within a set of standards. The idea is that without profiles, suppliers can make OSI products which are not compatible. But there is no guarantee that profiles will lead to compatibility and interoperability.

---

*MAP is still looked to by a world federation of MAP/TOP user groups.

9.6 Contradictions in the Process of Normalization

X/Open is a consortium of 11 international computer manufacturers with a stated commitment to bringing open systems to the marketplace. It was formed in 1984 as a loose affiliation and is now incorporated as an independent, nonprofit organization. Its members include AT&T, Bull, DEC, Ericsson, Hewlett-Packard, ICL, Nixdorf, Olivetti, Philips, Siemens, and Unisys. Many of these companies are also members of the SQL Access Group.

By adopting but also adapting accepted "standards," X/Open hopes to create a common applications environment that will allow the portability of software applications among different systems from various vendors. The organization does not endorse products; it publishes specifications.

X/Open is *not* a standards body like the International Standards Organization (ISO), the American National Standards Institute (ANSI), or the Institute of Electrical and Electronic Engineers (IEEE). It does, however, work closely with these institutes to determine what might be acceptable norms. For instance:

- X/Open has developed the X/Open Portability Guide (XPG), which is currently at Version 3.

- XPG specifies standard operating system interfaces across compliant Unix implementations.

XPG aims to provide a test suite for compliance, enabling compliant vendors to advertise adherence to an X/Open norm that appears on the product destined for the user organization.

X/Open's best-known work is with transaction-processing monitors (TPMs). The role of a TPM is to front-end the processing of high-transaction applications.

In 1987 X/Open published a TPM reference model, and in April of 1990 it issued a preliminary specification for the XA interface regarding communication between TPM and resource managers such as DBMS. Another goal of X/Open is to meet interoperability requirements, making it possible for heterogeneous databases to handle the same transaction coordinated by an X/Open-compliant TPM.

The first X/Open-compliant TPM was AT&T's System/T Version 4. AT&T's Tuxedo is one of the better TPMs currently available on the market. Running over distributed nodes, it has the capability to define a failed node, switching the request for information. (See Fig. 9.4.) Tuxedo is, however, challenged by OSF's Encina.

- Tuxedo is the first Unix TPM to comply with X/Open's XA interface specification.

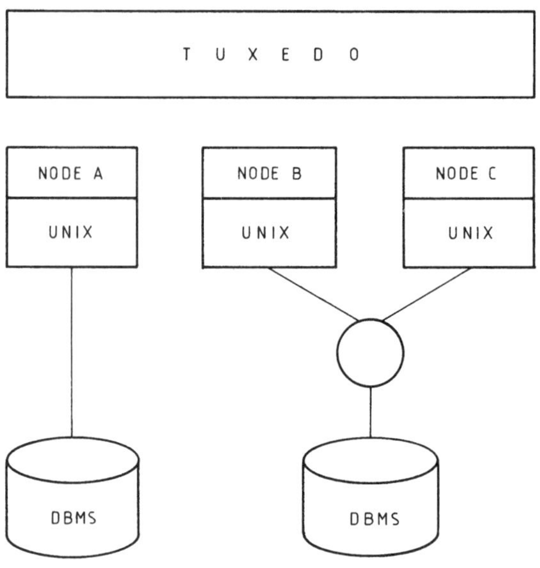

Figure 9.4 TUXEDO has the ability to define a failed node and switch the request to a server that still runs.

- System/T Release 4 incorporates the XA interface as the communications mechanism between the TPM and resource managers like DBMS.

Another goodwill organization, this one based in Silicon Valley, aims to productize ISO and ANSI standards. It has been set up by 42 different computer/communications vendors and user organizations, but IBM and AT&T are not part of it.

Known as the SQL Access Group (SAG), this cooperative body was formed in 1989 with the primary goal of productizing formats and protocols. Such productization of ANSI and ISO standards is necessary for interoperability between SQL-based relational database management systems.

Building upon the work done by the ISO remote data access (RDA) committee, the SQL Access Group has designed an interoperability specification which will be prototyped by each of its computer vendor members. The initial work focuses on three areas of specification:

- A precompiler API
- Formats and protocols (FAP)
- Procedure calls

At bottom, the various normalization and productization efforts just described are part complementary and part contradictory. All talk of "standards," but the standards they have chosen do not necessarily interoperate—which speaks volumes about norms.

Some experts say that at least some of the goodwill organizations described in this and the preceding section are not really working toward contradictory goals. Other experts disagree, though they accept that UI and OSF are not exactly the same kind of body:

- Unix International gathers specifications from hardware suppliers to tell USL what products to make.

- OSF actually makes products, which it then sells to its sponsors: IBM, DEC, Hewlett-Packard, and others.

That sort of distinction, the latter group of experts suggests, is not quite so clear-cut. Neither is it true that UI and OSF are as close together as might be inferred from UI's adoption of DCE.

X/Open is one of the nonofficial standardization bodies—not *the* body which aims to pull the industry together. Set up by some suppliers, X/Open seeks to bring out enough norms to cover all the basic functions of an open system, including POSIX and OSI—but so does OSF, with a different set of norms.

True, in one of its initiatives X/Open calls this a *common applications environment* (CAE). It also canvasses users in its Xtra market research, aiming to determine what standards are required. But all that adds up to just one normalization effort. It does not represent all of them.

Given the variety and to a significant extent the incompatibility of current standardization efforts, it is quite conceivable that vendor-dominated OSF and X/Open will both face competition from militant groups of users. Norms-oriented user groups have been forming, all specifying directions for suppliers.

The most important of these groups is Standards and Open Systems (SOS). After they formed SOS in 1991, the computer heads of blue-chip companies like Dupont, Eastman Kodak, McDonnell Douglas, and American Airlines wrote to suppliers listing a number of standards they wanted to be followed. These included de facto norms chosen to be among the best—even some not-yet-delivered standards such as DCE.

One of the aims of SOS is to avoid biased solutions resulting from pressures from particular suppliers. Another aim is to see to it that what is offered is made *open*.

SOS got in contact with the National Institute of Standards and Technology (NIST), which made the GOSIP profile for networking, suggesting that its *OSI workshop* be extended to make an *applications portability profile* (APP) covering the whole area of open systems and including de facto standards. This proposal could produce a rival to X/Open's CAE. And so on, and so forth.

9.7 There Is No Monopoly in Setting Standards

There is no monopoly in establishing de facto or de jure standards. All companies, goodwill efforts, and normalization organizations are equal, but the bigger ones and those having greater follow-up are more equal than the others. That's the way to bet.

In the 1960s and 1970s, IBM set the de facto standards, giving rise to a whole industry of plug-compatible manufacturers (PCMs). But that era has long since passed. Like the different maxi- and ministates which followed the demise of the former Soviet Union, the passing of IBM from the de facto standards scene brought into the picture a number of normalization organizations. We have examined several of them here, but none has the clout which used to be IBM's own.

One exception is the U.S. Department of Defense. It is, after all, by far the largest procurement agency of electronics, estimated to absorb the equivalent of 5 percent of whatever is produced anywhere in the world. Two de facto standards have been established because the DoD stood behind them:

- Unix

- TCP/IP

But the DoD did not take a firm stand in regard to graphics user interfaces, and today for better or worse there are plenty of them around.

One of the earliest examples of computer-aided design (CAD), pioneered by the graphics work of Dr. Ivan Sutherland, is X Windows. Developed in the mid-1980s under MIT's project Athena, X Windows was the first graphics user interface (GUI) available for Unix. X Windows (or a clone) is featured on most Unix workstations and is also supported by many nonworkstation vendors through the use of naive X Terminals—a funny breed.

One of the main merits of X Windows is that it provides user interface definitions which are portable across hardware platforms. X-based applications could therefore have a consistent user interface on heterogeneous systems. By separating front-end X server from back-end X client processes, X Windows permits a better distribution of applications processing across a network. As a result, it has become a de facto standard for distributed windowing, serving as a model for ANSI, IEEE, NIST and X/Open specifications.

It should be noted that the original development of GUI came from Xerox Laboratories, and also has its origins in the graphics work originated by Dr. Ivan Sutherland and Danny Cohen. Then, in 1984—though GUI predates the announcement—Apple Computers made the graphics user interface an affordable solution with Macintosh.

Next to Macintosh graphics in terms of popularity (measured in millions of copies sold) is Microsoft's Windows. It is followed, with a big gap in user numbers, by OSF's Motif. Motif is not the only GUI in the unix world. Another one is AT&T's Open Look which has also been derived from X Windows.

The impact of Macintosh, Windows, and Motif extends well beyond the graphics interface and into the core of the coming competition for mastery of the operating systems market. Among the other wild cards up its sleeve, Microsoft is betting on the fact that Unix has made a name among professionals rather than end users, where MS DOS is king.

Microsoft is betting on the fact that the Unix environment will not be taken over wholesale by the end-user population. The rich applications libraries under MS DOS and the much poorer libraries under Unix are a basic reason. Windows NT targets to:

- Overcome the gap which exists in operating systems for larger workstations*

- Exploit the huge applications libraries built over the years around MS DOS

- Bet on GUI as the vehicle of choice by end users through the 1990s

The most likely course of events is that NT will level off Unix and edge against both MVS and VMS by the end of the decade. Running just behind VMS is one of the artifacts which followed from X-Windows: DECWindows. But it appears to lack the necessary market penetration to support itself in the long run.

Motif, Open Look, and to some extent DECWindows are not the only GUIs in the Unix world. Among the not-so-popular GUIs (in terms of user population) are the Presentation Manager of OS/2, Character Mode and Block Mode. The proliferation suggests plenty of incompatibilities at the end-user level.

---

*Windows NT promises to do that, but also requires 12 megabytes of central memory and at least i486 power.

Vendors have to comprehend that there is no monopoly in standards setting. After IBM lost its market grasp by falling backward into the future in staying put with mainframes, the playing field became crowded and the market highly fragmented. Clear-eyed user organizations are able to capitalize on this fact.

Meanwhile new technology brings into perspective new processes and new normalization efforts. An example is the Boston-based Object Management Group (OMG). Object orientation is a key technology for a new kind of distributed computing now being delivered to the market.

The goal OMG set for itself is to persuade the industry to agree to one standard, the object request broker (ORB). This specification hopes to unite the rival static and dynamic approaches to linking applications in an object-oriented environment.

As noted in Sec. 9.1, another major effort is OSI's open distributed processing (ODP). It too has an object orientation, including a trading function which, in combination with other ODP facilities, performs a standardization role in distributed systems.

X3TC, the OSI normalization committee working on ODP, is part of an international effort which began around 1988. Its product is the Reference Model of ODP (RM-ODP, ISO 10746), which creates an architecture for standardization that integrates distributed computer applications and interworking basically aimed at supporting the two pillars on which modern solutions should rest:

- Interoperability

- Portability

This effort is co-sponsored by the International Standards Organization (ISO) and the International Electrotechnical Commission (IEC), through the Joint Technical Committee 1 (ISO/IEC JTC1). ODP is assigned to the subcommittee JTC1 SC21/WG7, which represents 18 countries and 7 liaisons.

Through a collaboration agreement, the Consultative Committee for International Telegraph and Telephone (CCITT) has combined its ODP-related efforts with WG7. As a technical arm of the Accredited Standards Committee X3, Information Processing Systems, X3T3 operates under the procedures of the American National Standards Institute. Let us hope that some generally acceptable norms come out of this effort.

10

Highly Distributed Processing

10.1 Introduction

In light of all the confusion surrounding open systems and the lack of real standards in computers, communications, and software, why should companies get out of the cocoon of mainframes and into a world of apparent uncertainty? What advantages are to be gained through client/server systems? Is it a really sound idea to pursue a course of highly distributed processing?

The reason is *competitiveness.* As we have seen in Part 1, international competition requires companies to operate on a global scale. This is true not only of big but also of small companies and of professionals.

The skills of experts in high technology are perishable. Innovation is everyday business, making the already acquired know-how obsolete. Just the same, one of the best business opportunities of small firms is to find a market niche in a more or less global perspective, a niche in which it can really be a leader.

It goes without saying that bigger companies are particularly vulnerable if they lose their competitiveness in the global market. Components of complex aerospace, computer, communications, automotive, and heavy-equipment products, among others, are now being designed in different countries, and the same is true of financial services as well as other sectors of the economy:

- A truly competitive product is typically designed and manufactured in several countries and distributed worldwide.

- Quite similarly, global securities trading, bids and asks, take place around the globe 24 hours a day, 7 days a week.

For global operations to succeed, information must be collected at point of origin and brought to the location where the work is being carried out. Therefore, the centralized solutions of the 1960s and 1970s are counterproductive.

Competitiveness sees to it that each knowledge worker must be connected to the global network, with some information services being generalized, while others are specialized or even localized. The former are served through communications channels and distributed databases, the latter through client/servers.

Not only does the execution of operations have to be real time, but also a radical simplification of work must take place. This is feasible only if the activities of the business are examined as a whole:

- First, through a grand design integrating them into a well-coordinated system

- Then, partitioning them into manageable pieces, each served by one or more networked client/servers

This flexible, integrative approach contrasts with procedures cast along the fixed lines of current organizational approaches. And it can in no way be served through computer centers of mammoth dimensions.

Organizations that retain the old structures with water-tight divisions of responsibility and twisted information flow patterns are not able to capitalize on business opportunities. Neither can they effectively use technology to achieve streamlined operations, reducing costs and drastically improving customer services.

In contrast to the centralized, inflexible approaches, one of the major objectives of client/server computing is to reduce the complexity faced by the applications developers. What makes programming for a client/server environment different from programming for a traditional host application is the placement issue:

- Where to place the processes and information elements

- How to deploy the technologies available to do the needed job

These are subjects treated in Part 1 from a business viewpoint. We will now examine more carefully what it takes in an organizational and technical sense. Both senior management and the technologists will be well advised to avoid mainframe-type adventures that can bring them into a business cul de sac.

10.2 Performance Expectations with Client/Server Solutions

After the decision has been made to use a client/server solution, it is wise to set proper performance expectations. The need for functionality must be weighed against cost and response time as well as other issues appropriate to each particular firm.

Monitoring performance during operations requires maintaining activity logs that are analyzed through expert systems. This will allow the evaluation of ongoing applications through regression testing as well as the testing of new applications and postmortem studies following major maintenance activities. A distributed database environment demands that such testing occur:

- At each location where processing may take place

- In a global sense for those processes operating networkwide

A major challenge in today's distributed environments inclining companies to keep a major central hub as the commanding authority is the lack of synchronization of existing computer-based production facilities with the models from which the applications were derived.

- Most of the legacy applications were not developed in accordance with a grand design.

- Maintenance is rarely if ever included in a model-driven optimization approach, even when the latter exists.

This mistake has to be corrected. Significant improvements in systems design and software/hardware performance are among the most basic reasons for the implementation of client/server approaches. This is true all the way to the choice of basic software.

An application in a client/server environment is either directly or indirectly connected to a DBMS. Direct connection is not quite advisable, since the systems programmer sets up controls that automatically lock the program to a given database management system. This reduces the polyvalence the application obtains through indirect connection.

- A program should be capable of reading and/or updating tables in multiple DBMS.

- It may commit in one location, connect to another DBMS, and proceed to issue statements for processing by still another DBMS.

This is particularly important with competitive-type applications. In a long transaction, for example, the computer program may continue with one DBMS as long as all the statements are processed by one database—but the program is always ready to exploit the contents of a group of other databases, as requirements develop.

As a matter of design principle, the distribution of information elements and applications must be transparent to the workstation user. The user should not even need to be aware that information from multiple systems was involved. Support services can be moved from machine to machine as end-user requirements change.

All this is part of the effort to make client/server computing a flexible and efficient way to answer ongoing as well as new requirements. An able implementation can help meet this strategy, thus permitting the business to gain a competitive edge and optimize its current computing investments while positioning itself for flexible growth.

In short, technology becomes manageable when industrial companies and financial institutions make smarter choices in their investments. The battle to remain competitive in today's environment may well depend on our ability to use computers, communications, and software more effectively than ever before in the face of:

- Market changes

- Product innovation

- Regulatory requirements

- Organizational assessments

- Resource evaluation

- Management planning and control needs

High performance at the end-user computing level is a key to this approach toward rationalization in the use of technological resources. At the same time, it imposes many requirements, of which the most important is a new systems design culture.

For nearly 40 years, computers were applied almost exclusively to simple transaction-processing and clerical operations. For these, the dumb terminals, naive protocols, and pseudo-client/server approaches used by most companies might be acceptable. But a highly competitive marketplace has shifted the focus of information technology implementation.

Knowledge engineering, and therefore expert systems, is a new type of software capitalizing on the fact that as technology develops, new business opportunities become available. They are also a sound way of answering higher performance expectations and of improving analyst/programmer productivity.

A quick look at the transition that brought us to where we are helps in documenting this point. As Fig. 10.1 suggests, in very old times of computer technology—that is, the *paleolithic age*—computer professionals and end users at any organizational level were two totally *distinct* crowds. The systems expert worked with second- and third-generation languages; the end users were fed with paper or were given nonintelligent terminals they could rarely use.

The mainframers would say that end users got nearer to the computer through nonintelligent terminals. This happened in the late

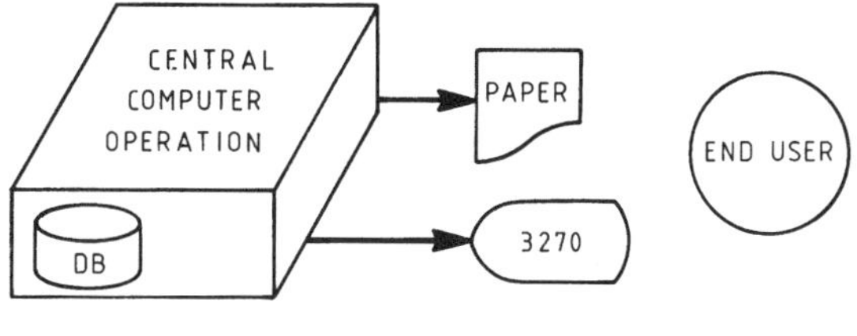

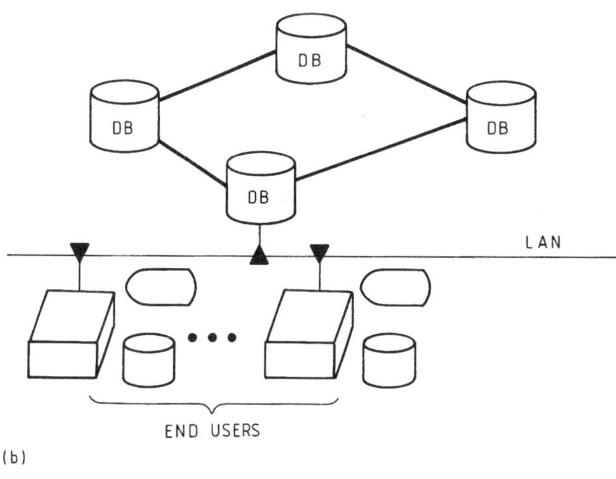

Figure 10.1   In old times paper, then slow nonintelligent terminals connected to the end user. Today's requirements are different. (*a*) Paleolithic age of computing. (*b*) Competitive solutions for the 1990s.

1960s and early 1970s. The argument is correct, but we are no longer in the 1970s:

- In the 1980s, end users got stand-alone PCs but still had to go on line to mainframes.

- In the 1990s, both databases and number-crunching servers were networked and brought near the end user. (See Chap. 11, on high-performance computing.)

This did not happen by accident. It was made feasible through technology in response to the drive by the market forces—a fact to be kept in mind when investment decisions are done.

Today, mainframe-based solutions dating back to the 1960s and 1970s are not just *retrograde,* they are counterproductive and damage the company which bases its future on them. As Fig. 10.2 suggests, there is a very significant difference between *legacy*-type and *competi-*

<table>
<tr><td>

Legacy Type

Synchronous

Mainly *simple transactional.*

For some time they may stay on mainframes, but as they become more massive, efficient solutions will have to be found.

Much of this work is still batch, and has to be converted to on line by means of client/servers.

</td><td>

Competitive Type

Asynchronous
Characterized by:

- Long transactions
- Complex queries
- Intensive communications
- Seamless database access

These need to be fully distributed, interactive, and focus on *database mining* and *analytics.*

</td></tr>
</table>

Figure 10.2 Two distinct types of computer applications require significantly different solutions.

tive-type applications. Companies that retain legacy systems are simply not competitive.

The change in terms of types of applications and systems approaches did not happen overnight. Even by the mid-1980s mainframe connectivity through nonintelligent protocols was passé thanks to the able use of local area networks. The proliferation of workstations and LANs brought up the need for a systems architecture and for normalization, as we have seen respectively in Chaps. 8 and 9.

10.3 Why Do We Need Information Technology Investments?

In any business, the purpose of information technology is to provide better services to customers, assure a platform for innovation, help in lowering costs, and permit management to gain access to corporate resources. Without investments in computers, communications, and software, the exploitation of these resources would have been slow and tedious—but throwing money at the problem does not solve it.

Sound technology investment goals can be summed up in one short sentence: "Strengthen the longer-term competitiveness of the firm." To reach and sustain this objective, we need a cooperative environment permitting seamless access to installed computers and the multimedia databases run by them.

Meeting this objective is do-able, but not through rusty concepts and centralized mainframes. A real challenge with client/server solutions is to develop applications that are innovative and that over the longer run can enhance:

- Market appeal
- Product development
- The quality of customer service

As we have seen in Chap. 8, to meet such goals in an able manner companies opt for open systems. But we also saw that these do not come in black-and-white; many tonalities of gray characterize an open architecture.

While variations do exist, what can be presented in a crisp manner is the decision to move out of a centralized approach toward a fully distributed interactive environment. As on-line transactions become increasingly complex, a client/server solution permits the transaction-processing monitor components to be put into separate address spaces for:

- Easier distribution

- Simpler control

- Better protection

Mainframers would say that easier distribution can also be achieved by putting the message manager on a front end and distributing only the transaction servers on multiple computers. From a longer-term survival perspective, this is nonsense. It is advanced only to perpetuate the status quo—hence, a bad situation.

Technologists who must adhere to time restraints appreciate that the increasing complexity of applications in business and industry, along with the heterogeneity of systems environments, has made centralized implementations inappropriate. Applications are best developed by means of distributed cooperative resources which, however, present new challenges in terms of:

1. Changes in cultural images

2. Representations of objectives

3. Complex interactions among the tasks required to achieve those objectives

The challenges posed by issues 1, 2, and 3 suggest that investments are made not only in software and hardware but also in the minds of people. Human beings are reprogrammable, but this can be done only through lifelong learning and appropriate investments.

- Priority should always be given to *human resources,*

- Technology is useless without people.

Next to the steady training of the human resources comes the direction in which technological investments will be made. Particularly important for modern business is an interactive transaction control system allowing cooperative tasks to interact by issuing transactions to shared objects stored in databases. Client/server solutions help in this mission.

A distributed cooperative model allows more local independence, flexibility, and reliability—in a much more efficient way than a centralized one. In a distributed cooperative model, applications are controlled by a set of tasks to be properly defined through a sequence of interactions. This means that several technical issues need to be addressed, including the way to observe and control the progress of an application that supports long-running activities.

The dynamic interactions among users can be complex and typically require iterative processes. Any authorized on-line user may change the cooperative objectives just like he or she affects the inputs and the outputs. This raises a number of queries:

- How can the shared resources be reliably manipulated?

- How do we define and determine when a cooperative objective is attained?

- What is the criterion for controlling interactions among multiple cooperative tasks?

Able answers to these technical queries must be given within the perspectives of the 1990s. These involve visualization at the end-user level, knowledge engineering, interactive prototyping, high-performance computing, broadband communications, and multimedia applications.

Developing appropriate software paradigms to support multimedia communications and computer-based cooperative work is one of the major challenges facing not only the computer and communications industry but also the user community. Solutions must firmly support distributed service implementation.

- The solutions necessarily involve heterogeneous database systems, object-oriented databases, and long transaction models. (This issue is discussed further in Sec. 10.6 and throughout Part 3.)

- They have to establish new correctness criteria for definition and control of interactions among cooperative tasks.

- They have to handle long-running applications, which can be achieved only through an iterative try-and-refine process.

Most importantly, the technical solutions that are supplied should be able to sell themselves to the users. Both the user community and the computer experts should appreciate that new technology is not just machines and software. It represents a major organizational and cultural change. Therefore, its implementation has to go well beyond installing the technical vehicle, into creating momentum for change.

The successful implementation of new technology rests on innovation—and innovation is value-driven, being successful only within a context of focused expertise. Therefore, when it evaluates new investments, management will be well advised not to spend a big chunk of money buying new machines without carefully focusing on objectives—studying and deciding on which platform to invest. Emphasis should be placed on:

- Recyclable OS
- Object DBMS
- Powerful graphics
- Efficient electronic mail

In conclusion, wise investments will primarily address the roots of a computer literacy program for everybody in the organization—starting with senior managers and professionals. Computer-illiterate companies cannot survive the test of the 1990s—and the same is true of people.

10.4   How Can We Follow a Policy of Renewal?

Without firm support by top management, the streamlining of architectural characteristics risks going nowhere in terms of turning around current technology and modernizing it. This is one of the key issues that must be explained in a convincing way to senior management and acted upon.

"The president is a very reasonable person, once things are explained to him," General Douglas MacArthur once said of Franklin D. Roosevelt. The dictum is just as true of corporate presidents and chief executive officers. What has to be explained to corporate management is that associated with the process of organizational renewal, and largely contributing to it, are two major, highly interrelated changes currently taking place in:

- Economics
- Technology

The economics issue has high sensitivity. Whether we talk of mainframes, maxis or minis—that is, machines of the 1950s to 1970s—we are referring to computers which are no longer being priced competitively. Their cost-effectiveness is so low that anybody investing in them needs to have his or her brains examined. Therefore:

A growing number of leading organizations move not only out of mainframes but also beyond LANs to client/server architectures. And they save a lot of money.

A pattern is now developing that speaks volumes about how user organizations feel and which investment decisions they make in terms of computer technology. At a May 28, 1992 meeting in New York, Oracle executives mentioned that the company's client base is rapidly changing:

- In 1989, some 60–65 percent of the Oracle DBMS business came from VMS.

- In 1992 more than 60 percent of the Oracle DBMS business came from Unix environments.

In other words, not only the mainframes but also the maxis and minis have proved to be a very bad investment—and top management must finally take notice of this fact. Mainframes, maxis, and minis cannot compete, in terms of price and performance.

- They are far and away outperformed by the new solutions with networked workstations and servers.

- They fall apart in terms of cost-effectiveness when compared with massively parallel computers.

Hewlett-Packard, for instance, has suggested that its new Business Systems Server will take care of 90 percent of IBM-installed computer bases—at a small fraction of the cost. The rich examples that Microsoft has given about the potential of its SQL server are another first-class illustration of the changing pattern of computer usage. We have already spoken of these issues but briefly repeating them helps keep them in mind.

Oracle, Microsoft, and Hewlett-Packard are targeting not only IMS database installations but also DB2. In terms of business, the IMS client base might have been plenty—they are said to represent an amazing $80 billion in investments:

- Both VSAM and IMS have a much broader client base than DB2.

- IMS and VSAM constitute IBM's soft underbelly.

Hence, the other vendors are targeting the IMS and VSAM environments, seeking to replace them. And they are after DB2 because it is costly and inflexible—a sitting duck. Precisely here lies the need for technological breakthroughs, and winner may take all.

Any vendor attacking the VSAM, IMS, and CICS installed base needs to be really strong in transaction processing. Its wares must feature high performance, high availability, and automated systems management—all that at a small fraction of Big Blue cost.

Every single one of the competitive features being mentioned requires a new OS departure with knowledge engineering and object orientation embedded into the operating system itself. Competitive vendors understand this reality.

- The policy of these competitive vendors is aggressively going after the IBM-installed base.

- The policy of IBM is, rather, a defensive one—and therefore a weak position.

The strategies are different, but incumbents and challengers by now use the same tools of knowledge engineering and object-based solutions—though on different platforms.

As the architecture of PINK helps document,* IBM and its challengers appreciate that closely related to the choice of an operating system is the selection of a very high level programming language—and it is just as critical. New programming languages are inseparable from viable solutions to the distributed database challenge.

When we talk of a new language, it is quite important to examine its features and benefits in cost savings, in terms of both development and maintenance as well as the guidance which exists in regard to planning able conversion strategies. As far as the users are concerned:

- There has to be documented evidence on how proposed tools help increase programming productivity and efficiency.

- Product life cycle must be evaluated, if the control of software costs is going to be a meaningful proposition.

All these references converge toward systems concepts that, when put together, lead to rules for systems architecture. We will look at the most important of these rules in Secs. 10.5–10.7, always within the perspective of assuring significant return on investment.

---

*PINK is the joint project for a new OS undertaken by IBM and Apple Computers.

10.5 Rules for an Overall Database Architecture

As we have seen in Chap. 9, a systems architecture employs design principles, defines relationships among components, and assures the interaction among attached devices: hardware, basic software, and applications programs. This definition is as valid of databases as it is of networks and of any other field in information technology.

The architecture defines formats that are compatible within an enterprisewide system, and is also a prerequisite to systems integration. Given the complexity of the computer industry today, a master plan is imperative—though, as the preceding sections underlined, such a plan has to be flexible and adaptable.

The architectural plan that is adopted should lead to the organization of a computer and communications environment that tries to overcome problems of poor performance, incompatible data structures, and high costs in information movements. This leads us to a major principle that aims to provide for continuity and unify all other, more complex efforts:

Develop a systems architecture, be sure it is valid, and stick to it.

Like any other systems duty, an architecture has to be properly studied—starting with *problem definition*. The flowchart in Fig. 10.3 suggests an approach followed by a manufacturing concern that a few years ago found it necessary to develop its own architectural solution, as none of those offered as commodities:

- Satisfied the company's specific goals in information technology

- Passed the test of completeness and performance

Since it searches to reconcile conflicting aims, the right architecture for database design, for example, must strike a sense of balance—and this takes lots of experimentation. For instance, in the case of response time, what constitutes good performance is application dependent, while the business goal may be application independence.

In addition, any sound architectural solutions should resolve contradictions between performance and cost. This issue is directly related to the amount of information flow involved as well as the level of usage. Main requirements include:

- Supporting fast response to analytical ad hoc queries

- Answering both global and local users' demands for information

- Capturing new data at the point of origin only once, but providing multiple uses

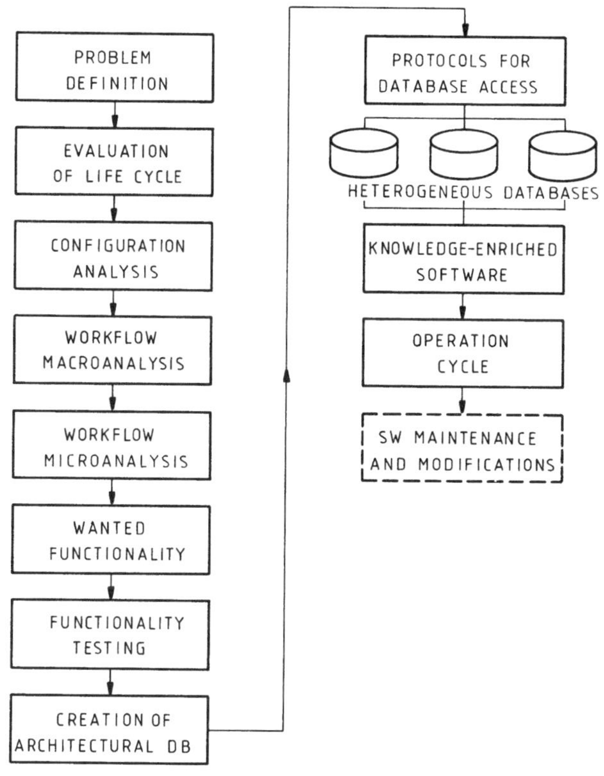

Figure 10.3 Studying what it takes to develop a systems architecture.

- Minimizing the movement of information elements around the network

- Providing for browsing facilities at the global level, to enable users to explore areas of interest

- Assuring a valid set of security mechanisms with authentication and authorization

These and similar requirements should fit well with the overall architecture. Though the latter will operate full time for many years, it must also be in a process of steady development with a persistent effort made toward renewal and refinement at an affordable cost. This leads to a second major principle:

Don't change the systems architecture, but keep its components flexible and able to evolute.

Continuity is very important through the life cycle of projects; that is why this chapter reflects on key issues affecting a systems architecture. But in no way does continuity mean ossification. When we have a master plan and know our goals, stability and flexibility can coexist.

- Projects do not need to be and should not be monolithic.

- Their components can nicely reflect new perspectives.

- Projects should be adaptive, but also fit within a well-chosen master plan.

The systems architecture should see to it that many of the projects that integrate into it complement one another—though the features that they show more or less reflect the prevailing technology. At the time of its development and market introduction, a given architecture should keep open all possibilities for future growth or downsizing in a modular form. A third principle holds here:

Products are designed for the user, and the database for the end user as well.

High technology is very powerful, but it is also a two-edged sword. The excitement of new developments can often lead us away from our goals into theoretical domains, at the detriment of meeting the precise objective we have set for our system.

To keep our feet on the ground and produce the results expected by the end users, we should adopt a *methodology* that brings together the meeting of user needs and prompt responses to a competitive environment through high technology. This advice is given in every chapter.

The design and maintenance of a database involve a steady cycle of development, where what we did today is superseded by what we need to do tomorrow. This is why clear concepts and definitions are needed, as well as the associated architectural perspectives of flexibility and modularity. A fourth principle comes into play here:

Any development effort should benefit from prototyping and should be done interactively on the computer.

As noted in preceding chapters, prototyping is a well-known concept in engineering and has been used since the 1930s with scale models. Today prototyping is done interactively on the computer through simulation:

- Shortening development time significantly

- Providing for dynamically updated documentation

- Doing away with paper-based systems analysis

The development of technological systems should be automated, like all other processes now based on communications and computers. Expert systems shells effectively aid the response to this requirement. But how many companies really profit from their availability?

10.6 Studying the Fine Print of Distributed Applications

The objective of this section is to provide guidelines for the design of distributed applications that can be implemented with available technology based on client/server computing. Both applications and databases must be projected in a way that can withstand changes in technology and in the marketplace.

Systems specialists with experience in distributed applications can appreciate that it is achieved in many ways, ranging:

- From an underlying distributed database manager

- To a distributed transaction manager with remote procedure calls and messaging

In either case, the system has to serve a number of workstations and their users, supported by servers that may be installed in different locations in the network, operating largely on a local basis but making themselves available for global events.

The proper placement and handling of database servers is a critical factor for success. Therefore, as we saw in Sec. 10.5, guidelines are required to facilitate their deployment. Such guidelines must include considerations of both information elements and process placement as well as security, backup, and recovery in real time.

The deployment of distributed applications necessarily means that some of the functions are executed on one machine while the remaining functions are executed on other networked systems. To achieve the proper distribution of functions, applications must:

- Be coded modularly

- Have well-defined interfaces

In this manner, different processes and functions can reside and execute on different computers utilizing distributed data stored across two or more servers that can be accessed by the application.

Needed information elements must be accessible by remote applications and remote users. Like the processes, such information elements may be distributed in different ways, each providing various degrees of access transparency with the higher degree being the better choice.

Any valid solution will face the fact that the distributed system will sooner or later have to cope with a heterogeneous computing and databasing environment where facilities may be required by any number of applications residing and operating in the network. The trend is to connect those computers in an integrated manner so that the whole aggregate can be regarded from a users' point of view as a single global distributed system.

As we will see in Part 3, heterogeneous database systems consist of multiple types of hardware running under different OS, under different DBMS, and communicating across a variety of incompatible protocols. (See also the sorting out of protocols from best to worst in Chap. 1.) Within such a perspective it is necessary to assure:

- Interoperability

- Site autonomy

As we have seen in other chapters, interoperability is necessary to support functional interactions between processes. Two or more entities are interoperable if they can interact to execute tasks jointly, whether they are residing on homogeneous or heterogeneous platforms. Their degree of interoperability is defined by the functions available across the network to be executed in an able manner.

Correspondingly, site autonomy is a basic requirement for viable distributed solutions. Client/server sites have locality, even if they must operate in a networked manner to serve regional and global processes. Besides this, if all communications links are down, the local processor must continue serving its end users until such time as the network becomes available again.

Each site must not only provide the appropriate security, availability, recoverability, and resource control but also assure the integrity of its information elements. This is particularly valid in a networked sense.

- Each local site and all of them in unison must transparently support distributed transactions.

- But read/write updates require a secure and virtually consistent database landscape.

Typically, for this purpose a *two-phase commit* protocol is implemented assuring an update over multiple databases either happens completely or does not take place at all. Different mechanisms have been developed to support this procedure. Some of them, for example, distinguish between initiation, prepare phase, and commit phase.

The prepare phase follows immediately after initiation. The transaction-originating node asks each of its filial nodes to commit or roll back its part when told to.

- When all filial nodes have been prepared, the initiating node flushes them the message regarding the transaction.

- The filial node indicates to its parent node that it is prepared, but cannot complete the transaction until told to do so by the parent (initiating) node.

During the commit phase, the node writes to its redo log that it is committed. Alternatively, it rolls back if there were errors during the prepare phase. Then, the parent node instructs each filial node to commit (or roll back), and the filial node informs its parent that it committed (or rolled back).

Locks are released after all nodes have committed (or rolled back), and this completes the commit phase. The crucial point of the procedure is the promise to commit, which assures that a common action is performed at some point as the transaction proceeds, supported through software.

These operations are not new. They have been executed for 40 years through computers, but typically have been done in batch. The two-phase commit requirements outlined in this example are particularly necessary for on-line, real-time execution, which—for reasons of efficiency and competitiveness is becoming increasingly popular.

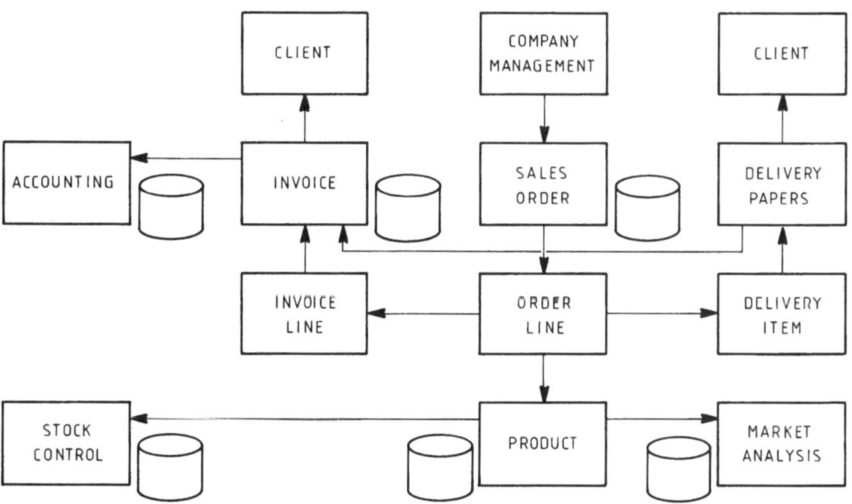

Figure 10.4 Changing from a batch-type discrete islands approach to an integrated on-line system.

The different processing blocks in Fig. 10.4 exist in practically every sales order handling, inventory management, and accounting procedure. Under batch implementation they operate as discrete islands, but this is an uncompetitive approach leading to delays, errors, overstocking, and high costs.

The advisable solution is to execute the processes on line. With this, different processes have to operate serially or in parallel as nodes of an integrated system—making necessary the type of phased commit approach examined in Sec. 10.6.

10.7   Project Control with Distributed Databases

An integrative approach to databases forms a network serving both global and local information elements over a wide area. Such an approach will see to it that all locations share an identical core database definition enabling common applications programs to operate consistently and without modification at various physical locations.

Core table definitions can be effectively developed within the perspectives of a given applications environment. For example, all the sales offices of a manufacturer or the branches of a bank may hold information about only the subset of customer accounts being handled—but such subsets overlap, and each customer account should be consistent throughout the network. Hence, there is a need for studying homonyms and synonyms.

At the same time, all applications must be designed to work against the principle of database consistency, within the distributed environment of operations. This will enable users to:

- Interact with one another and with database contents, updating their physical location's version of a shared table.

- At the same time, data migration and synchronization software handles the details of data access and data transfer.

Consistency and synchronization are very important as, in distributed database systems, information elements are not at one physical location but cover multiple physical and logical installations interconnected through local area networks (LANs) and wide area networks (WANs). (See Chaps. 12 and 13.)

For this reason, the Database Systems Study Group (DBSG) of the American National Standards Institute (ANSI) advises the wisdom of focusing on the organizational and software issues of database technology, starting with the fundamentals and proceeding with database management all the way to security and protection. DBSG also advises moving out of record-oriented approaches toward:

- Object orientation
- Multimedia
- Visualization
- New forms of storing and retrieving information

Such a transition is seen as necessary in order to accommodate the now developing requirements on database usage across an expanding topology with increasingly ad hoc query needs addressed to the system interactively by a myriad of users.

The able implementation of a distributed database solution must maintain the *integrity* of information elements. A DBMS does this by providing security, recoverability, concurrency, and referential integrity at local level but not necessarily networkwide. Besides this, other, even more important requirements are organizational.

The organization of any and every database project must be well defined.

Project organization should specify who does what and who decides on what. This is just as important during database design as it is in the course of operations and maintenance.

Many projects get into trouble because the organizational lines of command are not clear. They degrade not because of technological factors but for ill-perceived organizational reasons.

For instance, the functions of the database administrator are often stated in an inconclusive manner or not at all. In other cases they overlap with or contradict other people's functions. When this happens, the situation becomes chaotic both in a managerial and in a systems sense.

"A system becomes *chaotic*," advises James Gleick, "strictly by virtue of its unpredictability. It generates a steady stream of information, each new observation is a new bit."* Interdependencies as well as red tape are not just accumulated but also generated from connections that were not there before. Such connections are by nature uncertain, and the outcome may well be beyond management's control.

These issues are critical, because in many firms today the organizational lines of command are difficult to define. The reason is that we no longer talk of two-dimensional (line and staff) organizational structures but of multidimensional structures featuring:

- Profit centers
- Multinational operations
- Special assignments

---

*See James Gleick, *Chaos*, Heinemann, London, 1988.

Nowhere is this multiple dimensionality more true than with information systems, and it underlines the need for a well-stated definition of a project's mission, of specific responsibilities for handling the goals within such a mission, and of when the main task and its goals should be reached.

At the typical distributed heterogeneous database environment, we must account for the fact that the data structures will be different and the same is true of the formats.

Heterogeneous DBMS will utilize rather incompatible data definition and data manipulation languages, as well as data access mechanisms.

Efforts directed toward integrating such incompatible artifacts into a loosely or tightly knit federation of databases are conditioned by available skill, software offered on a commodity basis, the levels of diversion in the different structures, and the specific goals to be reached. Such goals may diverge at local and regional levels, but the chief technology officer (CTO) should see to it that they converge at the global level.

Five or even three years ago, answering interoperability requirements of the nature just described would have necessitated the development of custom-made expert systems. Today, this is no longer necessary because of commodity software that supports access to heterogeneous resources in a cross-database form.

High technology projects at large, and database projects in particular, should be undertaken only under strict timetables.

The definition of a timetable leading to and including the completion of a project, as well that of its component parts, is inseparable from the establishment of the mission. The same is true of the intermediate milestones, characterizing major steps toward the fulfillment of goal(s).

- A host of successful projects provides documentation that timetables should move rapidly.

- Projects, and most particularly database projects, should not be left to stagnate.

Whatever we undertake to do should be brought into operation—that is, practical application—without delay. Only then do projects offer results. Systems projects that overrun their timetables and their budgets should be killed. This is a basic duty in project control but is rarely exercised to the company's advantage.

The High-Performance Computer Is Another Server

11.1 Introduction

The high-performance computer of the 1990s is a scalable system, built with multiple microprocessors that can work in parallel. Performance is improved by adding more processors (scaling). Scalable massively parallel supercomputers deliver a great deal more power than traditional vector supercomputers (those with a large set of data elements) and cost much less money.

Since microprocessors double in speed and density about every 2 years, the performance of scalable parallel computers increases by so much. Essentially, it is the same microprocessor technology that

- A dozen years ago made personal computing possible at an affordable price

- Radically altered the approach to cost-effectiveness in the computer industry

Commodity microprocessors raise the supply of computing power and lower its cost. This is helping business and industry solve problems by identifying and analyzing the cost/benefit potential before making any commitments. But also, as we will see in this chapter it raises a number of prerequisites.

The best way to look at the challenges that lie ahead is by capitalizing on the strides that technology is making. The wise strategy is to consider the networked high-performance computer as another server. Running computations on such machines enables experimenters to:

- Build more detail into their models

- Conduct more analytical studies

The impressive cost/effectiveness ratio of high-performance computers opens immense possibilities in terms of their implementation. It makes affordable supercomputer power to the smaller and medium-sized enterprise—and this is important, because in the Western world small and medium-sized enterprises represent 90–95 percent of all companies and employ close to two-thirds of the workforce.

In today's fast-moving world, smaller companies and independent business units constitute the backbone of most national economies. Through their flexibility, short time to market, and responsiveness to client wishes, they also serve as models for larger firms. Indeed, many big companies are:

- Abandoning the vertical integration of the past for a network of smaller, more autonomous entities

- Emulating, in this way, the smaller company's ability to be agile and flexible, and to foster the entrepreneurial spirit

But smaller companies cannot justify the huge expenditures in hardware and software that the bigger ones have adopted without appropriate consideration of return on investment (ROI). For smaller companies, solutions have to be highly cost-effective in order to contribute to business survival.

Continuously greater effectiveness at less and less cost can be nicely achieved through client/server solutions, if the systems are carefully developed to be scalable. Scalability at the upper range of computing power is one of the roles assigned to a high-performance computer when it serves as a shared number cruncher on the LAN.

11.2 Choices That Make Business Sense

In the decade of the 1990s, the entire concept of computing will undergo a major change. Much of what is known at this time is becoming or will be obsolete, while new approaches will spring up. High-performance computing is one of them.

During the 1970s and a large part of the 1980s, innovation took a back seat to the perpetuation of the mainframe culture. But just churning out more bulky and more expensive versions of old machine designs does not work over the longer term in the communications and computer industry.

Innovation is the key to survival. It is therefore not surprising that today technology is rapidly refined and improved. A study by

Hoskyns,* done in 1992, sampled 258 user organizations in the United Kingdom and came up with the following results:

- In 1985, 90 percent of the participating firms replaced mainframes with mainframes.

- In 1991, only 47 percent among the sampled user organizations did so.

- By 1995, cognizant executives in the sampled firms suggested, this figure will shrink to 7 percent.

Fig. 11.1 dramatizes this sharp and rapid drop in mainframe orientation, in terms of new investments in computers and communications technology. Client/server solutions and cost-effective high-performance computing are the beneficiaries of this significant change in corporate policy.

To properly appreciate the role low-cost but high-power computers now play and will continue playing, we must look at strategies that really make business sense. Why should smaller to medium-sized firms pay so much attention to high-performance computing? They should because:

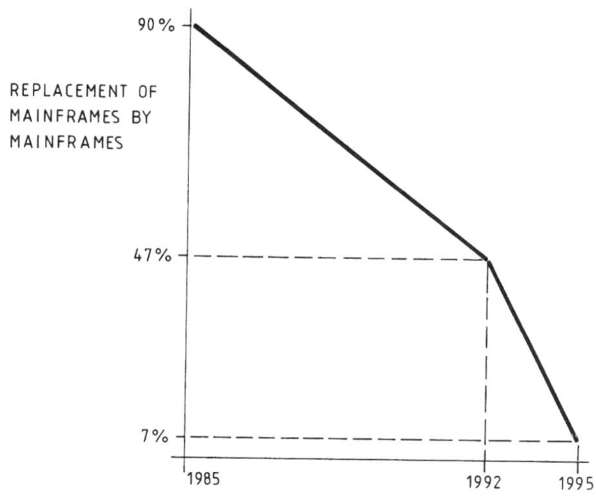

Figure 11.1 The policy of replacing mainframes with mainframes is radically changing to the benefit of client/servers and supercomputers. (*Statistics from Hoskyns, U.K.*)

---

*A British consulting company of the CAP GEMINI group.

- The interdependence between large and small firms has grown significantly in the past 10 years

- Smaller companies are closely tied as business partners to larger ones—hence, they must meet stiff competitive requirements

Computer vendors, for example, are actively developing a network of business partners who add software and service value to their products. These smaller business partners also help in product distribution and in systems implementation.

At the same time, bigger firms try to unload to the smaller firms some of their huge research and development expenditures. This started over 10 years ago in the aircraft industry but is now spreading into computers as the larger firms take a sharp knife to their R&D budget.

For instance, as one news article suggested:

> International Business Machines will slash its development spending by $1 billion, or 17 percent (in 1993)—an amount unprecedented in its history. The company spent about $6.6 billion in 1991, the last year for which figures are available. . . . While the world's largest computer maker remains a huge enterprise, it no longer can be expected to set the pace for technological innovation in the United States.*

"IBM as the IBM that defined computing is over; it's gone," said Nathan Myrthvold, Microsoft's vice president of advanced technology and business development. "As a result of new technology developments during the past 10 years, IBM's role in the computer industry has fundamentally changed."

The consequence is that what was once one of the world's most vaunted high-tech companies had been reduced to the role of follower, frequently responding slowly to the major technological forces reshaping the computer, communications, and software industry. This may be a blessing in disguise.

- Many investment bankers and technology specialists say that IBM's decline may instead mark the emergence of a new model for high-technology developments that will become powerful in its own right.

- Alliances of smaller, more innovative companies are now being formed and their combined forces come together quickly to attack crucial problems.

---

*See the *International Herald Tribune,* December 12, 1992.

An ever-increasing number of high-technology manufacturing suppliers presently are small and medium-sized companies, some of them resulting from joint ventures with some of the more dynamic bigger firms. Such alliances are aimed at developing new solutions for an increasingly segmented, but also increasingly demanding, marketplace.

Interestingly enough, several of those dynamic enterprises—and most particularly those designing and manufacturing high-performance computers—bear little resemblance to small firms of only 10 years ago.

- Affordable computers and communications technology have played a key role in strengthening the competitiveness of small companies.

- Processing power, which was accessible only to major organizations, is now found in service companies and small-scale plants of all kinds.

Client/servers and with them low cost, high-performance computers have a tremendous market ahead of them. In Western Europe, for example, some 15 million small companies are still making do without computers. As a result, they are not realizing technology's full potential to:

- Assist in developing innovative products
- Radically shorten the time to market
- Lighten the administrative workload
- Enhance managerial responsiveness
- Conserve scarce human resources

While no large organization would think of trying to operate without communications, computers, and software, it can also be argued that the smaller the firm, the more crucial IT (information technology) becomes. The more effectively each task can be performed, the more time is freed up to perfect products, processes, and market appeal.

Enriched with supercomputer power, client/server solutions permit management to exploit technology to full advantage, taking on competitors many times the company's size. Emerging implementation perspectives, such as multimedia, will make this even more true in the future, offering broad new possibilities to define a competitive edge.

The use of high technology at an affordable price by the smaller companies has led to an industrywide synergy in terms of developments but also to a shift in the definition of who is the major contributor to innovation and future progress:

- Small firms are becoming new centers of innovation.

- A number of very large development organizations—including IBM, Bell Laboratories, and Xerox—have slowly taken apart the engines behind their innovative contributions.

As a result, since we owe much of the future usefulness of IT to small firms, computers must adapt to them—not the other way around.

The ease-of-use requirements now benefiting companies of all sizes came first and foremost from these smaller companies. In turn, ease-of-use breakthroughs have been instrumental in offering ideas about market timing, in illustrating how these ideas can be applied in real time, and in simulating applied thought for additional forward-looking achievements. High-performance computing should be examined under this light.

11.3   Taking Advantage of the Economics of Massively Parallel Processing

In the late 1970s and early 1980s many computer shops turned to supposedly "new" technologies in an effort to resolve some of their power and complexity issues. These were heralded as an "innovative" generation of mainframes, but the results were trivial and the engines were very expensive as well as difficult to use.

The reference to difficulty particularly applies to the old and awkward programming approaches. Very few easy-to-use tools were provided by the "revamped" mainframers for end-user access, misdirecting the emphasis on managerial applications development to information retrieval. All this helped in:

- Perpetuating the "glass house" structure of the organization

- Strangling efforts that were truly aimed at new IT culture

The "innovative" approaches promised by mainframers proved to be nothing more and nothing less than the perpetuation of the obsolete mainframe culture, from which only the foremost computer user organizations were able to dissociate themselves. True innovation in computers, communications, and software largely rested on the fact that by the early to mid-1980s workstations, file servers, and local area networks began to gain a foothold as a solution to:

- The lack of any significant results or breakthroughs with mainframes

- The need for more flexible and rapid support to the end users

- The requirement to face, in real time, data redundancy and integrity problems

What happened during the 1980s in the domain of database management is a good example. As IBM's DB2 gained market share, it put a stamp of approval on the large-scale MVS shop, pushing user organizations into investing in relational technology and using it for large production systems all the way to the Systems Application Architecture (SAA).*

But in its fundamentals SAA is a business architecture and, over and above that, it does not necessarily answer the computing requirements of the foremost user organizations. At the same time, the typical MVS shop kept on suffered from the "glass house" syndrome of large systems—while high-performance computing solutions were available at lost cost.

- One of the many negatives lies in the fact that all information processing, from large, complex production systems down to ad hoc, simple data retrieval, has had to be performed by expensive, highly technical personnel.

- At the same time, end-users remained outside the glass houses and their pleas for support had little effect on the centralized processing side.

As leading-edge organizations found out the hard way, there have also been many other negatives. The glass house structure resulted in huge applications backlogs because the volume of requests could not be handled by the centralized computer staff. Large MVS shops are estimated to have a backlog of 3 to 5 years—and despite the long wait, the quality of the resulting applications software is substandard.

In addition to the "too little, too late" syndrome and the huge expenses characterizing glass house applications, there has been a lack of sufficient computer power to deal with the ever-growing computing problems:

- Database management and the DBMS handling the database work are heavy consumers of processing and input/output power.

- The DBMS is inevitably subject to growing workloads as the functionality and number of users increases.

With centralized solutions a growing workload creates a performance problem as more users seek to access database contents. This has an evident impact in terms of processing power, which is particularly dramatized in mainframe environments owing to the high investment cost.

---

*SAA is IBM's proprietary initiative to provide a common interface across multiple computing tiers.

Indeed, these facts have engineered the tremendous change in the way the market has looked at computers and communications during the last couple of years. Moreover, there has been a major switch not only in the thinking of user organizations but also in the manner in which the vendors themselves conceive their survival in an industry that has become more competitive than ever.

1. The long-running debate about how best to make computers thousands of times more powerful than they are now appears to be ending in a consensus.

2. Some of the vendors have outdistanced the crowd and are positioned to exploit the forces of the 1990s.

Taking American, European, and Japanese computer and communications manufacturers as a lot, among established computer vendors the two companies that leave the others behind are both American: Digital Equipment Corporation and Hewlett-Packard. Their strategies may be different; but they are forward-looking and they are sound.

Digital Equipment is now marketing the very high performance but low cost MasPar (massively parallel) computer as DECmpp 12000. Hewlett-Packard leads in true client/server solutions that compete with supercomputing in terms of cost-effectiveness.

There are, of course, other valid planners in the client/server domain such as Sun Microsystems, but when it comes to massively parallel processors the competition centers among four vendors—all of them present at the Fourth Symposium on the Frontiers of Massively Parallel Computation:*

- MasPar
- Intel Scientific
- Thinking Machines
- n-Cube

Some of the products of Intel, Thinking Machines, and n-Cube are hypercube architectures. MasPar features an X-mesh and Intel also offers mesh architectures. In addition, Encore's Infinity system uses a reflective memory and high-speed bus to connect processors, memory, and I/O channels. There is also Kendall Square Research, another high-performance computer company with an internal LAN-type

---

*The symposium was held in McLean, VA, October 19–21, 1992. Interestingly enough, IBM, Unisys, Bull, Hitachi, Fujitsu, NEC, and other mainframers were totally absent from the exhibits, the panels, and the conferences.

architecture—and this practically completes the roster of the upcoming computer firms.

11.4 Common Characteristics of High-Performance Solutions

Are there common characteristics among the high-performance computer designs advanced by these vendors and their wares? The answer is yes. As of 1992 the leading American computer designers seem to have agreed that significant change takes place not in one but in three directions at the same time. This is reflected in Fig. 11.2.

Every one of the three metrics shown in the coordinate system poses requirements that are a far cry from what is offered today by aged mainframes. The power such computers featured in the 1960s, 1970s, and 1980s is dwarfed by the new generation of computing equipment.

Specialists in the new generation of computers and communications stress that an important criterion is how square the solution is along the axes of reference Fig. 11.2 has shown.

- Peak gigaflops

- I/O bandwidth

- Memory bandwidth

The more balanced the design is, the more dependable is the machine and the solution to which it contributes. This is now an accepted principle.

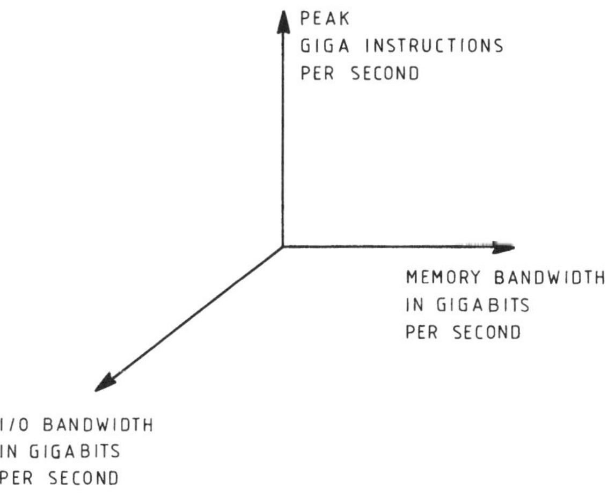

Figure 11.2 High-performance computing is measured along a coordinate frame of reference.

In fact, mainframes are not just suffering from very high cost per MIPS or FLOPS (floating-point operations per second) being delivered and from contention. They are also, if not primarily, limited by *their memory bandwidth*—which tends to invalidate the very expensive special-purpose processors they feature, although their vendors hide this important fact.

Besides the power, memory bandwidth, and I/O bandwidth, high-performance computers (supercomputers) today exhibit a feature that enormously increases their attractiveness: very low cost.

- A MasPar, massively parallel computer with 1,000 processors delivers 1,600 MIPS at a cost of $125,000.

- A 3090/600 with vector processor delivers about 120 MIPS and costs $8 million.

The cost/effectiveness ratio is 80:1 in favor of high-performance computing, and any executive who brushes such a ratio aside in favor of the beaten mainframe path will be highly irresponsible.

With mainframes, large processing bandwidth levels can be achieved at very great expense, which makes high power unwise because it is very uneconomical. Not surprisingly, a consensus is now developing in the American industry that old, slow, and expensive hardware is going to pass—which is an assault on the virtual monopoly in computing that the mainframes have held.

Because of huge investments in mainframe code, massively parallel computers will not replace all mainframes over a short period of time. It is also true that mainframes have no role to play as number crunchers in a client/server architecture. Economics dictate the use of supercomputer power.

Stated in a different manner, legacy problems bring under perspective the wisdom of establishing well-timed conversion strategies. One estimate in the American market, for instance, is that IBM customers have collectively been trapped with $1.3 trillion worth of software effort.

- Many user organizations have each put hundreds of labor-years on proprietary hardware and software systems, and for all practical purposes they have been locked in.

- Only recently have open systems software developments emerged, demonstrating the ability to move easily from one architecture to another—hence, in open architectural environments.

But arguments regarding legacy programs tied down to naive mainframes do not exist—and should not exist—with new, competitive-type applications. This is the domain of client/servers and of high-performance computing, combined through a flexible integration technology.

The reason client/servers and high-performance computers are mentioned together is that in many cases there will be a need for a number cruncher in a distributed computing solution. But as noted earlier:

- Mainframers wrongly advise their clients to attach their 20, 30, or 70 MIPS workstations to 50 MIPS mainframes.

- What users need is to attach their 20, 30, or 70 MIPS workstations to their 10,000 MIPS server or their 100,000 MIPS server. That makes sense.

The mainframe vendors are taking the user organizations to the cleaners. The user organizations that buy that line are just as guilty because they fail to take notice of the cost-effective solutions available to them—hence, to take responsibility for their decisions and actions. Yet there is a heavy responsibility for the prejudice they create to their own interests and those of their firm.

Beyond the trust issue is the realistic appraisal of the situation. Not only has hardware technology evolved, but also advances in programming techniques have convinced skeptics that a radical change is possible and the decision to make it is long due.

- Many problems were until now solvable only by large, bulky mainframe computers and, therefore, were very complex to analyze while some could not even be handled.

- Now these problems can be attacked at much faster speeds—and, more importantly, in a much simpler manner—by massively parallel machines.

Among leading-edge organizations, these factors are becoming a conscience, though to their discredit not all vendors espouse them. But, as Dr. Carmine Vona of Bankers Trust was to suggest: "End users now have a much better idea of what the procedures are and what they want to obtain."

This is indeed the right attitude. Said the chief executive of another financial institution: "The best central computer operations can do for their own survival is to help train the end users in computer literacy, steadily upkeeping that skill."

11.5 Benefits from Massively Parallel Computation

The Fourth Symposium on the Frontiers of Massively Parallel Computation, which took place at McLean, Virginia on October 19–21, 1992 identified some of the benefits we have seen in Sec. 11.4. The greatest strides are being made in hardware with 100,000 MIPS peak power already achieved—which corresponds to 800 IBM top-of-the-line mainframes.* Surprising is the size of the box that delivers such power.

- If we account for five huge buildings glass-housing mainframe computers, the 800 IBM mammoth-sized machines would require some 50 to 80 buildings.

- By contrast, the 100,000 MIPS peak power is delivered by a machine the size of a desk and fractions of it came as desktop models.

Who are the players in this high-performance market? Sec. 11.4 has already mentioned them. Who are the players with higher visibility?

Of the five American high-performance computer manufacturers—MasPar, Thinking Machines, Intel Scientific, n-Cube and Kendall Square Research—the first four were present both in the Exhibit and in the intensive program of Conferences and Discussion Panels of the McLean event. By contrast, IBM, Unisys, and the rest of the BUNCH† were absent.

In any case, they have nothing to offer in the frontiers of technology. DEC was present because of shadowing MasPar, whose computers it markets.

Interestingly enough, none of the leading Japanese computer vendors were present—as none qualifies in the frontiers of massively parallel computation. In fact, the Japanese computer companies are faced today with:

- Loss of market speed
- Loss of money

No massively parallel computers have been launched commercially in Japan, although a number of prototypes are now available. The furthest along seems to be Fujitsu's AP1000 engine, accommodating up to 1,024 32-bit SPARC processors.

To develop software for this machine, prior to launching a commercial product, Fujitsu has made several computers available for free, provided users share their software with the vendor. Fujitsu has also developed a massively parallel engine aimed at computer-aided design of integrated circuits (CAD/IC). Known as MAPLE, it uses up to 64K 1-bit processors like the Connection Machine of 1986.

---

*Though teraops operations are also considered technically feasible, machines approaching them are still very expensive.

†BUNCH stands for Burroughs, Univac (now merged into Unisys), NCR, Control Data (now defunct), and Honeywell (out of the computer business, succeeded by Bull).

NEC also has a prototype parallel machine named CENJU. It is configured for simulating ICs and has adopted a modular simulation algorithm where a circuit is partitioned into interconnected subcircuits. This leads to a coarse-grain computing approach.

- CENJU is not a massively parallel processor.

- It features only 64 CPU grouped into 8 clusters.

- A cluster bus connects the processors within each cluster and a multistage network connects the clusters.

The NEC engine uses a shared memory system where each processor element's local memory is mapped into a global memory address space. NEC says this avoids memory update problems—but it also has its drawbacks.

One can argue that the Japanese mainframers do a little better than their American competitors, as they at least try to bring some high-performance computers to the market. But in reality, both the American and the Japanese mainframers can attest through their painful experience that *loss of market speed and loss of money work in synergy.*

There is nothing from the mainframers' side (whether American, European, or Japanese) to match the 1992 announcement by MasPar of a 32-bit chip to equip its 16,000-processor computer—producing an affordable high performance computer which exceeds the level of 100,000 MIPS.

The new leaders in computer technology do not rest on their laurels. At the Fourth Symposium on the Frontiers of Massively Parallel Computation, MasPar, Intel Scientific, Thinking Machines, and n-Cube presented new models that outperform their preceding offerings as well as anything the mainframers had to offer. The consensus at the symposium was that mainframes constitute an unimaginative and costly approach to data processing.

- A significant number of the participants commented that mainframes will no longer be acceptable as a solution to current issues in information technology.

- Cognizant IT experts now find that true client/server solutions practically match supercomputing in terms of cost-effectiveness when compared with mainframes.

As defined in Chap. 1 of this book, *true* client/server solutions mean powerful but low-cost workstations, servers, and LANs. They do not mean the sort of rebaptized mainframes that Unisys, IBM, and others try to sell to their clients. These are misleading concepts.

In cost/benefit terms, massively parallel systems are a unique combination of state-of-the-art supercomputing hardware and software.

For the first time ever, supercomputers can now be profitably used not only for scientific applications but for commercial applications as well. They are:

- Providing a wide range of transaction-processing capabilities that go far beyond the performance of mainframes

- Featuring a cost per transaction per second (TPS) much lower than mainframes have ever provided

- Offering an architecture that is scalable, so that a wide range of configurations, prices, and performance rates is available

Capitalizing on a massive number of processors, for example, database blocks can be transferred among the computer's processors at as high a speed as is needed by the transactions being executed. Databases of up to billions of characters can be available in memory to serve thousands of users, an architecture that is unique to parallel computation.

11.6   Avoiding the Waste of Money on Obsolete Solutions

There is no longer a question that mainframes have become a huge waste of money. The question is: What is *our* company doing in order to capitalize on the new wave of technology?

Our company should not be languishing under the outdated mainframe mentality. It should not be suffering severe pains of its own making.

IBM, Unisys, Bull, Nixdorf-Siemens, the Japanese mainframers, and the EDPers at user organizations have this in common: They show:

- Few sparks of professional courage

- No clear vision of the future

Their intellectual powers are spent. They are out of ideas and have become prey to the lure of the easy, comfortable life of decay—which ends only when the resources have been exhausted.

Yet the foremost companies have shown how to follow a strategy of renewal. One of the developments in parallel computing is the networking of workstations into a system that can be used as a single large parallel computer, as the following example documents.

Researchers at Fermi National Accelerator Laboratory (Fermilab), in Batavia, Illinois, have combined 100 RS 6000 into a parallel computing farm. The system is used for reconstructing events that occur during the high-energy physics experiments in Fermilab's Tevatron superconducting accelerator.

- Each of these experiments collects data from millions of collisions of high-energy particles.

- The parallel farm allows experiments at a much faster pace than that of a classical vector supercomputer at much higher cost.

In a similar frame of reference, researchers at Oak Ridge National Laboratory and the University of Tennessee at Knoxville have developed software that links heterogeneous computers—from PCs to supercomputers—over a network to be used as a single large parallel machine.

These and similar examples help document that there is plenty of opportunity, but only a few companies know *how* to effectively exploit it. Those who do so appreciate that the computer hardware and software environment is changing rapidly as new technologies such as massively parallel computing are emerging at an increasing pace.

Newer, flexible solutions see to it that toolsets can be ported very easily to any platform. Portability across computers used today and those purchased in the future establishes the position of a given tool as the choice for advanced usage—including large, high-performance databases.

Both massively parallel computers and distributed deductive databases are needed for many applications central to an enterprise and its competitiveness. Aged systems do not provide able answers to fast-emerging requirements. Easy-to-use implementations are called for in areas like:

- Simulation and modeling

- Interactive design

- Telecommunications

- Network management

- Process control

- Materials handling

- Logistics

- On-line transaction processing (OLTP)

- 24-hour trading

- Multimarket arbitrage

- Relationship banking

Traditional, vector-type supercomputers such as those offered by Cray and NEC provide high performance for certain scientific applications. But they are not particularly suited for database applications in general and OLTP in particular.

- Like the mainframes they emulate at a higher speed, classical supercomputers are built to process a small number of operations.

- Their environment is that of operations performed on a very large set of data elements (also known as a *vector*), not the parallel exploitation of databases.

- Therefore, vector processors cannot handle long transactions and complex applications that differ from one another and need to be processed concurrently.

Solutions necessary to face the challenges posed by the new generation of problems must combine new hardware architectures with advanced software, taking advantage of massive parallelism. This

- Delivers high performance at a low cost per TPS

- Provides the decision support tools necessary in order to remain competitive

Efficient answers to the problems posed by long transactions call for flexible processor allocation. The number of processors employed for a given application depends on only the throughput needs of that application, and the available architecture must reflect allocation problems in an able manner.

Although multiple applications can share a particular processor, this is no longer the way to work. As chapter after chapter in this book has underlined, every time the number of processes exceeds the number of processors available in the system, the application is in trouble.

The number of processors employed for a given application is typically a function of the throughput needs of that application. But processing requirements change dynamically and so do priorities. Therefore, multiple applications can no longer effectively share one processor.

- Some applications may require only the throughput capacity of a single, dedicated processor.

- For many other applications, multiple processors may be necessary for effective handling.

Parallel computing solutions take advantage of new processing concepts. In addition to allowing multiple transactions to be executed in parallel on different processors, multiple processors are used dynamically to share the handling of a single transaction. For example,

- The decomposition of complex database queries can be done in parallel with multiple processors, each performing part of the task.

- Implementation capitalizes on the benefits of an architecture designed for high-performance, database-oriented transaction handling.

- The portability of flexible toolsets assures further strides beyond existing computer environments, adapting its software products to leading-edge hardware.

New and complex implementation environments call for flexible and rapid database management. This can be best achieved through massively parallel environments. Associated enhancements enable database applications running on very large numbers of processors to be

- Activated
- Deactivated
- Monitored
- Controlled in parallel

Backup and recovery mechanisms must also be fully supported. Backups of an entire database, or a portion of a database, can be done on line while the DBMS and applications using the database continue running, with no reduction in performance.

For security purposes, a record of all data modifications has to be maintained in log files stored on disk, thereby assuring that all database changes can be fully recovered in the event of a system failure. This, too, has to be executed in parallel and brings into perspective some of the software challenges associated with the new technologies and their implementation.

11.7 Visual Programming and Program Visualization

As has been often noted in Part 1, architectural solutions should see to it that developers can work out applications that are consistent, easy to use, and structured to access all attached resources. End users become more productive through agile, friendly, and fairly uniform interfaces that help them work faster in a comprehensive manner. Emphasis has to be placed on:

- Tools that are highly productive and user-friendly

- Concepts that are easy enough to understand

- Solutions based on industrywide norms and standards

The goal of this strategy is to make feasible the acquisition of a computer and software without worrying about problems of suppliers' compatibility. This makes many aspects of operations simpler to handle and protects investments. The key is the adoption of open systems.

High-performance computing suits the open-vendor environment. Open systems may not be the perfect solution, but vendor proprietary approaches are even less perfect—ending by locking the user organizations into a "this" or "that" approach that the vendor exploits to advantage.

Within this perspective, Chap. 8 has stressed the fact that a well-chosen and properly implemented systems architecture must support distributed, diversified, heterogeneous structures. It must be able to

- Integrate all the facilities offered by the computer industry, in the absence of firm standards and norms

- Lead toward a well-defined interoperability policy and practice

Openness, of course, applies to computers of all sizes, from workstations all the way up to large, old, and costly water-cooled systems, as long as they are still around. But a common denominator offered by open systems solutions does not necessarily respond to peak competitive requirements:

- The open-vendor approach should form the systems infrastructure both in a logical and in a physical sense. It should be provided through commodity software (packages) portable from platform to platform.

- By contrast, at the top of the pyramid of information technology solutions should be very advanced software developed through *visual programming* approaches by the organization itself.

Such a policy is in conformance with recently available statistics that help identify background reasons for the decision to migrate to a client/server environment as shown in Fig. 11.3.*

Among the leading-edge organizations on three different continents, in terms of new software departures, visualization was found to be the key word:

---

*These statistics are based on extensive research done by the author in America, Japan, and Western Europe during 1992.

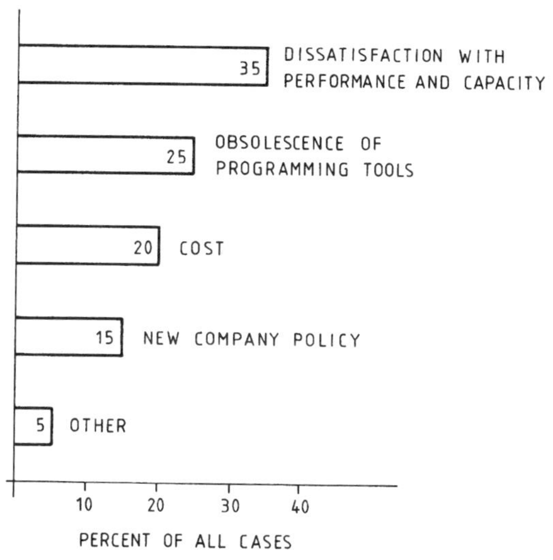

Figure 11.3 Background reasons for the decision to migrate to a client/server environment with open architecture.

- *Visual programming* affects the software development phase.

- *Program visualization* addresses software testing, implementation, and maintenance.

Notice that, in Fig. 11.3, the No. 1 reason accounting for 35 percent of the decision to change from mainframes to client/server and/or supercomputing is dissatisfaction with performance and capacity. Low-cost, high-performance computers are the best answer to this decision factor.

Coming second with 25 percent is the dissatisfaction with current programming tools. Here, visual programming is the answer. Taken together the No. 1 and No. 2 reasons represent 60 percent of the drive behind the wave of change in computing environments—but are computer vendors taking notice?

The dissatisfaction of user organizations not only with mainframes but also with the worn-out current programming tools has deep roots. In contrast to the hardware strides, software is a domain where not-so-significant advances have taken places—to the detriment of all concerned, vendors and user organizations alike.

Lack of breakthroughs in the software domain is the soft underbelly of new technology. This negative comment does not mean that new software developments are altogether lacking—but they are not what they should be. For example, in spite of $2.2 billion spent in 1992 by the United States government on massively parallel computing, the American industry has nothing similar to show to the fuzzy control manager (FCM) shell made in Germany. FCM was designed by 25-year-olds, with no government support whatsoever.

11.8 Visibilization and Visistration

The reason given by cognizant participants to the Symposium on Massively Parallel Computation for the lack of American software breakthroughs is that the U.S. government specified that the $2.2 billion should be spent on hardware, not on software. This thesis was severely criticized by many people at the symposium, in private meetings.

Government money is spent in a big way on hardware, because this is on what military supremacy depended for nearly 50 years. But, as Ross Perot aptly suggested in a television interview, the American government is still totally organized to fight the Cold War.

Of course, it takes more than money to have major software breakthroughs. Quite evidently, it also takes lots of imagination and initiative. The emphasis placed on program visualization at the symposium referred to parallel computers, and the examples presented were good. This is the way to bet for software breakthroughs during the coming years.

Indeed, in terms of program visualization there are some interesting developments to report, largely resting on interactive modeling and high-performance computers. Both deep models and surface models must be elaborated, leading to novel structures and experimental approaches. Issues at the top of the agenda are:

- *Visibilization,* the making visible of very small and very big times or concepts

- *Visistration,* making visible phenomena lacking a direct physical interpretation

The effective implementation of visibilization and visistration requires algorithms, heuristics, and high-performance computing—but also effective solutions to other infrastructural issues. An example is seamless access to distributed servers that run concurrently and independently. (See also the discussion on distributed deductive databases in Part 3.)

- Each server has locality but is also accessed in a global transaction sense.

- Each server is on its own processing node, with its own memory for database buffers.

- Each is enriched with its own set of backup and recovery processes.
- The entire system benefits from knowledge engineering processes making visibilization and visistration feasible.

We need a *macroscope* to observe the very big in a comprehensive manner, suggests Professor Terano of the Japanese Laboratory for International Fuzzy Engineering (LIFE). And we need fuzzy engineering capabilities to turn vague concepts into observable artifacts through visistration.

High-performance computing power underpins the ability to execute visibilization and visistration, the latter being the beginning of machines with abstraction capabilities and eventually with imagination.

- Very sophisticated algorithms and heuristics will be increasingly required to face the business challenges of the next 10 years.
- Some of the best brains to be found today in nuclear engineering and aerospace are indeed being redirected toward financial and business applications.

A practical example of the latter reference is the development of new, powerful paradigms for the American banking industry through *virtual reality* approaches. A group of major financial institutions is currently setting up a project development committee to which participate the Santa Fe Institute, Los Alamos National Laboratory, Brookhaven, Lawrence Livermore National Laboratory, and Argone National Laboratory.

Advanced research themes are currently being selected and are expected to have major influence on the financial markets and the management of banks and brokers. These themes include

- Nonlinearities encountered in economies and finance
- Fractals theory
- Chaos theory
- Butterfly effect focusing on aperiodicity and unpredictability
- Chance, uncertainty, and blind fortune
- Work on artificial life

The deeper goal is to solve problems that defy accepted ways of working. These projects involve discerning eye patterns, particularly patterns that appear at different scales at the same time. They also require ad hoc, on-line access to very large distributed databases.

Within a distributed deductive pattern, each server must handle the database requests of multiple clients. Associated with every parallel server must be a knowledge bank management system (KBMS) that tracks the current location of database contents in all servers. By using this approach, each networked workstation can acquire all the information elements it needs directly from intentional database structure.

Solutions must guarantee interserver data consistency. This also requires powerful languages that help in managing the distributed environment in an effective manner. Other important goals that powerful languages should fulfill are:

- Friendly end-user computing

- Rapid applications development

- Object-oriented paradigms

- Software reusability

Visual programming and program visualization help to effectively bring high-performance computer power at the end-user level. They also make feasible the exploitation of frontiers of technology, therefore permitting the handling of complex queries and long transactions—hence, competently facing the requirements of the 1990s.

In conclusion, during this decade the switch of emphasis toward greater cost-effectiveness, together with the evolution of fast interconnection of workstations and servers, will create *commodity supercomputing*. Visual programming will help assure a greater horizon of:

- Performance

- Reliability

- Applicability

Companies unable to capitalize on this mounting wave of cost and effectiveness, which brings solutions to many important problems, will see their role in the market diminished. But management should also appreciate that the limits in the able exploitation of the new technology can be overcome through lifelong training. If there is no change of the cultural image, there will be no results.

12

The Evolution of Local Area Networks

12.1 Introduction

In 1980 the local area network (LAN) was introduced as a novel form of communications. After a dozen years of steady evolution, both its technology and its mission have changed. During the better part of the last decade, LANs have proliferated to form the foundation for a wide range of communications solutions.

Starting with the fundamentals, by slightly adjusting the definition advanced by the IEEE 802 Committee, whose object is standardization in local area network technology, we can say that a LAN is a data communications system allowing independent devices to interconnect with one another. These devices fall into two broad classes:

- Workstations integrated at the work place, one per end user

- Servers assuring the functions we have examined in the preceding chapters of this book

Different types of servers can be distinguished: for databases or file management, number crunching, communications facilities (gateways), and other services such as printers and plotters.

The existence of the LAN and the facilities that it provides permits workstations and servers to share information and other resources. Essentially information is moved within a relatively small physical location—for instance, within a building, with the LAN acting as a common connecting medium.

The effectiveness of a LAN implementation is dependent not only on its cable but on its bus interface unit (BIU), workstations, and servers attached to it as well. There are some 13 factors affecting per-

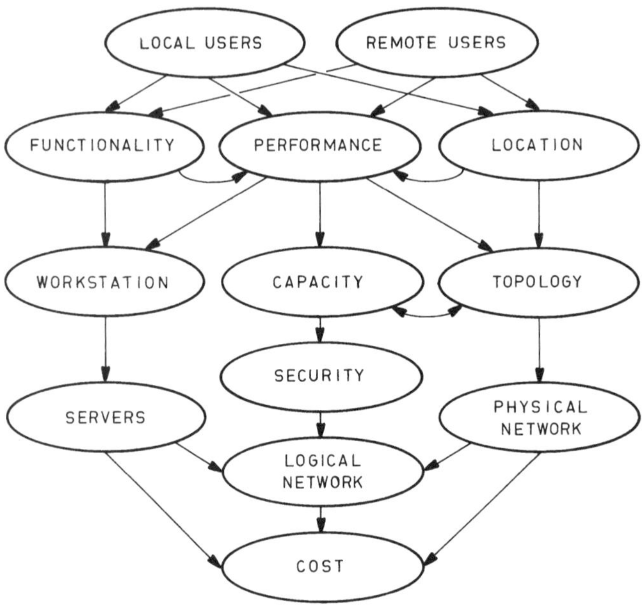

Figure 12.1   Thirteen key factors affecting the functionality of a LAN connection.

formance and they are shown in Fig. 12.1. The interaction among these critical factors and the technology behind them will assure that the perspectives of LAN implementation will continue to open up in the 1990s.

Supported through appropriate software, the shared wiring of a LAN can be conceived as dividing between a backbone and feeder lines. Both the backbone and the feeder lines must be managed in order to gain the benefits of the investments made in them. By and large, LANs fall into three broad categories:

- *Work group,* usually feeders

- *Campus,* representing a good example of backbone structure

- *Enterprise,* often evolving from campus LANs

Work group LANs respond to the need to share common information in file servers as well as peripherals. A dozen years ago the original development of a relatively low capacity LAN permitted work groups to effectively share product and process information, but as more users were added to the network LAN traffic increased. The need arose not only for greater channel capacity but also for architectured solutions.

12.2   Capitalizing on the Services Offered by LAN Technology

LAN technology was developed to provide in-house communications networks, linking together workstation, servers and various hosts. With work group LANs proliferating, backbones and bridges have been used for making interconnections:

- Campus LANs evolved when a number of work group LANs got interlinked over distances throughout a campus, a factory, or a city.

- Routers have been used to interconnect the work group LANs, providing enhanced network segmentation, better security, greater reliability, and larger bandwidth usage.

But as devices and protocols were added on campus LANs, a number of more comprehensive management solutions have been required—for instance, software programs residing in the bus interface unit acting as the interfaces between the network management applications program and the attached network devices, and network control centers (NCCs) to assure networkwide security, reliability, and quality of service.

The new generation of active LANs will offer both the systems manager and the end user much greater control. Rather than simply monitoring the network and keeping distant logs on individual users, an active LAN control center can configure the network to optimize its services according to the applications running on it.

Value-added services go beyond the original IEEE definition, which suggests that LANs address themselves to communications problems confronting a moderately sized geographic area. In this sense, distances run between 300 m and 1 km for baseband and 1 to 10 km for broadband. But with backbones and repeaters LANs evolved into metropolitan area networks (MANs).

MANs offer competitive advantages over plain old telephone service (POTS). The communications rates stand between 1 and 16 million bits per second (MBPS, or megabits) for baseband; up to 400 MHz for broadband and at the gigabits per second level with optical fibers.

Even a baseband LAN supports megabit data streams. At the 10 MBPS level featured, for instance, by Ethernet this is nearly two orders of magnitude better than the ISDN of POTS, which features two channels of 64 KBPS and a return channel of 16 KBPS (2B + D).*

---

*See also D. N. Chorafas, *System Architecture and System Design,* McGraw-Hill, NY, 1989; and D. N. Chorafas and H. Steinmann, *Intelligent Networks,* CRC Press, Boca Raton, FL, 1990.

Besides this, LAN technology is nowhere near the end of its evolution. The wireless local area network is growing along with mobile computing. In 1992 wireless LANs accounted for only 0.5 percent of worldwide LAN shipments, but some forecasts suggest that in 4 years' time (by 1997) they will make up 17 percent of all shipments.

Whether wire-based or wireless, the purpose of a LAN is similar to that of any computer application: to increase the productivity of its users. Slower and less efficient methods of sharing information and resources are always more costly, in terms of both time and investments. A local area network offers its users specific advantages:

- Direct party-to-party communication

- Media and topology independence

- A functional flexibility that can be implemented low in the architecture

- Coexistence and interchangeability of attached devices

- Cognizance and observance of some standards and norms

- Fairness criteria in the use of the communications resources

Such fairness criteria are put in action through the implementation of an access algorithm: Carrier Sensing Multiple Access with Collision Detection (CSMA/CD), CSMA with Collision Avoidance (CA), and Token Passing are the most popular protocols.

Although originally designed for long-haul communications, the Open System Interconnection (OSI) model of the International Standards Organization (ISO) is just as applicable with LAN, with the exception of lower layer restructuring. The physical layer has been split into two sublayers:

- Media access unit (MAU)

- Carrier, or transport medium

Correspondingly, ISO/OSI's data link layer has also been divided into two sublayers:

- Logical link control

- Media access control (MAC)

Distributed information systems can be viewed as a set of users and servers within the framework of this definition of protocols, which is presented in Fig. 12.2. A user wishing to communicate with a server first consults a directory to find its address, and then uses that address to send a message to the server.

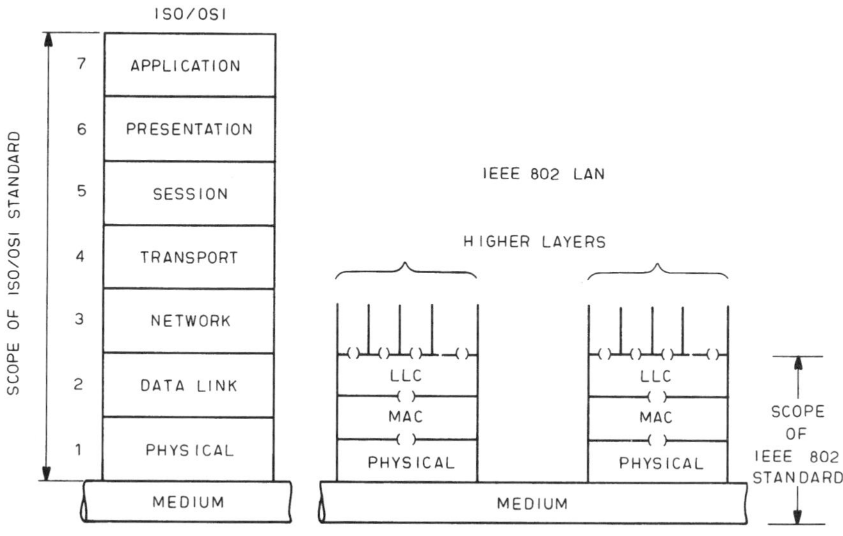

Figure 12.2 ISO/OSI and IEEE/802 reference models.

Messages contain sufficient information so that the server can reply to the user. In a local network environment, the user should follow the same procedure irrespective of whether the service to be accessed is on the same LAN or is on a distant one interconnected through a backbone, a metropolitan area network, or long-haul communications.

12.3 Nodes, Ports, and Teleports

Within one and the same LAN architecture, the nodes are identical and serve as connection points to the carrier. The LAN's ports are logical entities. In a baseband network, the node or bus interface unit will typically have one port and will be connected 1:1 with the WS or server.

However, these concepts and the devices designed to serve them evolve. The same is true of applications perspectives. In line with technological advances for higher transmission speeds and longer distances, the evolution of LAN technology has benefited from software support.

Not only does a network operating system (NOS) reside in the BIU and help in interconnecting attached devices, but also the use of LAN has gradually been expanded to multimedia. Today, the LAN is the carrier for the transmission not only of data but also of text, graphics, imaging, voice, and moving pictures.

Many aspects of usability may be addressed by engineering techniques, with choices depending on issues generally regarded as being in the sphere of implementation requirements. This goes all the way from basics (hence, hardware) to the aforementioned software aspects. From a wiring topology viewpoint, for example, currently available LANs are classified into three classes.

- Bus with branch implementation
- Ring (loop type)
- Star or group of stars (spider)

Such a classification is convenient for selecting an appropriate LAN solution as well as a configuration according to the distribution of connecting points.

Bus and star are more helpful with in-house floor applications, in a building. The loop type is preferable for connecting distributed buildings, and has been one of the earliest inventions by telephone companies (TELCOS). That is why the ring type shows its age—even when computer companies try to push it as the "better" LAN alternative.

There are several kinds of cables used for LANs. For short distances, such as up to several hundred meters, and when transmission speeds are 4 megabits per second (MBPS) or less, twisted-pair cables are extensively used. At higher speeds of 10 MBPS or, slightly more, coaxial cable is used. For 100 MBPS or more, as well as for backbones, the medium of choice is optical fibers.

Metropolitan area networks, mentioned further in Sec. 12.8, provide regional services and may interconnect several LANs. Wide area networks (WANs) cover larger areas than MANs, whether they are on a nationwide or on an international scale. (See Chap. 13.) WANs may contain central office equipment, trunk cables, optical fibers, microwave systems, and/or satellite communications from public or private networks.

There are several differences between LANs and WANs. First, LANs are generally fast, while wide area networks of the POTS type are slow.

- LANs carry great amounts of information over short distances, and are very good at it.
- WANs serve better when they carry small amounts of information over greater distances.

When a WAN transfers data, the receiving computer acknowledges their proper receipt either as each packet is received (an ACK/NAK transfer) or when the transfer is complete. This is known as a connection-oriented transfer. With LANs, data transfer is so to speak connectionless, which means there are no acknowledgments as such.

Information elements are packaged with the destination's node address and put on the medium for transmission.

Still another difference is that when we install a LAN, it is typically privately held and users do not incur additional expense by employing it. By contrast, WAN services charge the user as soon as the connection is made, whether or not the link is being used. This is one of the reasons that user organizations express so much interest in data compression and faster modems.

Of course, the capacity constraints associated with POTS-type WANs will change as the use of new technologies spreads. Both optical fibers and satellite communications systems are playing an important role in modern WANs and have been used commercially during the past 20 years. Satellite communications feature:

- Wide area coverage

- Simultaneous broadcasting

- Multipoint connectability

- Systems expandability

Satellite communications systems (VSATs) are used as links in computer networks owing to their ease of installation, their economics, and their ability to transmit voice, data, and moving pictures. A VSAT has a small antenna (of 1.2 to 1.8 meters in diameter), an outdoor unit (ODU), and an indoor unit (IDU).

In physical and logical structure, the network topology of a VSAT system is star type, with all communications passed via the central station of the topology—that is, the hub. One of the ways to obtain terminal access in VSAT is through a multiple-access method called Adaptive Assignment Time Division Multiple Access (AA/TDMA), which is an improved slotted Aloha approach.*

Connecting LANs to a WAN can be a challenging experience for the user organization, its applications, and its databases. Typically, applications designed for LANs usually assume fast transmission speeds and do not perform efficiently over a much slower WAN connection. But this too is changing because of the new generation of optical fiber—and satellite-supported WANs.

Satellite communications and radio links are promoting the use of *teleports,* to which are connected local area networks and private branch exchanges. Notwithstanding the differences among their

---

*Aloha is the seminal project financed by DARPA and executed some 20 years ago at the University of Hawaii.

respective orientations, all teleports offer an advanced telecommunications infrastructure suitable for a variety of leading-edge services.

Teleports will combine the provision of telecommunications services with business, industry, and financial services all the way to real estate development, assuring a unique market-product combination in real-life environments.

For a company with many operating centers, the interconnection of several teleports can enable advanced communications services to

- Promote a greater geographic coverage

- Contribute to the evolution of an integrative private network

In a wide area sense, teleports can form a backbone serving strategies for reaching wider markets. This, however, brings into the picture systems challenges, including plans for gateways, protocols, and network topologies for enterprisewide interconnections.

12.4   The Interconnection of Professionals and of Their Applications

An application is essentially a method of operation, or a process that the user finds appropriate, in that it allows certain tasks to be undertaken more easily and efficiently. Successful computer applications fit naturally into the user's work and produce intended results.

User needs are by no means static or universal. Hence, adaptation of the means at our disposal is very important and that is what we do through clients, servers, and local area networks.

- Today, many companies are beginning to realize that the growth of personal computer networks has placed between 90 and 95 percent of all processing power at the end users desk.

- After learning to perform personal productivity tasks at the workstation level, companies aim at achieving work-group productivity, and LANs play a key role in this task.

Management is particularly mindful of the availability of affordable connecting devices, such as gateways, bridges, and routers—which help not only in assuring necessary links but also in optimizing communications duties.

Gateway and bridges have been developed to create LAN-to-LAN interoperability.* Bridges actually allow messages to travel network-

---

*Some people say gateways are only for connection to mainframes. This is not a universal definition.

wide, even those between users not on the same LAN. As communications needs grew, and end-user requirements increased, this led to the creation of routers—that is, more intelligent devices able to keep routine traffic under control.

The switch to routers is to a significant extent a matter of utilization of bandwidth. Some companies are investing in routers exclusively for wide area connections to control traffic better and manage multiple protocols, while at the LAN environment they are sticking with bridges.

- Bridges are an older approach, but they are faster and of lower cost.

- Routers rely on sophisticated network addressing systems, sometimes confusing users that change locations frequently.

In contrast to repeaters, which make connected LANs a single logical system, bridges and routers make it easier to isolate file servers for better security. Only designated workstations are able to access the file server across the bridge or router.

The fact that repeaters, bridges, and routers can connect dissimilar types of cabling eases migration from one sort of cabling to another. It is possible to convert to structured wiring one department at a time, combining this transition with a reorganization that would in any case require moving and rewiring.

The alternative approaches presented here, as well as the business opportunity lying behind them, see to it that there is an explosive market for LAN products of all types. This is particularly true in Europe, where LAN implementation started somewhat later than in America.

As local area networks proliferate, in Europe alone a market is expected to reach more than $3 billion by 1996, with the largest segment being hardware: adapters, transceivers, and bridges, followed in terms of market potential by file servers, as shown in Fig. 12.3.

Down to the fundamentals, routers are part of the transformation taking place with LANs, and they are only an intermediate phase. As the LANs change from the passive channel for carrying data between different computers in a building, as they were 10 years ago to intelligent, active systems for distributing applications and multimedia information channels throughout the company, both the hardware devices and the software concepts supporting them are in an evolutionary stage. Along with bridges and routers, new LAN releases are equipped with a smart hub that is becoming the repository for internetworking functionality. The new generation of hubs supports many different types of transmission protocols:

- *Frame relay* is becoming popular, as a way to link LANs across the wide area.

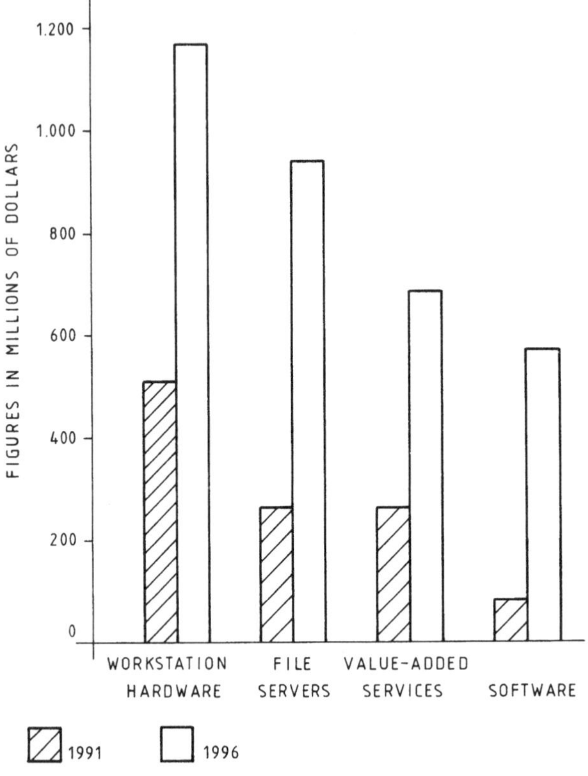

Figure 12.3 The four major products that will probably dominate Europe's market for LAN networks by 1996.

- Advanced network control functions are also becoming standard.

- Smart hub features are getting integrated with a multimedia orientation.

Sophisticated management of networks will go all the way down to the control of individual attached devices. By integrating what used to be rather autonomous functions, smart hubs will become a vital part of the information backbone, replacing the separate modules of bridges, routers, and gateways among networks. Eventually, this will bring the LAN that much closer to the wide area network.

Hub developers see the need to incorporate asynchronous transfer mode (ATM) services because they will allow them to support applications such as multimedia, which require high speed and high bandwidth. Along this line of development come broadband switches, designed to serve ATM requirements.

Such developments will see to it that a growing number of services will be supplied at various levels of LAN interconnection, permitting support for a growing range of functional applications requirements. Demand for a particular solution will arise from its ability to answer the challenges by specific user needs.

- Clear attributes of a particular service will be critical in determining its suitability.

- Families of similar services may be defined with attributes in common.

- Successful solutions will be those that can easily be reconfigured to fulfill changing needs.

Without doubt, the 1990s will see a rapid evolution in the needs of one and the same user to be manifested over a number of different occasions. Also, subtle yet important differences in the preferred method of working will become evident among individual users who share the same basic network.

These evolving systems characteristics are important, since most applications will be built on an integrated combination of suitable service primitives. To cover all possible applications perspectives, building blocks will have to fit together and interweave in almost any permutation, and this is one of the reasons that smart and eventually intelligent hubs are attracting so much attention.

12.5   The Move toward Wireless Solutions

Cabling options for local area networks are multiplying. Mixed-media installations are becoming increasingly common, and different alternatives such as wireless LANs are more viable than ever before.

Myriaprocessors featuring 10,000 or so interconnected devices are becoming popular. They are not so difficult to manage and are able to address the growing user requirements. Nevertheless, questions remain—as, for instance, the continuing usage of unshielded twisted pairs and the poor practice of running data and voice through the same wiring.

Sometimes, none of the existing types of cabling is well suited to the application. When just a few low-use workstations have to be interconnected in an old building, the cost of coaxial cable installation may be quite substantial. This tends to favor twisted pairs but also brings up the issue of wireless LANs.

The three most common types of wireless solutions are:

- Radio

- Microwave

- Infrared

Radio LANs typically use spread-spectrum technology, in which the signal is broadcast at a very low level over a range of frequencies instead of at a high level over a single frequency. Most spread-spectrum wireless LANs are slow, operating at up to 19.2 KBPS, but at least one solution by NCR, WaveLAN, features a 2-MBPS spread spectrum.

Microwave links are well known and widely practiced with wide area networks. The same is true, although to a lesser degree, with infrared bridges in connection to MANs and LANs. The following paragraphs highlight a project established to evaluate in-house LAN connectivity through an infrared approach.

The two-way infrared hub at the end of an optical fiber studied in connection with this project is shown in Fig. 12.4. The benefits this approach could provide include:

1. The freedom assured by cordless workstations, alleviating the need for fixed attachments at the walls of an office building and/or the use of floating floors

2. The ability to accommodate the requirements posed by developing species of hand-held and pocket computers, which will increasingly feature multimedia capabilities

In the opinion of the people who participated in this project, the two-way infrared hub idea has merits. Said one of the specialists: "In fiber technique we are anyway in the infrared region. Here we practically have the same principles and same elements."

One of the project's goals has been to exploit channel individualization per workstation and end user, with the background of a 1:1 channel allocation at least on a systems subarea. One criterion has been that such a solution should go beyond what a private branch exchange (PBX) offers today.

- Channel individualization could permit services in excess of "follow-me" on a PBX.

- It could make feasible reaching the respondent at any location.

- It might as well be used to unload calls stored to the personal voice-and-text mailbox.

The overall concept could be extended into an in-house microcellular infrared-based solution which, in its fundamentals, rests on the outlined premises. In this and similar projects prototyping is impor-

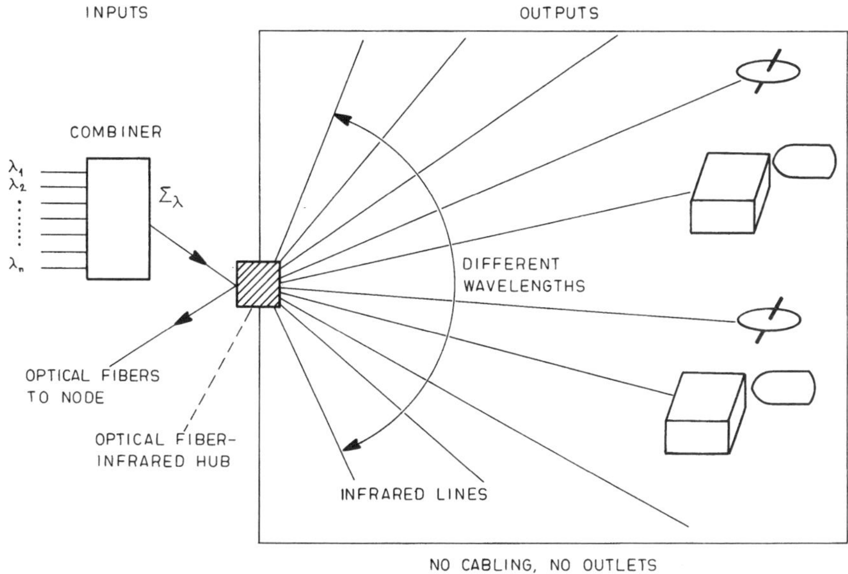

Figure 12.4 A wireless LAN study made for feasibility evaluation.

tant, since no company should plunge into technology just for the sake of it. First and foremost we have to

- Establish our perspective
- Put our act together
- Sort out our technical problems
- Distinguish the long-term advantage from the new solution

The guiding principle should be that interactions between users and network, to set up a particular combination of services, must be quick and easy. At the level of fine programmatic interfaces, dynamic reselection of services is necessary to support certain applications in particular user operating environments.

If microcellular infrared solutions are to fully meet these usage objectives, *flexibility* and *usability* will become key attributes of the overall systems design. The same is true of *reliability* as well as security and low-bit error rates.

In this and any other domain, a systems concept must be developed in a way representing a tool for users to call up, integrate, and employ service primitives in order to meet their applications needs. While such principles are just as valid for wired solutions, wireless ones do offer another degree of freedom—if they can reach acceptable dependability.

12.6 Placing Emphasis on Advanced Goals and on Service Quality

Some 10 or 12 years ago, the technical challenges posed by the deployment of local area networks were overwhelming and tended to mark the very important issues of service quality. While technical problems still exist, particularly with new technologies, as we saw in Sec. 12.5, performance goals and service quality are today quite vital.

LANs are installed for real-time services, but no longer are real-time applications limited to low-level control functions. They are now being used to monitor and control complex systems in dynamic environments that are not fully characterized by deterministic behavior like industrial control systems. Quite often in business and industry, the use of real-time problem-solving techniques becomes mandatory because of

- The lack of appropriate information

- The uncertainties involved in the market

Whether in manufacturing, in merchandising, or in finance, LANs are used for the implementation of real-time decision systems that are critical in nature. Hence, failures can have serious consequences.

A LAN may interconnect knowledge-based systems that work in tandem with more classical applications—as well as integrate different models designed and implemented to handle sophisticated control applications. In these cases, reliability is crucial, and the same is true of response time; both are aimed at providing performance guarantees for real-time problem solving.

In manufacturing operations, for instance, a realistic scheduling of real-time jobs has to be based on worst-case execution times of the tasks to be done. A fundamental issue with value differentiation based on client/server capabilities is that the worst-case execution time is often unknown or it can be much larger than average execution time. (See Sec. 12.7.)

- This can result in systems with low utilization if monolithic design criteria dominate, as is exemplified through centralized mainframe solutions.

- Even if variance of execution time regarding problem-solving tasks is not constrained, centralized conventional structures are likely to affect systems predictability.

Designwise, the execution time variance of problem-solving tasks manifests itself at two levels: *architecture* and *methodology*. To improve predictability, we have to tackle the background reasons for such variance at both levels.

The architectural level of representation can benefit from client/server solutions, provided the LAN, workstations, and servers integrate into a well-balanced system. This reference underlines the contribution of new design technology directed toward real-time implementation. One of the benefits is that it provides better ways to make tradeoffs between data space and computation time.

The aim should be to maximize the expected results. Along a similar line of reference, the use of knowledge-based reasoning can significantly benefit on-line real-time applications.

Expert systems can make a good contribution when an application program is likely to encounter a sizable number of related situations, each requiring the selection of one response from a set of possible responses.* In such cases:

- It is much more desirable to automate through knowledge engineering the process of constructing the response.

- The wrong approach is to bring results to the attention of a human operator who must screen all possible responses.

The message here is that LAN solutions should not be considered on their own, independent of the environment they serve. This approach is mistaken because it deprives the organization from a polyvalent effect.

Desirable as it is in terms of cost-effectiveness, the client/server model is only one of the key components in terms of an effective systems solution. An example can be taken from the use of file servers in connection with a sophisticated end-user-oriented implementation.

12.7   Reducing Database Search in
LAN Implementation

Sophisticated end-user-oriented applications require new departures in systems solutions. For instance, to reduce execution-time variance in a distributed environment, it is necessary to control the extent of database search through intelligence-enriched mining operations:

---

*See also D. N. Chorafas, *Expert Systems in Manufacturing,* Van Nostrand Reinhold, NY, 1992; and D. N. Chorafas and H. Steinmann *Expert Systems in Banking,* Macmillan, London, 1991.

- At the problem space level, the search can be reduced through the application of specific knowledge.

- At the knowledge retrieval level, the search can be controlled by such methods as data partitioning, downsizing the knowledge representation formalisms.

- At the physical level, the storage space can be partitioned by dedicating servers on the LAN by specific subject.

Partitioning the search space avoids looking into sections containing what is a priori known not to be applicable. Partitioning the data space allows us to avoid considering sets of data that are a priori known not to belong to the relation at hand.

All this is do-able provided we employ artificial intelligence tools, including both rule-based models and fuzzy engineering. Their use permits us to capitalize on acquired experience for better performance of the newly built systems.

In other words, we have passed the level where physical preoccupations and basic LAN software were attracting the most attention. We have come to recognize that real-time knowledge-based control must be embedded into computer programs, which often make tradeoffs between:

- The number of data operations actually performed per second and the response time needed to take hold of changes in the values of each of the variables being monitored.

Tradeoffs also include the number of servers required to store programs and data, including:

- The degree to which relevant information and associated computations may be underutilized within the chosen implementation perspective—or, alternatively, lead to servicing bottlenecks.

These considerations are particularly important to the design of client/server systems requiring clear definition of business goals, technical requirements, and associated characteristics. Often, these involve different degrees of uncertainty, and therefore their implementation must include the ability to restructure the system at run time—a proposition that can be served through client/server implementation.

- In classical, centralized real-time approaches, the problem usually entails providing the most faithful transformation of external control signals into physical actions.

- In contrast, a knowledge engineering enriched client/server model includes the ability to accept abstract job specifications and produce fast and flexible actions.

Since particular actions vary over time, intelligent real-time systems must be able to adjust timeliness, reliability, and performance to meet design goals during life-cycle operations.

The physical configuration of the system and associated costs should be changed, as well as the way in which the available resources are used. This is the reason for the emphasis placed in the logical constructs needed to run on a LAN, beyond the fact that a LAN's physical characteristics are also changing.

Current policies monitoring the performance of human systems are not so well developed. When users complain about performance, the usual queries that come are: Is channel capacity too low? Are there too many workstations? Is more disk storage required?

There is nothing really wrong with these queries. What is wrong is the fact that rarely are valid statistics available on which to base an answer. Here again is a field where the able use of expert systems can be of major assistance.

The incorporation of knowledge engineering into LAN-based modules leads to intelligent control systems capable of some degree of self-awareness. By this is meant the provision of:

- A knowledge bank with information about real-time constraints, essentially another server on the LAN

- The ability of knowing about and reflecting the capabilities of the processes running on a given LAN environment

Successful implementations of knowledge engineering help document knowledge and self-awareness as vital in establishing when a goal has been reached or a sufficient level of refinement attained. A further aspect in the administration of complex client/server systems is that dynamic requirements are given at multiple levels of abstraction, yet they must be expressed in a way able to satisfy real-time constraints.

A significant amount of research is currently being devoted to the constraints issue. In a modern real-time system, the specification of correctness contains constraints related to time and space in the real world. These may be expressed as explicit functions of time, or implicit in other constraints.

In a LAN landscape that can be easily redimensioned, a timing constraint may be negotiable at a particular moment if it can be relaxed—usually in exchange for obeying some other constraint. An example is a quality service constraint or one relating to systems performance and dependability.

In order to maintain as much flexibility as possible, intelligent real-time systems should be built with a modular design. They should be capable of translating operating goals into commands and should be enriched with a planning module. These notions must seep down the LAN design perspectives, in appreciation of the fact that we are moving beyond the classical LAN.

12.8   Are LANs Just a Better Sort of Mainframe?

Proponents of all-LAN solutions are quick to point out that they can have storage capacity equivalent to mainframe disks and a faster access time. Collectively, there can be a number of gigabytes on a LAN, which is able to move information elements between stations at former mainframe speeds.

At the same time, in terms of processing power the LAN's potential is the equivalent of a 3090 and in some cases it can provide more power. Distributed LAN-based systems have major cost advantages to show, and the list of references grows as companies move to client/server environments.

Advantages presented by LAN solutions as compared with mainframes are evident even when user organizations do not properly exploit the full capability of LANS, and therefore they are not getting the highest return on their investments. Underutilization becomes an issue because:

1. User organizations are not monitoring and effectively managing LAN operations

2. They are still exploiting them through largely mainframe-oriented concepts

LANs are *not* a mainframe in disguise, but this notion has yet to gain wide acceptance. As Secs. 12.6 and 12.7 have outlined, LANs provide a framework on which to build systems of distributed intelligence—a process which goes well beyond that of downsizing mainframes.

The discussion in Sec. 12.7 on database and real-time constraints is highly relevant to a sophisticated LAN environment for a variety of reasons. For instance, a LAN operates unattended, and unattended operations should include automatic backups and file transfers to be served through expert systems. The same is true of a number of optimization routines.

Under no condition should the client/server and its LAN be seen as another sort of mainframe, with all this means in terms of human operators, costs, and inefficiency. Precisely because there is no human interference from an operating viewpoint, the issue of automatic backups is quite important, the more so as the volume of data residing in workstations grows and much of it is critical corporate and work group data.

- Responsibility for information should not rest with the individual workstation user, who may or may not perform backups on a regular basis.

- Expert systems should provide automatic, unattended backup to protect critical data in the event of disaster.

Furthermore, as the preceding paragraphs suggest, expert systems should be used to provide performance monitoring, problem identification, optimization, load balancing, and the steady monitoring of response to user-defined conditions and requirements.

Contrary to the obsolete culture prevailing with mainframes, client/server expert system can be instrumental in problem diagnosis, disaster recovery, and capacity planning. They are also valuable in scheduling and initiating unattended operations in an evolving configuration management.

All constraints on resources, and the associated need for correct behavior, can be compounded by the fact that business increasingly requires real-time solutions. Security is another area where the impact of constraints can be well exemplified. It is also a domain of great importance to all user organizations, and can be served through knowledge engineering. Constraints should, for example, apply to authentication and authorization, in order to give a high degree of protection.

- Rules must go beyond simply requiring the applicant to quote a password or use an encryption key.

- There should be identification of the system user, ascertaining beyond doubt the identity of the applicant.

The multiple low-cost but powerful processors on a LAN make feasible such an approach, while centralized mainframe environments are both too inflexible and too limited in their ability to react. They are also too static.

Authentications have a finite and fairly short life. At its end, system users should be required to reauthenticate themselves. Doing so with mainframes means increasing the overhead, which is already way too high.

Authentication techniques should be extended to assure that after a user's identity has been established, the problem of controlling access to confidential information is also handled through appropriate knowledge-enriched constraints. This calls for classifying database elements and other documents, giving a corresponding access classification, which is dynamically kept up, to potential users.

As these examples help document, experience gained through successful client/server implementation has carried many organizations well beyond the original emphasis on the physical aspects of the local area network. No doubt, these concepts are also applicable to metropolitan and wide area networks, as the next section shows.

12.9   Using Metropolitan Area Networks

Local area networks are not always what the name says: local. Not only can the maximum distance between workstations and server on the same network be 2 km or more, but also a different LAN may interconnect through a backbone such as a metropolitan area network (MAN).

Presently available MANs can transfer data at the rate of 140 MBPS, 14 times the speed of standard Ethernet-type LANS. There is an emerging metropolitan area network market with systems in full development and fiber-based models reaching a 1.13 GBPS (gigabit per second) to 2.4 GBPS—hence, gigastreams.

Ongoing developments appear to offer faster and better quality communications at high speed, and are targeted as backbone applications to connect local area networks and imaging systems. Interconnected LANs and MANs can provide a suitable environment for the support of many applications involving the interaction of people within large organizations.

The IEEE 802.6 Working Group has decided to align its metropolitan area networking standard with the B-ISDN norms being developed within CCITT (but not yet formalized). This policy is significant because IEEE has been responsible for developing the most important international local area network standards, such as IEEE 802.3 (Ethernet) and 802.5 (Token Ring).

Since metropolitan area networks will have a growing impact in the 1990s, industry wants an early standardization of services, but at the same time needs assurance that protocols and interface will be compatible with future developments. There are two problems in this road.

1. The CCITT recommendation for B-ISDN are no longer as stable a frame of reference as they seemed to be. As a result, interim solutions are being made to satisfy industry demands. Such an installed

base will be difficult to dislodge at a later date because of the investments being made—and the associative competitive interests by vendors and users.

2. Current work on MANs particularly focuses on packet switching, but good old packet switching is becoming obsolete, to be replaced by frame relay. This change in technological solutions is particularly important, since MANs are seen as the main evolutionary step on the path to broadband integrated services. As far as we can see today, new services should be based on asynchronous transfer mode (ATM) packet-switching technology.

Compromises are evidently possible. In its review of the future of European data communications, the Conference of European Postal and Telecommunications administrations (CEPT) concludes that the MAN technology being defined by IEEE 802.6 "might be both applied as a distributed switch or access network for future ATM networks, but can also be used to offer a public, high-speed data service."

Along this frame of reference, CEPT envisions MAN technology fitting into the business communications environment, particularly for the interconnection of LANs. However, the suitability of 802.6 MANs for both data and voice is still a matter of debate among operators and manufacturers. The technical problems associated with a network capable of supporting high volumes of both connectionless and connection-oriented traffic can be enormous.

Since the 802.6 standard is based around an integrated switch, it also has to standardize a number of *adaptation layers* on top of the basic ATM features. The reason is that it allows for the support of other commonly available services, such as nonisochronous connections used in most LANS, including Ethernet.

Standardization of these adaptation layers within the 802.6 MAN may allow rapid support of the demand for MAN services and LAN-to-LAN linking, while at the same time facilitating a smooth evolution to B-ISDN once this becomes available (if it does). The counterargument is that as welcome as this approach may be, the protocols and standards are not yet in place.

There has also been skepticism about whether the integration of the telecommunications and broadcast sectors—both regulatory mine fields—through the deployment of broad and fiber-optic cable could be achieved in a rapid timeframe. Furthermore, uncertainty over the future demand for services, such as videotelephones and high-definition television (HDTV), has clouded the debate.

Wide area broadband communications, MAN, and HDTV are interrelated. They are also a pork barrel. Therefore, we now experience a politically charged battle over HDTV standards among Europe, Japan, and the United States—which has done little to allay uncertainties.

When truly broadband channels at MAN and WAN levels do arrive, they will turn the economics of providing traditional telephone services upside down.

- The almost infinite bandwidth available with fiber optics will probably mean that it will not be worthwhile charging for ordinary telephone calls or low-speed data traffic, such as electronic mail.
- Instead, subscribers could simply pay a fixed monthly rental based on the consumption of television or HDTV programs. We shall see.

Provided that what we see is convincing, the following scenario may characterize the mid- to late 1990s:

- A huge market may emerge to satisfy the demand of applications requiring high-capacity communications by means of suitable physical transmission media such as optical fibers.
- Multiple-service business networks will evolve capable of handling voice, images, and any kind of real-time and wideband traffic in a multimedia communications sense.
- The resulting infrastructure will be used for the transmission of broadcasting and value-added services, thus opening wide markets for advanced communications applications.

Oncoming logical and physical solutions will facilitate the identification of users in a sort of *communities of communication,* through the development of assessment methodologies based on knowledge engineering. Teleports could also be part of a support infrastructure for leading-edge applications. Given these possibilities, MANs could also play a strategic and practical role in terms of business competitiveness.

Backbones and Intelligent WANs

13.1 Introduction

As we have seen in Chap. 12, a network is a single entity made up of many component parts: nodes, links, control centers, protocols, software modules, and attached devices. These components should be designed, engineered, and built to work together, including the underlying network management software that allows the individual parts to operate as a single system.

When this synergy materializes, the resulting communications engine is greater than the sum of its component parts, if the latter are taken one by one. Compatibility, feature consistency, and seamless management of any of the networked resources must be hallmarks of any valid solution.

The object of this chapter is to provide a concise but comprehensive state-of-the-art review of today's networking developments, particularly in terms of wide area solutions:

- Assessing which concepts and products will predominate over the next few years

- Showing the reader how to prepare for future migration strategies that will minimize upsetting current investments

- Demonstrating ways and means for optimizing the ability to exploit new technologies as they become commercially available

Quite evidently, it will not be possible to deal in one chapter with the plethora of networking architectures and products of significance to today's managers, developers, and operators of information systems. These products include (but are not exclusively limited to): Accumaster, ACMS, Allink, APPC, APPN, ARPA/DDN, Banyan's

Vines, CICS, DEC DNA, DECmcc, DECnet, DSA, ECF, EMA, Encina, Fast Packet, FDDI, FTAM, FTP, GOSIP, IBM OS/2 LAN Server, ISDN, MAP, MS LAN Manager, MS NET, Net/Master, NetView, NFS, Novell NetWare/286, Novell Netwave/386, OpenView, OSF/1, OSI, PCSA, RPC, SAA, SNA, SNA gateways, SNMP, SONET, SQL Server, SUN ONC, TCP/IP, Telnet, 3270 and emulators, TOP, Tuxedo, Unix, X.25, X.400, X.500, XDR, and XNS.

Networking today involves a wide range of subjects: new systems structures, complex software environments, different classes of servers and workstations, a broader range of end-user services, whole new generations of LANs, MANs, and WANs. The more recent offerings feature fast-packet technology, broadband approaches, and other issues that radically change the nature of communications technology.

The goal of these advances is to provide a greatly improved networked speed, reliability, flexibility, configurability, manageability, ease of use, and transparency—at an affordable cost. To gain advantages from the evolving technology, user organizations must proceed with redefinition of functionalities, look at the convergence of environments, and be ready to handle multimedia products.

There is a golden horde of vital steps necessary for the achievement of successful cooperative processing solutions to handle voice, data, graphics, text, and moving image with equal ease.

Able solutions require that vendors and users make an increasingly serious commitment to the removal of current impediments to the deployment of cost-effective systems. We have to care for the proper integration of all resources in computers, communications, and solutions into corporate systems featuring automation of operations, improved end-user support, and the ability to merge the host of new products currently under development.

13.2 Communications
Solutions for the 1990s

Communications products operate in such areas as local area networks (LANs), metropolitan area networks (MANs), private branch exchanges (PBXs), modulators and demodulators (Modems), multimedia multiplexers (MMMs), very small aperture terminals (VSATs) for satellite communications, and many more. They are bought and employed to offer an increasingly sophisticated service which requires significant amounts of software to support business requirements.

Increasingly, the able answer to evolving business challenges demands the maximum utilization of resources at minimum cost. There is also a growing need for real-time connectivity between applications and users, to be made with significant flexibility and adaptability in order to face future requirements. This is what we call *future-proof* solutions.

The future-proof perspective is a relatively new concept, adding itself to the better-known needs for security, multimedia services, electronic mail, facsimile, and videoconferencing. Another important communications need is multilevel applications support for files, messages, queries, and transactions to be executed in a dependable manner with the minimum delay commensurate with acceptable cost.

Examined under the perspective of the requirements listed below, an effective communications network is the link between numerous components attached for long transaction handling, distributed processing, distributed databases, resource sharing, and other purposes. To efficiently interconnect multimedia workstations and servers, the network must feature an integrated architecture that

- Obeys open system prerequisites

- Is committed to future developments

- Has affordable costs for installation and operation

- Makes feasible an efficient utilization of assets

To reach such goals, user organizations must graduate to improved planning capabilities and adopt a policy of flexible but steady adjustment to developing user needs. This calls for an increasing systems dependability while also steadily expanding systems integration perspectives—interconnecting any user or device to any other user or device, and doing so end-to-end.

As shown in Fig. 13.1, from the user organization's viewpoint an end-to-end network can be seen as composed of five successive layers of communications services. These divide into two different worlds:

- One is wire-based, and is the classical way telephone companies interconnect with their clients.

This is a largely regulated market with old players and old plant, though Fig. 13.1 bets on fiber optics—hence, on its renewal. Most importantly, the norms regulating this market are more or less in place through the efforts of CCITT, CEPT, ISO, and other organizations—from technical issues to intercompany billing.

- The other and newer world is mobile and wireless. It is the modern way to make end-to-end interconnections, fully deregulated, with few standards and many new players which may be intracountry (global), cross-country, or only at metropolitan levels.

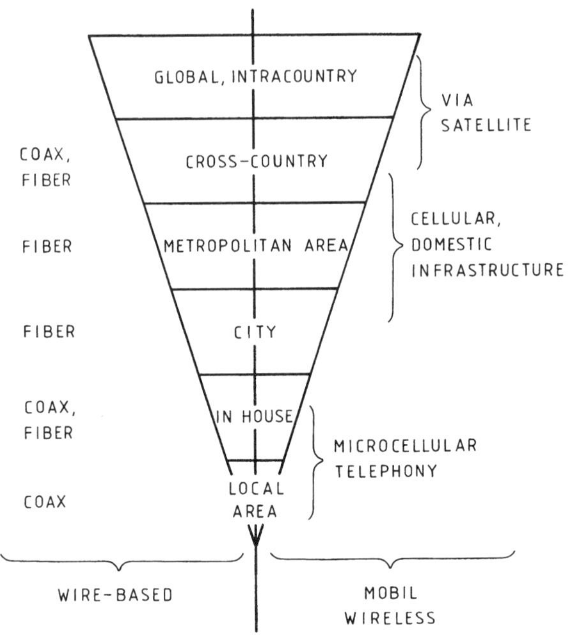

Figure 13.1   Communications solutions for the 1990s.

This means that a whole range of both technical and clearance services are up for grabs. Interconnectivity is required between the different carriers and minicarriers—and with this, settlement services. These are requirements from a business viewpoint.

From a technical point of view, as long as norms have not been established the mobile and wireless domain of communications will be in flux, requiring a great deal of attention in the handling of technical issues. Solutions are calling for significant expertise in the way the two different worlds of communications can be brought together to operate in unison to the advantage of the end user.

Like any other networked services, mobile and wireless communications support require, as they grow in importance and geographic coverage, systems software in the form of a network operating system (NOS), which itself must follow standards. This is written not only in protocol observance terms but also in basic operating terms, such as administrative duties, without increasing in an inordinate manner the amount of overhead.

When networked services and their interfaces are not built correctly, a host of technical problems arise, including:

- Addressing

- Naming

- Security

Many of the leading organizations that have started using the mobile and wireless communications opportunities think that what is currently available in terms of infrastructure is not enough. Among other issues is the need for global directory services which can assist in better supporting closed user groups—and therefore security services.

In other words, what is currently available in new communications disciplines are niche solutions which furthermore are not standard. A good deal of this criticism is also applicable to wired services which see to it that user organizations must carry higher network management costs than would have been otherwise necessary.

Apart from the technical issues reflected here, the whole domain of mobile and wireless communications involves a need for clearance and settlement expertise, to establish and administer a system of multicompany, multilateral billing. It is a job that must be fully automated; otherwise costs will become too high and profits will be wiped out as this market becomes increasingly competitive.

A practical example is *the GSM Clearing House.* This is the first of a new breed of clearinghouses aimed at simplifying the administration and billing involved with pan-European digital cellular networking.

- Telecommunications clearinghouses would develop in the coming years, with the goal of allowing customers to use the same mobile telephone in different European countries.

- The approach assumes the practical existence of different operators, offering clearing and netting services for, billing reasons.

A different way of making this statement is that the evolving requirements in the technical and financial domains require an infrastructural development of considerable size. Short of it, the user organizations will need to spend, for mobile and wireless network management purposes, a higher share of their communications budget than called for by corresponding wire-based services.

13.3 Developing the In-House Telecommunications Infrastructure

One of the significant trends in high-tech countries is the transition from an industrial society to an information society. The functional basis for supporting the requirements by an information society is communications, computers, and software. How far have we progressed along this path?

The transition from bare wire to more sophisticated services can be exemplified by the birth of the value-added network (VAN), which started in America in the 1970s, with prodding by the Federal Communications Commission (FCC). Its origin lies in the effort to bypass the regulated AT&T monopoly, which at the time was simply offering a bare wire service.

In other high-tech countries, the VAN concept came somewhat later. For instance, in Japan it started in 1982 with the authorization of information processing plus communication line reselling to small and medium-sized companies. Full-fledged VAN services appeared with the deregulation brought about by the Telecommunication Business Law of 1985.

There are differences between the American and the Japanese models of value differentiation in the communications domain. As shown in Fig. 13.2, in the Japanese approach to deregulation the still regulated areas:

- Were not classified according to the services provided, as was the case in the United States

- Were determined according to whether or not the telecommunications line facilities were owned rather than only rented

Such a definition may at first sight seem a little awkward, but the underlying difference provides interesting results. It has led to a wide

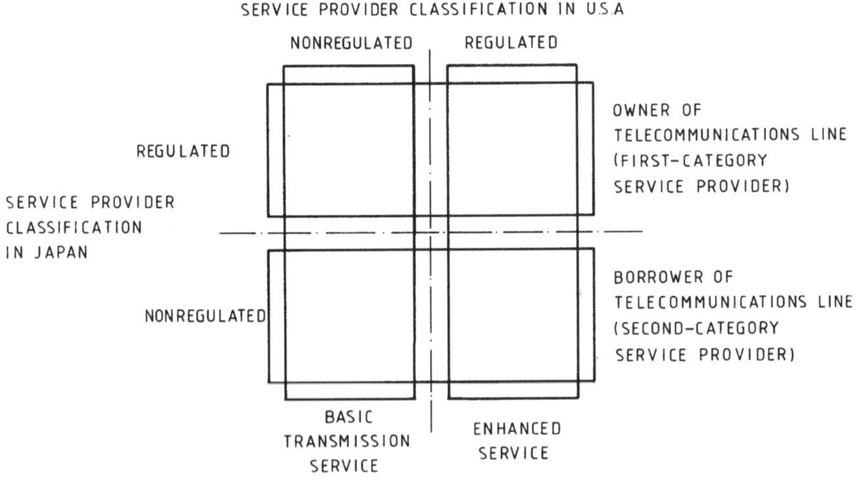

Figure 13.2 Deregulation of telecommunications services in Japan and the United States.

variety of services combining communications and information processing, which are now flourishing in Japan.

In its fundamentals, wherever it has been implemented the communications infrastructure in a VAN is characterized by low-cost, high-quality, and high-speed digital lines. Channel capacities of 1.54 MBPS (T-1 lines) or better* are being used, with further progress possible through the use of optical fiber transmission technology.

Optical fiber high-capacity links are implemented all the way from backbones for LANs, to MANs, and WANs. For LANs, in the recent years the most popular protocol has been the fiber-distributed data interface (FDDI), but it may well be overtaken by frame relay. (See also the discussion in Chap. 12.)

If a company is putting in a wiring system and wants a backbone, it should definitely go with fiber. For companies that do not want to pay the cost of fiber connections today but want the flexibility and performance that fiber offers for the future, experts suggest pulling a *dark fiber,* one that will not be used immediately.

In the general case, the extra cost of pulling the fiber along with a copper backbone is relatively small compared with later installing fiber in a separate operation. The rationale for a dark fiber is as follows:

- Fiber offers many advantages for LAN and MAN installations, among which is the fact that it can support longer cable runs than copper cabling.

- Laboratory tests show that fiber's information-carrying capacity is nearly limitless, at least under present-day perspectives.

- Fiber does not radiate electromagnetic signals, so it cannot interfere with other devices; at the same time, this feature increases security.

However, as far as infrastructural LAN implementations are concerned, despite its attractive qualities there is not yet a great deal of fiber in use. One problem has to do with protocols. While many users who are installing fiber look toward FDDI, most fiber-optic cabling today is being used to carry 10 MBPS Ethernet traffic.

- The FDDI standard is relatively new and not yet so stable, while it is also challenged by frame relay.

- Users want to give vendors time to work bugs out, particularly as regards interoperability of different FDDI equipment.

- FDDI currently costs about $10,000 per connection, while fiber-based Ethernet cards are available for much less.

---

*T-3 lines available today have a capacity of about 27 T-1 lines.

Hence, in connection with LAN implementation today fiber is typically installed only in the context of a long-term, companywide plan, or when a new building is built. Another opportunity is when a large company is rebuilding its entire infrastructure as a 5- to 10-year investment.

Whether current or latent, fiber backbone implementation should be made through a systems view. It should consider existing LAN installations and their protocols—most particularly the *class* of already installed access services. Figure 13.3 presents a bird's-eye view of the different protocol classes installed over the last 10 years.

The criteria for fiber usage are different with backbones for MAN, WAN, and in general VAN offerings. VAN offerings typically use packet-switching and circuit-switching technology.

- In some countries, like Japan, VAN circuit switching is employed to store and forward information for various communications media such as facsimile, voice, and data.

- By contrast, in VAN communications, packet-switching technology is essential in converting among different protocols, different speeds, and different codes for combining domestic or international computer networks.

One of the key advantages of fiber in VAN offerings is high reliability. The VAN must guarantee a stable and continuous operation. Besides fiber, in order to realize high reliability, redundancy arrange-

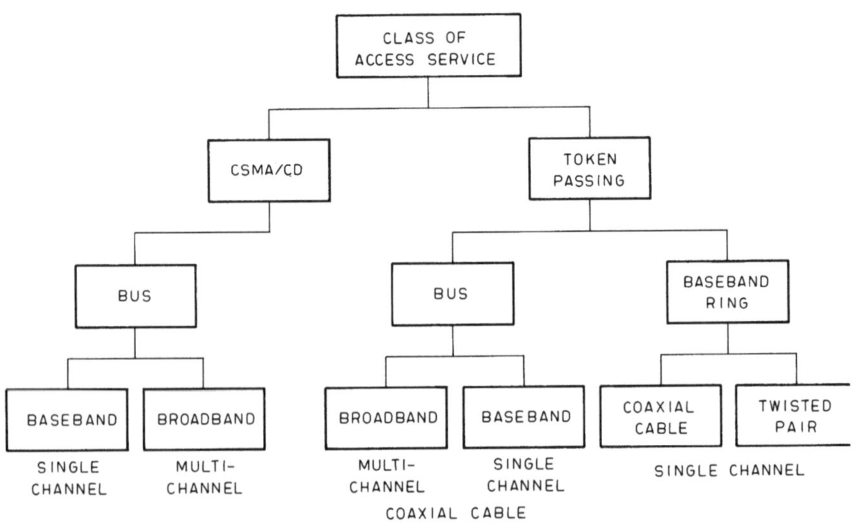

Figure 13.3   Classes of access services in CSMA/CD and token passing.

ments are made for such components as transmission equipment, switching equipment, and host computer systems.

Another vital feature is the network control center (NCC), which was mentioned in Chap. 12. A VAN consists of a complex combination of transmitting devices, switching systems and computers, which are distributed over a broad area. Hence, it is necessary to perform supervisory control and on-line diagnostics—the latter benefiting from the implementation of expert systems.

Finally, the communications infrastructure must act as a systems integration technology. Properly designed and implemented integrative facilities are necessary in order that communications and computer aggregates assure optimal service to the user organization.

13.4 The New Generation of Value-Added Networks

The currently available value-added networks are typically highly centralized. They were established in the late 1970s, and throughout the 1980s served as closed systems. This is why VANs find it difficult to promote the any-to-any free flow of commerce required to build tomorrow's *virtual companies.*

This is the main reason that open networks, such as Compuserve and Prodigy, have made inroads in the fee-for-service market but are mainly consumer-oriented. What is more, in all current network environments:

- Transactions are predefined and constrained

- Only a limited type of access is being provided

For instance, although VANs connect buyers and sellers, they do not allow flexible connections for buyers to communicate with other buyers, and sellers to connect with each other. This is a disadvantage for the corporate business relationship, which is more peer-to-peer in nature.

A new generation of VANs is therefore expected to develop, capable of exploiting the great competitive advantage in direct company-to-company relations. In essence, an organization wants to be able to hook up in an ad hoc manner with another organization that best fits the needs of a particular project—even if this is only on a one-time basis.

- Such connectivity requires flexible VAN supports as well as OSI's X.500* or similar directory service.

---

*X.500 is the ISO international standard for global directory (or naming) services. By providing specifications for directory services, X.500 defines a global directory standard for locating users by Email.

- It can also profit from value-added features that permit the user to find the required ad hoc information through a content- or attribute-based approach.

This type of navigation system, for instance, is being provided over a new network: EINet promoted by the Microelectronics and Computer Development Corporation (MCC) with wide area information servers (WAIS) technology.

WAIS is currently running on Internet, which was developed as a research network and allows only noncommercial interactions.

- WAIS features a distributed information retrieval service originally conceived and implemented by Thinking Machines, Apple Computers, Peat Marwick, and Dow Jones.

- WAIS provides access to information residing on hundreds of computers connected by the Defense Advanced Research Projects Agency (DARPA) of Internet

Through natural language queries (in English), WAIS searches the databases to find documents that contain the words and phrases in the question posed. Documents that match are ranked, and pointers to them are returned to the user for review and final choice.

The new-generation VAN is an *open* value-added network that must assure sophisticated, knowledge engineering enriched directory services in which companies can establish relationships and conduct business. For security reasons, it must provide users with an authentication capability, serving as a *trusted intermediary* to confirm that parties are who they say they are.

- This is the function to be assured through trusted systems, which have been on occasions described as notary public-type on-line services.

- Trusted on-line functions must include not only basic user confirmation but also prequalification of business partners (such as vendors and suppliers).

- Supported features must be enriched on-line through performance records, quality control measures, and information regarding the ability to meet specifications.

As an example, in addition to authentication EINet provides subscribers with technology to manage their own access services so that these organizations can control access to specific databases. Along this line, MCC makes available, to the companies that fund that particular project, confidential technical reports, but also offers nonconfidential reports and other information to a broader market.

As a third-party intermediary, the new generation VAN must be able to manage authentication services for a whole community of users. Not all of these user organizations will necessarily interact, but each can receive a rich array of support services in its own group.

In the EINet case, initial authentication and access control are being assured through Kerberos, an authentication server technology from MIT's Project Athena. Kerberos provides evidence of a user's identity and subsequent authorization to execute a program.

In the example above, MCC actually integrated the WAIS and Kerberos technologies for access control purposes to information made available through WAIS. Access control is critical if a company is going to conduct business through value-added networking leading to what might be called *electronic commerce.*

As in the case of mobile and wireless communications examined in Sec. 13.2, there also has to be a *clearing mechanism* for billing money to change hands. This remittance service requires fiduciary agents with network banking expertise.

These examples help document the developing need for a three-way approach focusing on a public technical infrastructure, user organizations, and financial clearing, as suggested in Fig. 13.4.

1. The public technical infrastructure provides sophisticated value-added networking capabilities, including a trusted system approach. Other features are directories, databases, and hypermedia—all the way to infrastructure for enterprise modeling. Specifically, the issue is how to build an *ontological* repository of models.

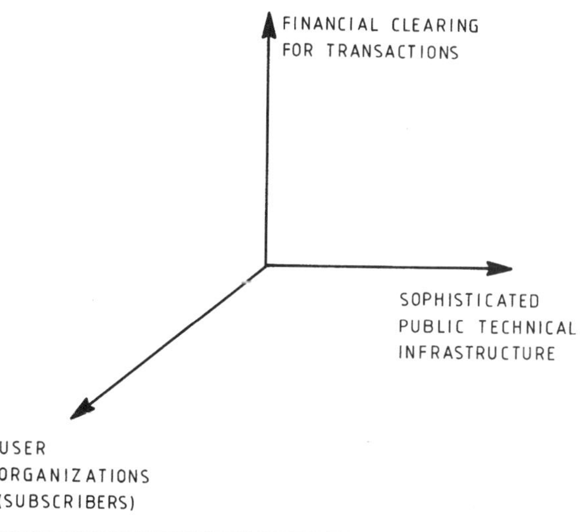

Figure 13.4 The new generation of value-added networks utilized in electronic banking.

2. On-line coordination of user organizations focuses on effective interconnection of individuals, teams, and organizations to integrate problem-solving efforts. This involves much more than data, including a whole range of multimedia services. Emphasis must be placed on the able handling of compound electronic documents and also on a new generation of voice support such as language translation, interpretive telephony, and teleconferencing.

3. A financial clearinghouse assures billing, payments, and in general debits/credits for user organizations, including merchants, information providers, VAN operators, and in general *information brokers*. Such capability goes well beyond the now classical electronic funds transfer (EFT)* services and requires advanced technology for its execution. Examples include intelligent networks, distributed deductive databases, and expert systems.

Solutions will not come over night. They will develop gradually, by major steps forward. For instance, NEC's Interpretive Telephone System (ITS) is said to eliminate the last obstacle in global telephone networks—that is, the language barrier—by automatically translating two-way dialogs in international telephone networks. ITS consists of three technological components:

- Speech recognition

- Machine translation

- Speech synthesis

Speech recognition converts spoken language into a sequence of words, machine translation translates it into another language, and speech synthesis finally converts it again into spoken language. These technological components, however, will not function properly in the ITS if they are simply combined together. They have to be tightly interrelated.

NEC started speech recognition and synthesis research about 30 years ago. Since then, the company has been very active in this field. At the TELECOM 83 fair in Geneva, Switzerland, NEC demonstrated an experimental automatic interpretation system based on a connected speech recognizer. Word identification used a word dictionary. Since then, syntax analysis and semantic analysis have made major strides.

Japanese-English and English-Japanese translation systems have been commercialized. A prototype of a multilingual translation system has been developed by NEC (known as PIVOT), which includes Spanish, Chinese, Korean, and Thai as well as Japanese and English.

---

*See also D. N. Chorafas, *Electronic Funds Transfer,* Butterworths, London, 1989.

13.5   Capitalizing on Network Intelligence

By the late 1980s, the feeling among telecom administrations and other network operators was that the integrated services digital network (ISDN) would provide the basis for the future public network. The facts of life obliged clear-eyed telecom authorities and independent companies to radically change their views.

While ISDN remains a selling slogan for manufacturers, the increasingly sophisticated needs of user organizations and the demands of a highly competitive environment have led telecom administrators to look for alternative methods of information delivery. Emphasis is on *fast, flexible,* and *economical* provision of new services in a manner attractive to the user, especially the business user. A major trend concerns the advent of the *intelligent network* (IN).* For user organizations, IN promises not only a host of significant communications services but also the option to create new opportunities by the users themselves without the intervention of network operators.

Under intense pressure to bring innovations to their networks in an atmosphere of increasing liberalization of network services, the telecommunications administrators see IN as a way to decrease the time it takes to develop new products and services. In addition, they believe IN will provide the platform for a growing range of income.

Although the concept of an intelligent network was first proposed by Bell Communications Research (Bellcore), the telecoms administrators, telecoms manufacturers, and computer vendors were quick to embrace it as the global network of choice for the 1990s and beyond. As a convergence between the data-processing and communications industries, alliance building will be even more important than in the past:

- One of the goals of the IN is to have network interfaces that assure operability among its manifold components.

- One of the factors delaying the launching of a range of IN features is the needed synergy between manufacturers, from components to architectural questions.

- One of the factors in the divergence of opinions on what is and is not an IN is whether intelligence in terms of expert systems, computer processing, and databases should reside in a digital exchange or should be in separate nodes.

---

*This is not to be confused with an AT&T offering under the same name that does *not* support the features described in this section.

- Another argument is whether such intelligence must be centralized for ease of maintenance, or distributed for getting resources close to where they are required.

By distributing intelligence in databases across the network, the IN holds the promise of cracking the software bottleneck that has delayed the introduction of new services, such as virtual private networks. Hence, it is being heralded as the key that will unlock the telecommunications service economy.

Intelligent networks also introduce the concept of software portability to network service provisioning. An IN architecture allows operating companies to deploy service control points (SCPs) in either a centralized or a distributed fashion, depending on specific needs.

It is conceivable that IN agents will be able to help the user concentrate on work and alleviate many of the difficulties presented with communications. In one of the ongoing projects, for example, two such agents are:

- The task manager

- The presentation manager

Both are dynamically exploited by means of user modeling and expert systems. Another agent, the networked information retrieval manager, also benefits in a significant way from knowledge engineering.

There is an interesting background to the idea of a task manager enriched by artificial intelligence. If the user was required to undertake all the problem solving necessary for operating the workstations and their controlling services, very few people would be willing or able to exploit the possibilities that on-line connectivity can offer.

For these reasons, it is felt that at the user level basic decision-making functionality must be allocated to the system, including:

- Proper user goal identification

- User action selection

- User action execution

- Feedback to the user

Such decision-making functionality will require sets of rules, both heuristic and algorithmic, which are sensitive to the state of the user, of the system, and of the application. Consideration must also well be given to dynamic allocation of functionality between the end user and the system.

The aforementioned characteristics of the user-system dialog are based to a large extent on an intelligent end-user interface. Dialog should include an analysis of help and tutorial subsystems, and must be sensitive to the different levels of abilities and experience of the user.

- The services to be embedded in the presentation manager must account for the fact that multimedia communication generates a highly complex range of problems.

- These concern the form of input/output information, as well as retrieval from heterogeneous databases and presentation of contents.

Multimedia information types will be text (linear and hypertext), graphical images, icons, and photographic images (single or moving), along with audio service feedback, voice generation, voice communication, interpretive telephony, high-quality sound, textually communicated data, visually communicated data, and orally communicated data.

In the general case, a few or all of these information types will be utilized within tasks that require telecommunications, such as interactivity between distributed work groups. Existing presentation techniques through graphic user interfaces (GUIs), such as windowing and icons, are a good way of assisting the end users in alleviating the ambiguity of information. But these techniques need to be further developed to encompass the simultaneous integration of multiple services.

Examples of GUIs are conversational messages, retrieval and distribution of information residing in remote heterogeneous databases, and other issues intended to avoid the obvious potential for confusions. (See also the discussion of networked databases in Part 3.)

Another major group of services to be provided by an intelligent network regards on-line diagnostics and the exploitation of quality history databases. Both should be executed through expert systems leading to the scheduling of preventive maintenance and to improvements in network reliability by an order of magnitude or more.

13.6   User-Oriented Modeling in a Layered
Network Structure

The advent of intelligent networks along the line examined in Sec. 13.5 will blur the boundary between public and private networking services through the provision of virtual communications facilities. In parallel to this, the deployment of fiber optics and associated photonics supports in the local loop will wave the boundary between switching and transmission. New flexible access systems hold the potential to

- Deliver true customer control at a reasonable cost

- Present the added advantage of almost limitless bandwidth, available on demand

By offering a steadily increasing transmission capacity at declining prices, fiber-optic transmission is forcing a change in the way public telecommunications networks are designed, built, and used. As a result:

- Commercial fiber transmission systems have more than tripled public-network capacity in only the past couple of years.

- Optically based connectionless switching schemes are blurring the differences between switching and transmission, challenging long-held tenets about network planning.

Beyond the level of physical supports, the greatest amount of attention will be necessary at the higher-up software layers. In the last analysis, it is advanced software which accounts for the sophistication of the solutions to be deployed.

A pivotal point here is *user modeling*, of which some basic concepts have been mentioned in regard to developing user interfaces to computer systems. In the past, most work has mainly been based on average user model characteristics with only small possibilities for the software products developed to adapt to the end user. Now we are talking of a totally different level of reference.

The basis for the new solutions being projected is to provide a greater ability to take the model of the actual user into account because of more intelligence in the equipment and the software developed for networks.

The network and its workstations will not only adapt themselves to the actual user. They will also support the development of user models and store parameters for further deployment. Such parameters will feature tutoring, smart interfaces, user profiles, and user skill adaptation.

The basic aim of all network intelligence efforts is to provide highly competitive services.

Among the key objectives is to produce the operational requirements for task management within an intelligent *user-window* interface. But user profiling will also involve helping manage the network itself, making it more adaptable to the evolving requirements for sophisticated communications services.

Another goal of user modeling is to produce the operational characteristics for presentation management through intelligent multimedia terminals. To reach such a goal, expert systems are needed to evaluate user modeling solutions, specify modeling levels for user-system interactions, and assist in developing methods for user assistance, training, and guidance based on the user-modeling work.

Just as important, in a network management sense, is to have usability metrics for evaluation of the results being obtained. "We measure everything that moves and we measure everything that does not move," said a senior vice president of AT&T in explaining the reasons for the success of the *Connect* credit card.

Most of the necessary metrics have to be developed, so to speak, from scratch, within the perspective of an intelligent network. A sound technical approach should be largely based on laboratory and field studies, using both knowledge engineering and cognitive techniques.

- In conducting such studies, the operational characteristics should be closely justified postmortem by data and be based on wide sampling.

- Operational requirements should be dimensioned through task analysis of a wide range of applications.

Not only are such studies demanding (and therefore not being done everywhere), but also the pace at which intelligent networks and flexible access systems are being deployed varies considerably from country to country and company to company. So far INs have received the most favor in deregulated regimes.

In terms of implementation, one of the key decisions to be made is whether to proceed with an overlay over current, often obsolete structures or a full-blown replacement strategy. A great deal of future competitiveness is embedded in this issue.

By articulating a set of basic elements regarding all network services, and providing means to combine and recombine these elements to create new services, INs will assure significant degrees of freedom. For instance, it will permit user organizations to switch vendors, creating services more quickly and at a lower cost than traditional architectures ever allowed.

13.7 The Impact of New Technology on Network Solutions

For user organizations, intelligent networks will make it possible to switch public network operators and manipulate to their advantage third-party software houses. For network operators, INs will make it feasible to create niche communications services for specific customer groups.

The intelligence embedded into a network will permit the decoupling of the software control architecture of public networks from underlying access and transport technologies. What is more, an IN service logic does not need to depend on any single underlying technology.

What this amounts to is an *advanced information-processing* solution encompassing a growing number of problem areas:

- Basic artificial intelligence techniques such as planning, searching, and problem solving

- The implementation of such techniques in a growing range of user-oriented activities

- The manipulation of processes connected to computer vision, speech analysis/synthesis, and interpretive telephony

- The development of trusted network systems—from the community level to the integration of large distributed databases and knowledge banks

Still other implementation domains include parallel execution of tasks connected to basic and value-added traffic functions. In the background of these applications lies the fact that they are indeed quite advanced compared with traditional applications. This is true for at least two reasons:

- Sophisticated implementations demand new principles for structuring and control based on peer-to-peer relationships.

- Modern network solutions are demanding in terms of memory and processor power, while the bounds of resources may not always be under control at execution time.

As we have seen in preceding sections, some degree of intelligence already exists in "this" or "that" network. But this is a smart rather than AI-based solution. For instance, equipment on customer premises is capable of simple tasks such as call forwarding. Networking equipment such as time division multiplexers is also increasingly endowed, allowing dynamic allocation of bandwidth and automatic rerouting of calls.

On the public network side, many systems operators are beginning to offer simple services, such as call waiting, to residential and small-business subscribers.

But all this is *déjà vu,* and the handling of the relatively simple tasks just described is quite different from the forthcoming need for fairly complex tasks.

- For simple and time-critical operations we can use a hierarchical, rather static, traditional design.

- For complex and not-time-critical operations we need nonhierarchical, peer-to-peer dynamic structures.

- For very complex tasks—that is, demand for knowledge engineering from an information-processing point of view—we need expert systems support.

The more demanding the task is, the more advanced algorithmic and heuristic solutions are necessary—but also the more difficult it is to produce a proof of successful, flexible evolution in the long run.

When we evaluate the degree of intelligence to be embedded into the system, we should keep in mind that as time goes by, the IN will be able to do a lot more than can be done with current technologies. Services are to be created, managed, and billed:

- Without modifying the infrastructure

- With standard interfaces so at least some of these tasks can be accomplished by third-party service providers or end-user organizations.

The message is that advancements toward intelligent networks are necessary because telecommunications systems are very complex and will be more so in the future. They can be managed only if good structuring principles are followed with the aim of combining reliable execution with advanced information-processing tasks.

Solutions must be provided not only in a local, limited manner but throughout the spectrum of network implementation, as shown in the layered structure of Fig. 13.5. Increasingly, user organizations will purchase from and certify suppliers according to their excellence in product and service, not according to an approach based on conformance to old procedures.

To understand this change in policy we must appreciate that the IN was conceived as a long-term effort to build an architecture able to simplify the introduction of new, more advanced telecommunications services. But commercial realities mean that many elements of the IN are already in place, though not in normalized form. This raises questions about:

- Telecom users

- Equipment manufacturers

- Systems operators

Such questions center around the necessity for IN standards. As each group is racing to introduce more advanced features into networks, norms and standards seem to have taken the back seat.

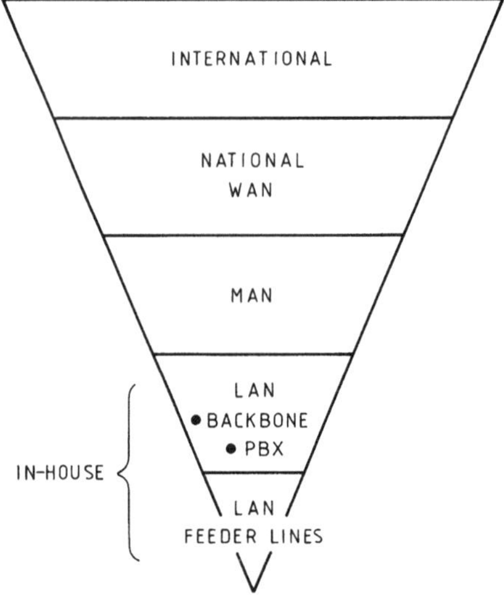

Figure 13.5   Five layers of networking where user modeling can give commendable results.

13.8   Facing Market Requirements for a Growing Rate of Services

One of the aims of the developments described in Secs. 13.6 and 13.7 is to create service-independent building blocks that can be mixed and matched to provide hundreds of communications services. The integration of knowledge engineering will enable services to be customized for individual end users.

Some network specialists think that ultimately the number of communications services will be practically equal to the number of customers. This is not unlike the plans being made in other industries to permit true customization of products. For instance, Toyota recently announced that by the year 2002 it will be able to produce a new car at customer specifications in just $3\frac{1}{2}$ days.

If such a feat can be achieved in the manufacturing industry, it will be even more feasible—and faster—in communications. The IN will be viewed as a set of services using databases and helped by expert systems to become a flexible platform in its ability to design and deliver customized services.

Today telecom operators do recognize the need to establish market requirements for a range of services, including security-enhancing solutions, automated diagnostics for better maintenance, quality histories of network performance, and significant improvement in bit error rate and in reliability. But the range of flexible, customer-oriented services goes well beyond all that.

- Since the provision of networked products is evolutionary, a major objective of the IN task should be to identify key enabling technologies wherever they may be found and to whatever discipline they subscribe.

- Another major goal is to technologically support a number of broad-based system trends, endowing them with suitable software techniques such as customer profiling and flexible programmability.

Efforts toward the development of intelligent networks include the evaluation of theoretical results via prototypes, in order to furnish the relevant feedback concerning IN-potential as well as to identify evolving business opportunities. A major part of the overall effort is requirements specification for better functional performance and flawless implementation.

Though there is a move by most telcos to retain control of central databases in an intelligent network, there is no technical reason why these databases cannot be operated by independent service providers or, even better, by the user organizations.

- The telephone companies do not need to divest control over the switching functions of their networks to competitors, though in the past they were obliged to permit the use of individual network components by competitors for the creation of value-added services.

- All the telcos need to do is to assure they are a flexible and dynamic part of the act in IN, rather than forcing their way into the business of others, which is that of databases.

It is simply absurd to think that large user organizations, or even private citizens, will ever permit the incorporation of private information into publicly controlled databases. This is the sort of thing that only the not-so-bright nationalized telcos (PTTs)* can imagine. Besides that, with their bureaucratic structure and closed mind, PTTs are not fit to operate distributed deductive databases or even intelligent networks. Their job is that of a utility supplier.

Ideally, the public databases should belong to information providers such as Dow Jones, Reuters, and thousands of others. Though a telco may own a public database company, the transport and warehousing

---

*Post, Telephone, and Telegraph companies, which are publicly run utility companies in continental Europe and elsewhere.

services for text, data, moving image, and other multimedia characteristics should be fully unbundled. Otherwise we will experience the worst monopoly we have ever seen.

To recapitulate, although in the coming years many more products and services will be offered through intelligent networks, what the IN effort now means is providing added value to the telecommunications lines, switching centers, and associated instrumentation. This value differentiation typically consists of:

1. *Knowledge engineering* constructs for transmission, switching, and on-line diagnostics

2. *Digitization* in channel transmission and switching

3. *High-quality* transmission and switching with low-bit-error rate (BER)

4. *High-capacity* channels with increasing broadband capability

5. *Nonblocking* solutions, although this is a relative term

6. Going *beyond on-line diagnostics,* through quality assurance databases and reliability studies

7. *Forecasting* and load planning for step-by-step expansion

8. A greater thrust in *innovation* and competitiveness, with corresponding investments in a steady flow of value added solutions

Intelligent network features do not come cheap—but when properly implemented they can save lots of money while at the same time helping to increase service quality and therefore building customer satisfaction and patronage.

As telcos look for ways to cut costs while bettering their services, they find out that the able implementation of the components of an intelligent network make a big difference in reaching this goal. Such components typically are intelligent nodes, intelligent lines, quality databases, analytical tools (both algorithmic and heuristic), simulators, and schedulers. The better-managed telcos appreciate this point and integrate such developments into their strategic plans.

Beyond LANs Come Networked Databases

Networked Databases in a Client/Server Setting

14.1 Introduction

Since the late 1970s, business applications have been increasingly hampered by the difficulties of deploying computers, communications, and software artifacts and by the lack of industry coordination in providing acceptable corporatewide database solutions for common user services. As we have seen in Part 2, these problems have raised user demands for the adoption of standards that can:

- Simplify applications deployment

- Bring discipline to information technology developments

- Assure a valid way of accessing remote databases

As a result of growing user demands, different approaches to database architecture are being developed by vendors to foster distributed business databasing, retrieval, processing, and control, while reducing the traditional burden of technical support at the file management side.

One of the drives in the development of efficient database management models aims at establishing criteria for access methods and the tools to use when retrieving and updating information repositories. At every stage of applications development, interactive users have different information requirements and need a model able to address developing professional perspectives.

Not only must databases be networked and accessed on line, but also appropriate sharing algorithms need to be established. The sharing of database resources must be achieved at two levels:

- A *lower level* where information is uniformly presented

- A *higher level* where user views can be employed interactively to build new models

Dynamic user views are usually complex and, up to a point, they are derived from lower-level views. In both cases, but particularly at the higher level, user views must be incrementally constructed and maintained in real time. Out-of-date views should be monitored automatically through *sunset clauses,* which indicate when stored information elements should be weeded out of the database.

As Fig. 14.1 suggests, in the distributed database environment, an information model can be of help in defining business views and their implementation. The key lies in a knowledge-assisted approach in storing and retrieving business data according to user requests in line with the existing database designs to meet the interactive challenges set out by the organization.

Knowledge of how the various information elements are used throughout the enterprise makes it possible to automatically prune the contents, weeding out unimportant elements through sunset clauses. Pruning does not necessarily mean throwing away. It may also mean dumping data in ternary storage, such as optical disks. This further increases the range of necessary cross-database access.

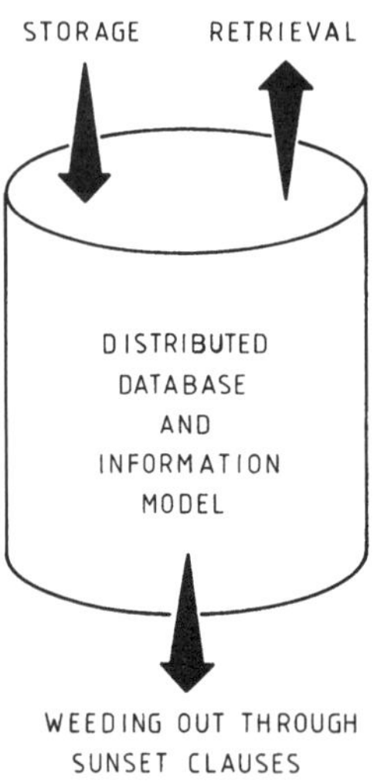

Figure 14.1 Sunset clauses should be used to automatically eliminate unimportant information elements.

14.2 Problems and Opportunities with Networked Databases

The need for file management has been understood since the beginning of industrial and business applications of computers. But it was not until the mid- to late 1960s that database management systems (DBMS) became commercially available, and with them the concept of a database was born.

Originally, databases were centralized and handled through mainframes. With the advent of minicomputers, databases became distributed and eventually networked by the late 1970s. The trend accelerated in the 1980s with the spread of:

- Workstations

- File servers

- Local area networks

Today, networked myriaprocessor configurations feature hundreds of intercommunicating databases. These constitute a distributed system consisting of hardware, software, and multimedia information elements (IEs).

The disk drives and their controllers are the hardware components; the database management system, data dictionary, and utilities constitute the basic software. Typically, the database network consists of a collection of cooperating but autonomous component databases which can be integrated to various degrees, although there are constraints on this process.

The software manipulating the component databases defines the degree of interconnection and integration which can be supported. This is just one example of an operation which needs to be consistent and normalized throughout the client/server model and its distributed databases.

Working at odds with the notion of distributed databases is the fact that the typical user organizations of the 1990s require multivendor information systems support. This brings up the important issue of *heterogeneity*.*

At the same time, user organizations need solutions with a much higher level of *functional integration* and *operational control* than has so far been made available to them by the different vendors. As corpo-

---

*Of course, heterogeneity in databases can exist even within the same vendor—for instance, having IMS, DB2, Adabas, Oracle, and Ingres DBMS under MVS, or having EBCDIC and ASCII data structures respectively on mainframes and workstations.

rations formulate plans for optimizing their use of information technology, a global reference model becomes necessary for organizing and managing corporate database resources.

Although the varied approaches used today appear to have similar architectural patterns to those followed in the past, they do in fact offer much greater scope and complexity. This is precisely what characterizes the new opportunities, as documented throughout Part 3.

Solutions for the 1990s must accommodate not only the current environment of multivendor database management systems but also future developments such as object-oriented databases, chosen to serve a growing range of business functions. Thus the need for successful approaches to architecting multivendor database systems becomes even more important.

The way information elements are structured and handled through a DBMS plays an important role in defining the architecture of an aggregate of networked databases:

- Each of the database components can participate in more than one federation of databases, as we will see in Chaps. 18 and 19.

- The term *federation* is used in a very broad sense, with degrees ranging from loose to tight coupling, according to the level permitted by the software supports.

Whether the coupling is tight or loose, the solution must be able to give unlimited on-line database access to all interconnected workstations and their applications. Interconnected devices must be able to store, retrieve, and update information concerning the applications they run.

The optimal solution will necessarily depend on many factors. Design criteria start with the answers to some basic queries: What business needs is the application addressing? How interactive are the workstations attached to the LAN? How should the application(s) address growing business requirements? How will database interactivity run across an enterprisewide model?

14.3 Bridging Database Requirements for a Variety of Users

Precisely because they are so flexible, client/server solutions need a representative information model, able to map ways and means for bridging database requirements among a variety of users. Able solutions must lead to valid specifications for answering the database requirement of the applications running on the network.

As we have seen throughout Parts 1 and 2, interactivity with database resources goes well beyond simple interconnection. It aims to:

- Allow the people who run the business to spend the least amount of time in technical tasks such as information retrieval

- Permit machines to access a growing range of incompatible, heterogeneous databases

- Generate accurate and powerful models that conform to the requirements of transactions and queries within the chosen architectural solution

Precisely for these reasons, one of the significant objectives of an integrative approach should be to enable component databases to continue their local operations while participating in the stated federation, or *multidatabase*. The integration of these components may be managed:

- Locally by the users, information technology scientists, and divisional database administrators (DBAs)

- Globally by the systems administrator in conjunction with the chief database architect

Generally, the amount of integration will depend on the architectural solution being adopted, the available software routines, the operating characteristics of the environment, and the needs of the federation users who have to share their databases.

The name of the game is finding an equilibrium of autonomy and communality in the databases participating in the system. The search for solutions is just as challenging when the databases reside in centralized sites as it is when there are multiple computer installations. In most cases, significant differences may exist in terms of:

- Hardware

- Systems software

- Data structures

- DBMS

- Communications protocols

Within an environment of distributed resources, the multidatabase will typically operate on multiple component units, each perhaps run under a different DBMS. Such a database system will be homogeneous only if the data structures and DBMS of all client/servers and other attached databases are the same. This is very rarely the case. More typically, the system will be heterogeneous.

To compound the problem, there are different levels of heterogeneity, each with its own drawbacks and opportunities. To face the former and exploit the latter, we must properly define applications, disciplines, and processes, which require global solutions in terms of planning, managing, and executing information services.

The evolution of a client/server structure should be based on the integration of systems management tasks reflecting a properly defined, open architecture. The strategy should be to evolve beyond the limits posed by current settings and introduce new functions for the management of database resources across heterogeneous environments. The proper systems view consists of:

- Defining current facilities and providing guidelines for a consistent user interface to the server databases

- Sustaining a flexible implementation environment for the development of advanced applications

- Supporting the multimedia needs of the users, workstations, number crunchers, and network(s)

Managing a client/server solution that is organized along these lines calls for effective interconnection of the database resources, continuous performance monitoring and tuning, capacity planning, and access control. All this requires systems management software as well as a methodology which enables users to gain interactive access to available information resources.

14.4   Data Modeling and Synchronization

Data modeling originated to meet the need for specifying structures in file systems. It was followed by the evolution of database management systems, leading to the introduction of the hierarchical and CODASYL (networking) models in the 1960s, the relational model in the 1970s, and object-oriented solutions in the late 1980s.

Hierarchical, CODASYL, and relational are today considered to be classical data models, each with strengths and limitations with regard to capturing, managing, and accessing information elements. Contrasted to these three alternatives is the emerging object-oriented database concept, which provides for superior performance, including modeling power.*

Emphasis on modeling power started with the relational approach which was proposed as a mathematical basis for the analysis of information elements. A basic aim was to provide data independence while addressing a variety of problems posed by database redundancy as well as estimating database structures in a more or less normalized way.

---

*See also D. N. Chorafas and H. Steinmann, *Object-Oriented Databases,* Prentice-Hall, Englewood Cliffs, NJ, 1993.

Subsequently, the object-oriented model made it possible to deal with inheritance, semantic values, integrity constraints, and the concept of layers and meta layers. This made feasible a more effective distribution and replication of rigorously specified information elements. The advantages of an object orientation are described in Sec. 14.7.

Of course, no data-modeling approach has a monopoly of advantages and/or of lower costs. A number of considerations are essential for comparison of DBMS facilities, such as:

1. Underlying theoretical concepts
2. Types of functional components
3. Assumed implementation areas
4. User interfaces
5. Applications interfaces
6. Levels of data abstraction
7. Supported modeling solutions
8. Record of object-level reference
9. Database system configuration
10. Issues related to transparency

While all database solutions and associated servers support simple integer and character data types, there are transparency problems with many of them, including challenges connected to varying character strings, date, time, decimal, and binary data.

The binary representations for different data types are often incompatible, not only for data-modeling reasons but also because of differences in the underlying hardware. Incompatibilities may also arise when software packages, in their minute details, differ from one release to another.

Any valid approach to data modeling should provide for a reasonable level of abstraction by hiding details of data storage not needed by certain users. The data model will be an incomplete tool if it does not do so. Abstraction is typically achieved through:

- Higher-level or conceptual models, as described in Sec. 14.9
- Object- or record-based implementation strategies
- Low-level physical mapping with emphasis on the actual physical file structure

Seen in this broader perspective, which spans four decades of evolving data-handling practices, the data model is an artifact that can be used to describe:

The structure of a database and its components

The *structure* of a database refers to the supported data types, relationships, semantic values, and constraints that help define the template of the distributed information resources.

The operations taking place on the distributed database

Operationally, the data model should assist in efficient storage, retrieval, and update, including insertions, deletions, and modifications. This is realized by modeling data into building blocks (or modeling constructs) through which the structure of a distributed database can be described.

The aim of this broader strategy of building blocks and their dynamic reshuffling is applications independence. Essentially, an *applications model* refers to the description of data for a specific applications concept.

In examining the applications environment as a whole and its component parts, we need to distinguish between the description of the database or *database schema* and the database itself. A database schema is:

- Designed for a given application or set of applications and users, achieved by analyzing their requirements

- Described through a data model that provides constructs in the form of language syntax or diagrammatic conventions

In some schemata, the data model is not explicitly defined but is implicitly present in given features. Whichever is the case, schemata usually remain relatively stable for most applications over the lifetime of a database.

Some evolution is possible, of course. During the process of database utilization, a schema may undergo transformation from one model to another. This, however, is a sound practice only when a strong theoretical foundation exists—for instance, relations based on set theory and first-order predicate calculus.

14.5 Logical Characteristics of Client/Server Databases

The client/server approach suggests that networked databases perform a growing range of functions. The overall structure can be seen as a multiuser system built from a set of discrete machines that are interconnected by a very high speed, highly reliable local area network.

With the introduction of servers featuring the ability to store gigabytes of data, the capacity of these LAN-based solutions exceeds that featured by most mainframes. Furthermore, the flexibility of such solutions helps put computing into the hands of end-user workgroups that can interoperate effectively even if the configuration is heterogeneous.

Each workgroup, and each individual end user, desires to exploit the best possible technology to solve ongoing and forthcoming problems. A number of requirements must be met in order to implement mission-critical applications. One is the proper understanding of the *logical* and *physical* characteristics of distributed databases.

Since companies confuse the logical and physical distribution of database resources, let us briefly review the fundamentals. In both a logical and physical sense, the original centralized database approach was designed for the relatively simple file management requirements that existed in the 1960s.

Today this classical model of file management is practical only with small databases. It simply does not fit current perspectives:

- The first implementation in a client/server sense has taken place, starting with a centralized logical concept on multiple physical devices.

- Multiprocessor architectures, which came alive in the early 1970s have been centralized, often with a unique logical internal schema—but such approaches did not prevail for long.

- User requirements led to the semidistributed databases referred to in Fig. 14.2*a*. Neither solution, however, lasted for a long time.

As mentioned in Sec. 14.2, even under the same operating system, there may be different logical schemata. For instance, under MVS may be DBMS as diverse as IMS, DB2, Adabas, Oracle, Ingres, and others. In fact, the diversity often leads to chaotic situations challenging database administrators and the company as a whole.

Misled by vendors, many DBAs believe that they have both physical concentration and logical homogeneity in their databases. This is not true at all. In reality, what they have is an uncontrollable heterogeneous database.

- Although irrational and fallacious, the concept embedded in this alternative prevails, creating the present unmanageable state of affairs.

- Figure 14.2*b* suggests that new solutions are needed—and this is where federated databases come into play.

The potential diversity between local and global databases calls attention to the crucial concept of *database views*. In database model-

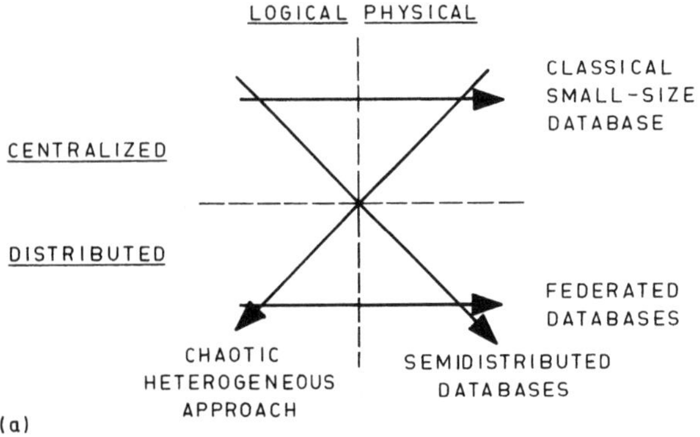

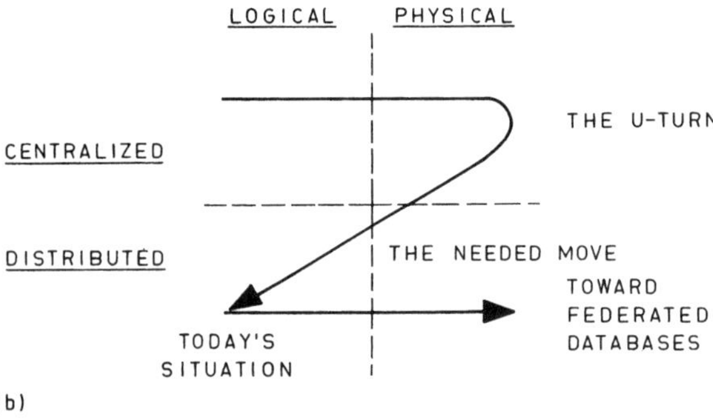

Figure 14.2 (*a*) Four alternatives in logical and physical database solutions. (*b*) The present chaotic situation and the next step.

ing, a view is a perceived model or mechanism by which a user and/or an application can:

- Record its specific requirements
- Define the explicit constraints

Most data models described in Sec. 14.4 provide a language to define an explicit requirement. One requirement, for example, is that in a distributed environment database views must be consistent. Achieving this goal requires logical synchronization of networked databases.

Synchronization mechanisms are indispensable to the proper operation of a database structure that is characterized by *locality*—hence, duplication of information elements—as is typically the case with client/server solutions. Synchronization approaches can be classified as pessimistic, optimistic, or hybrid and also as syntactic or semantic:

- Syntactic approaches concern the ordering of transactions.

- Semantic approaches relate to the type of information used in determining correctness of contents.

Synchronization mechanisms such as two-phase commit and time-stamp ordering can be considered *pessimistic* in their outlook. They synchronize operations of transactions first, then perform the tasks of the transactions.

In *optimistic* approaches, the task of the transaction is performed temporarily and then validated to see if a conflict has occurred. This, however, may lead to inconsistencies, particularly when implemented in very large databases.

Two-phase locking and timestamp ordering depend on the immediate validation of operations. They do not provide a facility to adjust serialization order dynamically to priority order.

- In optimistic concurrency control, the serializability test (validation test) is made only at the end of a transaction.

- In real-time transaction scheduling, an optimistic approach is expected to perform better than two-phase locking or timestamp ordering—with the risks mentioned above.

Another logical modeling issue that becomes important as the database environment gets more sophisticated is navigation among distributed information elements. A complex query or long transaction is a unit of activity that:

- Includes a significant number of retrieval operations

- Can be broken down into smaller units, with each one possibly addressing a different database

As far as the user is concerned, navigation through the networked databases must be easy and straightforward. Insulation from the mechanics of implementation issues is one of the major advantages of semantic data models over more traditional approaches, as we will see below.

14.6 Local Autonomy and Globality in Database Usage

As explained in Sec. 14.2, the federated database approach rests on the premise that the system as a whole is both logically and physically distributed. This can happen when:

- The attached file servers operate peer-to-peer

- There is no central authority commanding all servers in both a global and a local sense

One of the advantages of this approach is that it makes us lose our illusions about how databases should be managed. If we *really* appreciate that our database environment is bound to be heterogeneous, with no constraints from a central authority, we will see to it that the mechanisms provided for the federated architecture balance—by themselves—all conflicting requirements. Two of these conflicting requirements are outstanding.

- The component parts must maintain as much autonomy as possible, to serve local operations.

- At the same time, a good degree of resource sharing, in a global sense, must be achieved.

The requirement of *autonomy* encompasses at least four crucial factors. First and foremost is the fact that centralized authority is replaced by cooperative but coordinated activity among databases and supporting protocols. Thus, *federated* databases are in no way the same as *decentralized* ones.

- A decentralized approach remains focused on the center, which delegates to the periphery some of its responsibilities but retains ultimate control.

- A federated scheme is characterized by inverse delegation. The autonomous units in the periphery accept a coordinator function while retaining most of their independence.

A second crucial factor in supporting local autonomy while submitting to globality constraints is that each component database determines the IE that it wishes to share with the others in the network. This is important inasmuch as controlled sharing is a basic goal of the federated approach. Each participating database must be able to:

- Specify the information elements to be made available globally

- Define which other components may access global elements and in what ways

- Manage its import and export facilities (as described in Chap. 18)

A third factor is that each database in the global setting must determine how it will view and combine existing information elements. In a federated system, all access to the underlying IEs is mediated by a networkwide schema. At the same time—and this is the fourth crucial factor—a local database must have freedom of association with respect to the federation.

- Since the network is a dynamic entity, component databases must be able to enter or leave the federation.

- Each database must be in a position to modify its shared data interface, adding new IEs and withdrawing access to previously shared objects.

As a counterpoint to the features required to support component autonomy, the federated architecture must also provide mechanisms for object sharing through appropriate software modules. Among other facilities, this will require the services of a data dictionary.

As these examples of federated solutions help document, client/server computing offers many options in placing or distributing information elements. However, practical guidelines are needed on what to consider before these resources are placed. Rules must be concerned with the business requirements that are associated with the IE, including:

- Service level
- Response time
- Availability
- Performance
- Auditability
- Security
- Backup
- Recovery capabilities

The location of the data is evidently a concern, since the operational requirements have to be met not just once but steadily. In addition, a methodology is needed to produce a data model that will lead to a valid as well as dynamic database design.

The requirements posed by a dynamic methodology bring into perspective the role to be played by artificial intelligence. As we will see in Sec. 14.8, a knowledge engineering solution helps provide reasoning mechanisms, combining schemata with the flexibility for representing exceptions. Typically, it will also allow for *metalevels*—for instance, permitting a class to be an instance of another class in a superclass/subclass relationship.

In any federated database solution, identification is necessary to distinguish objects and classes—and to relate them to the real world that they represent. Identification is assisted by the expert system's knowledge bank, containing facts and rules, as well as by a set of strategies and guidelines for managing the knowledge bank.

Knowledge engineering can also provide agile human windows, with user-friendly external interfaces by which the user interacts with the system. This not only assists in user-machine communications but also helps to upgrade older applications, thus extending their life cycle.

14.7 Knowledge Modeling and Database Design

People and companies with experience in modern information technology appreciate that in a distributed, heterogeneous environment, data modeling and database design are neither simple nor straightforward. Hence, we should proceed with care and use the best available tools. Several preliminary concepts are described here. Chapter 19 offers an in-depth discussion of the role of knowledge engineering in database management.

A practical method of distributing the information elements is needed, so that business requirements are met in a way that is not only satisfactory to business units, end users, and processes, but also technically sound.

Data distribution and consolidation criteria have to be examined for applicability. Most likely, these criteria will include the following elements, which may vary depending on unique business requirements and technical factors:

1. *One entry,* many uses of information elements (IEs), which should be captured at point of origin

2. *Remote access* to the distributed resources and also consolidation of databases

3. *Partitioning* of the IEs to distribute and apportion prime data so that it can be made useful to all sets of users

4. *Level of sharing* among on-line users, versus keeping the majority of the IEs unshared

5. *Currency* of the IEs and whether they are being updated in real time or copied at a point in time

6. *Volatility* of the IEs in relation to how often they are updated

One entry, remote access, and partitioning should be studied closely together. If the distribution method chosen is copying the data, it is useful to categorize the data into master copy and business copy.

The *master copy* includes prime data and contains the most current committed instance of each entity. The *business copy* refers to point-in-time copies of the prime data, which form a stable base for query

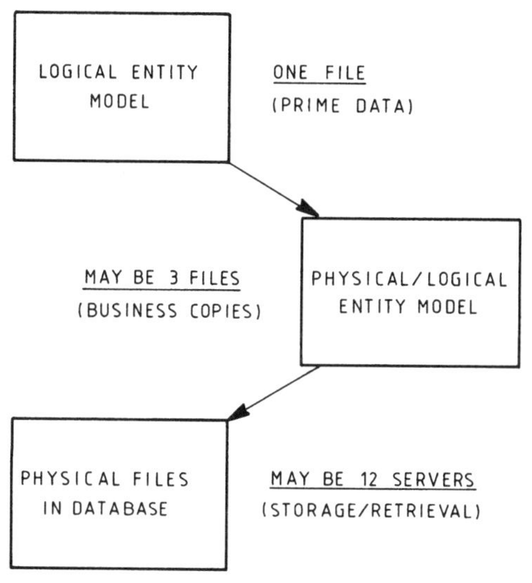

Figure 14.3 The performance of client/server solutions must be evaluated at three levels.

and decision support—but which should always present a *consistent* image to the prime or master copy.

Although these elements may suggest a discrete organization, they are actually indivisible from the physical and logical characteristics of the database. For instance, the plurality of distributed copies can be expressed in a schema similar to the one shown in Fig. 14.3. The same is true of the distribution of servers.

Such a schema reinforces the need for newer modeling concepts to meet the emergence of database applications that are too complex to be handled effectively by traditional methods. Examples of such applications include databases used for:

- Computer-aided design (CAD)
- Computer-aided manufacturing (CAM)
- Trading in foreign exchanges, options, derivatives, and securities
- Imaging and graphics
- Multimedia applications
- Computer-aided software engineering (CASE)
- Knowledge banks for artificial intelligence (AI)

This list goes on. For every item included in it, both knowledge engineering artifacts and semantic data models can help in addressing the requirements embedded in the particular application. Solutions must go far enough in expressiveness, have an inferencing capability, and be able to model behavior.

Knowledge-based and object-oriented systems can be very helpful in this connection. In general, organizations will be better equipped in dealing with such an environment if their client/server-oriented studies focus, at the outset, on basic supports provided by AI and the associated methodology.

Inference capabilities can be instrumental in elaborating the scope of the distributed environment and the way to handle its prerequisites. Following any grand design comes the need to concentrate on detail, but without proper definition of the overall objective, efficient results cannot possibly be obtained.

Knowledge artifacts also offer a focus on the functions to be provided. Distributed networked databases, for example, have four key characteristics.

1. *Multimedia communications requirements.* Each component database has a collection of objects, and other on-line databases as well as workstations may be interested in accessing some portion of the IEs. Exchanging consistent IEs is a primary activity in a federated setting—hence, the need for intelligence-enriched mechanisms to support real-time sharing.

2. *Knowledge management requirements.* Distributed database contents may be extensional (events, data) and intentional (rules, commands). The intentional layer covering the global database has to be properly elaborated. A clean job will require a significant amount of knowledge engineering, which underpins the intentional level.*

3. *Proper DBMS and data structure identification for each attached server.* Since the distributed database environment will have significant heterogeneity, a good description must be given of the different DBMS employed by locality. Identification should include their features as well as the data structures of their contents.

4. *Long transaction handling and sharing of IEs.* One or more of the local databases on the network may wish not to share its IEs directly, but rather to share operations upon them. This may be the case if the information is sensitive or has consistency constraints. Hence component clients and servers must be able to define transactions that can be invoked by other component databases as well to establish authentication/authorization requirements. This, too, requires knowledge engineering support.

---

*See also D. N. Chorafas, *Intelligent Multimedia Databases,* Prentice-Hall, Englewood Cliffs, NJ, 1994.

Furthermore, proper documentation, rich utilities, and automatic help services should be available on a networkwide basis. The core of the same support services should be available to all databases attached to the network, though add-on features may be also necessary by locality or region to answer local, parochial requirements.

In all these cases, the able use of knowledge engineering can assist in accurately modeling the environment by storing, manipulating, and using knowledge to:

- Draw inferences

- Make decisions

- Answer complete queries

Like semantic modeling, knowledge engineering uses an abstraction mechanism while providing for constraints and rules on operations. The scope of database utilization can be enriched by means of rules, the handling of incomplete and default knowledge, and temporal as well as spatial semantics.

14.8 Object Orientation with Networked Databases

Object-oriented and knowledge-based technologies play a key role not only in modern software development but also in the use of computer and communications systems—most particularly, networked databases. *Metamethodology* is becoming a key word in this domain, helping in the provision of a process management framework. (See also the discussion on semantics, which underpins object orientation, in Chap. 15.)

New tools are necessary to deliver efficient solutions, but technology alone is not going to produce the desired results. Equally important is a concept which helps us visualize how an effective cross-database connectivity can be assured. Further, remote database processing requires an appropriate architecture to define:

- Specific information flows

- Feasible interactions among resources

A valid solution should convey the intent and results of remote DBMS handling requests—a domain where knowledge engineering can contribute a great deal. It will also assure the connection between applications processes and database elements. Here, object-oriented approaches can be instrumental.

To accomplish this dual aim, the strategy should be able to describe the information flows that exist among participants in a distributed database environment. It should also define the responsibilities of such participants and specify when global interactivity could or should occur.

Connectivity goals include functionality, performance, integrity, and security, along with high-performance availability and network-wide recovery capability. An able solution will encompass the whole distribution of information elements, maintaining user protection and accessibility without undue complexity.

As we have seen in Chap. 13, *trusted systems* deliver their services by assuring a notary public type of function, where special software is able to guarantee both process dependability and security. This is written in the understanding that networkwide database interactions create many technical issues:

- How can the shared resources be reliably manipulated by concurrent cooperative processes?

- How do we define the attainment of a cooperative objective? How do we determine that it has taken place?

- How is a task informed about changes to an objective by other tasks? About changes to the environment?

- What is the criterion for controlling interactions among multiple cooperative tasks toward achieving an objective?

- How does a task observe what the reactions of other tasks are, after it modifies the cooperative objective or media types?

Visualization is a growing need in networked database environments, particularly for interactively steering applications and for facilitating collaboration among remote sites. These goals can be assisted through an object-oriented methodology and the use of knowledge engineering for distributed database coupling, as well as through fast file processing.

Figure 14.4 presents the interface between client and server which, in the case of distributed databases, should be extended in a global sense. In such a networked environment, the programmatic interface should enable client applications—written in any language that can be linked with, say, C, C++, Cobol, Fortran, or Pascal—to interoperate with the distributed databases.

Programming language statements should be passed as parameters and should not require preprocessors. This holds as much for the graphics browser as for any other interactive program. For instance, with Hewlett-Packard's object-oriented approach, OpenODB, the object manager, executes OSQL (Object SQL) calls made by the OpenODB clients.

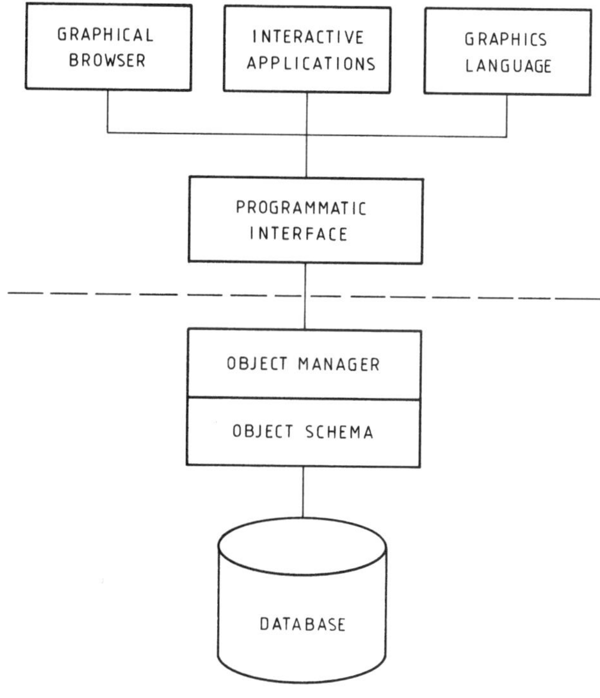

Figure 14.4   Procedural client/server interconnection in an operating environment.

- The object manager processes requests and accesses data and code from the internal data storage manager (relational storage manager) or passes the request to a subsystem outside OpenODB.

- The relational database performs the physical file management and database functions, such as multiuser concurrency, transaction management, on-line backup, and recovery.

In the case of OpenODB, which has knowledge of the relationships among objects, referential integrity can be maintained. For instance, if objects referenced by other objects are deleted, the system removes all dependencies. The user can specify whether to cascade changes or just to delete the immediate dependency.

The system should serve not only lower-level mechanics but higher-level business modeling as well. Facilitating tools such as those provided by OpenODB permit direct and effective modeling of business information. For instance:

- Each object stored in OpenODB has a system-provided, unique handler called an object identifier (OID).

- OIDs reduce duplication of information and relieve the developer from creating different keys to identify stored information in the database.

- Complex objects can be constructed from simpler objects, automating the management of relationships among simple objects.

In a typical object-oriented system, functions defined on a type can be inherited by one or more subtypes, rather than having to be redefined. Thus, it becomes relatively easy to extend the functionality of an application.

Just as important is the concept of overloaded functions. Multiple functions can have the same name with different implementations. The object-oriented DBMS will determine which code to execute, based on the parameter passed at run time.

As these examples help document, object-oriented approaches simplify the applications code, since the logic of determining which function to execute resides with the system. These solutions have not yet revolutionized programming and database management, but the evolutionary steps they incorporate are critical. The wise user organization will capitalize on them.

14.9 Macroscopic and Microscopic Approaches to Database Design

As we have seen, forward-looking organizations need modern and powerful tools in order to capitalize on technological advances. The same is true of the methodology that they adopt and employ in their daily work.

In an object-oriented inheritance model, for example, the qualities and characteristics of an upper layer are inherited by those below it. This is in conformance with applications practice in which *microscopic* decisions are typically made under the light of *macroscopic* ones, as the network in Fig. 14.5 suggests.

There are many merits in distinguishing between macroscopic and microscopic decisions. The former are of utmost importance, since they affect the work done at the lower levels. This is exemplified by the two-level schema in Fig. 14.5.

The macroscopic world presents an integrative view to be supported through heuristics, fuzzy reasoning, and intelligent control of unstable systems, as well as through image understanding and pattern recognition.

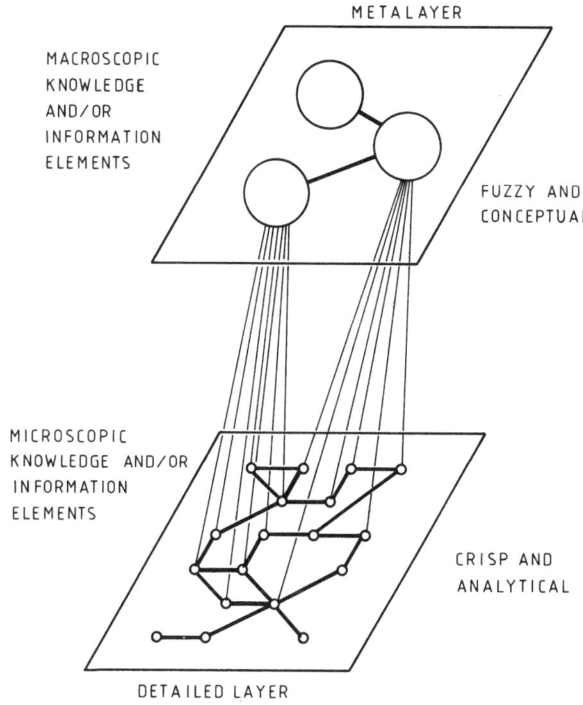

Figure 14.5 Perspectives in macroscopic and microscopic knowledge.

- When macroscopic solutions are properly approached, a valid framework is established for further usage.

- When macroscopic decisions are misguided, the microscopic views too will be misdirected—though they may be quite precise.

Generally, the coarser the grain of the microscopic design, the greater the lead time to implementation, the higher the cost, and the lower the quality of the resulting product. At the same time, with backward technology and without the needed on-line controls, it is very difficult if not outright impossible to assure that data processing does not get off the mainstream of user requirements.

Employed as a consistent methodology, a macroscopic approach facilitates both proper *systems planning* and *feedback control*. It helps in both directions because it constitutes a framework against which to gauge a finer-grain microscopic approach.

The macroscopic view is particularly important with nontraditional database applications like CAD, computer integrated manufacturing (CIM), treasury/forex, securities trading, and CASE (see Sec. 14.7).

The level of embedding in a macroscopic approach goes beyond the usual DBMS capabilities to support:

- Permanence of data
- Controlled sharing
- On-line backup
- Data-modeling constructs
- Support for inference
- Novel and extensible data structures

Examples are graphic images, voice, text, vectors and matrices, and versioning. The macroscopic view may, for instance, consist of a complex query and its processor as characterized in a long transaction. Or it may be a storage subsystem with interactive interfaces for complex queries.

Starting at the macroscopic level, the query processor will translate its component parts and associated operations into an internal relational algebra format. The latter is then interpreted against the information elements stored in distributed databases at the microscopic level.

This concept can be extended, for example, to include support for multimedia objects and/or to make visualization artifacts accessible from a number of programming languages through appropriate interfaces. The approach conforms fairly well to directives by the DB Systems Study Group (DBSG) of the American National Standards Institute (ANSI).

DBSG advises that the optimal way to focus on database technology is to start with the fundamentals and proceed to database management all the way up to the levels of security and protection. It also advises moving out of record-oriented approaches toward:

- Visualization
- Multimedia (text, data, graphics, voice, image)
- Object orientation
- New forms of storing and retrieving information

Both approaches are recommended in order to accommodate the developing requirements in database usage across an expanding topology, including increasingly ad hoc query requirements and the handling of long transactions. At the same time, it is wise to avoid coarse-grained approaches at the microscopic level—for reasons explained earlier in this section. The macroscopic view provides both insight and guidance by making feasible more accurate conceptualization as well as proper study and experimentation.

Apart from other benefits, this dual approach (through macroscopic and microscopic considerations) fosters optimal implementation of database resources. Optimization, however, has three prerequisites:

- How the data is structured

- How the database is partitioned

- What the hit rate is

One specific application environment, a network of 20 servers permitted 1,200 transactions per second because everything was done in parallel. It also assured that over the longer run critical success factors were reviewed and updated without upsetting the current structure. This is a vital contribution as:

- Technology steadily progresses

- Products and processes evolve

- The database structure evolves

- The organization changes

Here lies the wisdom of (1) reaching solutions which permit quick visualization at the macroscopic level and (2) using heuristics rather than procedural algorithmic approaches. Applied at the conceptual level, heuristics permit a flexible, imaginative response instead of a cookbook approach.

The macroscopic view is dominated by broad concepts. By contrast, at the lower, microlevel, detailed relationships can be defined among object types. This duality makes it possible to map the entity relationships of a conceptual data model explicitly.

- Starting at the macroscopic level, which supports the independent definition of structural information elements

- Progressing toward the lower level of derived object types, which interoperate but also permit analysis of aggregate objects already defined at the macrolevel

In this interplay between macrolevel and microlevel data properties are functions representing primary relationships, but there are also entity relationships which provide a shorthand mechanism for defining a collection of functions within the same domain. Macrolevel entities have relationships based on defined structural objects, a notion that goes beyond the simple attributes that single-level approaches typically support.

What Characterizes a Distributed Database?

15.1 Introduction

There is a growing acceptance of the need for architectural solutions to database organization and control. At the same time, improved technology has become available at the logical, physical, and user levels, as a growing market for database management systems has spurred research and development to provide increasingly better software support.

The vital impetus behind these developments is *interactivity*. User-information communications systems first came on line, with query and real-time update capabilities, in the mid- to late 1960s. Over the next quarter century they became distributed, polyvalent, and more user friendly, affecting both the logical and physical storage structures.

The macroscopic and microscopic approaches examined in Chap. 14 are held together by semantics, which play a key role in a distributed database structure. As suggested in Fig. 15.1, they affect architectural approaches at three levels:

- Systems concept

- User orientation

- Language and grammar

The systems concept defined through a macroscopic approach and mapped into a microscopic framework is that of a distributed database. It addresses applications perspectives, metaphors the computer can understand, supported internal schemata, and physical implementation.

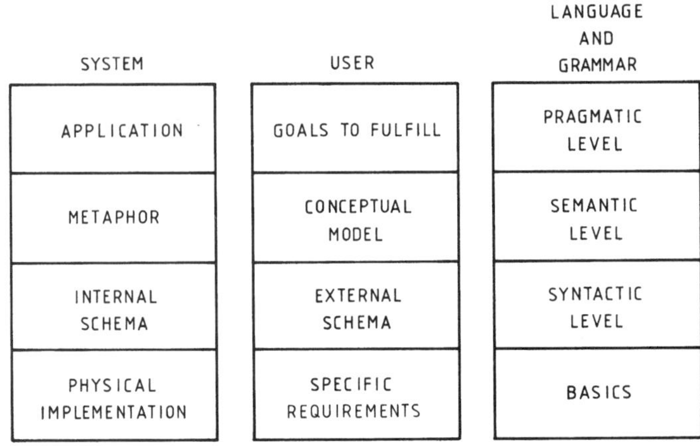

Figure 15.1   System, user, and language perspectives in a distributed database structure.

The systems user has goals to fulfill as well as a conceptual model which translates into an external schema. In terms of database interactivity, the user has specific requirements which need to be fulfilled. Language and grammar should start at the pragmatic level, focus on semantics, and include syntax as well as signs and rules.

An effective distributed database solution must integrate all the elements just discussed. It should reflect on applications issues using an appropriate applications program interface (API) for communicating across the network.

Through API, the systems solution provides a connection—more precisely, a thread—to the DBMS. The system processes the request for the applications program, passing the retrieved information elements and returning the codes back to the program.

In a distributed environment many language statements may be processed this way, ending when a request to commit the transaction (or to roll it back) is processed. The commit and rollback requests are triggered in different ways, specific to the DBMS products which enter into the operation. A client/server management function is responsible for coordinating this work with the transaction or query being executed.

In a client/server setting, distributed database operations will typically involve two or more DBMS interconnected to provide database services to applications programs. These may be homogeneous or heterogeneous—that is, the same or different products—as we have seen in Chap. 14.

Whether the DBMS are homogeneous or heterogeneous, any viable solution must be seamless to the user. (This issue is examined in more detail in Chaps. 18 and 19, on federated databases.)

15.2 Providing Multiple Access to Distributed Databases

In a client/server model, which provides multiple access to distributed databases, the supported integrity constraints must be independent of applications running on the system. This is necessary with centralized processing as well, but distributed databases tend to magnify the problem because of multicopy update requirements—as contrasted to keeping a single copy of information elements.

- Superficially, a single copy eliminates the redundancy and possible inconsistency of multiple files.

- Less visible is the fact that it also constrains database utilization to a small group of people and processes.

- Such a constraint tends to limit the usefulness of the system, significantly reducing the implementation horizon.

The distributed nature of databases in a client/server structure is fundamental to on-line interactive transaction processing. The same is true of ad hoc query applications as well as of the demand for:

- Higher performance
- Greater systems availability
- User-friendly interfaces

With the advent of workstations and local area networks, the trend toward distributed systems since the early 1980s has led to the concept of managing remote databases, thus adding new demands to age-old issues of data integrity, recovery, security, and privacy.

A duality of functions should attract great attention in any systems design. Modern, complex applications rest on data sharing among different programs. At the same time, data sharing among programs has been the first and most obvious requirement of a client/server architecture. Sharing implies:

- A reasonable degree of data independence applied in a network-wide sense, with or without the existence of backup servers

- The use of a data directory, which carries information about information elements in the database, but also proprietary characteristics such as locality and privacy

- The simultaneous handling of local and global database requirements in a way which assures data independence in a networkwide
  sense.

The objective of data independence is to insulate applications programs from the underlying database management technology, and
vice versa. It has been recognized since the 1970s that the way information elements are stored and accessed internally in a given
machine or machines—as well as the way files are restructured—
should be transparent to the user.

Data independence facilitates sharing by allowing the same information element to appear *as if* organized differently for different
applications programs, with the system performing the necessary
conversions. Resource sharing, data independence, efficiency, and
other prerequisites suggest a role that dedicated database computers
can offer within a given operating environment.

Storage hierarchies depend on the overall concept, the logical
media available, the storage access patterns, and program behavior
in run-time environments. Database design involves tradeoffs, capitalizing on the proper characteristics of distributed storage spaces,
including such parameters as:

- Access time

- Cost

- Capacity

Downsizing from mainframes to client/server solutions can follow
different paths. Figure 15.2 shows two alternatives that were first
benchmarked and then implemented in different parts of the same
business.

Alternative 1 followed a smoother transition by avoiding extensive
rewriting on code, mainly depending on the total translation of the
database into a server environment. This exercise involved only a
minor code conversion. As Fig. 15.2 indicates, over a timetable which
spans four quarters, databasing costs were cut in half. Still greater
savings are in store with the conversion of the files remaining in the
old database structure.

Alternative 2 was a more radical solution which permitted rapid
downsizing but also involved a significant amount of code conversion.
The database cost dropped dramatically to about 20 percent of mainframe costs. By the end of the third quarter the cost rebounded, but it
was finally brought under control.

In addition to the downsizing strategy which they share, the two
alternatives depend on a sustainable distributed database architec-

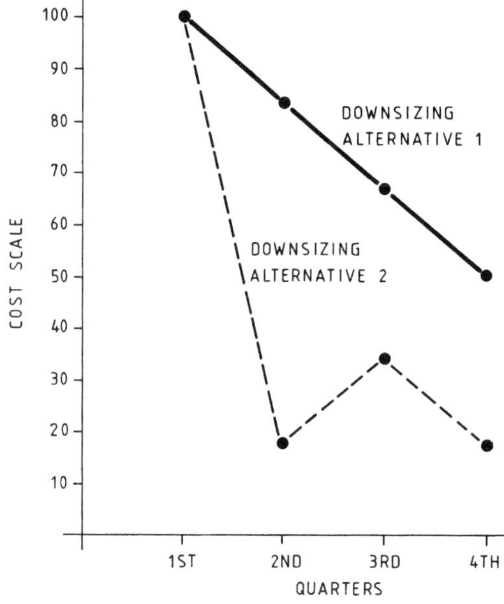

Figure 15.2 An object-oriented approach to exploiting the semantics of applications and information elements.

ture. In both cases this evolved over time, to permit maintenance of unification and simplification procedures used for database access and overall management. The lesson learned is that a networkwide database architecture must make it possible to:

- Establish efficient translation of data definition and data manipulation statements from one data model to another

- Demonstrate which features in the different available approaches are equivalent to each other

- Build a cost/benefit comparison into the different feasible alternatives prior to committing the company to one of them

A well-studied approach results in data models that are both better suited to the user organization and simpler to understand and implement. The choice of the proper networkwide retrieval scheme is the next basic requirement to be fulfilled in a multimedia sense.

Today multiple access to distributed databases has come to mean more than data, as the desired solutions move toward a multimedia orientation. In the past, large-scale computer-based text retrieval systems were inhibited by three factors:

- The cost of the tens or hundreds of gigabytes needed for comprehensive on-line text storage

- The not-so-effective data compression algorithms for compound electronic documents, including images and signatures

- The cost of entering and reentering text, data, and other information elements into the machine

Advances in memory technology, particularly optical disks and high-density disks, answer the first two challenges. Data transmission, facsimile, electronic publishing, and voice input alter the formerly restricted data collection considerations. But the data entry problem is not necessarily on its way to solution.

Data entry has long been a troublespot in information technology, and multimedia approaches promise little change. The problem is organizational rather than technical, and it is particularly pervasive with centralized operations, since few computer centers observe the sound principle, "One entry, many uses of information" of which we spoke in Chapter 14.

15.3 Semantics and Database Calls

Properly architectured client/server solutions can help in solving the reentry problem by following the principle that data and other information elements should enter into the system at point of origin. But the development of a valid distributed database architecture poses other challenges, such as:

- Identifying current and projected organizational needs in terms of distributed database requirements

- Reviewing and revamping existing data-processing perspectives to gain maximum advantage of client/server implementation

- Integrating the database organization, data communications, processing operations, and end-user presentation into a comprehensive system

Rather than force the different applications to coordinate a collection of distributed storage devices with separate files, the global database and its local entities should be managed as *a single logical structure.*

A concurrent system should be established and maintained. Existing applications should find their information elements to be completely compatible with the new local-and-global concept, with no changes required to exploit concurrency. Compatibility can be significantly assisted through semantic models.

As indicated in Sec. 15.1, the ability to exploit database semantics is of critical importance to the development of valid client/server solutions. This is true for simple passthrough applications as well as for federated databases.

Semantics signifies meaning, especially meaning in languages. Semantics is concerned with the nature, structure, development, and alteration of the meaning of forms. It is also the scientific study of the relation between signs and symbols and what they mean or denote.

Semantics plays a major role in our lives and in our businesses. Many of the things we do are full of semantic significance. Therefore, semantic modeling and associated notions have become important forces in the development of DBMS and of knowledge bank management systems (KBMS).

Semantic data models can assure more flexible data structures. Embedded into an object orientation, semantic notions:

- Help provide better logical facilities for storage and retrieval

- Assist in the automation of cross-database interactivity

- Assure a more effective concurrency control

With distributed database structures in particular, it is necessary to specify the semantics of both individual and collective resources. Each resource can be viewed as a set of objects, along with:

- The services necessary for its manipulation

- The rules for its use within the organization

As detailed in Chap. 14, objects can be concepts, models, IEs, applications programs, integrity constraints, and so on. The semantics of a resource reflects on the conceptual representation of objects, including their definitions, values, and the rules that operate on the entities whose meaning we handle.

Correspondingly, the semantics of software is expressed in terms of supported services: data model, language, and transaction model. Also to be accounted for is the semantics of the organization that owns the resource. This includes the rules defined by the organization and governing database usage.

Figure 15.3 suggests how this approach would work in an object-oriented environment that is rich in meaning. Three networked devices are shown:

- Workstation

- Number-crunching server

- Database server

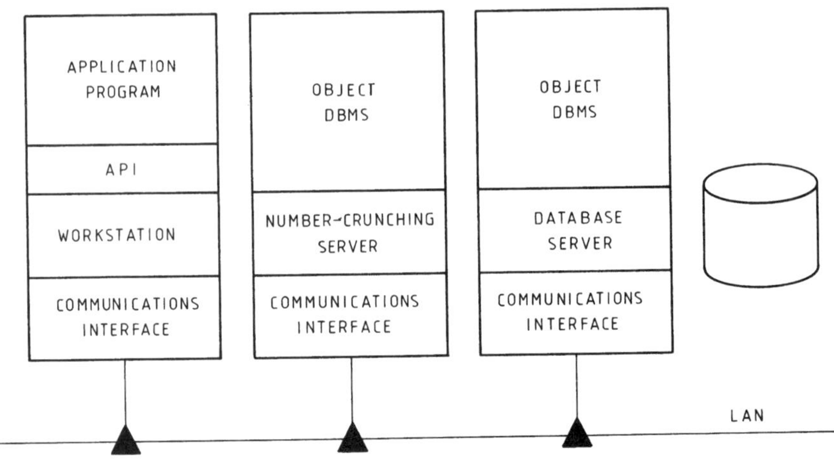

Figure 15.3 Getting out of mainframes and into client/server solutions. Note the difference in cost scale.

Software methods must respond to the level of cross-database access that is being implemented. In the case of the simple passthrough with drivers, the application can choose to use the different *optional calls* corresponding to each of the local DBMS capabilities reported by each specific driver. This permits an application to:

- Read information elements from all databases in the network

- Selectively demand more of those data sources capable of handling advanced requests

This is one of the better ways of tapping the power of full-function relational database servers. By contrast, nonrelational systems, even simple file access methods, can participate as data sources at a relatively low implementation functionality but also at lower cost.

This two-tier approach to the access of distributed heterogeneous databases presents competitive advantages. Equally important is the fact that the software needed for support reasons is ready and in operation through object DBMS—hence, it can be tested and benchmarked. Commodity object DBMS are a good short-term solution, particularly for:

- Analytical queries

- Management reporting

- Modeling

However, they are not necessarily a fool-proof approach toward heavy-duty transaction management. Distributed transaction handling requires tightly coupled solutions, and this is a demanding undertaking.*

Tight coupling in a distributed database environment is a complex and lengthy process that has been attempted in a number of cases with very limited success. Therefore, rigorous fundamental projects have started by setting software standards at the operating system level prior to addressing database management.

In conclusion, a distinction should always be made between short-term solutions, which we accept with some compromises, and long-term solutions, which have to be nearly perfect. The compromises to be made are not random. They require sound tradeoffs among cost, effectiveness, and the timetable of deliverables.

15.4   Top-Down or Bottom-Up End-User Service?

Accessing data from multiple sources, performing relational joins, creating and deleting external database tables, and modifying and inserting records in distributed databases are functions increasingly in demand in both business and scientific environments. The same is true of a number of other functions, such as:

- Automatically updating information elements at user-set time intervals

- Listing tables in an external database, or fields in an external table, in a consistent manner despite database heterogeneity

- Processing requests regarding IEs stored at a variety of external sources, many of which have locality and escape global control

The kind of multifunctional access that is usually sought must be assured not only for different relational DBMS but also for hierarchical code, Codasyl approaches (networking, owner/member), and inverted files—all the way to flat files and VSAM files.

Included in the class of basics is the ability to open and close database tables, browse through a table, and execute a simple query involving selection criteria. Also basic is the facility to fetch data, provide information about a function call that failed, and execute a command in the native language of the database.

Connectivity should be independent of the type of linkage being established, reflecting as a minimum the common denominator. The

---

*See also the discussion of the Multivendor Integration Architecture (MIA) by NTT in D. N. Chorafas and H. Steinmann, *Solutions for Networked Databases,* Academic Press, San Diego, CA, 1993.

latter constitutes the basic capabilities featured by all networked file management solutions that allow the application to connect to a driver, a server, and a database managed by the server. Beyond this common ground are basic functions determining the more advanced characteristics of the database being accessed. For instance:

- Supported knowledge engineering capabilities

- Programs helping in the conversion of data types and character sets

- Different ways of presenting and differentiating tables and fields in the database

Both basic and advanced features can be instrumental in assisting passthrough software developed for accessing a heterogeneous database environment. This is the practical strategy followed by all commodity offerings—from DataLens and Q + E on workstations to EDA/SQL on mainframes.

When the decision is made to use—at least over the short range—a simple passthrough software, attention should be paid to the version being chosen, since a specific release of commodity software can affect overall performance. Drivers must be dynamically linked in memory to host application(s) so that networked devices communicate at fast calling speeds, within all given constraints.

As noted at the outset of this chapter, a properly integrated client/server architecture must support a seamless logical view of networked databases. However, both integration and manipulation pose problems, given the incompatibilities arising from different data structures and heterogeneous DBMS. There are two approaches to the provision of an integrative solution: top-down and bottom-up. (These approaches are discussed in connection with database integration in Sec. 15.8.)

1. In a *top-down* approach, the conceptual designer decides on the redistribution of information elements and the partition of competences among local database units.

2. In a *bottom-up* approach, the main goal is to assure necessary linkages, so that the different databases can operate locally while supporting interoperability.

Quite often, top-down approaches seek to apply a partitioning scheme—based on languages that employ semantic variables and new classes of multiple identifiers—that allows the logical locations of the data to be quite different from the existing physical locations.

One alternative that has been tested but has not yet proved particularly successful is that of a superschema. According to this approach, distributed database integration can be viewed as an extension of schema integration. Serious flaws arise, however, because of conflicts among the concepts behind the local schemata.

To provide an effective solution it is necessary to resolve not only schema conflicts but also those existing between *data types* and *data formats* in the different local databases. It is also necessary to make a number of changes to render local conditions compatible with those of a more global architecture. This is not always feasible in a systems sense.

Bottom-up solutions can be simpler. What's more, they can effectively use a stream of products brought to the market by software vendors. Many among them have a general philosophy in common, as shown in Fig. 15.4.

Horizontal software for manipulating information elements (such as spreadsheets and report generators) and commands embedded in higher-level programming languages provide power and convenience. But they also need more flexible approaches to database access than ever before.

Spreadsheet users are often unable to manipulate data resident on servers, minis, and mainframes without having to go through a tedious data extraction step. In response to this need, Microsoft, Lotus Development, and other software vendors have brought to the market packages with versatile data access capabilities that any user organization would be well advised to text.

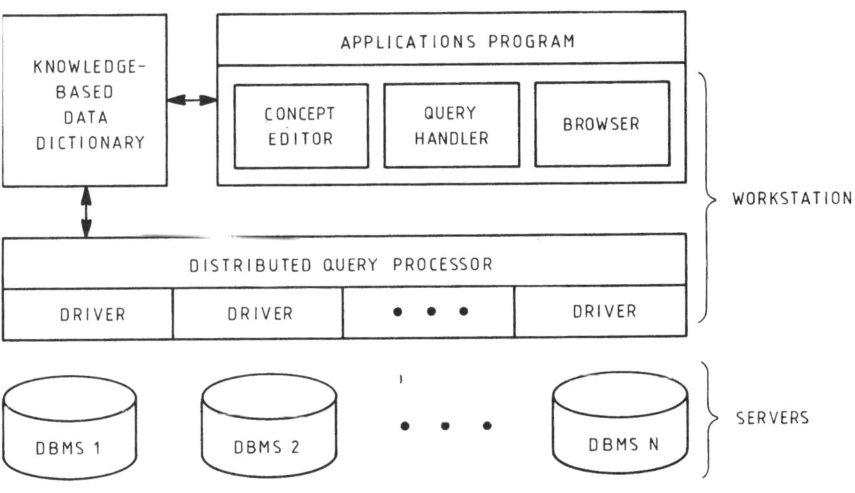

Figure 15.4   Real-time distributed access to different database servers.

15.5 Commodity Software for Cross-Database Access

Among other software vendors, Lotus Development has responded to the needs of sophisticated customers with the introduction of a product to pass real-time data directly into the 1-2-3 spreadsheet. Lotus Realtime sits between 1-2-3 and the communications drivers that gather data in the real-time feeds of financial information providers. The vendor describes this piece of software as an intelligent engine that can:

- Select and hold information from different information feeds

- Push it through to the spreadsheet at the appropriate time for further processing

For instance, securities traders can tell this engine which bonds, stocks, or other items they are interested in and which related information they want—such as opening, midday, and closing prices. The Lotus Realtime engine will hold this information in cache until required by the spreadsheet. The cache is constantly updated. Hence, when the spreadsheet starts calculating, it is provided with the latest information.

Other advances are more closely related to the integrated software running on the workstation—as is the case with Lotus Improv, the spreadsheet for the NeXT computer. It allows users to view information dynamically by means of plain English formulas instead of numerical syntax and to address multimedia databases.

In late 1990, Improv introduced a new spreadsheet feature, the DynaView, which allows users to view and compare data quickly without manually rebuilding the spreadsheet. Information elements can be viewed or arranged to:

- Compare data relationships

- Provide summaries which can be expanded to show detail

- Manipulate the display of the worksheet to reflect a new arrangement

Typical Improv applications include corporate financial planning, merger and acquisition analysis, market analysis, sales forecasting, what-if experimentation, and business graphics presentation. Some natural language aspects are associated with financial modeling programs.

In addition to charting capabilities, Improv offers a set of drawing tools and features to customize a presentation. Users can include spreadsheet tables or text annotation, also shading or sound, and enhance their presentations with clip art, logos, or photos.

Improv and similar programs permit users to display and print different views of data by simply moving icons around the spreadsheet, thereby bringing greater insight to the displayed information. Such programs also allow the user to name data locations (cells) in plain English instead of by letter and number, making it possible to spot errors more quickly and easily as well as to understand a spreadsheet created by another user.

Both spreadsheets and value-added solutions require interactive access to distributed, heterogeneous databases. Commodity software written to simplify cross-database access in client/server environments started appearing in early 1991. DataLens by Lotus Development is one of them.

To better understand the connection between DataLens and Release 3 of the 1-2-3 spreadsheet, it is necessary to differentiate between the component modules of DataLens and the database engine embedded in 1-2-3.

Differences and relationships between these two items also help explain why today the 1-2-3 spreadsheet is the only application supported by DataLens, though future developments could include any Lotus product—Graphics, Notes, and so on—as well as multiapplications packages.

Among the basic principles underlying the DataLens design approach is that information elements existing in a database landscape should not have to be modified in order to achieve integration of files from different storage media. Specifically:

- The local IEs should remain in place.

- Only a copy would have to migrate.

Existing applications should be modified, only if it is desirable for processing reasons.

Another design prerequisite of the Datalens approach is that users should not have to adopt a new language for communicating with the integrated system. They should be able to access local database resources independently, and the procedure should not have to change when additional resources are integrated.

The DataLens software helps the user envision the components of a systems solution in database-accessing terms, automatically defining relationships as well as interfaces. The use of drivers—one per DBMS being addressed—provides the stability needed for handling distributed databases.

Once the information elements requested by the spreadsheet have arrived at the requesting agent (client, user), facilities are available for transforming them within applications. This is good enough for many implementations in which the primary requirement is to be able to access IEs for a specific job, wherever they might be stored.

By working interactively with the spreadsheet, the user first defines the information required. DataLens then consults the data dictionary to establish where the requested data is located, and the appropriate drivers go into action to retrieve the data from the corresponding databases. (As we will see in Chap. 16, EDA/SQL works in a fairly similar manner, but runs on mainframes—hence on higher cost.)

After the information elements are transferred to the workstation that originally posed the request, they are translated into a common format in a way that is fully transparent to the user.

Any application can benefit from the fact that generic data translation programs exist to aid in the manipulation necessary after the access and transfer of data. This is a great improvement over most current approaches, in which the IE transfer itself is cumbersome and data translation is time-consuming.

It is quite sound to implement technical solutions which help eliminate manual methods of transferring data from databases—such as retyping the data by hand or changing tapes and floppies. Such manual approaches, found in many installations, are not only costly but error-prone.

Lotus Development perceives DataLens as a critical component of a *new generation* of software which is designed to assure multivendor data access across hardware and operating system platforms. The technology offers good connectivity that helps capitalize on existing computer and communications architectures, allowing users to transparently access information elements throughout diverse and incompatible database structures.

Clear-eyed user organizations have come to realize that the only elegant approach is to assure an on-line real-time connection to the distributed heterogeneous databases. The solution must preserve localized information to relieve the user from having to learn different 1-to-1 interfacing routines.

15.6 Database Autonomy, Organization, and the Quality of Data

One of the main goals of client/server computing is to permit the building and maintaining of applications and databases that can withstand rapid changes both in technology and in business conditions. This issue is of interest to the entire enterprise, and most particularly to the multivendor hardware and software platforms it employs.

Efficient access to distributed databases is a prerequisite for client/server computing. It is a service to be considered and provided in a seamless manner within the operating environment, as the ongoing applications require. Prerequisites to a valid solution include:

- Positioning client/server computing in the context of an overall systems architecture

- Evaluating the optimal placement of information elements, processes, and appropriate supports

- Considering organizational issues all the way to the quality of information

Companies, operating divisions, and other organizational entities that manage different databases are often autonomous—that is, they are under separate and independent control. People or companies that can control a database are often unwilling to let others share the data. In other cases, they will do so only if they retain control over their resources. Therefore, it is important to:

- Understand the aspects of component autonomy

- Study the best way in which they can be addressed

A component database participating in a federation may exhibit autonomy in relation to the data being managed, the data model(s), the query language(s), and the naming of information elements in the local and global space.

In addition, local autonomy of the conceptualization or semantic interpretation of the data may significantly contribute to the problem of semantic heterogeneity. There is, as well, an operational autonomy relating to the ability of a component organizational unit to exercise control over its database(s). For instance, design and execution autonomy may be an operational requirement.

Correspondingly, service autonomy requirements refer to the right of each organization or independent business unit to make decisions regarding the database services it provides to other organizational units. Such requirements relate to association and communications autonomy. In general, the dual need to be faced involves:

1. Maintaining local autonomy

2. Sharing data without conflicting requirements

Though many technical problems may impede interconnectivity, the most difficult ones to solve are those of a political or organizational nature. These relate to authority as well as responsibility.

Problems relating to the political issues associated with database manipulation are typically addressed through the database administration function, which must now be extended both to global networks and to the multimedia level. Solutions must be flexible, accounting for both organizational and technical issues.

Synchronization of cross-database access procedures as well as security and integrity are examples with both organizational and technical characteristics. In many client/server systems, one of the principal threats to data integrity arises from data duplication—which nevertheless is necessary for efficiency.

Maintaining consistency among several copies of the same information element is difficult and can pose a major threat to the reliability of a database. Though this problem relates primarily to distributed characteristics, it is proper to add that centralized solutions present risks to data integrity as well. In fact, multiple entry of the same information elements—characteristic of batch applications—is one of the most important sources of database inconsistencies and errors.

In general, the quality of a database and its contents depends on the quality and dependability of the data sources with which it is fed. Database quality also depends on the soundness of the design—in particular, on the criteria established for the various types of data being collated, sorted, and stored.

Whether distributed or centralized, a database cannot be constructed without active participation from the user community. Nor can it be designed, run, and maintained without a database administration function. Moreover, the users have to be equipped with state-of-the-art networked workstations, able to reach a myriad of databases in a seamless manner.

Standards must be devised to assure data compatibility as well as to assist in verification. Quality targets must also be defined to guarantee that, whether collected internally or purchased from external sources, data is consistently reliable.

Such controls must relate principally to the accuracy and comprehensiveness of the supplied information elements. Whether or not data is purchased from public databases, the work of harmonizing and quality controlling all information in a company's private databases must still be carried out.

The system has to be viewed from both a technical and a business perspective, with due attention paid to the long-term viability of the networked databases and the client platforms accessing them. This means that solutions must be designed to meet longer-term as well as short-term requirements.

Account should be taken of the fact that each user has a unique view of the same system as well as unique concerns regarding its operation. Therefore, well-defined and documented data- and process-modeling techniques must be used to produce a viable solution. The job is do-able in spite of the fact that user requirements grow and technology continues to advance. This is why innovative approaches are still emerging.

15.7 Placement Algorithms with Client/Server Solutions

Banks have branch offices distributed over a wide landscape, and manufacturing companies have factories and sales offices at multiple locations, regionally located warehouses, and customers and suppliers across the country and around the world. Therefore, the computer and communications network is a business tool supporting markets, products, and services at each business site.

Investments are made in computers and networks for business reasons—specifically, to utilize the organization's structure more effectively. Questions for management include: Where should business be conducted? What services will be offered at each site? With whom should we interface? How do expansion plans alter the current answers?

Valid answers to these queries must be found. Then comes the study of technological solutions, with a number of principles to be observed in designing, implementing, and maintaining distributed database systems. These range all the way from site independence to nonstop operations for long transactions and query processing.

- In terms of independence from site, the guiding principle is that local information elements should be managed locally.

- Though it should be made globally available, local data should not be affected by conditions at other sites.

As cannot be repeated too often, the sheer volume of IT expansion suggests that all sites of the distributed database system should be peer to one another. They should not depend on a central location for storage, retrieval, dictionary services, recovery control, and so on.

A similar statement can be made regarding independence from location. Users—whether persons, terminals, or applications—do not need to know the location of information elements they require. All data should be handled *as if* available in the local site.

Furthermore, even if records are partitioned and objects stored in a multiple number of sites, they should be handled logically as a single reference. Information elements should be partitioned and stored in order to yield high performance, but they should also be capable of reconstruction along the lines of an ephemeral hierarchy, as the application requires:

- Even if copies of information elements are reproduced, users do not need to know which site is the source or which data is the copy.

- If, for reasons of consistency and unique image, the objects are modified, their copies should be automatically modified as well.

To help in classifying information elements in order to create an effectively distributed storage facility, IBM suggests that the placement decision be based on the aftermath of a study that sorts out information elements according to:

- Single copy
- Shared
- Current

as well as on such criteria as:

- Centralized IE
- Partitioned
- Volatile

A single-copy criterion states that the information elements do not require sharing as such. Data would likely have no value to anybody other than a prime user. When the data is not intended to be shared, the other factors of currency, partitioning, and volatility do not come into play, and a single-copy environment is maintained.

When information elements are shared, a multiple-copy criterion is applicable. In such a case, the IBM algorithm suggests that only one location needs the current version of the data:

- This location is usually the "owner"* of the data, responsible for its accuracy.

- For all other locations, the data is current only to a point in time.

This algorithm is clearly false in the general case, though it may be applicable in special situations where real-enough-time (RET) data can satisfy user requirements.

In IBM's view, partitioning and volatility do not influence the decision for multiple copies. There are, however, business requirements such as security and confidentiality which can affect the partitioning

---

*"Owner" is a very misleading term in this regard.

of information elements and the distribution of their copies. Data is distributed because different business units need to share IEs in order to meet their operating requirements.

15.8 The Consolidation of Database Contents

Transactions alter the contents of databases, thereby increasing the volatility of the information elements. Indeed, the volatility of the data is an important factor in deciding the distribution algorithm.

- If IE volatility is very large, it will probably be easier to meet business requirements through consolidation, as is the case with airline reservation systems.

- If IE volatility is medium or low, wider distribution is the better alternative for reasons of autonomy, responsiveness, and efficiency.

Consolidation should not be confused with centralization. Consolidation may be nicely implemented through the client/server model, with a number of networked systems sharing a disk farm—as noted in Part 1. Proponents of centralized databases tend to forget that, in order to maintain their growing structures, they have to manage a horde of necessary pointers and indices. Nothing is simple in implementing oversized centralized structures.

Overall administration and housekeeping are more manageable when databases work in a federation. But there are tradeoffs to be made in adapting federative techniques in lieu of the more conventional monolithic solutions.

Consider a design approach that attempts to combine conventional database management with knowledge of the ways a distributed database system is put into use. In an effort to obtain the advantages of both, problems of integration are bound to emerge.

Besides being conceptually obsolete, and very expensive for that matter, centralized mainframe-based solutions tend to perpetuate dependence on operating systems and database management systems which have become awkward or even obsolete. By contrast, true client/server approaches observe the principle of independence of OS and DBMS. Specifically:

- The distributed database should work on different hardware platforms.

- The multimedia approach should run under different OS.

- The distributed database elements should be constructed from multiple DBMS, with a common interface provided.

Such an environment promotes consolidation by means of powerful algorithms and high-performance computing, as illustrated in Chap. 11. The solution is not only much more flexible and elegant, but is significantly lower in cost compared with the centralized database dinosaurs.

Consolidation procedures can be facilitated up to a point if the data model used to describe the integrated schema is a semantically rich form. There are two different viable approaches to integration in the database context.

1. The *top-down* approach is essentially view integration, with external schemata of cooperating applications combined into federated common schemata to be connected.

2. The *bottom-up* approach requires that the local schema of an existing participating database be transformed into the modeling language of the multidatabase system.

From such transformed schema subsets are created export schemata to be integrated into one or more common schemata. Notice that both approaches aim at schema integration but take different roads.

Just as vital in terms of a design which is easy to consolidate and manipulate is independence from the network. The distributed system should be constructed so as to integrate multiple network architectures and communications media—both local and wide area. These systems are already in place and they should be integrated.

Networked databases should work nonstop, operationally unaffected by the addition or deletion of sites and the modification of database configurations. Under less-than-ideal conditions, a minimal number of sites should be touched by the modification.

This principle of uninterrupted continuity is necessary to support distributed transaction management 24-hours a day, 7 days a week. Information elements in a multiple number of sites will be steadily renewed by a stream of transactions. Solutions must evidently support:

- Simultaneous update

- Data consistency among sites

- Recovery from systems failure

Every one of these issues should be assured. Possible deadlocks should be anticipated and avoided. The same principle applies to processing distributed queries, including analytical ones. All users should view and treat the distributed database system as a virtually homogeneous construct.

15.9   Assuring a Viable Means of Database Integration

Integration is at once the means, methodology, and practice of aggregating component parts of a system into a cohesive set. This work is typically done through interfacing, by understanding and preserving the interrelationships and interactions of the various components.

One of the basic goals of integration is to provide access to the distributed client/server landscape while disparate computer installations are converted into a more tightly knit aggregate. For instance, integration should provide seamless access to information that is *stored in different forms,* and *managed by different systems,* while preserving constraints and dependencies among various chunks of the distributed information resource during update. An associated goal is to make the programs that create or manipulate the information interoperable, able to invoke global services.

The integration of a distributed heterogeneous database allows users (people, workstations, servers, and applications) to combine information elements from multiple sources and create environments in which a growing variety of procedures can cooperate. This requires understanding and documenting the relationships and dependencies existing among information elements and procedures.

Establishing a common framework to handle dependencies and relationships can be a difficult task when the information elements are stored in heterogeneous databases and managed by incompatible DBMS. As a result, integration services need to hide or remove heterogeneities among databases and procedures by:

- Providing means to assure that dependencies are supported and constraints enforced

- Mapping both information and procedures with consistent names, formats, descriptions, and calling sequences

A factual and documented answer to these challenges requires systematic study of business unit locations and their requirements. In this way, given data entities can be identified by business unit *before* the distribution and consolidation criteria are considered. Current and potential operational needs, including security and performance, must be evaluated. The same is true for the resource monitoring necessary in a distributed environment.

In an integrated system, IE relationships among themselves and with applications must be traceable, expressible, and preserved—regardless of the heterogeneity of the components that store and manage multimedia elements.

Such a requirement, however, does not prevent each component from supporting specific internal relationships which are difficult to describe in a cross-component manner—especially when there are no common facilities for identifying related elements. The risk is that updates in one of the components are not always reflected in the others.

Integration is a prerequisite to effective interoperability. In multi-database systems, interoperability refers to the execution of applications using common information elements that are created by other applications and stored in a logically defined database—which physically may be widely distributed. In such an implementation, an agent mediates all accesses between applications and the local databases.

If all local databases are defined according to a single set of semantic conventions, with the multidatabase in mind, its universal schema would be relatively easy to construct. Most often this is not the case.

1. To assure consistency across the system, an integrative approach will make the heterogeneity of the underlying components and their information contents transparent to the user.

2. The masking of incompatibilities, in turn, will make components homogeneous.

Given the many aspects of heterogeneity and the constraints which need to be overcome, the level of integration is bound to be quite variable. The higher-level goal is to achieve a basis for cross-vendor interoperability, as detailed in the last two sections.

Existing studies and surveys compare integration levels, but there are really no standards for making such comparisons—much less for benchmarking. We can, however, define a multidimensional design space for integration which includes:

- Access to different DBMS and data models

- The support of transparency by end users

- Networkwide program interoperability

- Able mapping of all relationships

- Proper definition of dependencies and constraints

Constraint analysis includes logic-based representation of database semantics, specifications of database operations, updatable user views, and generation of rules for integrity maintenance. We will return to the issue of constraints and the requirements which they impose in Chaps. 17 and 18 when we examine ways and means to implement federated databases.

Information Warehouses, Client/Servers, and Remote Data Access

16.1 Introduction

The core of an open systems policy is an open standard supporting a variety of incompatible but competitive hardware and software products. Ideally such a standard should come from the International Standards Organization (ISO), as did the Open System Interconnection (OSI) framework.

Today's guiding standard is known as *remote data access* (RDA). It is elaborated by ANSI and ISO and productized by the SQL Access Group. However, it addresses only what its name says:—*data access,* particularly in the form of applications programming interfaces (APIs) and forms and protocols (FAPs).*

Despite pledges of support for standards such as the Structured Query Language and the SQL Access Group's remote SQL interfaces, the major database vendors are finding it hard to accept the concept of database interoperability through anything else but *their* individual solutions. There are many commercial—and technical—reasons for the vendors' reaction.

Beyond API and FAP lies a golden horde of problems that have to be solved in connection with accessing distributed databases for transactions, queries, and messages. As will be seen in this chapter, no norms exist for cross-database solutions; hence, vendors and users

---

*See also D. N. Chorafas and H. Steinmann, *Solutions for Networked Databases,* Academic Press, San Diego, CA, 1993.

tend to develop their own. Some of these home-grown solutions have utilitarian value; others are too restrictive; still others are very expensive in their implementation.

The potential impact of effective cross-database solutions can better be appreciated by keeping in mind that the full potential of the PC has never been realized.

- Self-interested computer manufacturers have kept the personal computer at arm's length from mainframes through low-key software and obsolete protocols such as 3270.

- User organizations and software houses need to devise sensible plans for the future in order to break this bottleneck.

Database interoperability through remote access places a premium on software that lets users interact with multiple, incompatible DBMS servers transparently. With this approach, individual server platforms are important players. However, user organizations and vendors have opposing views on database interoperability.

- Vendors look at DBMS servers as proprietary strategic products that can be used to drive sales of software and hardware.

- User organizations need servers for cross-database access to execute their applications, particularly those of an integrative nature.

Vendors that want to maintain the status quo can fight progress toward database interoperability, mainly by dragging their feet in building the servers needed to support it. However, having every major user organization reinvent cross-database software is not the solution to this wrong-headed approach.

16.2   Services Provided by an Information Warehouse

A wide range of cross-database solutions exist today. They are making the InfoCenter of the early 1980s unnecessary by providing access for query purposes to an impressive number of data structures and DBMS. Such solutions range:

- From the low-cost DataLens by Lotus Development and Q + E by Microsoft

- To the high-cost EDA/SQL by IBM, which is mainframe based

Since the foremost user organizations steadily emphasize the importance of commodity software for cross-database access, along with the software provided by SAA and AIX, IBM has given support to the Enterprise Database Access (EDA) construct.*

Up to a point, IBM's Information Warehouse and EDA seem to be complementary—or at least that is what the mainframer says. But in reality they contradict each other, because conceptually they present opposite approaches to making database resources available to the end user.

Many parochial solutions worked out by user organizations reflect the Information Warehouse approach of building up a separate, intermediate database structure—with all the delays, errors, perils, and costs involved. Although IBM's Information Warehouse is a much more polished and generalized solution than any of the others, it is still based on obsolete systems concepts.

IBM promotes its Information Warehouse as more than an InfoCenter. However, to the query "What's the difference?" the answer is given: "Conceptually nothing—except that the InfoCenter packaged up the data, while the Information Warehouse takes the opposite viewpoint." In principle, The Information Warehouse approach says:

1. Leave the information elements where they are.

2. Don't duplicate them and don't centralize them.

3. Don't move them to a single platform.

If this is really the case, then there is a great difference between the InfoCenter and the Information Warehouse, with the latter being a development in the right direction.

Of course, easy access to data resources remains elusive for most business users in spite of their corporate networks. As noted on several occasions, the major problem lies, not in the common difficulties associated with connectivity and networking, but rather in the systems concept necessary for integrating distributed databases and their contents.

NYNEX Corporation offers a good example of what is do-able. As a first step toward distributed database handling on its network, NYNEX consolidated dictionary references applicable to its many database structures. Then:

- It assembled all relevant databases and applications onto a virtually integrated relational framework.

---

*EDA was developed for IBM by Information Builders of New York. See also the discussion in Sec. 16.5 on the characteristics of EDA/SQL.

- Integration was achieved through the Data Interpretation System, an access tool made by Metaphor of Mountain View, CA.

NYNEX estimates that the consolidated databases now represent $80 million to $100 million in cost savings and additional revenue. Its analysts steadily use the consolidated information for database mining, to flush out the best prospective customers and other information vital to management decisions.

This example illustrates a fact often obscured in data-processing practice: The gap between end users and the information elements they want involves not only distance but logic—and the latter can be more upsetting than the former.

Although its first phase has been successful, NYNEX is not resting on its laurels. With a firm hold on usage patterns, management is considering bringing the consolidated databases to a client/server architecture that will reside closer to the end users. But there are other challenges as well.

In the first phase of implementation, NYNEX relied extensively on operational information which typically resides in transaction-oriented databases, including:

- Inventories

- Product orders

- Customer accounts

NYNEX and other companies active in this domain are concentrating much of their efforts on systems performance, including visual display of efficiency data. Their efforts aim to establish critical paths, locate performance bottlenecks, and guide management actions.

Hence, algorithms and heuristics are necessary to focus on the 10 percent or so of the corporation's operating data that is needed for optimization and decision making. Because powerful search and mining algorithms require considerable and expensive mainframe processing time, the client/server solution has come up time and again as the best alternative.

16.3 Database Management and Remote Data Access

The able use of database resources to assist managers and professionals can be assured only if standards are established at the applications boundaries. But as usual in the computer industry, products have been developed before norms could be worked out, leaving database integration a still unresolved problem.

As a growing number of cases help document, the main catalyst in the drive for improved tools for management information has been the realization that users must be able to control and simplify the ever-increasing number of information elements they need. They must also be able to cross-reference the information contained in the wide variety of databases required to do business.

In this connection, client/server approaches can present significant advantages, in terms of both efficiency and cost. Here are just two reasons:

- Ad hoc operations such as end-user queries require indexes and summary reports to speed data access.

- Such operations sap processing power, and when executed on mainframes slow transaction-processing performance.

The distributed solution sought by today's users must not only consider where data is accessed but also successfully resolve where and how ad hoc processing should occur.

Such a solution calls for a significant amount of flexibility as well as new tools. That is why many users have taken the InfoCenter model, which they relied on for many years, and put it to rest. Its basic concept rests on an old corporate truism—that most managers and professionals tend to run the same queries and reports against corporate databases day after day and year after year. Today nothing is more untrue.

Modern executive information systems, and the complex analysis requirements they pose, call for flexible ad hoc access to internal and external data sources. Access must be further enriched with the ability to provide interactive ad hoc database reports—in order to boost management productivity.

Responsive solutions to end-user needs require advances in distributed cooperative processing, the inevitable adoption of knowledge engineering tools, and an increased awareness of the problems of controlling the use of distributed information. In turn, this points to:

- The need to improve the facilities available for managing systems configuration

- The wisdom of building intelligent cross-database access schemes

Issues of data organization also have to be resolved before new technologies can be deployed. This is not just a technical problem. Distributed administration and licensing will remain reasonably complex issues until database applications based on OSF's Distributed Communications Environment (DCE) come of age.

Seen under this perspective, a key goal of IBM's Information Warehouse and similar approaches is to allow users to define the aspects of information elements that make sense for them. This, however, means that end users need powerful and friendly development tools to build their own reports, messages, transactions, queries, cross-tabulations, and computations.

In terms of requirements, end-user computing and client/server solutions cannot be defined in better terms. The concepts just explained not only make sense but also make lots of difference from the conditions prevailing today particularly, among EDP shops working with concepts and programs out of the 1970s and 1980s.

In the majority of cases, users still rely on their information systems departments to create data access routines for them. Yet companies could save big amounts of money just by letting users access their own data, provided the right tools and safeguards are put in place.

Object-oriented technologies offer an efficient generic solution to providing users with a valid data access method supported by a variety of front-end tools.*

■ Typically, the object databases contain both data and programs regarding the business.

■ Associated concepts include customers, accounts, products, prices, shipments, and other common business concerns, as well as issues unique to a particular enterprise and/or customer relationship.

An object technology offers distinct advantages over relational or other older tools. However, here again users are given a number of vendor-neutral and vendor-specific methods of defining objects and how to access them. The standards are still missing.

This is not to discourage active use of object-oriented tools and methods. Rather, such promising approaches are to be encouraged with the full understanding that there are no miracle solutions. Even interim solutions offer advantages, as we will see below.

16.4   Open Database Connectivity with Three-Tier Models

The long-established goal of a database management system has been to provide applications independence as well as data sharing among different users, applications, and locations. A new and increasingly

---

*See also D. N. Chorafas and H. Steinmann, *Object-Oriented Databases,* Prentice-Hall, Englewood Cliffs, NJ, 1993.

important goal is to answer the growing demand for a database capable of supporting multiple users.

Fast-developing requirements for enhanced database functionality call for handling distributed information elements in a more intelligent manner, simplifying applications system development, and providing seamless end-user access. The rise of networked workstations has increasingly brought into perspective an important dichotomy:

- The personal needs of an individual user

- The shared aspects of an integrated, multiuser enterprise solution

These demands are not necessarily compatible in terms of the functionality required. Therefore, the role of client/server computing is steered toward providing users with an appropriate environment, through essential access to shared data.

A growing response to multiuser requirements is the concept of database servers. Evolving concepts seek to strip database management to its essentials—that is, to view the process as a dedicated machine managing concurrent access to information elements shared by a large number of users.

An example of an engine designed to respond to new requirements is Microsoft's SQL Server.* It provides a database computing solution for corporate networks, enabling a wide range of client applications to effectively share information:

- Distributed data management handles remote stored procedures and two-phase commit for multiserver applications.

- Connectivity services extend access to corporate database sources in a networked landscape.

- An integrated server administration assures effective systems configuration as the dataflow and data load evolve.

In a May 1992 meeting in New York, Microsoft stressed the SQL Server's object-oriented characteristics. The SQL Server can also handle long transaction requirements through the procedure:

```
Begin Transaction
  Insert
  Update
If-Then-Else
  Savepoint
  Update
Commit Transaction
```

---

*Microsoft does not sell the SQL Server directly; it is offered through value-added resalers.

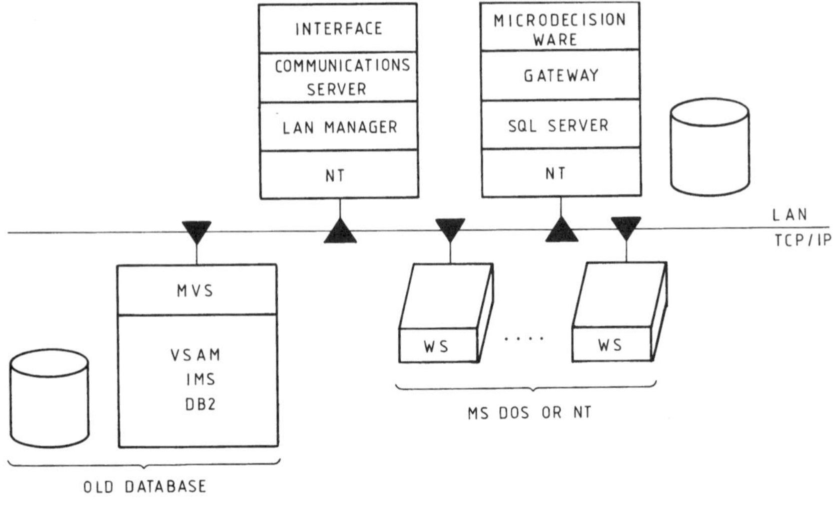

Figure 16.1 An SQL server with networked databases and workstations.

As shown in Fig. 16.1, in a distributed environment a master SQL Server will monitor subtransactions in a networkwide sense. Available software can roll back to savepoint, implementing a two-phase commit protocol.

The solution can support multiple communications servers, as evidenced by the practical applications adopted at Metropolitan Life Insurance and Con Edison. In one specific application, the system in Fig. 16.1 supports 400 workstations. The protocol is TCP/IP but it can also work under 3270 emulation. The latter approach is not advisable, except as a strictly transitory, interim measure.

- The networked SQL Server approach is technically more elegant than that of creating another, overlapping database through InfoCenter.

- The approach is more flexible in regard to the connectivity required to meet growing implementation needs.

Any viable solution, however, needs to be supplemented by the appropriate protocols. In this connection, Microsoft is developing a generic driver—the so-called Server Process Interface (SPI)—by means of open database connectivity (ODBC),* which is a version of API.

---

*ODBC works under NT and Windows, but not yet DOS.

In contrast to the offerings of ISO and the SQL Access Group, ODBC is a software-based concept which aims to combine RDA and FAP. It is proprietary but has been adopted by computer vendors like Hewlett-Packard and Unisys. ODBC connectivity aims to permit three-tier models.

As shown in Fig. 16.2, there is a significant functional difference between two-tier and three-tier connectivity solutions:

The two-tier models are much simpler and do not require complex software supported services.

The pseudo-server approach offered by mainframers falls into this two-tier class. Essentially it constitutes a PC-to-mainframe solution that has been around for about 10 years, and it has survived in terms of usage even if the point-to-point links have been replaced by a LAN.

The three-tier and n-tier models are more complex, given the heterogeneous database issues involved and the polyvalence of the connection.

But all by itself, the implementation of ODBC does not change a two-tier model into a three-tier one. This is achieved by the specific

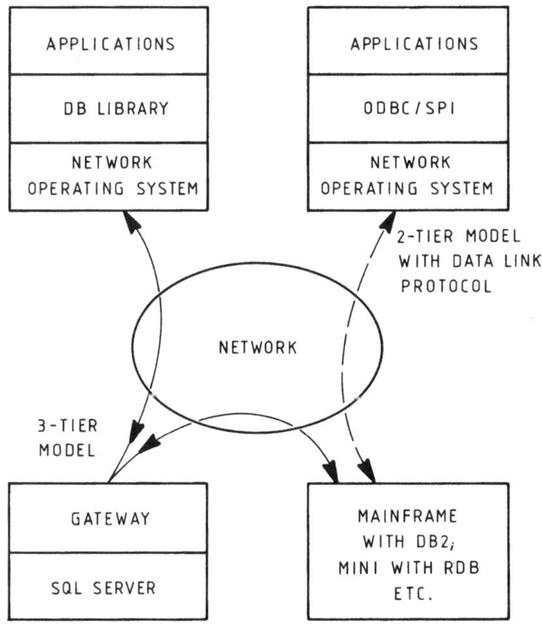

Figure 16.2 Three-tier and two-tier models for connecting networked databases and workstations.

systems architecture adopted—in particular, the advanced features that such architecture presents.

Of course, the two-tier processor-to-processor connection can be improved with a LAN. But this necessary step is not enough. Most of the interconnection software available from major vendors today can deal with one or two physical units at a time—not 500, 1,000, or more. Yet it is the myriaprocessor which will dominate the 1990s and beyond—hence the n-tier connection we are after.

Another hindrance that is often overlooked is the use of naive protocols in a networked environment. Particularly troublesome is the continuing use of 3270 emulation, which was designed for a much less sophisticated data-processing era and is highly ineffectual in networking clients and servers. Moreover:

- With 3270, implementation remains at character user interface (CUI) level.

- Today's overriding demand is for graphics user interfaces (GUIs).

Cognizant executives in leading user organizations are rightly concerned about such backwater connectivity. But vendor pressure turns management's attention around. Yet, if a user organization wishes to take advantage of sophisticated technical solutions, it has to focus on them. They will not come around on their own.

Two-tier and n-tier solutions are at a premium in an increasingly competitive environment where the cutting edge of technology makes the difference between profits and losses.

For simple connectivity, for example, a passthrough software such as DataLens by Lotus Development (see also Chap. 15) and Query and Edit (Q + E) by Microsoft will provide the service needed for point-to-point access to heterogeneous databases. EDA/SQL achieves the same two-tier connection, but at much higher costs.

Q + E and DataLens work under MS DOS on PC, at a cost of roughly \$2,000. IBM's EDA/SQL solution, which is examined in the next section, runs under MVS and requires a mainframe which costs upward of \$2.5 million. Since DataLens, Q + E, and EDA/SQL do roughly the same job, the difference in cost-effectiveness is three orders of magnitude. Still, many companies are willing to pay so much more money for so little return. Old tools and obsolete concepts die hard.

16.5 EDA/SQL: An Example of the More Limited Two-Tier Model

The database applications of the 1990s are those designed to manage large amounts of shared information elements. Efficient solutions are sought on the premise that databases constitute a critical component of the operations of any company. However:

- There are legacy problems to be dealt with, usually involving heterogeneous resources—another reason passthrough query-only capability is important.
- Solutions have to be found for the interconnection of incompatible databases, and the first commodity offering brought to the market reflected the two-tier model.

As a limited two-tier proposition, IBM's Enterprise Data Access/ Structured Query Language (EDA/SQL) has interesting features of possible appeal to companies operating in the IBM world—but it cannot perform miracles. There is no facility today that will:

- Take a DL1 call and unscramble it
- Ease the data access problem in so doing

The option for the user organization is to move its information elements wholesale to DB2. Such an option can be both very expensive and highly limited in terms of required functionality. Therefore, prior to deciding to move to DB2, users should be well aware of what they are getting.

Stripped to its fundamentals, EDA/SQL provides:

1. Access to distributed, heterogeneous databases, but for query-only purposes*
2. Facilitated access to duplicative storage the InfoCenter way

In reality, the first solution is the strength of EDA/SQL, aiming to provide data access to any language statement or tool that communicates requests via ANSI SQL.

The need for EDA in the IBM world comes from the fact that it is increasingly unwise to rely on homemade software for queries, reports, and data maintenance tasks—particularly if it is done through obsolete third-generation languages (3GL).

At the same time, studies have demonstrated that despite the growth of relational technology, much corporate data remains in non-relational form: VSAM files, DBMS such as IMS and Adabas, and so on. Again, this legacy data is critical to business, but only a small fraction of it is available in an interactive sense.

---

*Applicable to supported DBMS, as identified below in Fig. 16.4.

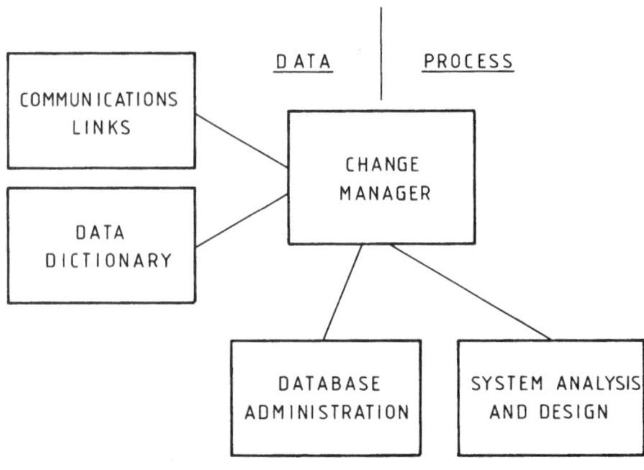

Figure 16.3 Change management affects both data
and processes in an EDA/SQL environment.

To make the data access process somewhat more convenient, one of
the focal points of the EDA/SQL architecture is change management.
As Fig. 16.3 suggests, change management affects both processes and
information elements, therefore requiring refined data definitions—
which in turn calls for first-class data dictionary assistance.

One of the pillars in change management is the provision of appropriate communications links. EDA/SQL supports a number of major
network protocols:

- TCP/IP
- NetBIOS
- Named Pipes
- LU 6.2 (APPC and CPI-C)
- LU 2 (3270 data stream)
- DECnet

EDA/SQL also aims to be a solution for open systems, enabling user
organizations to interchange software and hardware components
from different vendors. But this interoperability has to be implemented in a systematic cand methodological manner, and it cannot be easily dissociated from the IBM world.

Since some of the processes involved in the transition process can
be complex, IBM advises a cautious approach to change management:

- Going box by box
- Using the appropriate tools

The problem, however, is that a number of necessary tools still need to be provided. Moreover, as user companies confronted with change management are quick to stress, the most important issue is human resources. Not only does change management require a significant amount of training; it also takes time for the concepts involved to sift down through the organization.

EDA/SQL implementation also brings up issues of response time, issues that are dear to every user organization as well as to every single end user. Wisely, IBM makes no commitment on this subject. Instead, IBM suggests:

■ The level of depth at which a query enters IMS determines what the response time will be.

■ Link overhead can be better estimated, and IBM suggests that it stands at about 5 percent of response time on the query.

As an enterprise data connection, EDA/SQL aims to provide a uniform relational view of information elements regardless of their underlying organization, thereby making transparent:

■ Storage location

■ File architecture

■ Hardware platform

Data access, security, accounting, management of procedural libraries, and connectivity across platforms are provided, as the EDA server allows views to be created joining similar or dissimilar, relational or nonrelational files.

Available software routes the request to the appropriate server by means of *data drivers* corresponding to target formats, with answer sets returned to the user. This service is provided under the general heading of the Information Warehouse.

In essence, IBM suggests, there is *no global schema*. There is only an attempt to create better understanding through a global schema concept, although this is not a necessary precondition. "Experience says that global schemata don't succeed," suggested an IBM specialist. "Nothing happens and therefore the businesspeople get frustrated."

To the query "Does the underlying model have loose or tight coupling characteristics?" IBM replies that, to start with, EDA/SQL differentiates between *operational data* and *informational data*. It tries to unclutter the first from the second, aiming to create a more or less global selectivity while keeping data duplication to a minimum.

But why duplicate at all if the information elements can be read in place? According to IBM, EDA/SQL allows duplication because there are situations when such an approach is warranted.

A *data-in-place* strategy supports performance, but if the system is highly centralized it can lead to bottlenecks.* In such a case, the addition of a process operating simultaneously on the same information elements could have a negative impact on performance.

The *duplicate data* strategy aims to relieve the situation by diversifying information retrieval. This can, however, lead to other problems. Data must be maintained in its current state. And even though the production databases are updated on an ongoing schedule, the actual content of the management information database will differ from place to place. The results can be disastrous.

16.6   Read-Only Services While Reaching a Number of Heterogeneous DBMS

In terms of background development, EDA/SQL was derived from Focus. Information Builders spent much of its history developing database interfaces and languages. Focus is a fourth-generation language that can:

- Access data from 45 different DBMS and file structures

- Reside on 35 different hardware platforms and operating environments.

As IBM was to suggest during a 1992 meeting at the Santa Teresa Laboratory, EDA/SQL can be viewed as a Focus core with many drivers added to it.

EDA/SQL supports SQL as the standard database access language to relational and nonrelational databases. Variations in syntax, function-

---

1. *IBM mainframe-based:* IMS, VSAM, ISAM, QSAM, DB2, SQL/DS, Focus DB, IDMS/IDMSR, Adabas, Datacom DB, Model 204, System 2000, Total, Sharebase
2. *IBM RS 6000:* Oracle, Sybase, Ingres, Informix, Focus DB
3. *VSE/ESA:* VASM, SQL/DS, DL/1, Total, IDMS/R, Datacom DB
4. *DOS and OS/2-based:* DBase III, SQL Server, OS/2EE, Focus DB
5. *DEC-based:* RDB, RMS, Adabas, Sybase, Ingres, Oracle, Informix, Focus DB, Sharebase
6. *Hewlett-Packard:* MPE, KSAM, Turboimage, Allbase/SQL
7. *Sun-Unix:* C-ISAM, Oracle, Sybase. Ingres, Informix, Focus DB
8. *Other Unix-based:* ISAM. C-Isam, Informix
9. *Database computers:* Teradata

Figure 16.4   Data drivers supported by EDS/SQL.

---

*This point has been stressed all along: Information elements should not be centralized; they should be distributed.

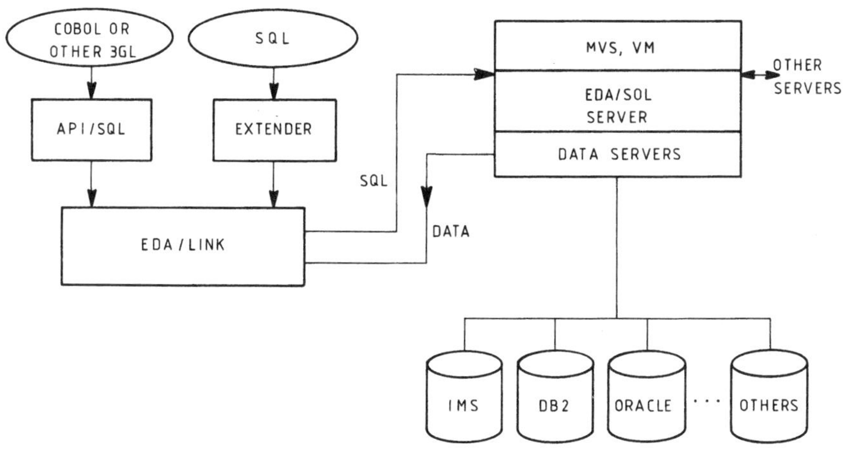

Figure 16.5 Access through EDA/LINK can be activated through SQL or 3GL, but database search transits through the mainframe.

ality, schema, data types, catalog names, and data representation are resolved through EDA/API. Thus there is no need to build and maintain homemade gateways and interfaces to file management systems.

Drivers currently exist on MVS and VM, but will also be added to a list of other OS—such as Unix V.4; Hewlett-Packard UX, VMS, and Ultrix; VSE/SA, OS/2, RS 6000, and MacOS. Figure 16.4 presents a list of the data drivers by supported OS. The EDA/SQL architecture is shown in Fig. 16.5.

It should be noted that some overlap exists between EDA/SQL and IBM's other product: DRDA. But there are also major differences:

- DRDA operates in a strictly relational environment, and at the present time addresses only IBM products.

- DRDA is *read/write,* and hence can help with transactions, while EDA/SQL is *read only.**

- EDA/SQL addresses nonrelational IBM products as well as non-IBM database products, but it is valid only for queries.

Neither EDA/SQL nor DRDA is stand-alone architecture. DRDA, for instance, uses the following software products as building blocks:

---

*But it is limited to networking four IBM-relational DBMS, which are incompatible to one another: DB2, SQL/DS, SQL/OS400 and SQL/OS2.

- LU 6.2
- Distributed Data Management
- SNA Management Services
- Formatted Data Object Content
- Character Data

It is the task of DRDA to tie everything together into a datastream protocol that supports cooperation among the different participating resources.

Correspondingly, in EDA/SQL a dialogue management facility (DMF) controls the exchange of information between client and caller. It allows a single remote procedure call to simultaneously actuate multiple remote procedures. The caller does not need knowledge of the details of data sources, since it is insulated from other software products.

As this discussion suggests, the warehousing and retrieval of information elements involves polyvalent functions able to support distributed environments.

- Data from everywhere in the company needs to be identified and described, but also translated and/or enriched.

- A data dictionary is needed to describe the information elements available within operations, as well as to act as a directory.

Within this perspective, EDA/SQL can provide a uniform, relational view of data, independent of database organization and fragmentation across hardware lines. In this manner, it assists the work of 3GL and 4GL, as well as spreadsheets and other software.

Translation from SQL to the native data language can be performed, where appropriate, with the SQL code passed through directly. The strategy is to accept that the database environment is heterogeneous. "We make it homogeneous with two products," suggests IBM:

- If data is relational, translation is done directly through SQL.

- If data is both relational and nonrelational, it is made to look relational through EDA.

As demonstrated in Fig. 16.5, this process works through data drivers and an array of independent, interlocking EDA/LINK modules supporting major network communications protocols. The set processing feature of SQL acts to minimize message traffic on the network.

EDA provides catalog facilities for complex, frequently used procedures. These may be executed simply by naming them, using run-time parameters. Navigating across heterogeneous architectures, the system returns an answer in response to a request. There are, however, two major limitations:

1. The service being provided is *read-only.*

2. The solution that has been developed and is supported is *mainframe-based.*

As stated in Sec. 16.4, DataLens by Lotus also operates in the read-only mode in response to queries and runs on PCs, not mainframes. The added value simply is not there for the much higher expense of EDA/SQL. Added value *might* have been provided, for instance, through:

- A parallel database exploitation approach, as some vendors, like MasPar, Thinking Machines, and n-Cube, try to do

- A fully transactional capability supporting the same range of heterogeneous DBMS DataLens features—but in read-write mode

The key to the parallel databasing approach is the ability to manage data currency on an ongoing basis, according to rules that are carefully projected and adjusted on a dynamic basis in response to user needs.

16.7 Access Parallelism and Database Utilities

The workload of a database server is inherently parallel. It is made up of a large number of relatively small, independent activities, originating from different and equally independent users.

This statement holds for all queries and transactions, but it is especially relevant to the new profiles which characterize the 1990s. Two deserve mention here:

- Complex queries

- Long transactions

In a 1992 meeting in Stockholm, Skandinaviska Enskilda Banken noted that the long transactions embedded into its new portfolio management programs require 1,000 disk accesses each, as contrasted with the 8 to 10 accesses typically needed for short transactions.

The now developing characteristics of sophisticated computer applications are in total contrast with traditional computer implementations of the legacy type—even those concerned with computer-intensive operations.

- The inherent parallelism of the new workload provides an opportunity for exploiting parallel platforms, provided that DBMS and transaction-processing monitors (TPMs) are able to retain and exploit this inherent parallelism.

- There is a growing need for minimizing the impact of required accesses to the same information (through serialization) in order to maximize concurrency.

Exploiting the parallel nature of a database workload is a key to the able use of hardware for database management purposes, since it directly affects the total systems throughput. Therefore, solutions projected for the 1990s should be able to identify and exploit opportunities for parallel processing within individual database operations.

Current practice suggests that parallel processing can be achieved through the dual approach of *data partitioning* and *function partitioning*. Data partitioning provides multiple instances of limited processes, with each process working against an independent partition of the underlying data set.

By contrast, function partitioning calls for structuring critical processes in such a way that the resulting separate functional sections can execute in parallel. This might be achieved automatically by compilers rich in knowledge of how the process works. Usually, however, it is done explicitly by the software developer, supported by tools such as parallel programming libraries and languages.

Database utilities are necessary to assist these operations. Their functionality must go beyond the *logical import/export* for migrating data and/or metadata to another database. It should help in on-line backup/restore and provide the means for checking and verifying the integrity of data structures. Other services, too, are important:

- An analysis utility can be instrumental in examining database page usage, space usage by tables, and number of levels of indexes.

- A statistical utility is needed for performance monitoring, and a dump utility is required for database analysis.

- A load/unload utility is needed on each table, along with tools for modifying the contents of corrupted database storage areas.

Still other services could be mentioned. The focus here, however, is on database utilities able to handle parallel processes.

The goal is to divide the database-processing workload among a number of processors, with background processes undertaking the necessarily serial work. A back-end database process performs the majority of the work involved in handling database requests, including reading data from disk into cache memory.

- This *one-process-per-user* approach exploits the existing parallelism in the incoming workload, with the operating system responsible for scheduling processes across the available processors of a parallel computer.

- Other supervisory processes (demons) are necessary to assure transaction integrity, so that a set of related updates applied in full to the component parts of the distributed database will *guarantee integrity*.

Quite evidently, this type of sophisticated solution cannot be handled by a PC with DataLens or Q + E software. But neither is it to be found in a mainframe environment with EDA/SQL—first because the mainframe is a serial engine, and second because the EDA/SQL software simply does not support it.

New departures are therefore necessary, and they must answer the parallel-processing prerequisites briefly outlined in the preceding paragraphs. They must also feature other systems characteristics such as concurrency, integrity control, and security.

Whether operating in a serial or parallel fashion, a multiuser environment must guarantee full concurrent access for storage, retrieval, update, and deletion.

Multiple applications should access the same database concurrently, and a snapshot mode should be available for increased cooperation in large-scale retrieval and report-writing applications.

Referential integrity must be provided with rollback of failed transactions, executed automatically but program-controlled for security reasons.

Integrity control necessitates transaction journaling with rollback recovery; afterimage journaling with rollforward recovery; and triggers connected to the execution of one or more actions when certain database conditions are met.

In its implementation, commitment control and recovery (CCR) has many component parts, and so far there is no international agreement on how they should be implemented. One approach is a commitment tree structure with a database in each node.

If a networkwide modification is done in a node, then all nodes from root to leaves must agree with the commitment. If one node does not do so, then no commitment can be made. Such globality is difficult to assure in a heterogeneous environment, which by nature lacks global referential integrity. No tools so far provide foolproof support.

For security purposes, database files must be fully protected, with rights to perform database operations kept under control and passwords steadily updated.

Such rights must be stored in the database and maintained by the database administrator (DBA) and must be updatable at any time. This is true not only of access control but also of views, data definitions, data manipulation operations, and database utility functions.

The good news is that standards are being developed for *trusted systems* that are able to handle a range of security functions. These have not yet been incorporated into commodity products offered by the major vendors. Yet it will not be difficult to add *notary functions* to some of the products examined in this chapter, particularly those products involving high costs.

Beyond Client/Servers:
The Federated Database Solution

17.1 Introduction

As Chap. 15 has documented before, an open systems policy can be implemented, several organizational prerequisites have to be fulfilled. Next comes the technical preparatory work toward a client/server solution. The approach calls for estimating the number and type of databases to be involved in the integration process and their information elements, size, topology, and concurrency.

An integral part of the prerequisite study is the transactional query requirements. Both tools and procedures are necessary in meeting end-user needs for the information embedded in the distributed database. Another important preparatory step is the clear knowledge and definition of the different approaches to global management which are feasible.

Both Chaps. 14 and 15 presented the concept of *federated databases* as the best possible state-of-the-art solution given today's environment of heterogeneous database structures run by incompatible DBMS.

But so far no detailed mention has been made of the principles underlying the virtual integration of distributed heterogeneous databases. To better focus on this subject, it is appropriate to redefine the meaning of federalism, as well as to make explicit that federalism is not just another word for decentralization.

Significant conceptual differences exist between decentralization and federalism, differences that have great impact on reaching manageable solutions:

- *Decentralization* implies that the center *delegates* certain tasks or duties to the outlying units, while remaining in overall control. The center does the delegating, the initiating, and the directing.

- Under *federalism,* the center is "granted" powers by the outlying units, in a sort of *reverse delegation.* The center, therefore, coordinates, advises, influences, and suggests—but it does not order.

Reverse delegation is precisely what happens when, in a federated database solution, each local unit works autonomously on transactions and queries of interest to it locally. At the same time, each unit is always ready to collaborate in global events.

This arrangement makes feasible a flexible and dynamic approach to database management. However, it should not be forgotten that organizations are made up of people, and people cling to habit. Thus procedures should be in place to assure that the federation does not lead to disintegration.

Implementation of the federation principle can be facilitated by a careful study of business practices:

- The concept of "less than 100 percent control" is bread and butter in business.

- It is fairly alien to many technologists, particularly to data processors.

In a way, federalism is how the board of management works in central European companies. The members of the board are equal or semiequal, and the chair acts as the speaker of the board, reigning by consensus. There is no president or chief executive officer with 100 percent control—but there are procedures that permit very effective coordination.

17.2 Alternative Approaches to Database Integration

Database designers who work on federated principles have not discovered a brand-new concept. What they have done is to apply an existing organizational solution to information technology—most particularly, to the management of distributed heterogeneous databases.

Whether they involve states, companies, or databases, federated enterprises are reverse-thrust organizations. The initiative, drive, and energy come mostly from the distributed units, with the center acting as the long-term influencing force. By their nature, federated organizations are rather *loosely coupled,* to use a technical buzzword.

This is the concept of federated databases which any database architect, administrator, or designer will be well advised to consider. In fact, there are alternatives: Three main methods are presented in this section (see also Fig. 17.1):

Federated Databases

- Leave databases as they are
- No global schema
- Only data dictionary handling of schemata
- Good for intelligent query systems—not for transactional ones

Schema Translation

- Virtual mode too complex
- Establishing universal schema
- Conversion of nonnormalized schemata

Interoperability approach

- Development of very powerful language
- Distributed object management
- Encapsulation and standard interfaces

Figure 17.1 Methods for integrating distributed heterogeneous databases.

- Federalism
- Schema translation
- Interoperability

A strict global schema is not part of this list for the simple reason that the concept has been tried and has failed. As a result, many organizations are using a simple passthrough, an approach examined initially in Part 1 and expanded in Chaps. 15 and 16 with the examples of DataLens, Q + E, and EDA/SQL.

As noted in earlier chapters, passthrough approaches have their place as an intermediate solution for query purposes—but not for transactions. Federated databases seek, as far as possible, to answer the requirements of both worlds.

Interoperability is particularly important in a transactional environment where delivering reliable service rather than bringing together existing hardware, software, and protocols is the measure of good performance. This issue is examined in considerable detail in Chap. 18.

In this connection, tools, measurement, and procedures will be key, but the same can be said about a federation of database services. Distributed services must be delivered to every desk in a way that is independent of applications development, while the designers must fully understand the product value chain of the company's databases and the role that they play.

To better understand the concept behind a federation of databases, it is helpful to return to fundamentals:

1. Loosely coupled systems have no global schema but possess passthrough capability.
2. Tightly coupled systems lack global schema but possess transactional interoperability.
3. Very tightly coupled systems have only global schema, which (as stated) is unrealistic in heterogeneous environments.

The federated solution fits in between alternatives 1 and 2—or, more precisely, might cover both of them, since it can itself have different degrees of coupling coherence. The options presented in the establishment of a multidatabase system can be expressed in the following terms (see also Fig. 17.2):

- Full integration might seem desirable, but technically it is very difficult to implement and quite often it is politically objectionable, owing to the facts of organizational life.

- Nonintegrated approaches demand too much skill on the part of the end user. They are slow, unstable, and very difficult to control.

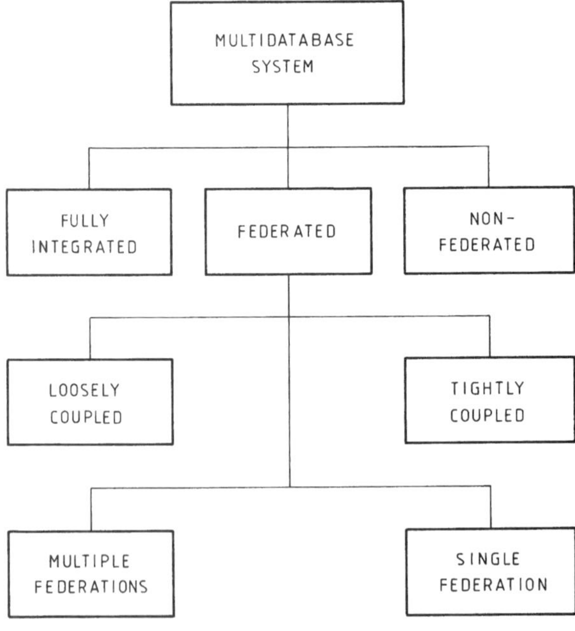

Figure 17.2 Alternative approaches to the establishment of a multidatabase solution.

- Federated solutions offer a good compromise. They do, however, come in several alternatives, ranging from rather loosely coupled to rather tightly coupled.

A solution is "fully loosely coupled" if it is the user's responsibility to create and maintain some sense of database cooperation and there is no tight central control enforced by the system and its administrators. A solution is tightly coupled if the database system and its administrator:

- Have the responsibility for creating and maintaining schema management, actively controlling the access to component databases

- Are authorized to express such responsibility by hiring and firing information scientists anywhere in the outlying units of the organization*

With both tight and loose coupling, sharing any part of the component databases or invoking operations on a component should be controlled in a way that permits a high degree of dependability.

This is the managerial element the two modes of operation have in common. The difference lies in their implementation:

- With tightly coupled databases, the corporate DBA has both the responsibility and the corresponding authority to assure that all attached data resources conform to unique rules.

- With loosely coupled systems, the corporate database executive is only a coordinator. Site management is under the control of the administrator of each local database.

Whether the database system is loosely or tightly coupled, a *reference architecture* is needed to clarify the various issues and choices within the database system. Each component of the reference architecture deals with one of the important issues regarding cross-database operability. Thus, understanding, categorizing, and comparing different architectural options for distributed database solutions is critical.

17.3   The Cooperation among Independent, Autonomous Systems

The term *federated database* was coined by Hammer Heimberger and Dennis McLeod.† Since its introduction, it has been used to describe

---

*The DBA also controls the salary and promotion of *all* IT personnel.

†University of Southern California.

several different but related database architectures, each with its own type of definition as well as established DBA rights.

As we saw in Sec. 17.2, a key characteristic of a federation is the cooperation among independent, autonomous systems. Since these can and often do feature different characteristics, the technical details of a federation are important for understanding and managing existing heterogeneous database structures.

The autonomous components of a federated database participate in a global aggregate which aims to assure partial but controlled sharing of information resources. Association autonomy implies that the component databases have control over the data they manage.

- They cooperate to allow different degrees of integration.

- There is no centralized control or centrally commanded access to their data.

There may, however, be real-time schema translation. As we saw in Chaps. 15 and 16, this helps in significantly reducing the complexity of a cross-database solution, although not necessarily its overhead. There are other reasons accounting for the favor a federated database approach is finding among user organizations.

One of the assets is technology—more particularly, the products expected to come to market within the next 3 to 4 years. "What is going to happen when you have a billion transistors on a chip is that all kinds of chips—even memory chips—will have central processing units on them," says John Moussouris, a cofounder of MIPS.

Let us put ourselves in the position of a user organization today. We are planning for solutions able to withstand the test of time, to survive at least through the 1990s, and we are informed about the next breakthroughs in computers and communications. Therefore, we would be professionally irresponsible if we did not account in our present work for these coming events as well as for pressing immediate requirements.

The fact that the coming wave of memory chips will feature embedded microprocessors is very positive in regard to schema translation strategies. However, real-time schema translation, though more than adequate for query-oriented solutions, is not enough for transaction processing.

In short, not all approaches to federalism support transaction management; therefore, we should be careful what we use in a transaction environment. There is a price to be paid for relative ease:

- Loosely coupled federated databases provide efficient solutions in query-intense applications.

- They assure both ad hoc approaches and the implementation of analytical queries, at relatively low cost.

- Knowledge engineering predicates can further extend this approach by having the queries executed with great simplicity.

These are the reasons federated solutions are on the way to being adopted as the main vehicle for assuring a virtually united environment of distributed heterogeneous databases, within the applications perspectives we are discussing.

Database federalism uses heuristics and partial-match algorithms to find similarities in the structures of two or more databases which communicate peer-to-peer. Moving information elements from one database to another involves assigning them as similarly as possible in the destination database. Two basic measures can be used in a partial-match process:

1. Comparing the category names, which essentially is a string comparison

2. Comparing category inheritance structures through knowledge engineering

When an information element is exported from one database to another, control data is carried along with it, indicating not only the specific category assignments in the source database but also something about the context in the category hierarchy.

In the destination database, the hierarchy is searched for matching classes, and if these are found, the information element is assigned to them. If no matching categories are found, an attempt is made to locate an appropriate corresponding category.

In a way, federation represents a compromise between no integration at all (forcing users to interface explicitly with multiple autonomous databases) and total integration. In the latter case, the autonomy of each component database is sacrificed so that users can access data through a single global interface. But as already stated, this is not a practical solution.

Federalism reflects the most recent technological developments and the fact that the methods preceding them did not provide by themselves the expected results, thus necessitating the search for better solutions.

A federated database solution succeeds where earlier attempts have failed because it leaves intact disperse and heterogeneous databases, as well as their schemata. As a consequence, the federated approach:

- Does not interrupt current operations or in any way alter them

- Does not imply a global schema definition and implementation
- Maps, in a data dictionary, the schemata characterizing the heterogeneous databases in existence throughout the network

There are, however, operational procedures to be followed. For instance, the database administrator must notify the data dictionary about any and every change in schemata, consistently updating their definitions. The DBA must also load new copies and assure through testing that real-time translation of schemata is properly carried out. And, quite evidently, the corporate DBA must work in close cooperation with local DBAs operating in the distributed environment.

17.4   A Real-Time Translation of Schemata

Real-time translation of schemata is carried out by the artificial intelligence constructs that command and serve the federated databases. But since a distributed database system is a dynamic entity, there is a need to assure that new schemata associated with DBMS implementation are known to the data dictionary.

- Part of the reason is that a federated database acts peer-to-peer, the system being physically and logically distributed.

- This contrast with the rather common solution available today, in which a database may be de facto physically distributed while management imagines that it is already logically centralized and does not take the necessary steps to that effect.

The often incomprehensive and contradictory policy of totally heterogeneous physical characteristics and an imaginary logical integration is resolved through the concept of *virtual* database distribution, also known as the *repository* approach. Each user operates as if there were a virtual disk nearby, while in reality the facility might be central or regional and miles away.

This alone negates the whole issue of networked workstations and server implementation perspectives, turning the whole system into a super-centralized, monolithic structure in which the chances of success are minimal. To operate it, the user organization must have logical homogeneity throughout the network, which by itself is also an illusion.

Let's look at the situation for just one vendor: IBM.

- VSAM, IMS, DB2, Adabas, Oracle, and Ingres DBMS (to name only a few) can run on the same mainframe with just as many different, incompatible schemata.

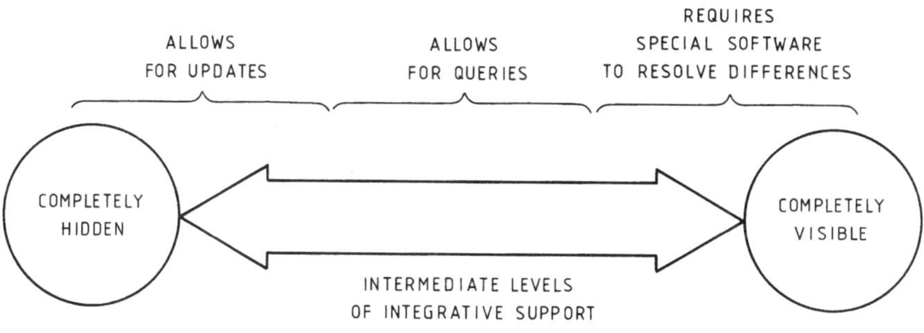

Figure 17.3 Different levels of integrating heterogeneous databases.

- Finding a common ground for so many different and incompatible schemata, from hierarchical to inverted and relational files, is a hopeless undertaking.

- What is feasible is to classify possible solutions along the lines of Fig. 17.3, which suggests a whole spectrum of connectivity regarding heterogeneous databases.

In the VSAM, IMS, DB2, Adabas, Oracle, and Ingres example, it matters little whether all six structures run on the same mainframe. Their coexistence amounts to nothing less than distributed incompatible databases whose heterogeneity is bound to be visible both to the systems analyst and to the user. This is the worst of all worlds.

Even if only relational databases from the same vendor were involved—for instance DB2, SQL/DS, SQL/OS 400, and SQL/OS 2—the resulting visibility would be very disturbing. That's why IBM found it necessary to develop DRDA. Its No. 1 goal is to hide the incompatibility existing in the distributed database environment, even if the cost to do so is exceptionally high.

Between the completely hidden and the completely visible alternatives there exist middle positions which are less costly as well more user friendly in their implementation. As we have seen in this chapter, the federated approach fills the middle ground, albeit at different levels of sophistication.

To properly choose the level of sophistication to implement, the user organization must accurately answer the query: What are the specific database issues in the company today? Two kinds of fundamental problems can affect the choice:

- Providing access to and distributing data upstream and down-stream

- Assuring the proper protocols for cross-database access

Distributing data upstream means moving IEs from the central or distributed warehouse(s)—whether on database computers, disk farms, or old mainframes—to the client/server platforms. The latter are typically LAN-based servers and workstations, as described in Part 1. Distributing data downstream means moving IEs from workstations and servers to the multimedia warehouse(s).

Multimedia information increases the requirement for a valid methodology to help the two-way distribution of information elements. Such a methodology must assure efficient information exchange, proper security maintenance and controls, and data integrity at all stages.

Whichever solution is chosen, it should account for the fact that ad hoc databases evolve on workstations using a spreadsheet and simple data management tools. Applications programs able to maintain this data often become critical to an overall solution. Hence their study is inseparable from the establishment of a valid database architecture.

As stand-alone applications evolve into networked LAN-based systems, distributive approaches need to be enhanced with a new generation of methods and tools. Their introduction must mesh with existing production applications—whether these are operating on client/servers or on mainframes.

- No organization can afford unaccounted-for information elements moving across the enterprise.

- The challenge is one of achieving a practical multimedia information distribution that retains local autonomy and control.

This is the gist of the advice given in Chap. 15 about integrating with existing networked systems structures. There are several ways to do so, and we have examined the most important alternatives here.

One alternative approach is the real-time translation of schemata (see Sec. 17.5). With workstations at 30, 40, and up to 100 MIPS, it is highly possible to empower the distributed database concept with information elements residing on different heterogeneous sites of a communications network. These sites:

- Feature different data structures

- Employ incompatible DBMS

- Use a variety of concurrency control mechanisms

Capitalizing once more on the power of the workstations, powerful algorithms can be used to assure the correct execution of all queries and transactions, even when they access objects residing on sites that have totally different characteristics. Until now, this problem has been approached by dividing user transactions into two types:

- *Local,* which access only objects residing on a single site and hence interact with a single concurrency control protocol

- *Global,* which access information elements residing on different sites and hence involve different DBMS and concurrency control protocols

More than likely, the federated database system will actually consist of several component databases functioning autonomously. But through a powerful data dictionary and real-time schema translation, the federation virtually works as one system, permitting controlled access to data in all component databases *as if* they had virtually homogeneous characteristics.

17.5 Research by Bellcore on Schema Translation

Schema translation software being developed by Bellcore is expected to be a critical component of a federated database toolkit. The concept behind this approach is to manage schemata and dictionary information in a federated database system. The tool aims to assist a user in performing several closely related database design and integration tasks, including:

- Developing a corporate logical data model (LDM) by integrating schemata of applications

- Integrating views when designing a large implementation

- Identifying related data used by two or more applications

One of Bellcore's research goals is to develop techniques that automatically integrate schemata at run time. The solution is not expected to handle every case and every DBMS, but it will address the majority of them. Considering the inability of current data models to capture the semantics of the real world, even partial integration is a breakthrough.

Both manual and automatic approaches are currently being studied. Manual integration involves activities performed with human input and reasoning and has limited practicality. Automatic integration requires knowledge engineering artifacts. A Bellcore extended

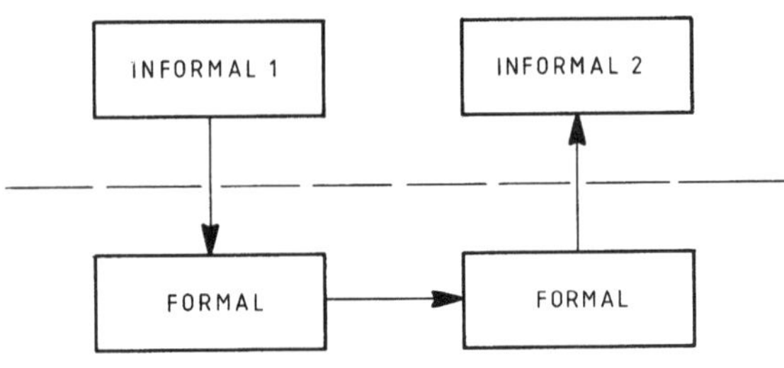

Figure 17.4   Informal-to-formal mapping as an approach to schema integration. Projected by Bellcore, this approach provides an easier mapping procedure.

entity-relationship (ER) model underlies this approach, employing metamodel concepts.

- A graphics interface permits creating and manipulating schemata that adhere to the integrity constraints of the metamodel.

- Forms are provided for entering and displaying dictionary information, as well as for updating the knowledge bank.

- A graphics query language has been developed for posing queries about the objects of the schema against the metamodel.

An informal-to-formal and formal-to-informal mapping procedure has been chosen, as shown in Fig. 17.4. The schema integrator can query the schemata using metalinguistics to determine the relationships among schema objects. The integrator can also use a set of operators for manual integration of schema objects.

- Schema objects include attributes and relationships in the ER model as well as classes (entity types).

- The procedure capitalizes on object-oriented solutions and exploits their semantic content.

For automatic integration, schemata are converted to a formal data model which provides the classification paradigm. Classification helps in formal reasoning to determine the superclass-subclass relationships among classes, as well as a complete set of relationships.

Other cross-database projects use object-oriented solutions to promote automatic real-time schema translation. They respond to the need for effective access and management of shared data across a wide range of applications. Such projects benefit from object-oriented data modeling and programming capabilities. In particular:

- They use both type and function abstractions.

- They help resolve mapping and schema integration problems.

Though the methodology from one schema translation project to another is not necessarily the same, the bottom line is always to provide facilities for applications needing to access and manipulate multiple autonomous and heterogeneous distributed database systems through a uniform interface.

These cross-database projects are not just front-end (passthrough) approaches. Their aim is to offer a complete data management perspective able to integrate various database structures and to do so in a more or less generic sense.

One approach to reducing the number of mappings between diverse data systems, an approach in use since the mid-1980s, is to define a common data model and language. Early efforts involved mapping the underlying data models to a relational data definition. However, a basic relational model is not sufficient to capture the integrated semantics of underlying systems.

Subsequent efforts have relied on a functional data model to represent the schemata of various existing databases. With this approach, a view mechanism defines the integration of local database schemata and specifies the rules for resolving data mismatches.

Such experiences, however, have indicated the need for a more extensible framework for dealing with the peculiarities of various DBMS. Thus, newer projects take advantage of object-oriented data modeling, using both type and function abstractions to deal with mapping and integration problems.

As used in this discussion, *function implementation* can be defined in an underlying database language—essentially a programming language with value-added features. Here in a nutshell are the basic concepts characterizing a cross-database model:

- Data abstraction and encapsulation facilities embedded in the model provide an extensible framework for dealing with various kinds of heterogeneities.

- The approach rests on the fact that heterogeneity is inevitable in traditional database systems, as well as with text, documents, and multimedia databases.

- An object orientation serves as a framework for uniform interoperation of multiple data sources with incompatible DBMS; the same is true of knowledge engineering.

Objects are uniquely identified by their object characteristics and may gain and lose types dynamically. Control is provided through metaknowledge. For instance, an object representing a given person may be created as an instance of a given type. Types have unique names and represent collections of objects with common characteristics.* The inheritance mechanism uses both object and AI concepts.

- Functions are the manifestations of operations helping to provide mappings among objects.

- Properties, relationships, and computations on objects are expressed in terms of functions.

A type can be characterized by the roles it plays in the arguments mapped into the procedure, and results of various functions are evaluated through knowledge artifacts. These are concepts which facilitate an effective federated object identification and associated operations mechanisms.

17.6   Implementing a Federated Object Identification

Object identification and its underlying concepts are basic parts of object-oriented databases. Object identifiers can be used to reference schemata. Within a single database, such identifiers are systems generated, unique, and immutable.

- They are used as references to objects, in relationships among objects, and as join attributes.

- They normally have semantic content in a systems sense but not from the user's point of view.

- The system may choose to encode the identifiers with certain internal informationI to help in automating translation and other tasks.

In an object-oriented DBMS that deals with multiple object databases, the query processor has to handle a mix of locally and externally generated identifiers. Identifiers belonging to other DBMS in the network—hence, external—may have different formats, to be handled through knowledge artifacts.

Because of name autonomy, identifiers might be assigned to the same application object; or the same identifier may represent different things in different databases. A federated solution has to deal with these issues through basic principles, the most important among them being:

---

*See also D. N. Chorafas and H. Steinmann, *Object-Oriented Databases,* Prentice-Hall, Englewood Cliffs, NJ, 1993.

- *Uniqueness.* Generating globally unique identifiers so that they do not conflict when different databases are interoperated

- *Local autonomy.* Preserving local autonomy in creating identifiers while assuring global uniqueness and object equivalence

- *Equivalence.* Helping to determine how and when two identifiers refer to the same applications object

- *Locatable objects.* Through object identification (OID), establishing an object location where most of the information about the object is currently stored

- *Implementation efficiency.* Managing the space for storing OIDs and optimizing the execution time of operations involving them

As these examples help document, one of the better means of approaching federated solutions is to apply the rich data-modeling capabilities provided by an object orientation to resolve problems of heterogeneous database integration.

Also, as noted in Sec. 17.5, while real-time schema translation solutions are not simple, they are more manageable when handled through flexible, semantically rich approaches. There are two key integration issues in an object environment.

1. Attributes of an applications object are stored in multiple databases with the intention to present a transparent view of an object and its properties. Such a view should be independent of the physical distribution of specific properties characterizing the underlying database systems.

2. Conceptually related objects and their properties are distributed in multiple databases while retaining a generalized view of these objects. This view should emphasize common traits and help in resolving the possible inconsistencies in attribute values.

At the modeling level, such problems can be addressed by exploring type and object relationships across multiple databases. For issue No. 1, a criterion for the object equivalence can be established. For instance, an object is identified by an ID in one database and a relation or attribute in another.

To perform queries that apply to a class of equivalent objects, an equivalence relationship between types in different databases should also be worked out. The system must be able to investigate the appropriate facilities that permit it to operate on equivalent objects.

For problem No. 2, the notion of generalization can be used as means of integration. This works in the opposite direction of the specialization process normally employed in developing new data-processing applications.

For integration purposes, generalization attempts to extract the *common properties* of existing object classes by defining a new metatype of the underlying types. In principle, the process of generalization:

- Permits the user to view the underlying systems at the metatype level

- Leaves the system to deal with the mapping of this view to the schemata of the underlying DBMS

In this sense, the behavior of a metatype can be defined in terms of the existing functions of the underlying subtypes. Furthermore, since the distributed databases can evolve autonomously, an integration process normally must deal with inevitable:

- Structural conflicts

- Domain mismatches at schema and data levels

There may be, for example, representation conflicts in which the same concept is represented by different modeling constructs in different schemata. There may also be dependency conflicts, with some concepts related differently among themselves in different schemata.

Key conflicts, too, are possible, with different keys assigned to the same concept in different schemata. Finally, behavioral conflicts may arise in which different operation policies are defined on objects of the same type in distinct schemata. We will follow up on this issue in the next section.

17.7 Dealing with Domain Mismatch Problems

Any approach to virtual database integration worthy of adopting must be capable of dealing with domain mismatch problems. For instance, the mapping between two domains, or perhaps a cross product of two domains with another domain, can be encapsulated in the implementation of conversion functions, with a defined conversion function taking various forms.

If the common model is rooted in a semantically rich object data model, some of the mechanisms for dealing with various representation conflicts may already be present in the artifact. Through this facility, metadata can be queried and updated as conveniently as user data.

Implementation also requires interfacing with client/server databases through a solution that maps the schema of an existing database to an equivalent user schema. This can provide query transformation functions and other services that are missing in one or more of the networked databases.

These approaches may allow applications to access and manipulate multiple databases, facilitating the interoperation of existing heterogeneous structures. Throughout this work, it is important to look forward to future applications designed around autonomous databases but intended to interoperate with other databases in the network.

The design of an architecture to address virtual database integration merits in-depth research in its own right. The same is true of a unifying data definition and data manipulation language. The data language should provide declarative statements that can handle multiple heterogeneous local databases, thereby creating:

- Types

- Functions

- Objects

Further, it must be possible to import specifications of types and functions from underlying local databases, integrating them into native schemata of the unifying language. We will return to this concept in Chap. 18 when we examine interoperability.

Not only must domain mismatch problems be solved a priori, but mapping facilities must be provided to generate a schema that gives a local data source the appearance of a virtually integrated database. Mapping can be instrumental in permitting the user to access heterogeneous databases through high-level queries.

- In principle, the mapping facilities should be modular, with a separate module for each local data model.

- A mechanism should be embedded in the module for specifying mapping between the data model of a given networked data source and the virtual database integration schema.

- The mapping and translation specifications can be fully or partially automated by means of appropriate tools.

The outlined approach will help make the distributed database a logically integrated entity which resides in multiple sites or among different machines at the same site. Once again, the essential goal is that the whole mechanism be transparent to the end user.

Under no condition should the end user need to know how the distribution has been made and which variety of data structures, DBMS, and other parameters it involves. The principle of transparency of technical details is one of the hallmarks of a valid design and the solution which it promotes.

This is the theory at least. In practice, building reliable and efficiently federated systems solutions is not that simple. Transparency is sometimes compromised by the need for simultaneous observance of a number of critical factors, such as:

- Any-to-any connectivity

- Site autonomy

- Widely distributed locations

- Seamless integration

- Concurrency in operations

- Networkwide integrity

- Image consistency at all times

- Avoidance of domain mismatch

As a way of fulfilling these requirements, systems designers talk of a *top-down* approach. Top-down presupposes that many practical problems have been solved and that both stable and efficient products are available. In practice, this is rarely the case.

Alternatively, a top-down approach can be implemented through flat orders issued at board level. Such a policy provides a landscape in which a top-down design can be applied even though technical database solutions may be lacking.

A technically elegant approach will make the end users job quite simple, with the environment resembling a single global schema even though in reality it involves many heterogeneous schemata. Such an approach takes account of the fact that not only do companies have an array of heterogeneous computers and databases, but they will continue to do so in the future.

Companies which took time to study the future effects of a policy of strict homogeneity found that for any practical purpose it cannot be sustained.

- Vendors tend to improve (read: change) their OS, DBMS, protocols, and other special software too often.

- Strict normalization, like standardization, leads to ineffective approaches in the face of technology's fast path.

- Locking into any one vendor for single sourcing results in an overall reduction in cost/effectiveness from the user's viewpoint.

Another major problem is that even with homogeneous DBMS products, the typical implementation of information systems has not adhered to a top-down design. The best that can be done is to define the objective of data sharing across the enterprise on a federated basis, with cross-database solutions supported by a reference architecture, as described earlier in this chapter.

Such an architectural solution should be specific to the enterprise working it out. Its overall perspective may be top-down, but its implementation will be bottom-up, designed to provide for interoperability among autonomous and heterogeneous database platforms.

17.8 Enterprise Models and RAID Services

The aim of the often-heralded concept of enterprise integration is to provide a commercial information infrastructure that connects people, computers, and software within and across enterprises. The background reason is competitiveness:

- Management must be able to develop, manufacture, sell, deliver, and support products and services.

- In today's world, it must do so with unprecedented speed, flexibility, quality, and economy.

Is this goal do-able? The technical issues raised here provide a good part of the answer: It is do-able if extreme care is taken regarding both the organizational and the technical aspects of the effort.

Although the user organization has to solve its own problems in connection with the organizational issues, it can profit from vendor assistance on the technical side. In the 1990s, computer vendors will be differentiated by:

- Their ability to assure and maintain seamless access to databases from text and data warehouse to the desktop side

- Their drive in finding able solutions no matter how heterogeneous the organization's on-line structures may be

The integrative perspectives offered by vendors should not only be efficient but also as low in cost as current technology can provide. A good example in the database domain is that of disk farms—or, more precisely, of redundant arrays of inexpensive disks (RAID).*

While only a small percentage of the engineering community has actually adopted RAID, the potential of disk farms is most significant.

---

*RAID systems first came to the market in the mid-1980s but are now being introduced as a new generation of very reliable structures. However, it would have been more accurate if the "I" in RAID stood for "independent" rather than "inexpensive" disks.

It is also indivisible from the federated database solution elaborated in this chapter.

Redundant arrays of inexpensive disks promise to provide a high degree of fault tolerance, which is a basic necessity for practically all networked environments. In addition, it is argued that federated RAID solutions can reduce the input/output (I/O) bottleneck that has plagued the computer industry for years.

- Some types of disk arrays offer so much bandwidth that they can even satisfy user organizations with huge I/O requirements.

- Disk arrays can perform a number of tasks that would be very difficult, time-consuming, and expensive to do otherwise.

So far, RAID solutions have been used primarily in the domain of supercomputing. Probably, this is so because the I/O bottleneck is most acute in high-performance systems employed for massive number-crunching and data reduction requirements.

In fact, alert systems specialists note that much of the business opportunity for RAID lies in the downsizing of computers from mainframes. As network computing becomes more prevalent, the need for hardware-based arrays of storage increases.

Supercomputing, of course, does not need to be the only domain for RAID. As we have seen in this and the preceding chapters, an expanding environment of information resources must serve the needs of a growing variety of applications. Different data types, database management systems, expert systems with their knowledge banks, and applications programs with their production facilities—all can benefit from the cost-effectiveness of RAID.

As can never be repeated too often, cost consciousness should be one of the pillars of any enterprise model for computers, databases, and software. RAID is different from other disk solutions, but then most available database resources are already incompatible with one another—from physical characteristics to syntax and formal semantics. This is, of course, the result of different:

- Hardware and operating systems

- Physical and logical data structures

- Informal semantics caused by different cultures

- Management rules

Enterprise information resources attempt to model some portion of the real world and necessarily introduce approaches to cope with incompatibilities. RAID is no different, except that it capitalizes on high storage capacity, greater reliability, and lower cost.

17.9   Choices with Redundant Arrays of Inexpensive Disks

Systems experts with experience in integration and in RAID suggest that, costs aside, the real value of redundant arrays of inexpensive disks is reliability in mirroring. Other systems experts respond that the more classical mirroring of selected files can do the job just as quickly and inexpensively *if* the user organization is interested more in random accesses than in I/O and database bandwidth.

There is some truth in both arguments. The approach known as *mirroring* (or striping) means writing all IEs onto two or more drives so that data is safe even if one drive fails. This approach is categorized as RAID *level 1* in the University of California at Berkeley paper that coined the acronym RAID in 1987.

However, when RAID vendors talk about disk arrays, most of them focus on higher levels. These levels employ powerful parity algorithms, to let users restore data when one or more drives go down. With powerful algorithms, techniques of error detection and correction rarely use much more than 25 percent of the total array capacity for parity, saving cost over classical mirroring.

In recent years, deciding on RAID levels has been a demanding task for potential users, but vendors now claim that the proper choice is not that difficult after all.

- CAD/CAM applications and others that have large block sizes and need high bandwidth usually call for RAID *level 3,* which uses one drive solely for parity.

- Transaction-processing environments that have small blocks and want good response time usually go with RAID *level 5,* which spreads parity across all the drives in the array.

Once the user organization has determined which RAID level suits its needs, as a whole and by application area, it must decide whether it wants a hardware or software array solution. In principle:

- Software systems are largely viewed as an inexpensive way to go.

- Hardware is considered a more performance-oriented, but also more costly, approach.

Software arrays use the host CPU and the existing controller or adapter to perform the necessary data assurance functions, eliminating the cost of special-purpose hardware. Hardware techniques use a dedicated processor on the controller board to create parity, perform error correction, keep track of data location, and handle other tasks.

Software offers a lot more flexibility—and is cheaper as well. But hardware proponents contend that software techniques have significant overhead in a RAID environment—though not as high as that encountered with mainframes.

There are, of course, a number of challenges posed by RAID decisions. Should departmental file servers be limited to a disk space-sharing function for connected workstations? Do they also have a role to play as full-fledged distributed databases? If so, can corporate resources then be distributed to departmental and remote sites? Can this be done on a much more extensive scale than present RAID implementations suggest?

The federated solution helps answer many of these queries in a positive manner. By integrating heterogeneous resources in a single environment, applications and users may interact to request and update information and, more generally, to execute tasks dependent on different resources. As always, the need for this capability is critical.

Strategic business applications that require: (1) intercorporate *linkage,* such as linking buyers with suppliers, and/or (2) intracorporate *integration,* producing composite information from engineering and manufacturing views of a product, are becoming increasingly prevalent. In turn, this promotes the concept of RAID solutions as a means of significantly improving upon I/O bandwidth and reducing costs.

As with the other approaches examined in this chapter, creating such an environment requires that the incompatibilities which can arise during query, update, and maintenance operations be resolved. But as we have seen, integration can be achieved even though the global view of the databases may be very different from the distributed local views.

Handling Heterogeneity in a Federation of Databases

18.1 Introduction

As we saw in Chap. 17, the concepts of federated databases and object-oriented solutions tend to merge. This is largely because they have common aims. In both cases, the goal is to allow types and classes of information elements to be viewed in a *meaningful* manner by their users.

Meaningful here refers to *semantic* orientation, a key issue to be expanded on in this chapter. In semantic terms, the *schema* is the *metadata*—a concept which introduces a third component to our model: knowledge engineering.

Effective interoperable database solutions must be able to accommodate various levels of abstraction and detail, supporting user-defined external schemata with both anticipated and unanticipated (ad hoc) queries. As the implementation of computers, communications, and software reaches senior management levels, as well as external traders and salespeople, many of the ad hoc queries will be fuzzy, requiring not only rule-based expert systems but *fuzzy engineering* as well.*

If one lesson can be learned from the most advanced applications available today, it is that dynamic solutions must:

---

*See D. N. Chorafas *The New Information Technology—A Practitioner's Guide,* Van Nostrand Reinhold, New York, 1992.

- Handle multiple viewpoints
- Be free of implementation details
- Feature physical data independence

Such solutions can be achieved through flexible client/server architectures, visual programming, and fuzzy engineering. By contrast, they are impossible with mainframes, Cobol, Fortran, 3270 emulation, and other technological dinosaurs.

Consider a fully distributed environment with four levels of reference: from microfiles on workstation, to workgroups, to departmental databases, and to a corporate warehouse (see Fig. 18.1). These represent the database levels confronting the systems designer.

- At each level, the information requirements are rather precise, but data structures and DBMS can generally be heterogeneous.

- Heterogeneity is increased with a global perspective, extending beyond the locality of the federated components.

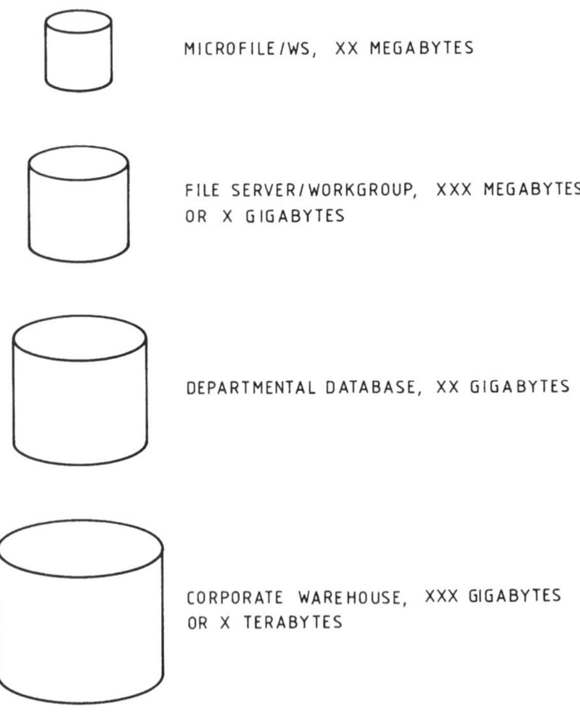

Figure 18.1   Levels of federated databases.

- The requirements faced by the distributed database structure should be described in an accurate (rather than precise) manner if the federated database system is to be manageable.

- Flexibility can be served through the development of interdatabase usage patterns, since customer requirements vary in function of time and location.

In a business organization, for instance, each subsidiary as well as headquarters wants to be able to interactively generate its own financial statements, limited only by the user's imagination and the database contents.

All these features are crucial to handling heterogeneity in a distributed database structure. The algorithms and heuristics used in managing the federation have to reflect the key points raised here.

18.2 Understanding the Classification and Organization of Information

A database study by an investment bank in New York identified significant overlaps (and incompatibilities) among 63 securities master files from different applications. Over the years, the massive weight of mainframe-based applications made such overlaps impossible to detect, so little could be done to streamline database contents.

In many other user organizations as well, the increasing *on-line* use of databases by managers and professionals points to the need for a thorough cleanup of available information resources. Interactive financial reporting is largely ad hoc, and to be effective it must answer queries on future business, not just on accounts and statistics of the past.

A factual and documented response to these requirements will make use of all four levels of distributed information elements shown in Fig. 18.1. This may involve interactivity with:

- Myriads of workstations

- Thousands of servers

- A significant number of text and data warehouses

Under no condition can this type of implementation be handled through the batch procedures that have characterized mainframes over the last 30 years. The use of, say, DXT to extract information during the night run is a workhorse approach that eventually leads to loss of competitiveness in the marketplace.*

---

*This statement is just as valid for the vendor of DXT as for the user organization.

A dynamic financial environment sees to it that a number of queries are posed simultaneously, each with its own pattern in terms of the data access and information elements it requires. Instead of opening a file, as legacy programs are designed to do, fuzzy queries choose one or two objects out of hundreds of different files—a service pattern that can be technically supported only through a database federation.

An industrial organization faced with a similar type of problem identified several handicaps confronting its main business. Among them:

- The current dataflow was been designed in 1969 for a 360/30 computer with sorting procedures which a quarter century ago were state of the art but today are obsolete.

- Sticking to old procedures has saddled the organization with a highly inefficient *card-oriented* approach while the disk memory approaches terabyte level.*

Setting aside the fact that end users are very badly served, managing a card-based approach with operations such as dataflow recovery leads to inefficiencies, such as having to fully rerun the job.

No wonder, then, that in company after company clear-eyed management has reached the conclusion that organization and methodology have to change. At the same time, it is not possible to change every database structure around because of *lack of:*

- Money
- Time
- Skill

A number of leading-edge organizations have therefore concluded that whatever does not change must be federated according to organizational and classification requirements.

- Classification should not be confused with identification.

- Classification is taxonomical; identification provides a running ID number.†

---

*Still another organization has found, following a benchmark project, that using card-oriented imaging on disk ends by using only 5 percent of the available disk capacity.

†See also D. N. Chorafas, *Handbook of Database Management and Distributed Relational Databases,* McGraw-Hill, New York, 1989.

Classification is a methodology that has its prerequisites. Before viewing specific information elements, users need to understand the classification and organization of the information at their disposal.

Understanding the contents and semantics of the information elements in the database is a relatively easy job *if* all data, text, images, and objects contained in the distributed resources have been classified. Their identification (not necessarily their classification) has to be transparent to the user.

Classification offers significant assistance in implementing an object-oriented solution. Classes appropriate to a balance-type query may contain the following information, to be provided in a network-wide sense:

- General ledger account
- Responsibility center
- Current balance
- Month-to-date aggregation

Month-to-date aggregation may include all daily balances since the beginning of the month. The month-to-date average balance can be easily calculated algorithmically. The same is true for the beginning-of-year balance—as well as balance change, by day, for a period n.

Unlike policies and procedures followed in the past, these queries will not be posed one at a time. Nor will they concern just one account. They will cut across comparisons—for instance, in terms of costs, income, and business activity. Able answers can in no way be supported through old methods.

18.3 Facing the Challenges Posed by Complexity

Organization and classification of information elements are important in facing the challenges posed by today's complex on-line environments—the long transactions and polyvalent ad hoc queries which must now be supported. Such transactions and queries address:

- From any workstation, and any procedure running on it
- Any networked database, whether designed for local or global service

Superficially, the example presented in Sec. 18.2 looks *as if* the requirements it poses have been rather common with legacy-type applications. In reality, a cross-database balance query poses a number of other issues which require looking at the distributed resources as a collection of generic structures.

Each database structure, along with its contents, has specific semantic integrity constraints and primitive operations. It also has its own characteristics in terms of data types and DBMS. In order to operate as a network:

- Database structures must support the specification of objects, object classifications, and interobject relationships.

- The semantic integrity constraints of the global database model must specify restrictions on current states and transitions between such states.

- In spite of multiple accesses with diverse goals, database contents must accurately reflect all information required by the dynamic applications environment.

Simpler solutions regarding constraints can be given by codes. For example, a class code may specify whether an account is classified as an asset, a liability, and so on. A group code can identify an account as belonging to a certain set of accounts within a given class.

It sounds like old stuff, but it is not. The expanding database environment alters all past notions. Static limits and constrained parameters can be used in a one-tantum approach, which may be valid in a static, fairly centralized database environment, but not in a globally distributed architecture.

Old solutions are predominantly static, and therefore cannot handle the requirements of ad hoc queries, which are in steady evolution. In a banking application, for instance, an authorized cash limit typically specifies a limit to be maintained within a location. But the globality of widely distributed and polyvalent customer transactions today calls for an approach that is at once more secure and more flexible.

An end-user-driven, interactive approach should permit ad hoc definitions as the need arises. It must also be able to handle a dynamic redefinition of parameters and metalevels of constraints:

- Alert parametric approaches should allow the user to specify factors that represent ad hoc requirement(s).

- Parametrization may need to be done by ledger account/responsibility center, in a global sense or in any other frame of reference.

Transaction records will typically contain information on transaction code (debit or credit), source code (point of entry), "as *of*" date (the actual day the transaction is to take effect), value date, "as *if*" date (for experimentation purposes), and so on.

Ad hoc queries and special-purpose reports may address each of these variables across the system or all the variables in a given location. They may focus on a certain account and its subaccounts, or apply to all accounts in a cross-database sense.

- Transactions may be *long,* in terms of both their execution and the number of subtransactions they involve.

- A transaction may create an object, delete it, update its attributes, or ask for responses to specific queries prior to executing transactional parts.

Such a transaction can be either an input entered at point of origin or a derived internal action—for instance, one created by a rule. The rule may be derivative, or it may be triggered by an object update done by another transaction.

All this points to the complexity of the applications which now need to be handled in real time. This is another way of saying that centralized mainframe approaches and Cobol programs can no longer toe the mark. Efficient answers are to be found in:

- Client/server solutions

- Visual programming approaches

For interactive users, understanding the dynamic aspects of information classification is one element of computer literacy. This can be easily explained through paradigms derived from the user's professional practice—most professionals use *deviation rules* in their daily work.

Deviation rules provide a means of handling database system heterogeneity. They can be enacted by means of a higher-level model built on top of the distributed database environment. Supported by this approach, solutions involve both metadata and metarules—hence artificial intelligence constructs.

In a major departure from the beaten path of legacy-type applications, expert systems help exploit in a networkwide sense transaction journals, trial balances, and general ledgers. The user thereby gains total flexibility in defining:

- Interactive management reports

- Ad hoc analytical financial statements

Flexibility in both areas is important, since significant differences generally exist in the philosophy and practice of accounting from one subsidiary or operation center to another. Differences also exist in the manner in which information flows into the general ledger or is reported to headquarters.

The message is that information systems solutions should map and assist the organization's way of doing business. They should not straightjacket the enterprise just because meeting the end users' agenda is not a prime target of the EDPers.

18.4 Multidatabases and Federated Nodes

A *multidatabase* is a federation of local, independent databases which are networked. As already discussed, for most functions, these databases work locally and regionally, but for some functions they work globally by preference in a seamless manner.

As noted in Chap. 17, the goal of federated database solutions is to provide integration perspectives with access transparency to preexisting information resources. Reaching this objective requires:

- A graphics ad hoc query language that is easy to use and operate in an efficient manner

- Knowledge tools for inferencing and recursive queries as well as for handling formalisms regarding schema integration

- A framework that helps in design and implementation, including consistency checking

Consistency checking is typically applied to the *federated nodes* of the multidatabase. Consistency and integrity must be assured while local autonomy is preserved.

At the same time, users at a given location should be able to conduct the bulk of their business without the long-haul data communications characteristic of centralized mainframe approaches. Hence, federated nodes should:

- Collect information elements in real time or in real-enough-time

- Maintain these information elements in raw form on site for future cross-database usage

The federated concept already embraces all information elements necessary for business operations, not just some of them. Different design approaches can be taken to reach this goal, depending on the implementation environment and the tools available.

For example, one objective may be to reduce the dependence on telecommunications during the business day, taking advantage of typically cheaper overnight data transfer rates. Another objective may be to provide a better response time locally to on-line users.

Database updates made to a location should be handled through coordinating nodes, allowing a limited number of machines to manage the migration of data between interested locations. Coordinating nodes typically have store and forward facilities. In a transnational implementation, for instance:

- Each country may have a national node for managing customer information and other data shared on a national basis.

- Information that is maintained and shared at a broader regional level may be managed by a regional node.

However, it is not absolutely necessary to have a regional node—or to install only a single node at one location. In certain cases, a separate regional node could be designated for each major class of information elements. Of course, administration clearly becomes more complex as the number of regional centers grows.

Federated nodes may contain not only discrete information elements but also different algorithms to exploit them. Further, on a country-by-country or region-by-region basis, information in the general ledger may be reported in one way to management and in another to the government.

The law of the land in one country may require audit trail references and consolidation procedures in a different presentation mode and/or contents than that required in another country. Since headquarters will probably have still another type of consolidation procedure, regional and headquarters differences must also be handled in a global database sense. Both cases require the application of rules and metarules, or constraints embedded within the structural component of the global model.

In short, the federated nodes of a multidatabase will need to follow both global constraints and locally expressed rules in order to make a universal solution feasible. The manipulation of elements can be assisted by knowledge-enriched software.

The specification of a particular database construct using these local-purpose and general-purpose structures and constraints is an expression of conceptual schemata. A family of database models will consist of:

- General-purpose and special-purpose collections of primitives that support transactions and queries applied to the networked databases

- Knowledge-enriched operations that facilitate the manipulation of information elements within the perspectives implied by a given conceptual schema

This strategy has been found to offer significant support with incompatible database environments.

Another approach to accommodating heterogeneity in a federation of databases is to deal with it on a component *pairwise* basis. This however requires n^2 intercomponent translators for a federation with n components—an intricate and expensive proposition.

As we will see in Chap. 19, still another approach is to provide a powerful common language which permits all components to communicate, sharing information services. This approach presents opportunities as well as problems; and whether a federated architecture or a common language is used, artificial intelligence concepts and tools must be part of the solution..

18.5   The Concept of Federated Schemata and Their Transparent Usage

Knowledge engineering and object orientation in a federated architecture allow a collection of database systems and their components to:

- Unite into a multidatabase in order to share and exchange information

- Make transparent any differences in the constituent databases participating in the federated solution.

This strategy respects the fact that users of existing local databases participating in a distributed environment have expended considerable resources—in terms of skills as well as software and hardware—to develop their solutions. Therefore, they will be quite reluctant to lose control of them.

At the same time, changes in the structure of existing databases must be weighted against competing demands for continuity. Any lasting solution will focus on political factors as well as the technical problems in the real integration of existing databases which is, in general, most difficult.

An important problem in this regard is that the same information elements may be contained in several networked databases, yet they may be represented by different conceptual structures.

If a tight integration approach is used, one of these conceptual representations must be selected and the others changed to comply with it. As a result, applications using the other representation will need modification—which in terms of consumption of human and financial resources can be a bottomless pit.

In light of these difficulties, it is appropriate to pursue the multidatabase architecture that allows the existing networked nodes to maintain their autonomy, while providing a substantial degree of information sharing. This advice has, of course, been offered to the reader all along.

The goal should be to define mechanisms for database interconnection that minimize central authority, yet support partial sharing and coordination among database systems. Here is where federated schemata come into play.

A federated schema approach can offer full data distribution transparency and is quite powerful from the user's point of view. But such an approach can be limited when applied to information systems that have no schemata or schema models—for instance, simple file management and text and image information resources.

The problem is that virtually federated schema cannot unify such databases. Solutions need to be enriched with object-oriented concepts such as encapsulation, applications independence, and data abstraction, as well as with metaconcepts and inheritance capabilities.

Recall that through a federated schema, users and applications are presented with the illusion of a single, integrated, and homogeneous database. Users need not be aware of semantic conflicts that may exist among the different distributed heterogeneous databases.

- Explicit resolution of conflicts can be handled through knowledge engineering.

- Implicit differences can be approached by means of metalevel representations.

The emphasis on metalevels of reference regarding schemata and DBMS functionality—even if these are heterogeneous between and within different client/server environments—is important, because in a network of autonomous database components the only way a federation can function is through implicit cooperation. We have seen several examples of what this statement means.

- Cooperation requires the ability to initiate a potentially complex series of actions, including negotiated data sharing.

- A framework of federated nodes can collectively achieve a substantial amount of sharing while each maintains essential control over its information elements.

Each federation of databases must have a single federal dictionary, whose information province is the federation itself. The federal dictionary supports the establishment, maintenance, and termination of a multidatabase. The main difference between the federal dictionary and more parochial ones is its *globality*.

Existing data dictionaries can play a global role, but a better solution is to build meaning—hence semantics—into data definitions.* Among the stored values should be metadata acting as interpreters of data. This higher-up layer, distinguishing metadata from data, creates an *explicit self-representation*. In an object-oriented environment, for instance, objects can access and modify their metaobjects through tracing, using inheritance and equilibration. Metaobjects further assist the user in understanding object:

- Functionality
- Limits
- Constraints

The metalevel is in complete control of the object level, with the linkage being provided through environmental interactions to assist in the implementation of federated schemata and their transparent usage. But the metalevel also implies other requirements best be examined through import and export characteristics.

18.6 Export/Import and Dynamic Binding in Federated Databases

Communications among members of a federated database are set up, initiated, executed, and terminated by the component servers as well as by the attached workstations. The facilities provided by the global data dictionary should support a list of constraints as well as schemata and metadata. Knowledge engineering artifacts should be able to distinguish between *global* schemata and *local* schemata.

The local or private schema describes that portion of a component database that is local to and therefore stored at the component database. The larger part of a private schema is devoted to describing the applications data available in a locality. To a point, this function corresponds to that of a nonfederated environment.

However, though some of the information will remain local to the component, a portion of the applications data and associated transactions will be *exported* to other databases in the network. Furthermore, in addition to application-specific information, private schemata will most likely contain a small collection of elements relevant to participation in the federation by the local database.

---

*See also D. N. Chorafas and H. Steinmann, *Solutions to Networked Databases*, Academic Press, San Diego, CA, 1993.

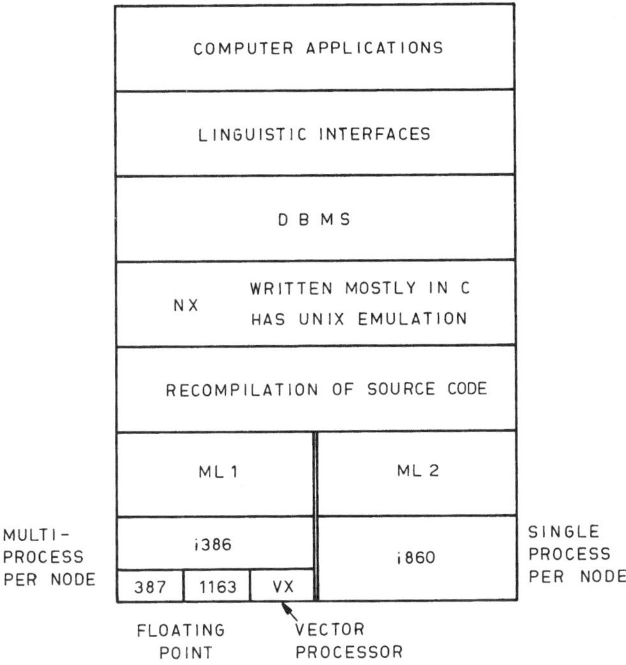

Figure 18.2 A layered approach making the hardware details transparent. *ML 1 and ML 2 are incompatible.

According to the *export/import* model, such information is exported by the component database for use by other components, particularly the federal data dictionary. This information may:

- Be descriptive of the local database, such as its name and network address

- Consist of primitive operations for data manipulation

- Relate more specifically to characteristics connected to the import and export schemata.

Since existing export/import applications are limited, it is difficult to provide a widely valid basis for discussion. Therefore, an example is taken from the strategy adopted by Intel Scientific.

The Intel export/import example, shown in Fig. 18.2, permits recompilation of source code without rewriting between:

- Machine language 1 (ML 1), is applicable to the i386 microprocessor and associated gear (387,1163 chips and a vector processor)

and

- Machine language 2 (ML 2), designed for the reduced instruction set computer (RISC), the i860 chip*

ML 1 and ML 2 are incompatible. However, this becomes transparent to the user, since there are four software layers covering the recompilation level.

A similar concept can be applied to federated heterogeneous databases, with the upper layers supporting schema exchange—which itself is served by the export/import mechanism. We will return to these notions in the following section.

Many specialists believe that to a very substantial degree the issue boils down to *integration versus transparency*. But is there really a difference between the two? Is there a true choice?

- In essence, integration and transparency are *not* two different things, but two faces of the same concept.

- Transparency is a *measure* of integration—more specifically, of the elegance with which it has been done and its dynamic binding characteristics.

In a number of cases transparency may need to be overridden. In CAD, for instance, a user may wish to have different views, each *as is,* rather than being given a unique or standardized version. Typically, however, transparency is a basic design requirement.

The principle of flexibility requires that users be provided with the ability to dynamically search information in their operating environment. But in the presence of a large number of information domains—that is, in practice—the construction of integrated schemata is difficult to obtain.

- Compared with very tightly coupled integration, the federated database approach avoids building a global schema.

- It provides a collection of local schemata along with a federal dictionary and a negotiating language.

---

*The i860 chip has been withdrawn from the general market but continues to be produced and implemented in the high-performance parallel computers of Intel Scientific.

- This collection is most flexible *if* it is subject to an organization hierarchy which is created ad hoc as dynamic requirements imply.

- Such an approach leads to more flexible information sharing among client/server databases.

Federalism permits autonomy and dynamic binding flexibility. *Flexibility* and *autonomy* are very important factors in a cooperative information-sharing environment.

Any attempt to enforce a centralized scheme would be unacceptable to a large number of individual users. Local database administrators should be in full control of the information stored in their databases—and of the associated schemata which enter into the federated solution. Nonetheless, the integration of these component parts should be as fully transparent as possible.

Such a requirement can be met if the available tools enable interactive on-line sessions from workstations, using flexible formatted screens, and allow the facility to set up ad hoc connections. The system should permit the user to access and employ semantic directories.

This is the role of object-oriented databases, which provide additional capabilities above and beyond those of relational technology. By value-differentiating on the relational level and its flat files, object-oriented flexibility and evolvability assist in significantly reducing the long periods of planning, coding, and testing.

18.7 Supporting the Concept of Autonomous Databases

The effective implementation of autonomous databases requires rather significant modeling and abstraction power, explicitly supporting the specification and enforcement of semantic integrity constraints. Such a strategy facilitates graceful database evolution as well as a wider diversity of modalities of database objects; it also provides for higher-level user and program interfaces.

What is more, implementation can be fairly simple if emphasis is placed on concepts, principles, and techniques of semantic database solutions.

The relationship of autonomous databases to more traditional database management approaches must be carefully examined, with mechanisms developed to substantiate user-to-database and database-to-database communications.

Figure 18.3 presents an example of an export/import mechanism to help assure dynamic binding in a federated database environment.

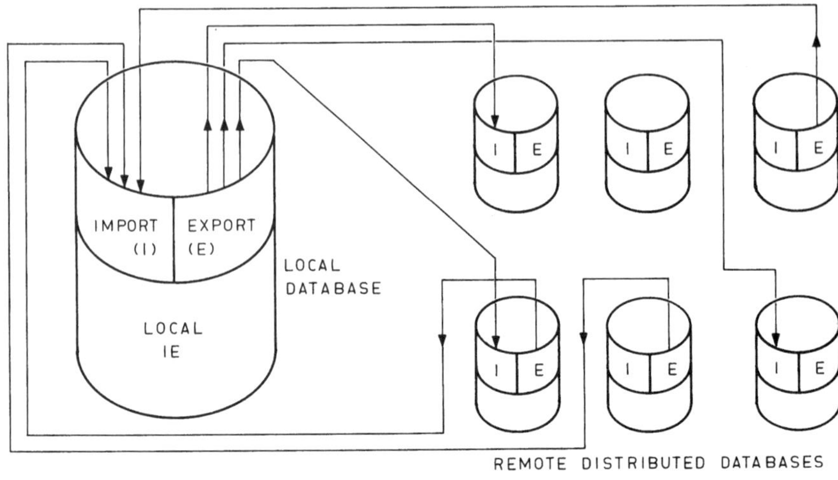

Figure 18.3 Export/import in a federated database solution.

- A semantic data dictionary exists at every database location, along with a sharing advisor.

- From database to database, the connection is export-to-import, as briefly described in Sec. 18.6.

Basically, in a federated scheme each component functions as an *autonomous database,* with three separate schemata. Each of these schemata consists of a collection of types and maps describing some class of information important to proper global functioning. The three schemata are:

- Local
- Export
- Import

The export schema of a component specifies information that the local database is willing to share with others in the federation. This will most likely consist of a collection of types and maps denoting the data to be exported to other components.

- The exported information is divided in federation-specific and application-specific schema.

- The federation-specific information is quite similar to that of the private schema, since it is derived from it.

- Correspondingly, the application-specific schema is extracted from the application-oriented portion of the private schema.

The import schema of a component specifies the information that the component database desires to use from other databases. Each imported information element has a definition property specifying how that object has been derived from the underlying export element(s) of another database.

Schema exchange, and therefore schema import, is a fundamental information-sharing operation in client/server databases working as a federation. It may, however, be necessary to modify a component's import schema by gaining access to some element of exported information.

Typically, import and export information needs to be encapsulated. In terms of housekeeping, each database participating in the federation must know what information is available networkwide. This is accomplished through the federal dictionary, which allows each component to find the names and network addresses of the others. Subsequently, a component may contact other components, using a predefined protocol.

To help the component databases perform these functions in an able manner, the global data dictionary should include (or import):

- Data structures

- Access methods

- Description and manipulation language(s)

All attached client/server databases have this information in their local data dictionaries. The challenge is to create a federal repository out of it.

Export/import interfaces are also needed, but their role is not as explicit as that of the export/import schemata. The primary interface function is to provide direct support so that each component is able to define its own view of information elements. Finally, translation procedures may be necessary. These can be implemented through software or firmware.

18.8 Export/Import Elements and Global Constraints

Import elements can be seen as foreign data to be localized, while export elements can be viewed as local—to be communicated to other databases in the network. The act of communication, and not just that of processing, brings into perspective two other basic characteristics of a client/server environment:

- Behavioral aspects, which may include specific binding procedures, preferably with the latter being generated parametrically

- A model involving both structural and functional connections as well as knowledge artifacts

The knowledge bank management system (KBMS) that will best serve this approach can be regarded as a generalized collection of concepts, mechanisms, and tools. It is in place to support the definition, manipulation, and control of databases for a variety of applications.

Underlying this strategy is the principle that, for a number of technical and economic reasons, one desirable property of resource integration is to keep existing applications intact.

- The applications should be usable as before, but should simply have access to additional information when appropriate.

- The applications should need only to be extended, not changed, in order to make use of an expanding client/server landscape.

Therefore, solutions should aim at integrating separately developed database resources in a way that assures the stated properties. Integration must be achieved at the semantic level, with different databases mapped to the global perspective through a set of axioms and tools.

Queries and updates against local views can be translated globally, as described in Chaps. 16 and 17, and then retranslated back to local views. From the viewpoint of a local application or user, everything appears the same as before integration, except that queries may return additional relevant information.

Such a solution is intended to provide the functional capabilities extending over the independent existence of databases through a conceptual level of data abstraction. The export/import mechanism supports the query and modification of databases and also accommodates the evolvability of both logical structure and physical organization in response to changing information, evolving usage, and diverse performance requirements.

Primitives and higher-up rules should uphold semantic integrity, assuring that the database is an accurate model of its applications (real-world) perspectives. They should also promote security, concurrency, and recovery. Mechanisms should be in place for restoring the database in the event of a failure of any type. This is an integral and indispensable part of global database management.

Such mechanisms do exist in response to local database management requirements. The latter are answered by the DBMS installed at every site. The global requirements will be attended through a KBMS whose rules will tailor the distributed resources to specific applications environments.

As we will see in the discussion of intentional and extensional databases in Chap. 19, at the core of this approach is an AI-enriched database model, which acts as a mechanism for specifying the structure of the logical client/server solution and the instantiated operations that can be performed on the information elements in the global resource.

Once again, the object orientation is quite helpful in this respect. Whereas the now classical hierarchical, network, and relational models have a definite structure, an object-based system is flexible.

- It acts when instantiated.

- It handles a hierarchical structure which is ephemeral.

In so doing, an object-based system helps combine flexibility and evolvability with greater operational efficiency. It also avoids setting a priori global constraints, which can be quite harmful in terms of systemwide efficiency and client/server interoperability.

This is particularly true under current conditions, where successful solutions to heterogeneous database technology with embedded major applications are still in the making. Even today, most financial and industrial applications: rely on centralized data resources which are massive and inflexible. Hence, data used by one application is rarely shared by others.

However, since end-user requirements evolve rapidly, this situation is changing. Today applications have to share data resources—and this, once again, calls for interoperable database systems. But we should not, as some vendors suggest, reduce a priori our degrees of freedom through global constraints.

Critics of this approach may argue that even though the need for flexibility is generally recognized, proposed solutions find little widespread accord. If so, the reasons are both philosophical and technical. The philosophical problems revolve around:

- Newer distributed environments

- Older centralized structures

A significant amount of cultural inertia must be overcome to replace old concepts, which largely depend on one central authority, with approaches that make truly peer-to-peer systems feasible.

As we have seen on several occasions, technical problems relate to the transition from centralized control toward greater autonomy. When a network's nodes impact on other nodes, autonomy is more or less lost. But if the distributed environment rules are not in place, this can lead, among other things, to:

- Lack of two-way commit interfacing

- Uncoordinated locking mechanisms

- Local and global performance problems

Precisely for these reasons, the export/import model and other solutions suggested in this chapter are designed to provide significant flexibility—as contrasted with the monolithic approach of applying systemwide constraints which have been carved in stone. Newer solutions can also assure global accuracy, as the next section documents.

18.9 Global Accuracy, Precision, and Completeness

The concepts which prevailed with centralized databases—in particular, with accounting-type applications that used the first relatively large files—led to the design of database systems under assumptions of *precision* and *completeness*. In reality this may not be true of either (1) the information elements they store or (2) the requests to retrieve them.

In other words, the assumptions of completeness and precision are often false. This is the direct result of a fast-expanding database structure which, in today's financial and industrial worlds, contains rapidly changing information elements.

It is clear that centralized approaches and their worn-out tools cannot meet the completeness and precision requirements of modern business. In addition, we must appreciate the fact that today there are two large families of data that contradict each other in terms of characteristics and requirements:

1. *Hard data* are typically historical facts and accounting values.

2. *Soft data* are forecasts, projections, and extrapolations.

Sales statistics are hard data; sales forecasts are soft data. As Fig. 18.4 suggests, soft data is obtained from hard data through an algorithmic and/or heuristic approach. The softness of data is part of the price we pay in order to obtain timely information results. Sales statistics give results which merely reflect the past.

Soft data may be accurate (or so we hope), but they are not precise. In an organizational pyramid—from transaction processing to decision support—both soft data and hard data are necessary for doing business.

Normally, both families of information elements will be served through a distributed database environment. Within this perspective, the contained information elements may need to be:

- Absolutely precise for local purposes, such as bookkeeping

- Much less precise for global purposes, such as management accounting

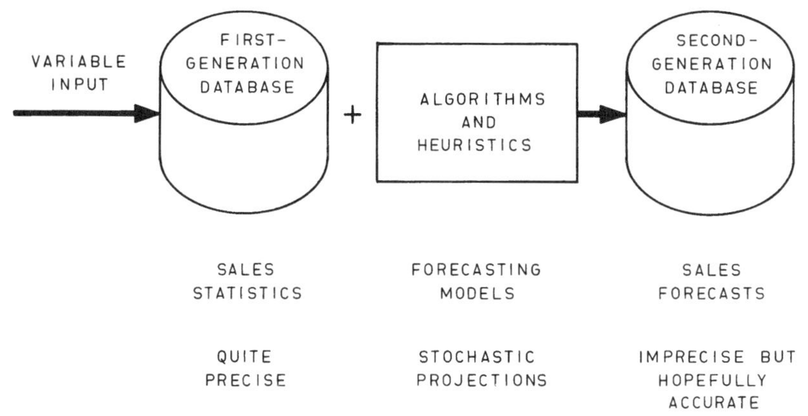

Figure 18.4　Dynamic binding in a federated database environment.

For these reasons, in recent years considerable attention has been paid to issues which have been wrongly characterized as representing imprecision and incompleteness in databases. The correct terminology is *crispness* versus *fuzziness* of response, with approaches available to address both issues in a meaningful database sense.

Indeed, considerable work is currently being done on models that extend the prevailing database concepts to represent *imprecision*—within an acceptable level of accuracy. Representations of accuracy and of imprecision are both important, and the same is true of appropriate query evaluation algorithms.

We need a mechanism able to support the specification and evaluation of vague queries made in a federated database setting. Quite interestingly, heuristics—and most particularly fuzzy engineering—provides a way to bypass certain aspects of database heterogeneity and thereby manipulate information about the quality of the data in regard to:

- Validity

- Accuracy

- Completeness

Subsequently, other heuristics artifacts can use this information to qualify the answers being received. One such tool is fuzzy-set theory, which has been adapted and applied to various financial and other applications.*

---

*See also D. N. Chorafas and H. Steinmann, *Expert Systems in Banking,* Macmillan, London, and New York University Press, New York, 1991.

Heuristics and algorithms are necessary to tackle the problem of accommodating the controlled sharing and exchange of information elements among a collection of distributed heterogeneous databases. Database mining operations must be examined from a number of viewpoints:

- Some projects focus on an experimental approach to information sharing, with pattern recognition as a focal point.

- Other projects aim at the coordination of autonomous and heterogeneous databases which should be operating together.

Multidatabases, intentional databases, superviews, object-oriented solutions, and virtual databases all stress the need to provide a unified global approach to a collection of existing heterogeneous databases. Each approach seeks to handle the issues of accuracy, precision, and completeness in a virtually homogeneous sense.

- Intended use should be kept in perspective in the design of any integrative approach.

- The solution to be provided should be application-independent and parametric so that dynamic adjustments can be made.

Not surprisingly, the experience gained so far demonstrates that valid solutions require new departures, necessarily involving both structural and functional knowledge in an AI sense.

Structural information alone is inadequate in finding a dynamically valid solution to federated databases. Many of the fundamental con-

	INFORMATION ELEMENTS	TOOLS
HIGH LEVEL	CONCEPTUAL SCHEMA	SCHEMA MODEL
LOW LEVEL	MULTIMEDIA INFORMATION	LANGUAGES SUCH AS C++

Figure 18.5 Quarter spaces in a semantics-oriented environment.

straints are embedded in the schema definition. These have functional aspects and may be used to resolve federation issues. Value classes of attributes can also provide information that is useful in facing ambiguities.

Within the context defined by this approach, Fig. 18.5 suggests that consideration must be given to both the information elements in the client/server databases and the tools being used. This calls for a high level of reference, involving the conceptual schema(ta) as well as the schema model(s).

Within the distributed database environment, issues such as local and global accuracy, precision, and completeness particularly interest the left side of Fig. 18.5. At a low level, the latter will concern the multimedia information elements and commands expressed in a language such as C++.

One last aspect to be considered in an integrative client/server landscape is the methodology for semantic integration of autonomous information resources—and how it can be served through intentional databases. This is the subject of the next and final chapter.

19

Knowledge Engineering and Interoperability in Client/Server Environments

19.1 Introduction

Interoperability assured through powerful linguistic constructs is one of the strategies used to create a homogeneous background out of heterogeneous databases. The methodology takes a different road than that of federated databases (examined in Chaps. 17 and 18), relying on language artifacts rather than a common layer of reference.

The transfer of schemata from one database to another by means of some code is not unlike the transfer of DNA in living organisms.

- An agent carries with it a genetic description that can serve to integrate it into a new environment.

- The procedure utilizes the export/import paradigm described in Chap. 18 but also features value-added characteristics.

Under some conditions, the agent being used transforms itself, affecting its basic structure, to accommodate a homogeneity prerequisite. Unfortunately, at the present time we lack the powerful linguistic solutions needed to try such a biologically inspired approach in very diverse database environments.

Early attempts at schema transfer focused on situations with a common DBMS background, particularly relational. More diversified solutions have *not* been particularly successful because of language deficiencies.

As a result, the interoperability method has taken a new turn, seeking to integrate diverse database elements and knowledge engi-

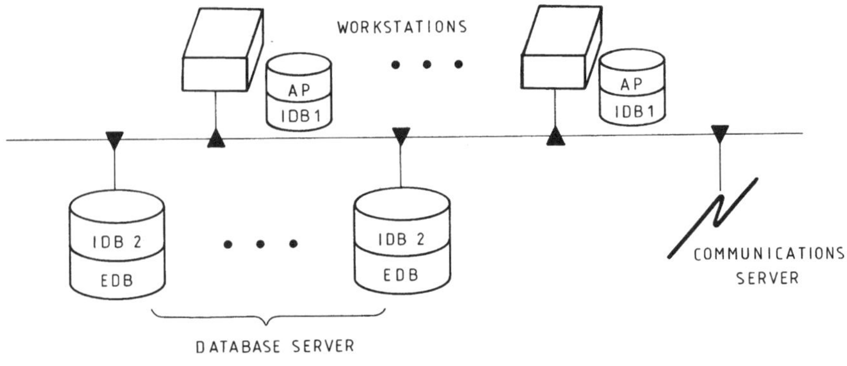

Figure 19.1   Interoperability can be assisted through intentional database facilities acting on extensional structures.

neering artifacts within an *object-oriented* background. One of the better-known efforts in this direction relies on:

- Intentional databases (IDBs)*

- Extensional databases (EDBs)

- Guarded horn clauses (GHCs) as the language

The whole concept rests on an artificial intelligence implementation. Intentional databases are enriched by knowledge engineering and act as a metalayer which directs and controls the behavior of heterogeneous extensional databases residing both in clients and in servers.

Intentional databases, too, reside at client and server levels. At the workstation level, IDB 1 makes transparent to the user the diversity existing in terms of the networked databases—from data structures to DBMS and other issues. It also assists the appropriate cross database access through data dictionary facilities.

At the server level, IDB 2 acts like logic over data, facilitating access to the information elements required by an application as well as acting as cache to the EDB. The extensional database can be relational or object-oriented, or of an older model such as hierarchical or Codasyl. Figure 19.1 shows where each of the IDB 1, IDB 2, and EDB facilities is located.

Central to this concept of IDB and EDB is that of *metadata*. We have encountered the meta concept on many occasions, and will fur-

---

*See also D. N. Chorafas, *Intelligent Multimedia Databases,* Prentice-Hall, Englewood Cliffs, NJ, in press.

ther consider metadata and the management of constraints in Sec.
19.3.

19.2　Promoting a Business-Oriented Interoperability Approach

According to an article in *Communications Week International*
(February 3, 1992), companies that are most advanced in their thinking about interoperability tend to invest in systems that give primary
support to the sales and marketing functions. In these projects, the
development of database interoperability starts by rationalizing customer data, which is typically spread over order processing, billing,
and accounting.

Once the needed cross database infrastructure is set in place, a language based interoperability becomes more sophisticated, aiming to
exploit distributed resources, many of which have so far been islands
of applications.

- In manufacturing, interoperability may concern an integrative system of sales orders, accounting, inventory, and warehousing.

- In banking, interoperability might focus on links between such
  areas as loans, export financing, investment advice, and portfolio
  management.

In the past, these applications areas were not necessarily connected,
yet they address business relating to the same customer.

The manufacturing paradigm can be extended to computers and
databases operating on the shop floor, permitting the different systems components to work together toward common goals. Another
vital business extension is in the direction of an interoperable aggregate running all business functions from R&D to distribution and cost
control.

Every one of the aforementioned examples can benefit from a homogeneous IDB layer, at each networked workstation, which commands
over heterogeneous EDB resources. There are, however, barriers to
interoperability that go beyond the lack of powerful linguistic constructs noted in Sec. 19.1.

The most important barrier is cultural. Many systems professionals
feel lost when confronted with databases that seemingly are unable to
interoperate.

Another constraint is the lack of reliable international standards to
support interoperable applications. This is unfortunate, because as
far as the lower part of the information pyramid in Fig. 19.2 is concerned, legacy applications available today in isolation cover most of

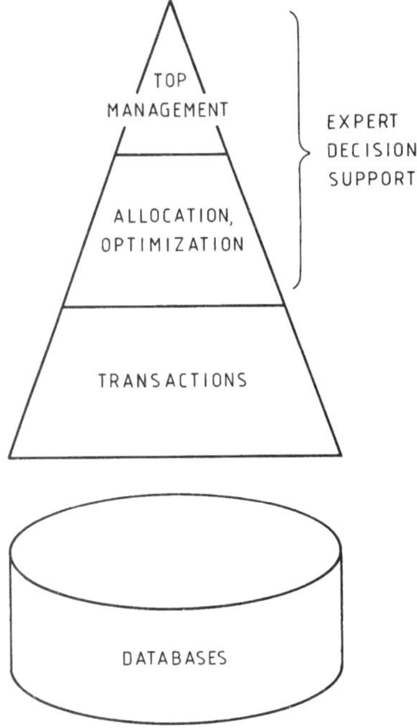

Figure 19.2 Of the three levels of sophistication in information technology applications, only the lower one is covered; however, this lower level is also fragmented.

the obvious business functions that relate to money flowing in and out of the enterprise.

Stated in different terms, without an integration of the legacy applications at the transactional and accounting levels, and corresponding virtual database homogeneity, it will not be possible to support in an able manner the expert decision applications. That is why there are overwhelming business pressures to make future systems follow the interoperability model.

An often-mentioned benefit of interoperability is an increase in managerial productivity—and therefore in span of control. Flat organizational structures effectively reduce the white-collar work force, since more business functions can be carried out under one manager without being subject to overwhelming centrifugal forces.

Seamless interoperability solutions can also improve the product value chain, from raw material to consumption. For a long time senior executives have looked to their IT directors and telecommunications specialists for advice on how to shorten this chain, thus saving money and gaining competitive advantage.

Far from being academic, these issues are highly practical, reflecting the fact that cultural constraints may be much greater than technological ones. A valid solution depends on organizational support:

- People must be quite willing to accept change as a state of mind, capitalizing on the benefits it makes feasible.

- Alterations of past images must be tolerated in return for the benefits of improved organization and effectiveness.

The results of cascading seemingly diverse information elements, subject to a series of actions, often surprise even experienced users. Such results, however, require continual fine-tuning of databases to more closely mirror their requirements.

In an organizational sense, the support of intentional and extensional databases may have a deep impact on business practices. To a significant extent, such support helps to redefine what is do-able and what is not in terms of coordinating production, inventory, and sales, handling customer relationships, and so on.

Apart from other benefits, interoperability provides a clear view of the synergy between computing and telecommunications and how the two function together. As a result, more value can be extracted from existing LAN investments:

- Without seamless on-line database access, local area networks and personal computers are relegated to domestic chore work: word processing, spreadsheets, electronic mail, and so on.

- At the same time, the high cost per workstation has led companies to demand that their users access more resources, thus obtaining greater value from existing investments.

Another, highly touted benefit of interoperability is that it strengthens the user's hand in dealing with suppliers, since the implementation of metalevel concepts makes it feasible to support an open-vendor policy. Thus, when it comes to providing a valid interoperability approach, the role of vendors is diminishing.

19.3   Models, Metamodels, and Metaknowledge

Precisely because the discrete island approaches and the proliferation of incompatible databases led nowhere in practice, many worthwhile projects were aborted. As result, leading-edge information scientists reverted to coupled systems able to integrate distributed heterogeneous databases. This shift in focus brought into perspective the importance of paying due attention to *constraints*.

Constraint analysis is not a new concept. The challenge today is to apply it to the study of distributed database operations, and at the same time to identify possible side effects. Such a process helps in refining the scope of a global database view based on appropriate constraint identification.

Constraint analysis can be instrumental in providing a formal basis for representing vital factors associated with semantic data models. Once such a basis is established, database operations can be specified through integrity maintenance rules.

When advanced database and network technologies are merged, the resulting client/server applications can take full advantage of network resources while remaining independent of underlying protocols. At this point in time, development is not quite so simple, but it is doable.

Indeed, one of the goals of object-oriented approaches is to make such a strategy feasible. Cross-database transparency put at the service of the end user is a good measure of integration. The basic dimensions affecting a transparent solution lie in the:

- *Data model* and its primitives

- *Database schema(ta)* descriptions

- *Structure* of information elements

- Programming *primitives*

- *Data sources,* including locations and derivations

- *Dependencies* and relationships (including semantics)

- *Time and cost* of providing an interoperable solution

Several key questions arise in qualifying and quantifying these issues: How are entities and relationships represented? Can behavior be specified, and if so how? How are aggregates formed? What is the best form of a query language? What should its key features be? How are constraints expressed?

Solutions should focus on domain modeling in a way which permits behavioral representation leading to explicit specifications. They must provide for schema evolution as well as account for data and knowledge distribution in reasoning about:

- Metadata

- Metaknowledge

Are metalevel concepts negating the experience accumulated through 40 years of data processing? The right answer is that they don't negate at all; rather, they constitute *a major evolution* which necessitates a number of changes. Such an answer can be appreciated only by people with a culture open to the future, rather than one locked up in the past.

During the 1987 annual meeting of the American Association for Artificial Intelligence (AAAI), W. J. Watson of Texas Instruments made the statement: "Most of us think that AI per se will lose its identity within about 5 years." He then explained that he did not mean the recent surge of interest in commercial knowledge engineering applications would begin to wane. His thesis can be summed up as follows:

- If anything, the artificial intelligence industry is maturing and becoming better established.

- Therefore, classical data processing and knowledge engineering will merge.

- As a result, all new developments in information systems will have a significant artificial intelligent content.

Present-day experience suggests that Watson's forecast has materialized. In fact, the merger of two disciplines has produced results not only in the processing side of information but also in the management of distributed databases. The latter issue is of particular interest to client/server landscapes.

Figure 19.3 expands on the concept of intentional and extensional databases brought forward in Sec. 19.1. It also integrates the concepts related to services provided by a knowledge base management system (KBMS), as discussed in Chap. 18.

The implementation of artificial intelligence to enhance database and networking functionality promotes greater efficiency in computer, communications, and software systems. Efficiency is all the more important, given the fact that as networks grow with usage two additional objectives come to the fore:

- Flexibility

- Extensibility

The result is more sophisticated software able to handle a growing number of databases, newer workstations, and other processors of different manufacture and architecture, along with diverse OS and incompatible applications programs.

Database and network intelligence sees to it that greater architectural flexibility can be provided through only minor changes to the existing system structure. Resources, particularly information resources, can be shared among clients in an able manner. The bottom line is greater cost-effectiveness and better service.

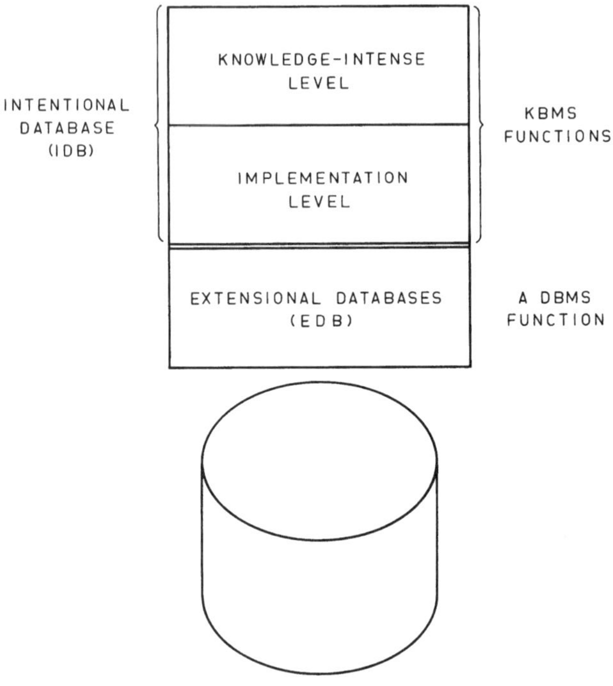

Figure 19.3   Intentional and extensional databases in a client/server environment.

19.4   The Contribution of Intentional Databases

Through intentional database approaches, metalevel concepts can be worked out to reflect on ways which permit a dual modality—that is, having object transparency and object visibility at the same time.

A solution that integrates multiple data models must provide mapping between concepts in one model and those in another. This can happen by degrees, with action triggered through successive metalayers, according to the metaknowledge paradigm examined in this chapter.

When differences between data models are completely hidden, it looks *as if* each of the members in the heterogeneous database landscape is defined in terms of the same primitive concepts. The other extreme is that all differences are completely visible.

- When schema disparities are visible, the user must provide routines to resolve the differences.

- At midrange, the solution allows for seamless queries but not for seamless cross database updates on transactions.

- When schema are transparent, heterogeneity in the structure and semantics of elements is completely hidden.

With every project, it is important to define the degree of transparency an integrative solution should provide. In the general case, there will likely be different feasible implementation strategies—each with its own constructs—that produce about the same level of integration.

Available technology has defined a variety of systems that hide certain aspects along a number of dimensions. Implementation choices are likely to resolve some of the integration issues better than others. In all these cases, cost/benefit considerations help to define the practical levels of an integrative solution.

Through an ingenious exploitation of constraints and metaknowledge, network operating systems are evolving to the point where sophisticated resource sharing becomes available.

- Through this approach, client/server computing allows workstation programs (acting as client) to direct service requests to one or more servers.

- Such service requests interface through the intentional database (IDB) layer, which is able to interpret and act upon the heterogeneity at server level.

- Redirection is transparent to the user and the application, thus assuring better sharing of databases and relatively simple messaging.

Seen in this perspective, the client/server model is evolving to a distributed network computing model. It is enriched through the provision of directory services, such as naming and location. The latter make it easier to assign missions to server machines on the basis of changing user requirements and server capabilities.

The able implementation of a metamodel permits a server to direct requests to another server, that is, to act as a client, providing generally distributed service features. However, the growth of an environment of distributed resources leads to additional requirements for:

- Ever more powerful servers

- High availability features

As this discussion helps document, several systems management needs must be addressed. Here is where the issue of metamodels and constraints comes in. It can help in dynamic systems management, providing an effective way to distribute applications software, establish and maintain version control and security, and handle other crucial issues.

19.5   The Distributed Computing Environment (DCE) Effort

The type of interoperability we are investigating here lies above the seven-layer Open Systems Interconnection (OSI) of the International Standards organization (ISO). Its implementation calls for intelligent (that is, knowledge engineering enriched) applications, including:

- Query algorithms

- Transaction programs

- Database search mechanisms

It is worth noting that all the methods examined in the last three chapters—interoperability, federated databases, and schema translation—depend on knowledge engineering. By contrast, the application of a network-wide global schema rests on brute force.

If we wish to use brute force, then the arbitrary definition of a universal schema is the way to go, but we must keep in mind that attempts made in the past have failed. The relatively simpler approach is to work through knowledge engineering and data dictionaries.

Figure 19.4 consolidates this approach through the strategy of a general directory able to integrate *n* schemata. The same resource should also include security clauses and supervisory processes for the access mechanism.

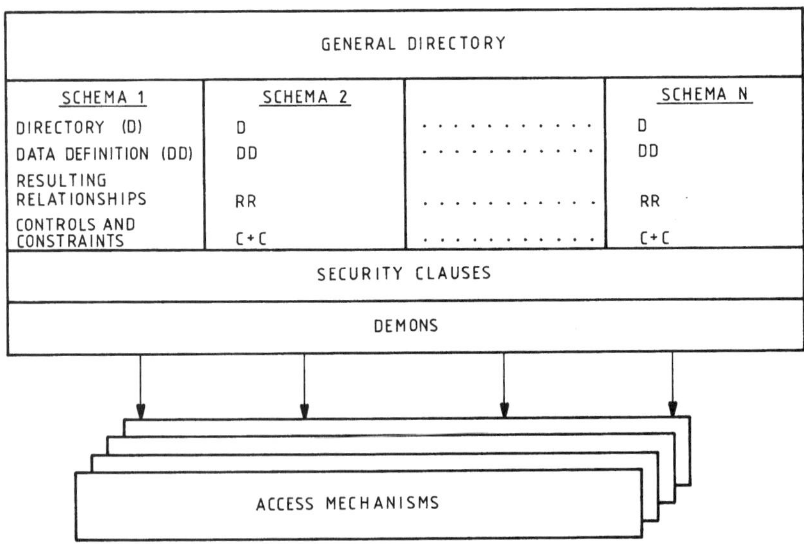

Figure 19.4 Implementing data dictionaries in connection with access mechanisms.

- The approach will perform well for managerial duties and ad hoc queries, but may not answer transaction requirements.

- For future applications, a normalization method should be chosen that is able to respond to the evolving database interoperability.

- Both transactional and managerial requirements should be served through a normalized approach.

In fact, a key difference between the interoperability solution advanced in this chapter and the relatively loosely coupled databases discussed in Chap. 17 lies in the ability to handle transaction-processing requirements.

If a transaction-oriented interoperability strategy is adopted, as transactional applications are transferred from mainframes to client/servers, normalized schemata may be the way to go. This will, however, call for wise choices concerning the *normalization* method to be followed all the way from data structures to DBMS.

Needless to say, normalization presents serious problems beyond technical competence. For one thing, most normalized schemata today are proprietary—that is, they belong to one of the main vendors in the computer business. Therefore, adoption of one of them can be a major handicap to an open-vendor policy.

- Normalization does not come in the abstract; it needs firm foundations which must be defined, not just described.*

- The whole idea of schemata was born with DBMS and their usage in connection with applications.

- If there are so many schemata around, it is precisely because there are so many different and incompatible norms.

Hence, the normalization of schemata may also be seen as the antithesis to an open-vendor policy—though an open-vendor policy is a very sound approach. As a result of this contradiction, a company may outwardly promote an open-vendor policy while following an adjunct policy that reduces the many current schemata to a low one-digit number.

A similar statement can be made in connection to communications disciplines. In many current applications, hardware and software from one vendor merely coexist with devices of other suppliers. These are capable of working together only by means of expensive interfaces. Yet users want to:

---

*Description leads only to a myriad of interpretations. This is what happened with the ISO/OSI reference model.

- Interconnect those diverse systems in an ad hoc manner
- Freely move applications from one platform to another
- Handle software environments on several systems of different sizes and capabilities

In other words, users are demanding interoperability among heterogeneous computers not only in regard to databases but also in connection with all other resources. This is a prerequisite for a cost-effective distributed environment in which the processing power and the information elements are federated over a network.

In a technical sense, a comprehensive effort toward this goal is the Distributed Computing Environment (DCE) software, developed by the Open Software Foundation (OSF).* DCE focuses on problems such as:

- Provision of opportunities for growth in applications
- Diversity of operating environments
- Need for OS homogeneity
- Drive to maintain security

DCE effort reflects the fact that the 1990s are seeing dramatic changes in the process and economics of connectivity. These changes are characterized by the appearance of a technology to interconnect computer-based resources over high-speed links to create large networks.

- By the year 2000, over 80 percent of the computers used in business, industry, and finance will be linked to one another by local, metropolitan, and wide area networks.

- Interconnecting those organizations that need to share information in databases is a prime objective of many current efforts.

- Cross organizational links open up new applications possibilities, allowing business partners to exchange information needed in their daily work.

As more organizations are linked together, however, multivendor environments become a necessity. This leads to the need for normalized protocols, data access methods, and applications programming interfaces (APIs). It is just as important to standardize basic software practices as it is to create new designs.

---

*OSF is an industry-supported research and development organization of hardware and software vendors, user organizations, and research institutions.

These concepts may not be universally accepted, but they are based on already available experiences. A careful study adapted to a company's own database problems may reveal novel and interesting issues that can be nicely incorporated into a cross-database strategy, forming the basis for future integrative approaches.

Database development teams are often surprised by the range of novel requirements discovered through focused research. Several of these involve the analysis of existing bodies of knowledge; others are the result of putting a chosen method to practical use. The development of further possibilities through successive refinements is a particularly relevant paradigm.

19.6   A Strategy for Making Interoperability More Effective

The best policy for establishing interoperability among heterogeneous databases is to take a proactive stance, coordinating appropriate procurement and implementation strategies. As Citibank has discovered, user organizations must be prepared to devote considerable time and resources to understanding the issues involved in cross-database access in order to avoid expensive errors.

- The choice of appropriate standards helps, but more is needed than norms and standards.

- The way standards are implemented among different vendors often leads to incompatibilities.

- Information exchange becomes blocked when "standards" are interpreted in different, incompatible forms.

It is important to understand that there is no such thing as off-the-shelf interoperability. Therefore, development of conformance testing procedures should start with this premise—the realization that there are going to be differences.

Since universal norms are *not* the rule, a sound approach is to focus on internal norms to be observed by all departments and divisions and on conformance testing by the user organization. Again, however, there are no norms for such tests, and no two vendor companies take the same approach.

Despite this drawback, a conformance testing procedure implemented by the user organization can be instrumental in flushing out major incompatibilities. These are bound to exist even between computers and communications products for the same ANSI and ISO standard.

Functional tests are necessary, but they are not enough. First of all, the user organization must decide which standards should apply.

Though de facto standards can serve as good starting points for evaluating vendor offers, international standards are a better alternative. Key queries for vendors should include:

- Whether the product conforms to those standards

- How conformance will meet specific user requirements

Vague promises that "My product is ISO/OSI compatible" should not be taken at face value. One case involving eight vendors vying for the same contract is illustrative.

One of the vendors offered SNA, evidently not an ISO/OSI model. The other seven stated that their solution was fully ISO/OSI compatible—but when tested these seven solutions were found to be fully incompatible among themselves.

User organizations will be well advised to insist on real interoperability within a properly specified internal environment as a principal condition of sale. A contract should also include:

- The tests to evaluate conformance

- The time frame within which conformance is to be achieved

- The penalties to be paid if the vendor fails to meet the interoperability condition

Another basic issue that deserves attention concerns the procurement of new hardware and software—as well as the evaluation of what is already in house. In this regard, conformance tests may not reflect the real-world environment in which the product will operate. Running a real-life, multivendor network involves:

- A heavy but fluctuating traffic load

- An environment subject to many random events

Using software and equipment in this setting can be quite different from running tests in a laboratory, especially in regard to interoperability requirements. Therefore, such tests should provide some weighted factors able to account for deviations from real-life requirements.

Not only must test sequences verify that the products operate in accordance with the chosen standard, but each function must be tested both in isolation and in unison with other functions. Dual tests allow software and equipment to be evaluated in a factual and documented manner, assuring that attached resources will interoperate with another vendor's products.

In short, it is not sufficient to evaluate isolated protocols, or products that operate adequately in a single-protocol environment. These may well fail to meet interoperability criteria when multiple sourcing solutions are used, and multiple sourcing solutions will be the rule rather than the exception in the 1990s.

Beyond prototyping and laboratory tests comes the need for fine-tuning (at least with a small-scale system) under real-life operating conditions.

- Fine-tuning constitutes an advanced level of interoperability testing for decision purposes.

- It is aimed at enabling the acquired product(s) to achieve the best possible performance.

Such a strategy is an integral part of the proactive stance described at the beginning of this section. The earlier in the procurement process the user organization takes account of interoperability, the more likely it is that the new system will function properly in conjunction with hardware and software already in place.

19.7 From Legacy Applications to Client/Server Solutions

Figure 19.5 recapitulates in graphic form the strategy outlined in Sec. 19.6. An interoperability study should start with the functional specifications, establish the go/no go criteria, proceed with the standards to be chosen, follow up with the tests, and find fulfillment in real-life implementation. This study must focus on two areas simultaneously:

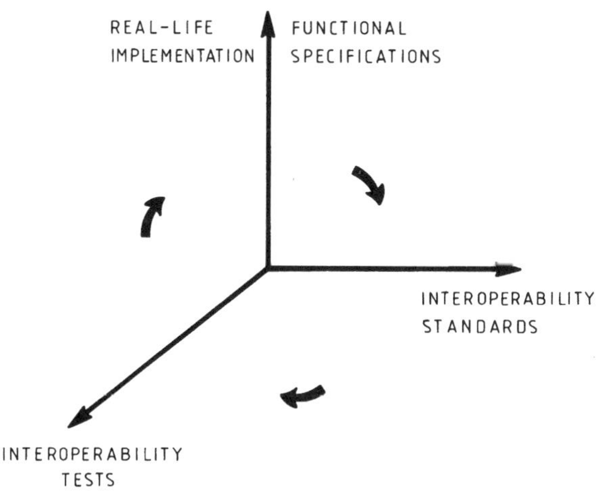

Figure 19.5 A strategy for interoperability support, from functional specification to actual implementation.

- The new, competitive client/server solution chosen for implementation

- The legacy-type applications in existence, whose databases must integrate into the system

Since legacy applications are typically (though not exclusively) run on mainframes, the changeover is not going to take place overnight. Hence, an interoperability study must fully account for the transition period, which might extend to a couple of years.

An article by *Forbes* has this to say regarding efforts to get over the hurdles presented by legacy type applications:* "Aetna's technology vision is clouded by both technical and cultural obstacles that prohibit rapid change. The company, for example, has a huge capital investment in mainframe-based computing. Fifteen IBM behemoths are at work...."

As the technology of leading firms shifts to client/server solutions and *desk area networks* (DAN),† companies that find themselves at the forefront of the big switch gain significant competitive advantages. These are documented through flexibility and adaptability, presenting a cutting edge that no outdated, proprietary solutions can ever match.

It is *not* sufficient to install thousands of personal computers while leaving the mainframes and their culture intact; and it may as well be counterproductive. In the late 1980s the Teachers Insurance and Annuity Association (TIAA) tried this approach and got no satisfactory results. Subsequently, a courageous management threw out the mainframes and replaced the entire system with 350 networked Sun workstations and servers. This is a *client/server solution by excellence.*

For another leading financial services organization in New York, the transition from mainframes and other quite diverse hardware platforms to a homogeneous, interconnected client/server environment:

- Took 15 months of study, preparation, benchmarking, and preliminary testing

- Necessitated only 12 months in actual conversion procedures, a four-step process that was phased-in every 3 months.

Yamaichi Securities of Tokyo originally interconnected through hyperchannel, global trading run on IBM computers, with research done on Hitachi, back-office support on Unisys, and dealing support on

---

*Forbes ASAP, May 1993.

†A project financed by DARPA and conducted by MIT, the University of Pennsylvania, IBM, and Bellcore.

Vax. Then management decided to eliminate the batch solution, converting to real time with client/servers and optical fiber connectivity (typically FDDI protocol).

Such a conversion was advisable in order to modernize the dealing and back-office support system—but the job could not be done by presenting discontinuities in database access. Hence, the interoperability issue between the old and the new solution was crucial during the transition period.

In both the American and the Japanese examples, the client/server solution presented significant advantages. Among them:

- Conversion to full real-time operations

- Implementation of a knowledge server

- Intentional database application for queries and answerback

- Incorporation of knowledge artifacts

- Significant cost savings.

However, no matter how important these advantages were, they could not be considered to constitute a practical implementation unless interoperability was fully supported. Here lies the importance of seamless database access, as emphasized throughout Part 3.

A basic premise in systems design for the 1990s is that one workstation per desk should be performing everything its user needs. This imposes the requirements of:

- Modularity

- Compatibility

- Networking

- Human engineering

- Expandability

- Predictability

All six have been found to be focal points for the success of a new systems solution. Just as important is the ability to understand that the real challenge of the coming decade is not computation, but communication.

Transaction-oriented applications provide a good example of how computation and communication compete for the No. 1 post in systems attention. Real-time transaction execution has different requirements from query-only and simple update solutions.

All told in terms of advanced information technology implementation, there is an important distinction in the systems design perspectives of different types of applications. Taking a case from the financial industry, we can distinguish among three:

1. A dealing support system takes stock exchange feed and brokers' trade information, applying a market data filter to provide a reference database.

2. A trading system uses knowledge engineering artifacts but needs to be updated in real time—and because of past commitments it rests on incompatible databases, like the Yamaichi example earlier.

3. A back-office system handles settlements and the upkeep of accounts. It simply cannot operate efficiently (if it can operate at all) without simultaneous access to diverse and incompatible databases.

In the past, both hardware and software suppliers have had an easy ride in the sense that they could ignore interoperability requirements and duck their heads when it came to observing established standards. But those days are over. Both vendors and user organizations need to understand the importance of networkwide interoperability and adapt their strategies accordingly.

19.8 Planning the Changeover to Client/Servers

Conversion to new and therefore lesser-known systems should be done step by step, bringing together both the lessons learned by the early starters and a comprehensive appreciation of the user's work. Among the key background factors to be considered are rising expectations in user-information communications, particularly the users' demand for on-line processing and databasing.

Another crucial issue to be addressed through proper study is the cost saving to be achieved through client/server solutions. Costs alone can provide plenty of justification for a change to client/server architecture—for several reasons:

- The inefficiency of centralization with its poor response time, relatively low reliability, and high costs

- The benefits to be derived by capitalizing on the falling processor and main memory costs, which are visible with client/servers

- More end-user control, therefore greater data information technology accountability both in performance and in prices

- The ability to be flexible and stay flexible as changes in implementation perspectives increase competitiveness

The changeover from mainframes to client/servers must be accomplished in a well-timed, step-by-step manner. The prerequisite study cannot be done piecemeal. It requires a global approach to network solutions which include interoperable databases.

A client/server implementation with good chances for success calls for well defined implementation plans and the proper study of technical infrastructure. Cost-effectiveness should be a key preoccupation throughout.

The conversion to a client/server solution is a unique opportunity for the implementation of a *grand design* which can be valid for at least the next 10 years. As Fig. 19.6 suggests, this requires insight, foresight, and flexibility at every stage—from software to computing to communications.

The communications challenge will be that much more pronounced as broadband networks with a capacity at the level of present day LANs begin to take over a wide range of implementations. They will help in creating systems which bring computer power, access to huge databases, and communications-intense features under every desk. The main reason for this development is economic.

Communicating databases are the answer to the overwhelming requirement of controlling sprawling paperwork, which, after 40 years of computer practice, still defies classical data-processing approaches. Enriched with very efficient supports such as optical disks, communicating databases enable the effective utilization of technological innovation.

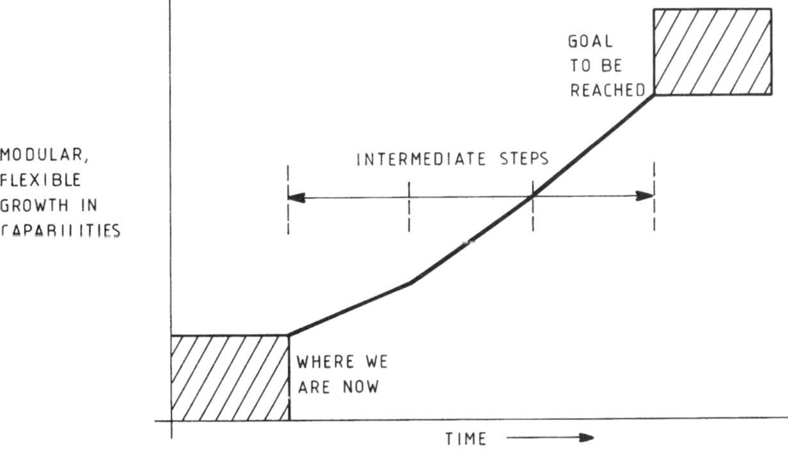

Figure 19.6 In order to remain valid for at least a decade, the grand design requires insight, foresight, and flexibility.

Experience teaches us that the implementation of advanced technology often occurs in two stages. These can be summed up a nutshell in the following terms:

1. The innovation is exploited to perform in a better way the same tasks that were once done by other means.

2. Implementation leads to the development of new applications that could not reasonably have materialized or even been foreseen, prior to the change.

Thus, the real challenge lies both in improving upon what is currently done and in identifying new fields of applications made possible by advanced technology. Able solutions for communicating databases make feasible the maintenance of a viable independence between systems. But, as always, there are prerequisites to be met.

The communications, computer, and software system—focused on the needs of the end user—must provide knowledge-enriched procedures able to build and edit multimedia files, handle missing values, and transform key variables. Software should assure not only cross-database interoperability in spite of heterogeneity but also the ability to define and redefine data models of interest to the end user.

Effectively communicating databases do influence the design and operation of computer networks, just as they make feasible complex transaction execution. Communicating databases become especially vital as networkwide on-line access enhances human productivity with services never before available to the end user.

Widespread access capabilities also underline the need to enhance reliability, since a physical or logical failure—even if it can be confined to one subnetwork—affects the interactivity of the end user. Only if the network is reliable will the end user be able to effectively exploit the contents of distributed databases.

Therefore, the goal should be to assure a dependable and robust system in spite of component node failures, the eventuality of an improper use of facilities, or even loss of information resources. This is another way of saying that the identification of the behavior of systems components must receive proper attention. Evaluation must be made of:

- Ways and means for effective monitoring

- Timely recognition of systems violations

- Possible vulnerability of database(s)

- Integrity controls, audit tools, and audit trails

While these components pertain primarily to databases and end-user computing, they also have a great impact on networks—both wide area and local. It is simply not possible to effectively construct a network and choose an appropriate protocol without establishing precise interoperability goals.

- Such goals start at the end-user level and should consider all requirements: present and future.
- Once established, goals affect workstations, databases, networks, human windows, and linguistic supports.

Finally, as stated on many occasions, the handling of communicating, interoperable databases in a networkwide sense should be enriched through artificial intelligence constructs. The network systems we build today are destined to live past the year 2000. Both the systems architecture we choose and the integration means we apply should anticipate this life cycle.

Who Can Help in the Transition Period?

Doing what the 19 chapters of this book have outlined will require all types of information technology skills. What that means in practice is that the different systems specialists will increasingly work together as polyvalent project teams, across departmental boundaries, to deliver specific end-to-end applications and functionality.*

Interoperability may signal the end of discrete island data-processing approaches, but it also requires a great deal of know-how to be implemented effectively. Who should provide that know-how? In other words, who is the ideal partner in the transition?

The evident answer is that the company to be chosen as a partner should be able to make a real contribution by helping to get out of the mainframe culture into an elegant and cost-effective client/server architecture. It is evident that an organization which has been working with mainframes for decades needs help in the conversion which has to be done.

- What are the alternatives in getting help for this job?

---

*See also the discussion in Chap. 5, Sec. 5.6, on the choice of a partner for the conversion from mainframe to client/server.

- Who are the reengineering players in the market?

- What skills can they offer?

From IBM to Unisys and others, mainframers try to convince their customers that they can handle the conversion to client/server. That is, they claim to have both the skills and the impartiality to act as the user organization's consultants.

This is, of course, a boastful lie at least. It seems ludicrous to call the mainframer to save the user organization from its mainframes. Moreover, with their incompatible product lines, OS, DBMS, and protocols some of the mainframers are sinking their own ship. They are not going to live long, especially since they lack the skills needed to do job.

- Mainframers don't have the client/server skills because they don't have the products.

- They don't even believe in true client/server know-how. They just try to strike a deal.

Open-eyed organizations know the pitfalls. But not all companies are aware of the facts or care to read what careful research often reveals. Yet some research findings are quite accurate and can help in avoiding lots of errors.

On July 24, 1989, *Communications Week International* published a survey by Forester Research of Cambridge, MA. According to the report, 100 of the 1000 largest American corporations feel that IBM has yet to discern that communications must lead computing in the 1990s.

This is the user organizations' perception of IBM's communications skills. Five years down the line the projections made by Forester Research proved to be true, say recent statistics from other sources.

Table A.1 presents statistics compiled at the end of 1992 by the Common Market Executive, XIII Directorate General. It documents that as a communications equipment manufacturer, IBM is tenth in the world, considerably below French, German, Japanese, Swedish and other American firms.*

In fact, the major American corporations participating in the Forester survey suggested that IBM should make fundamental changes in its strategic communications approach. Included in these

---

*NEC of Japan, for instance, is doing three times more business in communications equipment than IBM.

TABLE A.1   The 15 Leading Communications Manufacturers in the World

Company	Origin	1992 business in communications*	Percentage of total business
Alcatel	France	17,344	91.8
AT&T	USA	10,000	16.4
Siemens	Germany	9,575	22.4
Northern Telecom	Canada	7,915	100.0
NEC	Japan	7,210	26.5
Ericsson	Sweden	6,900	93.9
Robert Bosch	Germany	4,640	23.6
Motorola	USA	3,510	30.7
Fujitsu	Japan	3,200	12.9
IBM	USA	2,530	4.0
Ascom	Switzerland	2,090	100.0
Phillips	Netherlands	1,920	6.5
Italtel	Italy	1,740	94.7
Nokia	Finland	1,565	42.2
Oki	Japan	1,330	27.1

*In millions of dollars.

changes was the addition of a modern, open, multivendor approach to networks.

"If IBM restricts itself to maintaining its traditional communications systems," said the Forester report, "large U.S. companies will slowly defect." The study also pointed to IBM's waning influence as:

- Support for international standards grows

- Downsizing policies slow down mainframe sales

This observation applies to every mainframer, of course, and developments in the past few years suggest that it is accurate. It is also a good reminder of the pitfalls of entering the mainframers' consulting web.

Today, computers have become commodity products, and computer manufacturers must rely more and more on communications gear and software sales to keep their margins from slipping. But the major computer vendors of the past have conceptual bottlenecks in house, and they find it very difficult to get out of them. The intransigence of mainframer culture is the heart of the problem.

In the late 1980s strategic directions at IBM included a major switch in business focus. The concept looked impressive:

	1989	1992	1995
Software and consultancy	30%	50%	70%
Selling hardware	70%	50%	30%

This switch in emphasis and in sources of income seems fine on paper, but is it really convincing? Unfortunately for IBM, the answer has been no.

When the above projections for IBM were made public in 1989, Wall Street securities analysts asked themselves two questions:

1. How is IBM going to accomplish the needed *cultural change?*

2. How will IBM act as an *independent system integrator* and *consultant?*

Underlying the second question, of course, is the fact that the large majority of IBM's business is in proprietary hardware and software: SAA, SNA, MVS, VM, AS/400 OS, OS/2, DB2, IMS, SQL/DS, OfficeVision, and so on. Did IBM really intend to downplay these products?

In other words, even assuming that IBM's goals were properly chosen, was the company positioned to meet them? Could such aims be attainable with the current IBM culture and product line? The evident answer was no, Wall Street analysts concluded, and as a result there were going to be few surprises.

Business planners at IBM's corporate headquarters, of course, should have detected that such a turnaround could not be made so fast—if it could be made at all. For instance, in the second quarter of 1989, IBM's software revenues grew by only 6.2 percent, down from increases of 15 percent prior to that period. This hardly suggests that the mainframer would be able to reach its self-imposed goals.

The advantage of hindsight is having hard evidence on which to base a statement: IBM's self-imposed 50–50 goals for 1992 were never fulfilled.

To be sure, this entire scenario is valid for any mainframe vendor. The fact of life is that *the world is moving from machines to brains*—a concept which has settled in only the most advanced people, and in the leading-edge companies.

Winston Churchill once recounted a story told to him by Josef Stalin. Once upon a time, the story goes, a bear terrorized a village. When enough was enough, the villagers decided that they had to kill the bear if they and their children were to survive. They came up with a plan.

A special poisonous powder was prepared and carefully stored in a paper packet. A peasant agreed to approach the bear and blow the powder in its face. Everything went as planned until the last minute. Then, just as the villagers saw salvation in their grasp, something terrible happened. The bear blew first.

Don't let the mainframers blow powder in your face.

About the Author

Dimitris N. Chorafas is an independent business consultant who specializes in strategic planning, technology transfer, and the evaluation and design of information systems. He is the author of more than 40 books on management and computer-related topics, including *Handbook of Data Communications and Computer Networks*, 2/e; *Local Area Network Reference*; and *Designing and Implementing Local Area Networks,* all published by McGraw-Hill.